*What All Americans Should Know about
the Most Recited 31 Words in American History
and the Flag They Honor*

# THE PLEDGE OF ALLEGIANCE
# &
# THE STAR-SPANGLED BANNER

## A Patriot's Primer on the American Spirit
## and
## A Citizen's Guide to Restoring the Republic

## John White

Our cause is noble; it is the cause of mankind!
— George Washington

## Dedication

*Children are 20% of the population but 100% of the future.*

To my grandchildren Brandon, Katherine, Sean, Amalie, Carson, Madeleine and Devin,
to my grandnephews Jeffrey and Jamie,
to my grandniece Danika and my grandnephew Braden
and to Angelica, Jessica and Sydney.

*May they and their children's children know liberty and justice for all.*

# ACKNOWLEDGMENTS

Portions of Chapters 1, 4, 7 and 16 are drawn from my book, *Enlightenment 101*.

Sidebar 1 is reprinted by permission of Freedoms Foundation, 1601 Valley Forge,Valley Forge, PA 19481.

Appendix 5 is reprinted from the 1994 book *Uncommon Sense: The Real American Manifesto* by "A Real American" (William James Murray) by permission of America West/Global Insights Publishers, 675 Fairview Drive, #246, Carson City, NV 89701.

# CONTENTS

## Part II: The Star-Spangled Banner

**Foreword**

# THE PURPOSE OF THIS PRIMER

> Educate and inform the whole mass of the people... They are the only sure reliance for the preservation of our liberty.
> – Thomas Jefferson

> Knowledge is, in every country, the surest basis of public happiness.
> – George Washington, First Annual Message, 1790

> Knowledge will forever govern ignorance: And a people who mean to be their own Governors, must arm themselves with the power which knowledge gives.
> – James Madison

When Thomas Jefferson wrote the Declaration of Independence, he tells us in an 1825 letter to Henry Lee, he intended it to be "an expression of the American mind." He wanted "not to find out new principles, or new arguments, never before thought of, not merely to say things which had never been said before; but to place before mankind the common sense of the subject, in terms so plain and firm as to command their assent, and to justify ourselves in the independent stand we are compelled to take." The Declaration of Independence changed the world profoundly and for the better.

I have similar hopes for this book. I call it a primer because, like the famed New England Primer for colonial schoolchildren, it covers the basics—the fundamentals necessary for intelligent and responsible participation in the society and government of America. It is a text for intellectual, civil and moral education of Americans (and all who want to be). I have tried to ground it in the facts of American history, the principles of American sociopolitical theory and the highest aspirations for our nation expressed by our Founders, and, like Jefferson, to place it before mankind in terms plain and firm, clear and persuasive.

However, my perspective is that of someone who is not only an American but also an inhabitant of Planet Earth. My reason, research and personal experience have brought me to a global—indeed, cosmic—view of "the course of human events." When Jefferson wrote for "mankind," he had little more than the British Empire and Europe in mind. Although that included several dozen nations, feudal states and kingdoms, they all arose from a common culture known as Western civilization. Today "mankind" is the nearly 200 nations and 7,000,000,000-plus people of the world who live in an enormous range of social and political systems arising from vastly differing cultures and civilizations. With the benefit of several centuries' hindsight on the subject of the American experience, and with a long involvement in spiritual traditions for higher human development, I offer commentary intended to be useful not only to the future of America but also to the entire human race.

Unlike Jefferson's view of the Declaration, however, I believe there are "new principles or new arguments never before thought of" in this book. They relate to the subjects of patriotism, global society and God-in-government. Unlike Ecclesiastes the Preacher, I believe they are something "new under the sun." Therefore, at the outset, I will point to the eight aspects of this book which I think are genuinely innovative and, equally important, beneficial to all:

1. The recognition of the Declaration of Independence as a spiritual document as much as it is a political document.
2. Reviving the distinction our Founders made between the War for Independence and the American Revolution.
3. The distinction between liberty and freedom.
4. The definition of liberty (social-political freedom) as a subset of an all-encompassing condition, liberation (spiritual freedom).
5. The connection between American patriotism and the family.
6. The connection between American patriotism and enlightenment.
7. The creation and use of the term *liberative* to denote a higher-level political perspective based on spiritual freedom and recognition of its source, God, so that the connection between liberty and liberation is emphasized.
8. The identification of America as a theocracy, albeit a new and better form than all others.

On the basis of the principles and arguments set forth here, it is possible for humanity to rise above its perennial divisions, with all their terrible expressions of man's inhumanity to man, to attain a new understanding and mode of behavior which honors the sacred and transcendent source of life in everyone, regardless of their name for that source and the outward condition of life in their society. In other words, ***in its ideal form the American mind can become the basis for a universal mind of love and respect for the whole of humanity and its home.*** From that will naturally follow "peace on Earth, good will toward men." That step toward human unity is the purpose of this primer on the American Spirit. Thus, this book is not about nationhood so much as it is about planethood and global community, and how America can lead us there.

# Introduction

## FREEDOM IS NOT FREE

To be born free is a great privilege; to die free is a great responsibility.

– Anonymous

• In a New England elementary school, boys and girls stand beside their desks, face the national flag and cross their heart with their right hand in the ancient sign of fidelity. Then, with solemn faces, they repeat after their teacher, "I pledge allegiance to the Flag of the United States of America..."

• At the start of the annual meeting of a mid-sized company in the South, the Chairman of the Board asks the assembled shareholders to stand, face the flag and recognize with him that one of the blessings of liberty is the free enterprise capitalist system of America which allows them to own and operate their business. The Chairman asks them to say aloud with him the words they know well: "I pledge allegiance to the Flag of the United States of America..."

• In a Midwestern church where Boy Scouts hold their meetings, the troop and its leaders stand at attention while a color guard of Scouts presents the American flag. Then, with the Scout hand salute performed by all, they follow the designated Scout who leads them in saying, "I pledge allegiance to the Flag of the United States of America..."

• In the City Council chambers of a small city in the Southwest, the Mayor asks all to rise as a color guard from the Fire Department takes its turn among local civic, service, fraternal and youth groups in presenting the colors at the monthly City Council meetings. When the color guard has turned around to face the roomful of citizens who have assembled to participate in the evening's agenda for local government, a Councilor leads the audience: "I pledge allegiance to the Flag of the United States of America..."

• At a military outpost where U.S. soldiers stand guard against enemies of freedom, the daily morning ceremony proceeds. The flag is raised aloft smartly on a flagpole. All is quiet except for a bugle call on a loudspeaker. As the men and women render the military salute to their country's flag, the loudspeaker carries the words across the parade grounds to them: "I pledge allegiance to the Flag of the United States of America..."

• In courtrooms across America, the presiding judge for that day takes his or her seat, then stands and faces the national flag. The Clerk of the Court calls out, "All rise for the Pledge of Allegiance." The judge, with right hand over heart, intones, "I pledge allegiance to the Flag of the United States of America..."

• At a ceremony conducted by the U.S. Citizenship and Immigration Services, a group of immigrants are about to say the Pledge of Allegiance for their first time as American citizens. They have completed the educational process of preparing for citizenship. They finish saying the Oath of Allegiance which naturalized citizens must speak aloud to renounce loyalty to any "foreign prince, potentate, state or sovereignty" to which they previously belonged. Then, while their families and friends look on with happiness and pride, these newest citizens of the United States of America say together, "I pledge allegiance to the Flag of the United States of America..."

• In the capitols of all 50 states and in the Capitol of the United States of America, legislators rise from their seats at the start of the day's business. They face the flag standing beside the podium on which the presiding officer's chair rests. The presiding officer then turns to the flag, places his or her right hand across the heart in the ancient sign of fidelity, and begins, "I pledge allegiance to the Flag of the United States of America..."

• In a remote Prisoner of War camp, weakened and haggard men of the armed forces of the United States face a makeshift American flag. It is about the size of a handkerchief. It has been furtively stitched together from rags, colored with homemade dyes and carefully concealed from the eyes of their captors. In the dim morning light, with some men in the most distant cells unable even to see the flag, the POWs stand at attention, render a salute and, with barely audible volume, whisper in unison as they have done each morning for their months and years of imprisonment, "I pledge allegiance to the Flag of the United States of America..."

• In memorial services across our nation, families, friends, neighbors and community members gather to show their care and support for the grieving men, women and children who lost loved ones in the terrible events of September 11, 2001. A priest, minister, rabbi, imam, chaplain and other religious leaders conduct the services. They begin with an invocation to God. Then, with heightened appreciation for the words which the gathered citizens have so often recited, they repeat them once more: "I pledge allegiance to the Flag of the United States of America..."

Why do we Americans pledge allegiance? To what do we pledge our allegiance?

In the aftermath of the September 11, 2001 terrorist attacks on New York City and Washington, D.C., it has become commonplace to say that everything changed for America. That is true in one sense; our open society was heinously abused by people who intend us great harm. We must indeed change to strengthen national security and be more determined than ever to protect the blessings of liberty which we enjoy as citizens of this nation. Freedom is our birthright, but freedom is not free. The price of freedom is eternal vigilance—moral and intellectual vigilance in the civic, economic, political, governmental and military realms—and often, sadly, the blood of patriots. Our freedom must be protected and defended by each new generation of Americans.

However, it is also true that some things have not changed at all—specifically, the ideals, principles and values on which America is founded. They are eternal, immutable. They are the bedrock of our nation. But to remain meaningful, they must be learned and understood by each new generation of Americans—and acted upon faithfully.

The resurgence of patriotism which swept over America after the tragedy of 9/11 is heartening, but if that patriotism is to be more than "flag-deep," if Americans are to be more than the "sunshine patriots" whom Thomas Paine criticized for their superficial loyalty during our War for Independence, we need guidance and deeper understanding. The Pledge of Allegiance can be a guide for every American to what is true, timeless and unchanging about our country, and worth pledging our lives, our fortunes and our sacred honor. A short listing includes liberty, personal sovereignty, inalienable rights, justice for all under the rule of law, equality of opportunity through a classless society, and human dignity for all through a form of government—democratically elected representatives serving in a constitutional federal republic—which reflects the divine source of all that and exalts the individual citizen above the state. The flag of the United States, rightly understood, symbolizes all that.

As Western civilization in general and America in particular finds itself engaged in a great clash of cultures, internally as well as externally, it is more important than ever for the good of Americans and all humanity that the meaning of the Pledge, the flag and patriotism be well understood. Why? Quite simply, **America in its ideal form is superior to all other nations and societies** in terms of liberty, justice and prosperity for all, equality of opportunity for all to pursue happiness, inalienable rights and other important indicators of political and social well-being which are universally recognized, such as public education, public health and protection of life, property and privacy.

That statement is not intended to denigrate anyone; it is said without false pride. I recognize that all nations and cultures have various forms of wisdom and beneficial traits and aspects which are valuable for the world. However, it *is* intended to declare that not all nations and cultures are equal. Our democratic society and our republican form of government—which together make up the *American nation*—when conducted in accordance with our founding ideals, principles and values—which together make up the *American way of living*—offer an avenue for establishing a veritable heaven on earth. Moreover, we can do so in a manner which allows *all* nations and societies to coexist, if they are peaceful and respectful of all others, in accordance with Jefferson's phrase which used to be our national motto: *E pluribus unum*, "Out of many [states, nations, societies], one [global community]."

This book deals with the essence of America—our ideals, principles and values, our history, our national objectives, our social and political functioning. It looks at the past, present and future of America, and what that means for us—for "we the people." [1] It also deals with our social and political malfunctioning. It focuses on the noble but doesn't overlook the ignoble. By unpacking the deepest meaning of the two quintessential expressions of America—the Pledge of Allegiance and the flag—it seeks to reawaken the American Spirit across our land so that the best of our country's heritage is publicly recognized and reasserted as the basis of our personal, local, state and national life and our international relations. (I explain the term "American Spirit" in the first chapter.) Some of this book is descriptive, some is prescriptive. It contains history, philosophy, practical information, personal commentary and opinion. (It also has a touch of humor because I mean to be serious but not somber.) Certain phrases and key ideas are repeated in order to reinforce them and to have the chapters, sidebars and appendixes stand as self-contained statements for reprinting.

In addition, this book seeks to extend the American Spirit around the planet, peacefully and cooperatively. It seeks to make a better home for humanity based on the American experience—the good life and life which is good. It seeks to develop a global civilization based on our spiritual and sociopolitical heritage, so that a world community emerges which provides liberty, justice, prosperity, health and equal opportunity for all to pursue happiness. Toward the end of the book, I offer my vision of such a world community because, as the Bible puts it, "where there is no vision, the people perish" (Proverbs 29:18). I hope it helps America to transcend the hateful harangue going on across the nation of Democrat vs. Republican, liberal vs. conservative, Left vs. Right, progressive vs. neoconservative. There is a higher perspective, a clearer understanding of America than that, which I offer here. It is neither right wing nor left wing, but upwing.

You may wonder: Who is this person offering his views and opinions? Simply a concerned citizen. My biographical profile is in the back of this book. I'm a teacher and writer by profession. Governmentally speaking, I am a Jeffersonian constitutionalist. Religiously speaking, I stand with the Founders of our nation who recognized that God is the author of our being and the source of our freedom, our sovereignty, our equality, our rights, our justice and our human dignity. Economically speaking, I am a free enterprise capitalist. Politically speaking, I am registered as a Republican but I put principles above party and am therefore first of all a republican. Philosophically speaking, I am in the conservative wing of libertarian thought.

No one can be totally objective, but you can be honest about your biases. Those are some of mine. To boil it all down: I regard myself as neither liberal nor conservative, but *liberative*. Liberative means "that which frees you." I coined the term (*liberal* + conserv*ative*) to name the perspective which recognizes both the strengths and the shortcomings of the liberal and the conservative stances, and which integrates the best aspects of them while discarding their errors and excesses. Liberative denotes spiritual freedom and the source of spiritual freedom as the basis of everything in our lives, including liberty. (See Appendix 7 for a discussion of the meaning.)

The century just passed has been called The American Century because of our nation's supreme importance in global affairs. Now, as the world enters a new millennium, I urge all Americans to take action—as I explain in the last chapter—to turn The American Century into The American Millennium. It is, I maintain, humanity's only hope for a truly free and peaceful world.

---

## FOOTNOTES

[1] Consider this powerful summary statement of our political history I've taken from the 1953 textbook *Adventures in American Literature*, which I used as a student in high school: "When George Washington took the oath of office as first President of the United States, Louis XVI reigned in France, there were a Holy Roman Emperor, a Russian Czar, an absolute monarch in Sweden and in Denmark, a Sultan in Turkey, an Emperor in China. All these have been swept away down the swift current of history. Yet the American nation is today the oldest republic, the oldest federal system, the oldest democracy in the world, and its Constitution is the oldest written constitution in the world."

## Prologue

# THE NAME OF OUR COUNTRY

We'll begin this exploration of the fundamentals of America with a simple question: How did our country get its name?

The word "America" is derived from the name of an Italian merchant and traveler, Amerigo Vespucci of Florence (1454-1512). The Latinized form of his name is Americus Vespucius. He was skilled in astronomy and navigation, and explored the New World at the end of the 15th century and in the early 16th century. [1]

Christopher Columbus is credited with discovering the New World in 1492 in the name of the King of Spain. (Previously he had approached King Henry VII of England for financial aid in undertaking a westward voyage in search of India, but Henry turned him down.) Columbus made three other westward voyages—in 1495, 1498 and 1502. Convinced he had had sailed to Asia and found a new way to the old world, he called the islands the Indies.

After Columbus's initial success, France, England and Portugal realized its importance and quickly joined in the exploration, competing for territory and resources. In 1497 Henry commissioned John Cabot, who sailed to Labrador or Cape Breton—the exact site is uncertain—and claimed what is now the east coast of the United States in the name of the king of England. The first French explorers in the New World are unknown, but by 1504 Cape Breton had been named; it is the oldest French place-name in North America.

In 1499, Vespucci went as one of the pilots on a voyage to the northern coast of South America, under command of Pedro Cabral, who was searching for India in the name of Portugal. In 1501, Vespucci sailed from Lisbon in a Portuguese fleet of three ships to Brazil and skirted the coast as far south as the La Plata River. He made a third expedition to the southern continent and in 1504 wrote letters giving an account of what he had seen in the *novus mundus*, the "new world," as he called it to distinguish it from the Old World. He declared that he had found a continent in the south "more populous and full of animals than our Europe or Asia or Africa and even more temperate and pleasant than any other region known to us."

Vespucci's account found its way into print in 1504 at Augsburg, Germany. It was the first published narrative of any discovery of the mainland. The account went through many editions; the 1505 edition, published in Strassburg, mentioned Vespucci on its title page as having discovered a new "Southern Land." This is the first instance hinting at the continental nature of the new discovery, as separate from Asia.

### Proof of an Unknown Continent

Vespucci's voyages were of great importance because they proved the existence of a new continent. They showed that South America was not part of the Indies discovered by Christopher Columbus, who insisted he had found a new way to the old world. He therefore failed to realize the true situation. Previously, some geographers had suspected there was a great southern continent; they called it the "Fourth Part," with Europe, Asia and Africa being the three known parts of the world. Vespucci's voyages confirmed the existence of this Fourth Part; they also secured Brazil for the Portuguese crown and resulted in giving the name "America" to the Western Hemisphere.

## The Name of the New World

The New World had no name until 1507. The name "America" stems from a letter Vespucci wrote about the beauty of the New World, which was widely read in Europe. A copy of it came into the hands of a German professor, Martin Waldseemueller, a teacher of geography in a little college at Saint-Dié-des-Vosges, in eastern France. In 1507 this letter and others by Vespucci were printed by the college press as an appendix to a new edition of the popular *Geography* of Ptolemy. The book contained a map which was the first to show the New World surrounded by water and, therefore, definitely not part of Asia. It also contained the suggestion that the newly found land should be named America in honor of Vespucci because Waldseemueller supposed he had discovered it. "The New World having been discovered by Americus Vespucius...I do not see what fairly hinders us from calling it Amerige or America, viz., the land of Americus," he wrote. 2

The name "America" was placed on the maps of that time. (Other names given the southern landmass about that time were "New India" and "Land of the Parrots".) Waldseemueller wrote it across the space for Brazil, but intending it to name all of South America. Waldseemueller's map was the first to depict the Americas as a separate land mass, not connected to Asia. The northern continent was left unnamed on the map, possibly because it was not yet recognized as a separate continent. However, by 1528 Columbus's Indies were known as the Americas. (In 2003 the Library of Congress acquired the only known surviving copy of the Waldseemueller map. It is a woodcut print on paper in 12 sections, measuring 8' x 4.5' altogether. It has been called America's "birth certificate" and "baptismal certificate" and is on display at the library.)

Mercator, the Flemish geographer, was the first to use the name for the entire land mass of the Americas, and others followed his lead, extending the name of America to the entire Western Hemisphere. The first geography of America was issued by Enciso at Saragossa, Spain, in 1519. By the 1530s, nearly all of Europe referred to the new land as America. When it became clear there were two continents, they were designated North America and South America.

So it came about that the continents were named by an obscure German professor in a French college for an Italian navigator in the service of the king of Spain.

## Columbia, the Gem of the Ocean

Thus, Columbus was deprived of the great honor of having his name given to the new world he had discovered. However, in the early days of our nation, there was much sentiment in favor of calling it Columbia in honor of Columbus. A popular song expresses the sentiment: "Columbia, the Gem of the Ocean." Likewise, Joseph Hopkinson's poem "Hail, Columbia" names our land as such, and our nation's capital, Washington, is located not in any state but in the District of Columbia. Cities such as Columbus, Ohio, and Columbia, South Carolina, honor Columbus, as does the university named Columbia. The first space shuttle was the Columbia.

## The United States of America

That explains the history of the last part of our country's name. But what about the first part?

In February of 1776, Thomas Paine wrote of "Free and independent States of America." The terms "United Colonies," "United Colonies of America," "United Colonies of North America," and also "States," were used in 1775 and 1776. However, the term "United States of America" was first used in 1776 at Philadelphia in the opening line of the Declaration of Independence, which begins "The Unanimous Declaration of the Thirteen United States of America..." [3]

Now, let's look at what that means for us today—and also for our descendants and the rest of the world.

---

# FOOTNOTES

[1] Although Columbus is credited with discovering America, there is ample evidence that he was not the first European to visit our shores. Native Americans, of course, have been in the western hemisphere for at least 20,000 years, and some evidence indicates their presence in one or both of the Americas for 100,000 years or more, although scientific opinion is divided on that. But an astonishing archeological find in Kennewick, Washington, in 1996 indicates caucasians—which originally meant people of the Caucasus Mountains in Europe—were here as early as 7,400 B.C.E. A skull and nearly complete skeleton of a 5' 8" man (now called Kennewick Man) discovered there lacks the classical mongoloid characteristics of Native Americans.

As for modern Europeans, the earliest known contact is attributed to Phoenicians; at Mystery Hill, New Hampshire, Phoenicians from the eastern end of the Mediterranean Sea apparently set up a colony about 480 B.C. which existed for several hundred years. In 551 A.D., Brendan the Bold, an Irish monk, reached the coast of North America; earlier in the same century, another Irishman, St. Finbarr, did likewise. Leif Ericcson, a Viking, sailed to Newfoundland about 1000 A.D. and Vikings lived there for more than a century. In 1171, Prince Madoc of Wales sailed to America. In 1398, Prince Henry Sinclair of Scotland led an expedition to the New World, reaching Nova Scotia, Massachusetts and Rhode Island. These claims are disputed among archeologists and historians, not completely settled, but it is almost certain that Columbus was not first.

[2] For more details see Toby Lester's *The Fourth Part of the World: The Race to the Ends of the World and the Epic Story of the Map That Gave America Its Name* (Press Press, 2010). A challenge to this long-accepted view was made by Rodney Broome in *The True Story of How America Got Its Name* (MJF Books, 2001). According to Broome, "America" most probably is derived from the name of Richard Amerike, a weatlhy merchant of Bristol, England, who helped fund English explorations in the New World/ North American mainland in the late 1400s. Broome cites records which indicate that Bristol ships visited Newfoundland to obtain fish from the Grand Banks at least twelve years before Columbus sailed to the Caribbean. "A letter discovered in 1955 in the Spanish National Archives...established that Bristol merchant ships had sailed to America considerably earlier than Columbus had..." Broome writes (p. 107). The letter

was written in Spanish by Johan Day, a Bristol merchant, to Christopher Columbus in 1497 or 1498.

Broome contends that Martin Waldseemuller's attribution of the name America to Amerigo Vespucci was a mistake which Waldseemuller admitted and tried to correct by removing the name America and reference to Amerigo Vespucci from later editions of his map.

As for Amerike, he sponsored John Cabot's 1497 voyage to North America, a territory which Cabot (a Venetian mariner whose real name was Giovanni Caboto) knew of even before Columbus made his initial voyage. It was customary for explorers to name new lands after their financial sponsors and Cabot, Broome says, promised Amerike to do just that, although he later reneged on the agreement, calling his discovery Newfoundland. But seafaring people around Bristol, Broome contends, were aware of Amerike's role in Cabot's visit to North America before Columbus ever set foot on Hispaniola.

**Chapter 1**

# "I PLEDGE ALLEGIANCE TO THE FLAG": WHY IT IS RIGHT TO BE LOYAL TO AMERICA

There is nothing more common than to confound the terms of American Revolution with those of the late American war. The American war is over, but this is far from the case with the American Revolution. On the contrary, nothing but the first act of the great drama is closed.
— Benjamin Rush, Signer of the Declaration of Independence, 1787

What do we mean by the Revolution? The War? That was no part of the Revolution. It was only an effect and consequence of it. The Revolution was in the minds of the people, and this was effected, from 1760 to 1775, in the course of fifteen years before a drop of blood was drawn at Lexington.
— John Adams in a letter to Thomas Jefferson, 1815

The War for Independence which founded our nation is over, but the American Revolution goes on because it is a spiritual revolution of global dimensions. Our revolution is unique in history: the proclamation of liberty for all, individual sovereignty, self-determination, inalienable rights, equality of opportunity, justice under the rule of law, and human dignity for all, derived from God and guaranteed through constitutional republican government of the people, by the people and for the people—all for the purpose of enabling us to find individual and collective happiness. Implementing that revolution is called the American Spirit.

The call of that revolution speaks powerfully and positively to the full range of our human nature. It draws from us that which is latent, waiting to be unfolded. It urges us to strive for something better for ourselves, our families, our communities, our nation, our world. It expresses itself physically, mentally, politically, socially and spiritually—in all aspects of our lives. It taps our capacity for growth in a way which contributes to the good of everyone. It brings us to the realization of our own highest potential as individuals and as a society, and it urges us toward actualization of that potential. In short, it promises a better world of peace, prosperity and fulfillment for all.

Thus, in the course of two centuries-plus, the American Spirit has blossomed across our land. Today, the United States of America has ascended to preeminence among the nations of the world. Economically, technologically, commercially, politically, militarily, culturally and in so many other ways, the American Spirit has produced enormous changes for the better in civilization around the globe. No nation in history has done so much for the common person as America. No nation in history has been such a force for good. Emma Lazarus's beloved sonnet about the Statue of Liberty rightly proclaims:

Give me your tired, your poor,
Your huddled masses yearning to breathe free,
The wretched refuse of your teeming shore.
Send these, the homeless, tempest-tossed to me.
I lift my lamp beside the golden door!

It's been said that immigration is the sincerest form of flattery. If so, people all over the world have voted with their feet on the question of which is the best nation of all. (An apocryphal sign at an anti-American demonstration overseas reads, "Yankee go home —and take me with you!")

There were missteps in the revolution, of course. We're not yet perfect. There were major failures to live up to our ideals, our principles, our values. There were bad choices in governmental and social policy and practice. There were shameful wrongs, such as slavery and segregation, the suppression of women, child labor abuses, and the mistreatment of Native Americans and other minorities. Those wrongs stained our national honor. They were not unique to America, but they were wrong nevertheless and cannot be overlooked. There is an undeniable dark side to America.

However, the American Spirit strives toward wholeness and health in the body politic, toward "a more perfect union," as the Preamble to the Constitution puts it, with liberty and justice for all, as the Pledge of Allegiance puts it. Thus, the American Revolution is self-correcting of missteps, failures, bad choices and wrongs by Americans who had not—and perhaps have not yet—fully awakened to the nature of our revolution.

For example, slavery is a millennia-old worldwide institution, but America eliminated it through a great civil war. [1] Since 1865, the sheer evil and unacceptability of that institution has been imprinted upon the conscience of humanity. Racial prejudice and discrimination still exist here to some extent, but in America today, people of color have full equality under the rule of law. [2] While we have not yet achieved full integration as a society—because that is a matter of mental attitude and cannot be legislated—we certainly have complete desegregation throughout the nation and equal opportunity for all.

For another example, the entitlement to vote was originally limited to white male property owners who were 21 or older. Over time, however, America has extended the vote to non-landowners, to people of color, to women and to citizens as young as 18.

The employment abuses of children outside a family concern have been eliminated. Young people are now protected by law against the exploitation which forced them to work long hours under poor workplace conditions for extremely low wages, without benefits.

As for Native Americans, they, too, now have equal rights under the law. They may live anywhere in mainstream American society or reside on reservations where tribal law and culture reign. Although poverty and poor health are problems sadly afflicting some Native Americans, that condition is not exclusively theirs, nor is it due to governmental action. [3] Moreover, the prosperity brought to some tribes by their entrepreneurial ventures into tourism, gaming casinos and other businesses has generated the means to proudly showcase their ancient ways of life for non-Native understanding. The National Museum of the American Indian in Washington, D.C., is a highly visible center to preserve their traditional culture. The casino income is also used to provide jobs and services for tribal members.

Why has all this "course-correction" to the course of human events occurred? The answer is simple. We are a nation based on the highest and most universal value: freedom. America is therefore known as the Fortress of Freedom. Our government's primary purpose is to assure our freedom as individuals and to protect us from those who would abuse it or abolish it. All other government functions are secondary to that. That is why the allegorical female figure atop our nation's Capitol is named "Freedom" and is a symbol of hope to people everywhere. [4] That is also why our national bird is the eagle. It appears on the Great Seal of the United States and on our coins because the eagle is the most able to soar heavenward, its flight symbolic of the freedom we enjoy and the object of freedom. [5] And that is why our nation's highest civilian award, like the Medal of Honor for our armed forces, is the Presidential Medal of Freedom.

Freedom is central and fundamental to the American way of life. It is our essence, our *raison d'etre*. As President Ronald Reagan put it, "Freedom is the deepest and noblest aspiration of the human spirit." Freedom serves the interests of everyone; it transforms lives and revitalizes societies. Freedom releases creative energy; it is the engine of all progress—technological, intellectual, cultural and spiritual. Freedom moves the hearts and minds of the American people. It is the key to unlocking our human potential, individually and collectively. And **the human potential can change the human condition**.

The Liberty Bell is inscribed with the words of Leviticus 25:10: "Proclaim liberty throughout all the land unto all the inhabitants thereof." The American Spirit proclaims liberty and its blessings throughout all the world unto all its inhabitants. Millions upon millions outside our country have heard that proclamation and come to our shores to embrace it in "the land of the free." The political experiment called America, begun in 1776 when we declared our independence from British rule, [6] is Earth's greatest opportunity for every human being to use his or her talents, effort and resources to pursue happiness, to build a satisfying life in a context of freedom—responsible freedom which encourages creative individuality, caring and stable family life, civic involvement, social and environmental concern for the well-being of others, and spiritual unity.

## What Is Freedom?

Freedom, Mr. Webster tells us, means the absence of necessity, coercion or constraint in one's choice or action. **The essence of freedom is having a choice.** It is having—to quote Mr. Webster again—the power to do as you please or not being subject to another's will, not having to ask permission. A person is free to the extent that he or she can exercise choice. The opposite of freedom is coercion, subjugation, involuntary servitude, bondage, imprisonment, slavery.

In America, freedom of choice is regarded as our fundamental condition and inalienable right. We Americans speak of the right to live our lives as we choose—the right to self-determination, the right to create our own destiny. The American way of life means freedom from arbitrary or despotic control; it also means the exercise of social, political and economic rights and privileges. It means the unhampered right to pursue the opportunities of life. We ask our children, "What do you want to be when you grow up?" because, unlike so much of the rest of the world, they have the freedom to choose a way of life for themselves.

However, rights always carry responsibilities; otherwise, liberty becomes libertinism, which is the abuse of rights. As James Wilson, a signer of the Constitution and generally regarded as the most erudite of the Founding Fathers, observed, "Without Liberty, Law loses its nature and its name, and becomes oppression. Without Law, Liberty loses its nature and its name, and becomes licentiousness." Rights exercised without regard for responsibilities become wrongs. Choices must be responsible choices, ethical choices, moral choices so that their consequences do not harm others —that is, they do not violate the rights of others. For example, someone may drink to the point of intoxication, but if that person then gets behind the steering wheel and drives on the highway, that is choosing irresponsibly, as Mothers Against Drunk Driving and others who have lost loved ones in DUI accidents can attest. Similarly, someone may perform activities which generate toxic waste, but if that person then disposes of the waste improperly, that is choosing irresponsibly, as former residents of the Love Canal, New York area can attest.

Freedom and responsibility are therefore inseparable. Think of the connection as one person put it: *freesponsibility*. Freedom without responsibility is lawlessness; responsibility without freedom is slavery. (See Sidebar 1.) Freedom is never license to do as we please, but only to do as we ought. (I explain the meaning of "ought" and its implications for human happiness later in this chapter.) In other words, freedom is the right to be wrong, not the right to do wrong.

Moreover, freedom is indivisible. It embraces every aspect of our humanity—both outer and inner, external and internal. It applies to our physical, mental, social and spiritual dimensions because we have the capacity—the free will—to choose what we do and how we behave in all those dimensions of life. If freedom is reduced in one aspect, that bears on all others. To quote President Reagan again, "Freedom is indivisible—there is no 's' on the end of it. You can erode freedom, diminish it, but you cannot divide it and choose to keep 'some freedoms' while giving up others." Moreover, since freedom is indivisible, so is responsibility. We have the freedom to choose in all aspects of our lives, but we also have the responsibility to choose wisely, morally, well.

Human history is a story of increasing freedom for us. The story has two themes: freedom *from* and freedom *to*. We have increasing freedom from the harsh constraints imposed on us by nature and by people who seek to control us through force and subjugation. We also have increasing freedom to act as we wish, for better or for worse, for good or evil.

*Physical freedom* means freedom from the elements and other dangers of the natural world, and from hunger, thirst and other physical needs. It also means freedom to move about and travel. The development of agriculture, for example, provided surplus food and thereby freed us from the necessity of roaming the land as hunter-gatherers. The domestication of animals freed us from the burdens of traveling by foot and carrying heavy loads. Medicine freed us from many diseases and debilitating conditions. Aviation and spacecraft freed us from the limitations of gravity. All that gave us more time and freedom to create, to produce, to travel, to increase our knowledge and raise our standard of living.

*Mental freedom* means the absence of fear or coercion in our thinking and our emotions; it also means unfettered access to information, as in freedom of education and freedom of the press. Together with physical freedom, it allows us to advance civilization, to build a higher culture.

*Social freedom* takes the physical and mental freedom of individuals and extends it to members of a community or society, so that the institutions of that community or society are likewise structured to remove obstacles or barriers—both physical and mental—to exercising choice and self-determination. Social freedom means, for example, we can associate with others, select our occupation and, if we want, change jobs, marry whom we choose, live where we want and as we want  Some societies do not extend freedom to all its members; slavery and suppression of women, minorities and underclasses are sad examples of social unfreedom. Children, of course, naturally have less freedom in the family and the community than adults because they're not capable of handling freedom maturely, but as they grow up, as they learn to exercise self-control and become educated into the ways of society, their sphere of thought and action—their physical, mental and social freedom—increases.

Although *liberty* is often used as a synonym for freedom, strictly speaking it is not. Liberty (from the Latin *liber*, meaning free rather than slave) is the sociopolitical aspect of freedom. It is external or outer freedom. A person may be captive, enslaved or in prison and thus not enjoying liberty (sociopolitical freedom), but he or she may nevertheless be free from hatred of his or her captors, slave masters or prison staff, as saints and holy people have demonstrated. Likewise, a person may be oppressed yet bear no ill will toward his oppressors. Mahatma Gandhi's struggle for India's political independence is exemplary of that; so is the equally great struggle by the Dalai Lama, spiritual-political head of Tibet, against Chinese Communist invasion and occupation of his country. (Significantly, his autobiography is entitled *Freedom in Exile*.) Conversely, a person may have social and political liberty, but nevertheless be captive, enslaved or imprisoned in his or her own fears or vices and self-destructive desires, and thus not enjoy that liberty, not know happiness. So liberty or external/outer freedom is no guarantee of internal/inner freedom.

## Spiritual Freedom—the Highest Aspect

This brings us to the highest aspect of freedom: *spiritual freedom*. In the entire spectrum of human knowledge, exploration and aspiration to unlock the mystery of existence and find enduring happiness, there is only one key, one answer: spiritual freedom. It was stated clearly by Jesus Christ when he said to his disciples, "And ye shall know the truth, and the truth shall make you free" (John 8:32). Similarly, Gautama Buddha, with his dying words, said to his followers, "...those who shall be a lamp unto themselves, shall betake themselves to no external refuge, but holding fast to the Truth as their lamp, and holding fast to the Truth as their refuge, shall not look for refuge to anyone beside themselves—it is they who shall reach the very topmost height" of spiritual freedom.

In other religions and sacred traditions, there is a similar understanding of spiritual freedom as freedom from self-ignorance and self-delusion, from vices and character flaws, from negative emotions, destructive compulsions and anything else which generates human unhappiness and prevents us from living God-centered lives of love and service to humanity. That perspective, which is the collective highest wisdom known to humanity, is called the Perennial Philosophy. [7] It is also called the Ageless Wisdom, the Timeless Wisdom and the Primordial Tradition. [8]

Spiritual freedom is what life is all about. Spiritual freedom based on understanding the absolute truth about the nature of reality: that is the goal which all major world religions and sacred traditions have for humanity. It is their common doctrine, their transcendent point of unity. They are in concord when they say that our Creator—our Divine Source—wants us to remove from ourselves all the spiritual blindness, self-centered thought and immoral behavior which separates us from the realization that we are one with the Divine Creator because that realization can transform the world into what it should be—heaven on earth.

Just as the world's religions and sacred traditions have many names for God, so too they have various names for the spiritual truth which makes us free. The most common term in English is *enlightenment*. Synonyms for it are spiritual freedom, liberation, God-realization, cosmic consciousness, unity consciousness and nondual consciousness.

The Declaration of Independence states the theory of freedom governing America, and it is based on the spiritual truth which sets us free. The Founders of America held two intimately related principles which they expressed in our founding document. First, God is the mighty author of our being and the ultimate moral authority for our laws and government. Therefore, we have a duty to reverently acknowledge God in our lives. Second, we are made in the image and likeness of our Creator. Therefore, by virtue of our spiritual nature, human beings are sacred, sovereign and inviolable. All else in our free society flows from that: our liberty, our equality, our rights, our justice, our human dignity and the primacy of the individual over the state. As James Madison put it in his 1785 *A Memorial and Remonstrance*, "before any man can be considered as a member of Civil Society, he must be considered as a subject of the Governour of the Universe." (See Appendix 3 for an elaboration of this point.)

From the American perspective, freedom is given to us by God, the source of freedom. It is given to be used responsibly to show forth God in our lives—that is, to glorify God, who is also the source of morality and law. God is the supreme lawgiver; the purpose of human life is to reflect the law of God and thereby glorify God. We have the free will to use our freedom irresponsibly and to break God's law of moral, righteous living, but *the divine purpose of freedom is to realize the presence of God in every aspect of our existence and to ever-deepen our capacity for expressing that realization*. Therein alone can we find unalloyed happiness and ultimate certitude about the human condition. That is the highest metaphysical wisdom of our nation. That is the spiritual truth on which America is founded.

All which follows from that philosophy of freedom is therefore based on the idea that we are primarily spiritual beings with a divine purpose and destiny. We are born free and morally equal, and are endowed by our Creator (not by people or any systems they devise) with rights which are inherent and inalienable. Government's purpose, from the American perspective, is primarily to guarantee that freedom and those rights for all. In the words of Rev. Stanley R. Allaby, because the Founders believed that man was created in the image of God as a free, moral agent, it then follows as a political corollary that man must be given as much freedom as possible, so that he may make moral choices within the context of freedom and apart from pressure or coercion.

Achieving that condition would be a seamless integration of internal and external freedom—a society of self-governing people whose thoughts, words and deeds are controlled by a profound sense of the truth which makes us free. Thomas Paine, author of the first American bestseller, *Common Sense*, which rallied the colonists to seek independence, recognized the linkage between the internal and external forms of freedom and commented, "Spiritual freedom is the root of political freedom... As the union between spiritual freedom and political liberty seems nearly inseparable, it is our duty to defend both."

## The Moral Imperatives of Freedom

Beyond that, since freedom and rights carry responsibilities, we must be responsible for ourselves. As a self-governing society, we must govern ourselves personally and use our freedom properly—that is, morally—as God intends.

Please note this well: ***The American political experiment in self-rule begins with everyone ruling himself***. James Madison stated it explicitly: "We base all our experiments on the capacity of mankind for self government." The two essential elements which undergird self-government are freedom and personal responsibility. Without that, the self-government which we Americans enjoy will degenerate either to tyranny or anarchy (which would soon be followed by tyranny).

Self-rule, therefore, must always be moral—can *only* be moral. Freedom cannot exist without morality. The moral imperatives of freedom are inherent and nonnegotiable. The moral superiority of freedom to all other approaches to government can only be demonstrated by righteous people living in a godly society. We must "walk the talk." Anything less than that undermines our happiness, our security and our future. The preservation of freedom is everyone's responsibility and it begins with moral alertness and moral commitment. Unless we have sufficient character (moral rectitude) and self-discipline (moral fortitude), we will not be able to govern ourselves, individually or collectively.

Our Founders understood that, as Madison put it, men are not angels. They understood, with Jefferson, that "virtue is not hereditary." They understood that the difference between liberty and libertinism is moral self-restraint and respect for the rights of others. They understood elected officials would be drawn from the seedbed which produces all candidates for office, the American society. Without a moral citizenry committed to public virtue, they said, this republic will not endure. Virtue and morality, along with an alert, informed and involved electorate, are the best safeguards against political corruption.

Therefore our Founders spoke of America as "a republic of virtue." [9] Without virtue in our citizens, without a moral citizenry, this republic will not endure, they said.

The idea was derived from Montesquieu's 1748 *The Spirit of the Laws*, which discusses different political systems, from tyranny and monarchy to a republic. Montesquieu says that each regime has different requirements of its people. A tyranny must cultivate a capacity for fear in people, a monarchy must cultivate a capacity for honor and a republic must cultivate a capacity for virtue. Our Founders, echoing

Montesquieu, said that without virtue in its citizens, without a moral citizenry committed to public virtue, this republic will not endure.

Listen to the Founders:

In his June 20, 1788 speech to the Virginia Ratifying Convention for the Constitution, James Madison said:

> Is there no virtue among us? If there be not, we are in a wretched situation. No theoretical checks—no form of government can render us secure. To suppose liberty or happiness without any virtue in the people, is a chimerical [vain] idea. If there be sufficient virtue and intelligence in the community, it will be exercised in the selection of these men [to hold federal office]. So that we do not depend on their virtue, or put confidence in our rulers, but in the people who are to choose them.

John Witherspoon, a Founding Father and signer of the Declaration of Independence, put it simply: "civil liberty cannot be long preserved without virtue" and a republic "must either preserve its virtue or lose its liberty."

Patrick Henry, the American Revolution's "voice of liberty," said it plainly: "Bad men cannot make good citizens:...A vitiated state of morals, a corrupted public conscience, is incompatible with freedom."

Likewise, Benjamin Franklin warned that as nations become corrupt, they have "more need of masters" [dictators] and therefore "only a virtuous people are capable of freedom."

George Washington agreed in his Farewell Address: "It is substantially true that virtue or morality is a necessary spring of popular government." While praising the Constitution, he said that it would survive "only so long as there shall remain any virtue in the body of the people."

So did John Adams: "The foundation of national morality must be laid in private families....Public virtue cannot exist in a nation without private [virtue], and public virtue is the only foundation of republics."

So did John's cousin, Samuel Adams. "He therefore is the truest friend to the liberty of this country who tries most to promote its virtue and who, so far as his power and influence extend, will not suffer a man to be chose into any office of power and trust who is not a wise and virtuous man...The sum of all is, if we would most truly enjoy this gift of heaven [a free and independent nation], let us become a virtuous people." [10]

A free and virtuous nation consists of free and virtuous people. Lack of virtue among the electorate will lead to election of nonvirtuous officials. Misuse of freedom—nonvirtuous action—ironically results in slavery to our appetites and addictions, which in turn leads, via the political process, to anarchy or dictatorship.

That is why **the first level of government in the American system is the family**. That is where newborn citizens receive their basic education in self-rule and have their character moulded to take personal responsibility for that understanding. That is where they learn self-control, respect for property and the rights of others, respect for duly constituted authority, the value of education, thriftiness, civic responsibility, public decorum and other fundamentals of the American way of life.

Our primary identity as Americans is as sons and daughters of God. **That means our society is really a single, holy family.** (The meaning of this is expanded later in the chapter—see "Patriotism and the Family".) Our nation and our citizenship in it are predicated on being subject to the rule of God, whose principles of operation for humanity and the world are expressed in the Declaration of Independence and are codified in the U.S. Constitution. **Together they provide the theory and practice of enlightened government.** That theory and practice addresses all levels of our being. (See "A Vision for Americans" in Chapter 13 for an elaboration of this point.)

God is the foundational and overarching reality of the cosmos, and America is a deliberately constructed reflection of that. When we recognize that God is the reason we exist and that we are always in the presence of God, it requires us to recognize that for others as well. We are all children of God the Father. At the soul level of our existence, we are all brothers and sisters in the family of Man. The Declaration of Independence states it with eloquent simplicity:

> We hold these truths to be self-evident, that all men are created equal, that they are endowed by their Creator with certain unalienable [11] rights, that among these are life, liberty, and the pursuit of happiness.

Rev. Martin Luther King echoed this with equal eloquence in his famous 1963 Address at the March on Washington, better known as the "I Have a Dream" speech, which was about more than just sociopolitical liberty:

> I have a dream that one day...the glory of the Lord shall be revealed, and all flesh shall see it together....
> When we allow freedom to ring, when we let it ring from every village and hamlet, from every state and every city, we will be able to speed up that day when all of God's children, black men and white men, Jews and Gentiles, Protestants and Catholics, will be able to join hands and sing in the words of the old Negro spiritual, "Free at last! Free at last! Thank God almighty, we are free at last!"

To the voice of King should be added that of Anna Julia Haywood, born into slavery in 1858 who rose against great hardship to become the fourth black woman in American history to earn a Ph.D. Long before King, Cooper wrote, ""The cause of freedom is not the cause of a race or a sect, a party or a class—it is the cause of humankind, the very birthright of humanity."

## The Government of God

The system of government devised for America matches the principles of the universe's "operating system" more closely than any other form of political organization does, and therefore it most closely reflects what has sometimes been called "the government of God"—that is, the laws governing creation, the structure and process of the cosmos, the way reality works. [12] John Adams put it this way: "Human government is more or less perfect as it approaches nearer or diverges farther from the imitation of [God's] perfect plan of divine and moral government." In his First Inaugural Address, George Washington pointed to "the eternal rules of order and right, which Heaven itself has ordained." [13] That set of rules—that heavenly government—is true, even though some of our Founders' lives were not completely in keeping with the perfection of the principles set forth in the document they wrote. For example, Washington and Jefferson owned slaves, but if they had behavioral flaws or inconsistencies, that doesn't make the principles any less true. Even Thomas Paine, a self-declared religious skeptic and non-Christian, said amid the dark days of the War for Independence that he was not so much of an infidel as to suppose that God "has relinquished the government of the world, and given us up to the care of devils…" (Paine was a Deist who rejected institutional religion.)

The thrust of all human experience is toward the discovery of God—not the anthropomorphic image of God held by a child's limited understanding, but the God whose ultimate form cannot be known because it is beyond all words, images, concepts and thoughts. In contemporary language, that discovery is the direct realization of Spirit, Godhead, the Ground of Being, the Great Mystery; in more traditional language, it is awakening in the depths of our being to the Divine Creator or the Source of Existence. In that discovery of the nature of ultimate reality is a second, correlated discovery: spiritual freedom—the greatest human value, the goal of human life.

The Founders of America understood that perspective to a significant degree. (See Sidebar 2 and Appendix 3.) They were products of the Age of Enlightenment, and although that term actually refers to an era characterized by the employment of philosophic, scientific and religious reasoning rather than the transcendent, nondual consciousness of the enlightened sage, their unique and unprecedented political experiment called the United States of America embodies their understanding—and does that well. The foundation of America—the self-evident truths which the Declaration of Independence names—is a spiritual vision congruent with the Perennial Philosophy. *The Declaration of Independence is a spiritual document as much as a political one.* The historical outworking of that has profound importance for the development of global governance and a worldwide wisdom culture, as I will show in the final chapter.

## The Attainment of Spiritual Freedom

The attainment of spiritual freedom transforms a person. [14] Since God is the innermost aspect of all creation, and since God is righteous and moral, it follows that the innermost nature of all creation, including us humans, is righteous and moral. Whatever sin or evil proceeds from us is secondary and a result of ignorance of our true self who is God, the Self or the Supreme Identity of all creation. As we come to know God better, as we become more God-centered, we become less self-centered. We become less concerned about our own will and more concerned about God's will. The goodness which is the "godness" at the center of our lives shines ever more brightly.

Sin, strictly defined, means "missing the mark," as in the process of aiming at a target. The "target" is God, and our deepest urge, the thrust of all our experience, is to turn away from self-centeredness and become centered in God. (That includes our sins and mistakes, which eventually teach us to redirect ourselves toward the target. As the hymn "Amazing Grace" puts it, "I once was lost, but now am found, / Was blind, but now I see.") *Spiritual freedom is being centered in God—on all levels and aspects of our existence.* The enlightened person can be said to have hit the mark, to have attained a bullseye, to have realized his or her true nature. He or she rests easily in God; there is no moral, emotional, intellectual or spiritual unease or dis-ease in the person. There is only the ongoing, abiding sense of the presence of God. There is only the ongoing, abiding sense of his or her unity with all creation. There is only the ongoing, abiding sense of the "fruits of the Spirit."

That presence, that unity, that Holy Spirit guides the liberated person, speaking to him or her through consciousness and conscience, constantly reminding the person—and likewise us, if we listen—that the cosmos has a moral foundation, a code of righteousness built into it reflecting the moral nature of God, who is the "withinness" of the cosmos. Conscience is "the still, small voice of God" which constantly whispers to us in the center of our being about that code, about that which is true and good, eternal and immutable. George Washington, in one of his early writings, described conscience as "that little spark of celestial fire." Likewise, John Adams wrote in 1775:

> Human nature itself is evermore an advocate for liberty. There is also in human nature a resentment of injury, and indignation against wrong. A love of truth and a veneration of virtue. These amiable passions, are the 'latent spark.' ... If the people are capable of understanding, seeing and feeling the differences between true and false, right and wrong, virtue and vice, to what better principle can the friends of mankind apply than to the sense of this difference?

When we begin to pay attention to the center of our being through prayer, meditation, contemplative practices and humble self-observation and self-reflection, we discover that we are one with the Source of all being and that we have a built-in "operating manual" for how to live a godly, righteous life. The holy scriptures of the world's religions and sacred traditions have expressed in their various cultural forms the essence of that operating manual for attaining a condition of existence which is permanently God-centered or enlightened, with all its inherent reward: spiritual freedom, enduring peace, unconditional love and universal wisdom.

From that attainment flows a behavioral expression of freedom in all aspects of the person's existence. It powerfully affects those around the enlightened person and aims to do so for the entire society in which he or she lives. (Liberation frees us *for*, not *from*, the service of God.) Its ultimate aim is transformation of the world to a condition which recognizes and expresses the presence and the glory of the Divine Source in everything.

## Reflecting Heaven on Earth

There are many terms for such a utopian society. They are drawn from the world's religions and sacred traditions, and reflect their understanding of the divine nature of reality and the transcendent metaphysical realms which seek to guide our development here on earth. Christianity and Judaism speak of the kingdom of heaven, but other traditions likewise name the ideal society. In Tibetan Buddhism, it is Shambhala. In Taoism it is the World of the Immortals. Islam has its Garden of Paradise. Native Americans speak of the Happy Hunting Ground. The highest lokas (heavens or celestial realms) of Hinduism and Buddhism are similar images of a perfected condition, as is Plato's World of Ideas, the Greco-Roman Elysian Fields and the shaman's Imaginal World. Although the imagery may differ from tradition to tradition due to cultural overlays, the underlying unity of understanding about human destiny is unmistakable.

Thus, it is no accident that our Founders—notably, George Washington, John Adams, Benjamin Franklin and Thomas Jefferson—saw in America the potential for human perfection and therefore sometimes spoke of our country as the New Jerusalem and the New Israel, just as the Puritans had spoken of America as the Promised Land. [15] By that they did not mean a Jewish nation but rather a God-centered society whose collective will was to reflect heaven on earth. [16] As John Adams put it: "I always consider the settlement of America with reverence and wonder, as the opening of a grand scene and design in Providence for the illumination of the ignorant, and the emancipation of the slavish part of mankind all over the earth."

Heaven, it should be noted, simply means unbroken communion with God (Mr. Webster's definition) and is not necessarily limited to a postmortem condition. (That is the teaching of Jesus and other sages.) God-realization, liberation, cosmic consciousness, unity/nondual consciousness, spiritual freedom, enlightenment: these are terms for unbroken communion with God while still alive in human form. Jesus Christ was the prime exemplar of that for Western civilization, and he explained it with this statement: "I am in the Father, and the Father in me" (John 14:10).

Therefore, America, for all its shortcomings and unrealized promise, is a magnificent experiment in human living which has never before been made in the history of this planet. It is an experiment based on the idea of **expanding individual freedom in a context of family and community relationship, social and environmental responsibility, and religio-moral guidance to create a society which reflects heaven on earth**. It is an experiment which aims at fulfilling humanity's perennial moral aspirations for a godly society. [17] Our Founders were quite conscious of that. The symbols which they created for America, such as the flag and the Great Seal, embody that (as I'll discuss later). However, it is an unfinished experiment and will not be completed until the entire human race enjoys the blessings of liberty we Americans now have. Patriots seek to benevolently extend the best of the American way of life to all the world in the name of God and our common humanity.

Thomas Jefferson put it this way in his final letter, written June 26, 1826, as he lay dying at Monticello, his Virginia home. (He died eight days later, on July 4, 1826.) Jefferson's letter was to the citizens of Washington, D.C., expressing regret that he was too ill to accept their invitation to join them for the fiftieth anniversary celebration of the Declaration of Independence. He told them of the global vision he and the Founders had for their political experiment based on freedom and self-rule. One day, he said, the experiment would spread to the entire world. "To some parts sooner, to others later, but finally to all," he wrote, the American form of republican self-government would become every nation's birthright. This worldwide triumph was assured, he went on to say, because "the unbounded exercise of reason and freedom of opinion" would soon convince all people that they were born not to be ruled, but to rule themselves in freedom. "All eyes are opened, or opening, to the rights of man....For ourselves, let the annual return of this day forever refresh our recollections of these rights, and an undiminished devotion to them."

That brings us to the question: What is patriotism and its significance to America?

## Defining Patriotism

The word "patriotism" is derived from the Greek word *patrios*, meaning "of one's father," and is defined as "devotion or loyalty to one's fatherland." More commonly, patriotism is understood as "love of country." That can be considered broadly to mean "undivided allegiance, unfailing love and eagerness to defend one's country against all enemies."

However, patriotism is not simply an emotion, even a deep emotion such as love. Patriotism is a sentiment, and sentiment, Mr. Webster tells us, means "thoughtful emotion" or "refined judgment prompted by feeling." Patriotism, therefore, is thoughtful and refined love of country. It is feeling grounded in judgment, and that judgment arises from a moral basis which recognizes absolute values and right vs. wrong which have been revealed by God, via religious teachers and spiritual leaders, throughout history in all times and places. In short, patriotism is informed, intelligent love of country.

Patriotism results from a process which, over time, unites head, hand and heart into a clear vision of what a nation is all about. In other words, patriotism is not inborn; it is learned by speech and by example. It is learned from parents, teachers, public figures and others in positions of authority and influence who demonstrate patriotism in their words and their lives. It is absorbed from the culture, directly and indirectly, in the process of becoming responsible, mature citizens. Native-born children learn it growing up; immigrants learn it by assimilating into the cultural mainstream of the country in which they take citizenship.

Please note that I am talking about countries or nations in general, not America in particular. Patriotism in America is different, as I will show in the following pages. America breaks the pattern, **America transcends the age-old perspective and establishes a new definition, a new meaning for patriotism**.

My concern is this: Without a clear understanding of the nature of patriotism, America will not endure, nor true world community grow. Properly understood, however, **the essence of America is the future of the world**. (I will show that in the final chapter.) If America succeeds in fulfilling its potential, all the world will benefit; if America fails to attain its promise, all the world will be the worse for it. **The future of America is the future of freedom, and the future of freedom is the future of the world**. In that regard, it is profoundly significant that the true name for the Statue of Liberty is "Liberty Enlightening the World." The torch Miss Liberty holds aloft at the gateway to our nation sheds what the song "America the Beautiful" calls "freedom's holy light." The ultimate form of that holy light—the ultimate form of freedom—is enlightenment. **[INSERT SIDEBAR 2 HERE]**

## Patriotism Is Not Nationalism

First, let's distinguish patriotism from nationalism. In America, they are not the same thing, as I will explain below. I am advocating national pride, not nationalism. Patriotism is different from nationalism, which seeks to elevate one nation above all others. (Hitler's motto *Deutschland über alles*—"Germany over all others"—is an example.) Nationalism is contrary to the attitude of our Founders, who had a "live and let live" attitude and advised people to walk modestly before God. The Declaration of Independence speaks to the world about America assuming a "separate and equal station" among the powers of the earth, not a loftier station. George Washington said in a prayer which he wrote for the nation in 1783 at the end of our War for Independence, "Almighty God, ...dispose us all to do justice, to love mercy, and to demean ourselves with that charity, humility and pacific temper of mind which were the characteristics of the Divine Author of our blessed religion and, without a humble imitation of Whose example in these things, we can never hope to be a happy nation." (See Chapter 4 for the complete quotation.)

Americans have great reason to feel proud, but the self-evident superiority of America to all other nations need not—indeed, should not—be proclaimed boastfully. [18] Our good deeds speak louder than any words can. Because of those deeds, all the world recognizes America as the land of greatest freedom and opportunity. (See Chapter 5 for numerous examples of good deeds.) True love of America is the opposite of what British intellectual H. G. Wells, during World War II, called "the crazy combative patriotism that plainly threatens to destroy civilization." World War II brought America into conflict with an alliance of aggressor nations—the Axis powers—trying to assert through military might that they were culturally superior to all others. That's nationalism. Americans rejected the proposition that might makes right, and we continue to do so. It is patriotically proper to defend one's nation against aggression; it is quite another thing —and morally wrong—to try advancing one's nation by making war upon others. Our nation's emphasis is on military prowess for defense, not militarism.

## Patriotism Is Not Chauvinism or Jingoism

Let's also distinguish patriotism from chauvinism or jingoism. Patriotism does not support the notion of "my country, right or wrong." That is ignorant and irrational love of country—blind devotion or misplaced loyalty which doesn't recognize the moral foundation and political theory of America. John Quincy Adams wrote in 1847, "And say not thou 'My country right or wrong'/Nor shed thy blood for an unhallowed cause." Abraham Lincoln put it this way: "I must stand with anybody [who] stands right, stand with him while he is right, and part with him when he goes wrong." In a similar vein, Theodore Roosevelt agreed: "Patriotism means to stand by the country. It does not mean to stand by the President or any other public official save exactly to the degree in which he himself stands by the country....It is unpatriotic not to tell the truth—whether about the President or anyone else."

If a public policy or governmental action is clearly wrong or immoral—that is, unconstitutional—it should not be supported, no matter how loudly an advocate proclaims that "it is best for America." It should be opposed and denounced. Although someone in a position of authority may "wrap the flag around himself" as he or she pursues that which is bad for America or contrary to American ideals, principles and values, patriots should declare it is not in the best interest of the American people nor in accord with the Constitution, which is the supreme law of our land and a clear reflection of God's law for Creation. (I expand on that in Chapter 4.) They should oppose it through the soap box, the ballot box and the jury box. [19] As the 18th century writer Samuel Johnson said about exposing wrongdoing in high places, "Patriotism is the last refuge of a scoundrel." The Framers of the Constitution, who expected virtue, morality and good character in public officials of the new nation (again, see Chapter 4), nevertheless recognized the potential for wrongdoing by them and wisely provided the means for correcting it—impeachment.

## Patriotism Is Not Isolationism

Last of all, let's distinguish patriotism from isolationism. Patriotism does not mean cutting all ties with the world, raising the drawbridge and turning completely inward. That would be totally contrary to the intent of our Founders, who understood that America had to be involved with the rest of civilization. Trade, diplomatic relations, mail, immigration—all these aspects of our national life were regarded by them as important and were therefore addressed in the Constitution.

Today, with transportation, communications, finance and commerce so rapid and so global, America cannot isolate itself. Nor should it even try. Those who advocate a hard-line American isolation from global affairs are neither realistic about America's history nor cognizant of America's destiny. On the other hand, we Americans should not give up our national sovereignty to unelected international bureaucrats who rewrite our laws, regulate our internal affairs, redistribute our wealth and override our process of representative government. It is not isolationism to stem the flow of illegal immigrants across our borders. It is not isolationism to protect American jobs and the balance of trade from unfair foreign practices. It is simply good sense: putting America first for reasons of national security against forces hostile to our sovereignty and our economic, social and political freedom. Independence is not the same as isolation.

## Patriotism and the Family

If patriotism is not nationalism, chauvinism, jingoism or isolationism, then what is it?

Patriotism is broadly defined as love of country and I've further defined it as informed, intelligent love of country. Even more precisely, however, **patriotism is the national form of love of family.**

Love is first expressed within one's family. Patriotism is simply an extension of the inborn impulse which humans have to love their parents, siblings and others who nurture them. That love becomes the basis of their self-identity. As children grow up, the natural love which they express for their family, the fundamental social unit, extends to larger and larger social units (unless the child is taught to be prejudiced and intolerant).

Patriotic love of country is no different in kind from love of one's neighborhood, town or city, and state. It is simply familial love and self-identity expanding to ever larger social units. That is why countries are called fatherlands and motherlands, meaning "parent-like nurturing social contexts defined by a nation's territorial boundaries." By a completely natural process, children come to love their country and to identify with it. Thus, in every country of the world, patriotism is nationalism.

*Except for America.*

America is an exceptional nation. First, we began as an exception to the millennia-old pattern of nationhood based on loyalty to a person, place or past. Instead, our Founders acknowledged God as the supreme lawmaker and the foundation of our society. Second, the divine right of kings to rule people was replaced with a radically new idea: the divine right of people to rule themselves. We pioneered a new way of living based on freedom and equality. That has provided the means for Americans to become exceptional—meaning self-fulfilling and self-exceeding—in every aspect of our lives, individually and collectively. It also provides the maximum opportunity for every citizen to pursue happiness and contribute to societal progress.

That difference is why this blessed land of ours is unique and why, finally, there can be a true world community enjoying all the blessings of liberty which we Americans enjoy. I'll discuss that more fully in the last chapter. What I'll discuss now is the most fundamental aspect of American exceptionalism.

If patriotism is the national form of love of family, why should that love end at the borders of a country? Why arbitrarily limit the expression of lovingness? Patriotism, as a manifestation of the God-given impulse to love and value others, has room in it for the ultimate social unit, the human family. Patriotism does not conflict with a concern for world community; patriots can legitimately "pledge allegiance" in spirit to Earth and its inhabitants. That is practical as well as philosophical because, obviously, no country stands alone in isolation. Each country is involved in world affairs, and in today's global society, many conditions and situations require regional, hemispheric and even planetwide efforts to handle them safely, efficiently and effectively.

To understand what is different—and better—about America, we must ask: Since all countries display patriotism, what distinguishes American patriotism and why should we prefer it?

The answer is simple but profound.

American patriotism is rooted not in love of a territory or a common ancestral group; it is rooted in love of freedom and the source of freedom, God. It is *focused* on the territory within our national borders, but it is *grounded* in recognition that our freedom comes from God, not government or any other human source. The foundation of America is spiritual, not material; celestial, not terrestrial. Freedom is, as Thomas Paine said in *American Crisis*, a "celestial article" made valuable by heaven. In the words of the Declaration of Independence—which has four distinct references to deity— the foundation of America is "Nature's God," "Creator," "Supreme Judge of the World" and "divine Providence." Understanding that expands the meaning of patriotism to universal proportions.

In the American theory of government, God is the source of our liberty, our sovereignty, our equality, our rights, our justice and our human dignity. God is the mighty author of our being and the moral authority for our laws. As John Adams wrote, our rights are "antecedent to all earthly government" and are derived from "the great legislator of the universe." Another of his terms for God was "the Spirit of Liberty."

Thus, American identity is not national, but spiritual, and American patriotism is love of the Spirit of Liberty expressed in thought, word and deed. ***America is founded on a transcendent vision of the divine unity of creation under the governance of the Creator***. American patriotism recognizes timeless spiritual ideals, principles and values at the base of our existence as God acts in the world and in human affairs. It honors the presence of God in the life of each individual. So, ***American patriotism is not bound to a place or a people or a past, but is essentially a state of mind, a deepening of spiritual vision, a growth in human consciousness of God's presence and God's action in the world to have us fulfill our destiny.*** Our national motto says it well: "In God we trust." (Chapter 4 elaborates on this.) Our pledge of allegiance to the republic acknowledges that we are "one nation under God."

## Planetary Patriotism and Global Governance

If patriotism is essentially extension of our God-given impulse to love and value people, and identify with them, there is no reason for it to stop at a national border. It can, and should, encompass the world. Properly understood, therefore, American patriotism—love of the American family—can be extended to embrace the entire human family and all creation. It also can provide the global ethic of respect for the planet which would terminate the rape and plunder of Mother Earth. That is because American patriotism is fundamentally grounded in God, whose primary quality, all the world's sacred traditions say, is love. As God's love is reflected in us, it spreads outward, embracing all humanity, all life, all the cosmos. It is inclusive, not exclusive. It recognizes the dignity inherent in all life—indeed, all creation—and treats it with respect and love.

As such, America is—to repeat—an experiment in human living based on the idea of expanding personal freedom in a context of family life, community relationship, social-environmental responsibility and religio-moral guidance to create the ideal society—a heaven on earth under the spiritual direction of God, whose laws are written in our hearts. However—again to repeat—the experiment is unfinished and will not be completed until all humanity enjoys the blessings of liberty we Americans now have.

Happily, that is possible. The territory of America has expanded greatly since the original thirteen colonies banded together, but the essence of America—the American Spirit—has remained unaltered. American patriots are loyal not simply or even primarily to our territory, but to the animating force behind America—the Spirit of Liberty, or God —and to the recognition that the animating force, the hand of God, moves within humanity, calling us to realize its presence, calling us to God-realization, to liberation, to unity/nondual consciousness, to spiritual freedom, to enlightenment. The key to that is not territorial conquest but self-conquest.

## The Formula for American Patriotism

It has been said that America is more of an idea than a place. That is true. However, America is not simply an idea—it is a *universal* idea. It arises from a universal source and applies to all humanity. American patriotism therefore proclaims liberty and its blessings throughout all the world unto all the inhabitants thereof. It seeks to extend the best of the American way of life—the best of the American family—to all people through peaceful means such as education, fair trade and commerce, humanitarian aid, charitable works, people-to-people exchanges, moral suasion and compelling example, rather than through exploitive business and financial practices, colonialism, militarism, clandestine intervention and manipulative foreign policy serving special interests and elite power groups. Our national foundations are spiritual faith in God and moral insight into the nature of reality and the design of creation. Our foundation documents—the Declaration of Independence and the Constitution—express that in the absolute values of God-given liberty, personal sovereignty, inalienable individual rights, and equality and justice under the rule of law. [20]

This can be summed up in a simple formula: *American patriotism = faith + family + freedom.* (Of course, the terms of the formula must be understood in all their depth, not simplistically or superficially.) In the American experience, faith, family and freedom are intimately blended in a process which requires everyone to be responsible for themselves and the liberty they enjoy while respecting the life, liberty and pursuit of happiness of all others. Living that understanding is the key to making America work for all.

*America! America!*
*God shed His grace on thee,*

*And crown thy good with brotherhood*
*From sea to shining sea!*

American patriotism recognizes that our national identity consists of the ideals, principles and values which flow (as the Eye of Providence on the reverse of the Great Seal of the United States depicts) from the metaphysical to the physical, from the transcendent to the mundane, from God to the nation, where they are embodied in the institutions, customs, laws and practices of our civil and political life. That is what unites us—a geographically, racially, ethnically and religiously diverse people—into one nation. That is our common culture. That is our credo.

American patriotism is therefore appreciation and respect of our country's spiritual foundations and her past, present and future. It is best shown by responsible citizenship to preserve freedom and the blessings of liberty for ourselves and our posterity. (See Chapters 5 and 8.) Through a direct and unadulterated extension of our political heritage, American patriots can fashion a society which builds world unity while honoring diversity, exactly as the words *E pluribus unum* on the Great Seal indicate, and which removes institutional forms of bondage and barriers to freedom, justice and equality of opportunity. However, without that citizen involvement, without "walking the talk," our ideals, principles and values will fade away like the colors of a weather-worn flag. As George Washington said in a September 5, 1789 letter to the Legislature of Pennsylvania :

> It should be the highest ambition of every American to extend his views beyond himself, and to bear in mind that his conduct will not only affect himself, his country, and his immediate posterity; but that its influence may be co-extensive with the world, and stamp political happiness or misery on ages yet unborn.

In short, American patriotism is an understanding of this nation as a means whereby God is building His kingdom on earth. [21] By offering to all nations the privilege of joining the Union, a United States of the World [22] could develop around the earth. Humanity could, at long last, pledge allegiance to "one Nation under God" in a magnificent act of planetary patriotism and global self-governance, with liberty and justice for all. I will enlarge upon that in the last chapter.

For now, think of the Pledge of Allegiance as a guide to our heritage and our potential as Americans. The Pledge is a vital expression of why it is right to affirm our loyalty to this nation. It is also a reminder of our solemn duty as Americans to preserve that precious heritage for all citizens, keeping it free from distortion and safe from co-option. And as the deeper meaning of the words of the Pledge arises in you, think of the Declaration of Independence and the U.S. Constitution as providing the theory and practice of enlightened government, reflecting the law of heaven, where the ideals, principles and values undergirding our nation are embodied. The Declaration of Independence and the Constitution should be posted in the entryway of every school in the nation as a clear, direct expression of the foundation on which education is conducted here. (See Appendix 7. See Appendix 9 for curriculum suggestions.) And think of those schools as providing "education for enlightenment."

In light of all this, American patriotism is easy and simple to define:

**American patriotism is preserving, protecting and defending the Declaration of Independence and the Constitution against all enemies, foreign and domestic.**

---

# FOOTNOTES

[1] The institution of slavery is at least 10,000 years old. It has been practiced in all cultures for millennia. People of every race and color were both slaves and enslavers, around the world. Europeans enslaved other Europeans for centuries before the first African was brought across the Atlantic to America. Likewise, Africans enslaved Africans for centuries before the Americas were discovered. Moreover, slavery existed in the Western Hemisphere before Columbus arrived; Native Americans such as the Choctaws, Chickasaws, Cherokees and Seminoles owned slaves, as did the the natives of Latin and South America, and the Kwakiutl and Nootka clans of the Pacific Northwest.

How was that ungodly worldwide institution overcome?

The intellectual history of freedom on Earth begins circa 1000 B.C.E. with the ancient Hindu scriptures known as the Vedas and the Upanishads. They declared *swaraj* or psychological liberation, a condition in which the moral and spiritual identity of all humanity is seen to be one with the Supreme Being. However, that concept was not applied as a critique of social institutions such as caste or chattel slavery.

In the fifth century B.C.E., Plato described freedom not as the democracy of Athenian society, but as the liberation of the soul from bondage to fear, ignorance, illusion and vice. Again, however, there was no critique of the institution of slavery. That did not occur until Christianity arose.

Although democracy began in Athens—and was a significant step in world history toward liberty for all—the Greeks were not truly egalitarian; they were a slavery-based society, as were the Romans. The disapproval of slavery began with the christology of St. Paul when he wrote in his epistle to the Galatians, "There is neither Jew nor Greek, there is neither bond or free, there is neither male nor female: for ye are all one in Christ Jesus" (Galatians 3:28). That statement marks the first appearance of the egalitarian spirit which eventually led to the global abolition of *state-approved* slavery. Paul reinforced it in his second epistle to the Corinthians: "Where the spirit of the Lord is, there is liberty" (2 Corinthians 3:17). Likewise in his letter to Philemon, he states that a master should treat a slave "no longer as a slave, but more than a slave, as a beloved brother" (Philemon 1:16).

Christianity emphasized the infinite worth of each individual soul and the moral equality of all individuals, whether freeborn or slave. It brought the concept of freedom into the social-political dimension of life.

The movement to abolish slavery therefore began where Christianity dominated, in Euro-America. In Africa, the Middle East and Asia there was no religio-spiritual principle equivalent to Paul's which applied to their social institutions. Pre-Christian Jews had slaves, all the way back to Abraham. Muhammad and other Muslims had slaves, as did Africans. (The notorious African slave trade existed only because, first of all, Africans captured and enslaved other Africans. They also captured Europeans—at least 1,000,000 between 1530 and 1780, according to Robert Davis's *Christian Slaves, Muslim Masters*.) Buddhism, while advocating spiritual liberation, was not a social reform movement, nor was Hinduism. Likewise, the religions of Confucianism and Taoism ignored social class and caste, including slavery.

Although Christendom failed for centuries to implement institutional change based on the spiritual oneness which Paul enunciated, the abolition movement, begun by Quakers in England in the 1700s, brought the question of slavery to prominence. A few individual protests had been made in England in the 17th century, and in America some German Quakers denounced the trade as early as 1688; other Quakers did so in 1696. The first corporate protest, however, was made in England in 1727 by the Society of Friends. Pennsylvania Quakers followed suit in 1730 and other Americans soon joined the abolition movement.

The Declaration of Independence carried forward the idea of emancipation; Jefferson's draft of the Declaration had a long section condemning chattel slavery (see the next footnote). (But when Georgia and South Carolina protested, it was removed by the Congress to keep unity among the colonies in fighting against Great Britain.) By 1839, when the Amistad slave ship incident occurred (see my poem "Singbe's Dream" in Chapter 6, Footnote 5), abolitionists in America had great strength and were helping large numbers of slaves escape to freedom in the North and Canada via the Underground Railroad.

Although America was not the first nation to abolish slavery—Denmark was—the state of Massachusetts was one of the first governments in history to abolish all slavery permanently. The Massachusetts state constitution, written by John Adams, ended slavery by declaring all slaves citizens eligible to vote. The Massachusetts constitution was ratified in June of 1780, just two months after Pennsylvania became the first state to abolish slavery. In 1777, Vermont, which was not yet a state, became the first territory to abolish slavery. No land other than the American states would abolish slavery until Denmark did so in 1796.

The American Civil War sealed the rightness of abolition in the consciousness not just of our nation, but of humanity itself. That doctrine is the basis on which slavery in America was finally eliminated, while India still has a grievous caste system and Africa still has slavery being practiced in some regions.

When chattel slavery (as distinguished from the state slavery of totalitarian regimes such as Communism—still prevalent in the world today) was finally eliminated from the world as a socially approved institution, it was the Christian foundation of Western culture which brought about the abolition and it was the American Civil War which provided the exclamation point to the historical record of the end of that horrible institution. There were no national wars fought after that over the issue of slavery because the inherent right to be one's own self—to "own" your self—was established in the collective consciousness of humanity, and thereby slavery was abolished, in principle, from society around the world. Sadly, pockets of slavery linger in the world today in Africa and Asia, especially with regard to women. The condition of women in many parts of the world approaches—and in some cases is—slavery, but at least the concepts of equality and fundamental human rights are universally established among nations.

Ominously, however, state slavery (under socialism) is entrenching itself more and more throughout the whole world.

2 Our Founders have been criticized for not applying to slaves the principle of equality enunciated in the Declaration of Independence. In finding fault with them, especially Jefferson and Washington, the critics unfairly overlook the following.

Thomas Jefferson strongly condemned slavery in his draft of the Declaration of Independence. Previously, his first act in political office, as a young member of the Virginia House of Burgesses in 1769, was to introduce a bill allowing slave owners to free their slaves; however, the bill did not pass. He raised the issue again when he went to Philadelphia as a member of the Second Continental Congress and wrote the Declaration of Independence.

Jefferson's draft of the Declaration was about one-fourth longer than the final, published version. It stated numerous reasons for America's severance of ties with England, including the immorality of slavery. The Congress deleted that and much else. (There were 86 amendments proposed to the draft before it was finally approved.) Here are Jefferson's words charging the King of Great Britain with yet another crime in his "long train of abuses" against his American subjects since, Jefferson pointed out, the slave trade was ultimately sanctioned and subject to regulation by the Crown, which chartered trading companies.

> He has waged cruel war against human nature itself, violating its most sacred rights of life and liberty in the persons of a distant people [Africans] who never offended him, captivating & carrying them into slavery in another hemisphere, or to incur miserable death in their transportation thither. This piratical warfare, the opprobrium of INFIDEL powers, is the warfare of the CHRISTIAN king of Great Britain. Determined to keep open a market where MEN should be bought & sold, he has prostituted his negative for suppressing every legislative attempt to prohibit or to restrain this execrable commerce. (*Thomas Jefferson: Writings*, edited by Merrill D. Peterson, Literary Classics of the United States, Inc., New York, 1984.)

This language was removed at the objection of two colonies—Georgia and South Carolina—who threatened to leave the Congress and the struggle for independence if slavery were abolished. In responding to the objection, the collective sense of the Continental Congress was that America could not fight two wars at once—the external war against Great Britain and the internal war against slavery. Unity was necessary to face the external danger, they felt, so the issue of slavery was put aside until the War for Independence was concluded.

At the Constitutional Convention in 1787, the issue was revived, resulting in the compromise to ban the importation of slaves after 1808. In 1806, when Jefferson was President, he reminded Congress that the time was near when it could prohibit the slave trade, and urged that it be done. Congress then outlawed the trade as of January 1, 1808, and Jefferson signed the bill into law.

Although Jefferson may be described as a racialist, because he thought the black race had certain biological and psychological traits which were inferior to those of the white race, he was in no sense a racist. His idea that all people have inherent and equal moral value transcending those traits extended to blacks in the most fair-minded way. He once wrote, "The spirit of the master is abating, that of the slave rising from the dust, his condition mollifying, the way I hope preparing under the auspices of heaven, for a total emancipation, and that this is disposed, in the order of events, to be with the consents of the masters, rather than by their extirpation."

George Washington was, like Jefferson, a slave owner. Also like Jefferson, he was no hypocrite. As a young man, he had been acquisitive, increasing his slaves from the dozen he inherited from his father to 135 in 1774. But, Terence P. Jeffrey states (*Human Events*, 11 February 2002, p. 7), leading the American forces in the Revolution worked a change in Washington's heart—a moral transformation. The fight for independence forced him to confront his personal attitude, and the nation's, toward traffic in human flesh. In 1786 he wrote to Robert Morris, a signer of the Declaration of Independence, "There is not a man living who wishes more sincerely than I do to see a plan adopted for the abolition of slavery."

Washington reiterated that position in writing to others, not only because of its moral rightness, but also because he clearly foresaw the social, political and economic turmoil which slavery's continuance would bring. In short, in his later years Washington recognized that slavery was not morally or economically tenable. For example, as President he approved and signed the act of Congress known as the Northwest Treaty, which prohibited slavery in the new U.S. territory. He wrote to his wartime friend LaFayette that he considered the prohibition a wise measure and expressed his hope that America would become a confederacy of Free States.

In his will Washington ordered all his slaves to be freed upon his wife's death. (Jefferson did not so order because of his huge indebtedness in his old age, as Saul Padover explains in his classic 1942 biography *Jefferson*. To do so in a planter society would quickly lead to bankruptcy because slaves were "property" and subject to the claims of creditors. Nevertheless, Jefferson did emancipate five beloved male slaves in his will.) "In his last act," Jeffrey notes, "the Father of Our Country sent an unmistakable message: Freedom is for all Americans, and all men, regardless of race. In this he bucked the trend of his time and the customs of his state."

It is unfair to apply present-day standards retroactively to Washington and Jefferson—and indeed, to all the Founders and Framers—to judge them as worthless "dead old white men." They were products of their time. But they were superior products because they outgrew the standards of their time with regard to slavery. They became advocates for societal change which led to those very standards upheld today by which some critics find fault with them. Such judgment is simply unfair and undeserved.

[3] The Indian trust accounts appear to be an egregious exception to this. There are an estimated 500,000 current individual accounts which have been created by the federal government since 1887. The Department of the Interior (DOI) is responsible for administering them and ensuring the fair and proper payment of due compensation to Native Americans from leases it arranged for timber sales and for oil, gas, minerals and grazing rights on Indian trust lands in the West.

Native Americans claim that their rights have been disregarded and that the government has cheated them of billions of dollars. According to the Blackfeet Reservation Development Fund web site (www.indiantrust.com), after Congress ordered full disclosure by DOI, after three DOI Cabinet secretaries have been held in contempt by a federal judge for not doing so, and after four trials which ruled in favor of the Indians, the federal government still cannot certify the accuracy of a single one of the half-million accounts. The Treasury Department's commissioner of the Bureau of Public Debt testified that the United States has used the trust funds to reduce the national debt. However, "no one knows how much of our money was used to reduce the debt load of this country or how many years the U.S. government used our trust money for these and other important government purposes, such as building dams and major power projects in the West." Moreover, according to the DOI Office of Historical Accounting, 40 million acres of Individual Indian Trust land have simply vanished from their original ownership. The web site comments:

> Records have been, and continue to be, lost, systematically destroyed, corrupted and, in many cases, never kept. In short, the government has no idea what the proper balances in our trust accounts should be. It doesn't know how many trust accounts it should be managing today.
>
> It has admitted, however, that at least $13 billion in nominal dollars has been collected from Individual Indian Trust lands. But it doesn't know what happened to this money or the compound interest this money was earning for generations.
>
> And remember these are accounts the government created for some of the poorest Americans. We Indians had no choice in the matter. The government unilaterally decided we were incompetent to handle our own funds and created the trust in 1887.

4 The bronze statue by Thomas Crawford was commissioned in 1856 and cast at a foundry in nearby Bladensburg, Maryland. It is 19.5 feet tall and weighs 14,985 pounds. It was placed atop the Capitol on December 2, 1863, during the Civil War. It was raised in sections as a huge crowd watched. President Lincoln, however, did not see the event; he was in bed with a fever. Upon completion of the task, a 35-gun salute was sounded from the 12 surrounding forts which then protected Washington, D.C. Placing the statue signaled completion of the construction of the Capitol after 70 years of work on it by architects, artists and craftsmen. Total cost: $23,796.82.

"Freedom" wears a helmet surmounted by an eagle's head and feathers, and encircled with stars. Originally, Crawford had given "Freedom" a liberty cap inspired by antique classical models and associated with freedom from slavery. Secretary of War Jefferson Davis objected to the symbolism from the Southern point of view, declaring that such a depiction would only further inflame pro- and antislavery passions which were sweeping the country. He was right, but the change of headdress was insufficient to avoid the Great Debate.

There is a little-known aspect to the statue's creation which exemplifies one of America's greatest missteps: slavery. "Freedom" was cast by a slave named Philip Reid. Although Reid actually earned his emancipation through his work, his owner received the compensation for the foundry work.

5 Although the foundation of America involved a most extraordinary collection of men of wisdom, they were not all saints or sages, and the disputes among them over various issues along the way from the War for Independence to the creation of the Constitution—and even afterward—are legendary. George Washington and George Mason, once good friends, fell out over the Constitution. John Adams and Thomas Jefferson likewise became estranged for years due to political differences (but resumed their friendship in the twilight of their lives). One dispute involved our national emblem, the bald eagle, and lasted for six years. Benjamin Franklin called the eagle a bird of "bad moral character" because it stole food from other birds. Moreover, he argued, other countries were already using the eagle as their symbol, so why adopt something so commonly used? He proposed the turkey instead. He was overruled, but when Congress decided in 1782 to adopt the Great Seal of the United States, it was the bald eagle, unique to North America, not the golden eagle of other countries, which appeared on the obverse (front) of the seal.

6 The roots of the political experiment called America include the first constitution of Connecticut, known as the Fundamental Orders. Voted upon and adopted in January 1639, the Orders marked the beginning of Connecticut as a commonwealth. The annual *State Register and Manual* of Connecticut notes that their spirit was that of a sermon preached by the Rev. Thomas Hooker a short time before their adoption, in the course of which he enunciated the proposition "The foundation of authority is laid in the free consent of the people." Hooker also preached that "the choice of public magistrates belongs to the people as does the right to limit their power." He closed with the challenge: "As God has given us liberty, let us take it."

The Fundamental Orders recognized no allegiance on the part of the colonists to England, but in effect set up an independent government. The *Manual* further notes, "The historian John Fiske was justified in his statement that this instrument was 'the first written constitution known to history that created a government and it marked the beginning of American democracy'."

Constitutional expert W. Cleon Skousen notes in *The 5000 Year Leap* that the Fundamental Orders were based on the principles recorded in the first chapter of the Book of Deuteronomy. "This constitutional charter," he wrote, "operated so successfully that it was adopted by Rhode Island. When the English colonies were converted over to independent states, these were the only two states which had constitutional documents which readily adapted themselves to the new order of self-government. All of the other states had to write new constitutions." (*The 5000 Year Leap: A Miracle That Changed the World*, National Center for Constitutional Studies, 1981, p. 18.)

7 The name "perennial philosophy" comes from *philosophia perennis*, a Latin term coined by the 17th century German philosopher Leibniz. *The Perennial Philosophy* is also the title of a book about this global wisdom-tradition which Aldous Huxley published in 1944, adapting Leibniz's phrase. It was the first book on the topic to get wide public notice. It deserved such notice because it is a magnificent work about the human condition and our potential to change it for the better.

In the midst of World War II, Huxley wrote *The Perennial Philosophy* to offer a solution to the problem of man's inhumanity to man. To put it simply, he said there will never be a better world until there are better people in it, and the place to begin building better people is with ourselves, through spiritual practices which bring our lives more and more into awareness of the unity of the human family under the parentage of Creator-God.

Yet the world's religions, from which most spiritual practices are derived, seemed at that time as divided from one another as the Allied nations from the Axis nations. Their potential as a force for universal good will and spiritual brotherhood was unrealized. Earth's political bodies and religious bodies alike were in deep division and struggle. What might end the warfare and unite the human race?, Huxley wondered.

The only solution, he said, lay in seeing the essential unity of the world's major religions and sacred traditions. What is that unseen unity? In a single word: enlightenment. Enlightenment, he said, is the core truth of the world's major religions and sacred traditions, no matter of what era, no matter from what civilization or culture. It is the "highest common factor"—not the lowest—among the world's spiritual traditions, religions and sacred lifeways. *The Perennial Philosophy* was intended to show the universality of that core truth behind the multitude of names and forms which the religious impulse—humanity's search for God—has taken throughout history.

The rudiments of the Perennial Philosophy, Huxley wrote (p. vii),

> may be found in every region of the world, and in its fully developed forms it has a place in every one of the higher religions. A version of this Highest Common Factor in all preceding and subsequent theologies was first committed to writing more than twenty-five centuries ago, and since that time the inexhaustible theme has been treated again and again, from the standpoint of every religious tradition and in all the principal languages of Asia and Europe.

There are three aspects to this timeless collective wisdom, Huxley explained. First is a *metaphysic*, namely, the fundamental idea that Reality—with a capital R—is a divine substance; all things, he said, including lives and minds, are forms of that divine Reality, traditionally called God. Second is a *psychology* which says that the soul of each individual is identical with divine Reality; in other words, the ultimate identity of everyone is that divine Reality, traditionally called God. Third is an *ethic* which says that Man's final end—that is, the goal toward which all human life is striving—is vital awareness and understanding of that divine Reality, of the immanent and transcendent Ground of all being, traditionally called God.

To put it more simply, God or divine Reality is the source of all creation and we human beings are one with the source at the soul-level of our being. The purpose of human life is to consciously realize that divine source within us and then align our lives to express it throughout all our activities. We must let the Ground of our being become the basis of our doing.

That is God-realization, liberation, cosmic consciousness, unity consciousness, nondual consciousness, spiritual freedom, enlightenment. That is the core truth of the world's major religions and sacred traditions. That is the final solution to the problem of man's age-old inhumanity to man—a spiritual solution. Huxley's research demonstrated that convincingly in his book and it has been confirmed many times over since then by scholars and spiritual teachers alike around the world.

8 The term "Ageless Wisdom" comes from the Theosophical tradition begun by H. P. Blavatsky in the last 19th century. The term "Timeless Wisdom" was coined in the last century by American philosopher Manley P. Hall, founder of the Philosophic Research Foundation in Los Angeles. The term "Primordial Tradition" was coined by American professor of philosophy and scholar of religion Huston Smith, author of the classic bestseller *The Religions of Man* (now retitled *The World's Religions*).

9 Arthur Lee, an American diplomat during the Revolution, wrote in 1769: "Liberty is the very idol of my soul, the parent of virtue, the nurse of heroes, the dispenser of general happiness because slavery is the monstrous mother of every abominable blight and every atrocious ill." He was voicing a widely shared understanding of liberty, according to Prof. Daniel Robinson's first lecture in *American Ideals: Founding a "Republic of Virtue"* (The Teaching Company, www.TEACH12.com).

10 Adam's full statement, in a 1776 letter to Mercy Warren, was: "Public virtue cannot exist in a nation without private [virtue], and public virtue is the only foundation of republics. There must be a positive passion for the public good, the public interest, honour, power and glory, established in the minds of the people, or there can be no republican government, nor any real liberty: and this public passion must be superiour to all private passions."

11 Jefferson wrote "inalienable" in his draft of the Declaration of Independence, as facsimiles show. After the Continental Congress approved it and ordered it to be disseminated, a printer's error changed "inalienable" to "unalienable" and that is how the official text of the Declaration now reads, although "inalienable" is the better usage.

12 For the century-plus of Americans who were educated in reading and writing from *McGuffey's Reader* grade school textbooks, God was defined quite simply as "the great moral Governor of the universe." McGuffey was echoing James Madison (quoted above) and others such as John Adams who described God as " the governour of the Universe." Likewise, America's first constitution, the Articles of Confederation—drafted in 1777 and ratified in 1781—refers to "the Great Governor of the World" as presiding over the hearts of the delegates to the Congress. All told, between 1836 and 1920 *McGuffey's Reader* sold more than 120 million copies. The understanding that God is the governor of the universe was widespread in that era and therefore was simply "common sense"—that is, a commonly held and commonly understood belief about the nature of reality which is so plain a truth that mere statement of it makes it self-evident. It is therefore correct, in that regard, to say that as America drifts from its religious, moral and philosophic moorings, America is losing its common sense. (That understanding is so fundamental to America that the man whom I described above as a self-declared religious skeptic and non-Christian, Thomas Paine, author of *Common Sense*, would likely weep over the loss.) For an elaboration on this point, see Chapter 4.

13 In anticipation of Chapter 4, I will quote the context of this statement by the Father of Our Country: "No people can be bound to acknowledge and adore the invisible Hand which conducts the affairs of men more than the people of the United States....We ought to be no less persuaded that the propitious smiles of Heaven can never be expected on a nation which disregards the eternal rules of order and right which Heaven itself ordained."

14 The process of attaining spiritual freedom is the subject of many books, courses and teaching organizations. There are far too many to mention here. I will simply refer readers to my own books, *The Meeting of Science and Spirit* (Paragon House: St. Paul, MN, 1990), *What Is Enlightenment?* (Paragon House: St. Paul, MN, 1995) and my forthcoming *Enlightenment 101: A Guide to God-Realization and Higher Human Culture.* Note that the process of attaining spiritual freedom is alluded to in the quotation by John Adams at the head of this chapter. Adams reiterated this key idea in a second statement: "The Revolution was effected before the war commenced. The Revolution was in the minds and hearts of the people... This radical change in the principles, opinions, sentiments and affections of the people was the real American Revolution."

15 A portrait of the Israelites crossing the Red Sea was proposed by Benjamin Franklin for the Great Seal of the United States. (For more on the Great Seal, see Chapter 4.) As for human perfection, George Washington, in his January 2, 1783 Newburgh Address to his officers amid anonymous calls for overthrowing Congress and establishing a constitutional monarchy, said, "And you will, by the dignity of your Conduct, afford occasion for Posterity to say, when speaking of the glorious example you have exhibited to Mankind, had this day been wanting, the World had never seen the last stage of perfection to which human nature is capable of attaining."

Thomas Jefferson, in a 1799 letter to William G. Munford, said: "I consider man as formed for society, and endowed by nature with those predispositions which fit him for society... his mind is perfectible to a degree of which we cannot yet form any conception."

John Adams expressed his vision for America this way: "I always consider the settlement of America with reverence and wonder, as the opening of a grand scene and design in Providence for the illumination of the ignorant, and the emancipation of the slavish part of mankind all over the earth."

16 Some Americans declare that America is a Christian nation. They are correct in one sense but wrong in another. As I point out often in this book, there are two fundamental aspects to the American nation: our society and our government. Neither in itself is sufficient to encompass the meaning of "nation." Together, they do.

By choice and careful design, the *government* of America is secular, not religious. The First Amendment to the Constitution prohibits any establishment of religion being created or supported. There can be no religious test for holding political office. So in a governmental sense, America is secular, not Christian.

However, the *society* of America is decidedly religious and overwhelmingly Christian. The First Amendment also prohibits government from interfering with religious expression. American society has been a religious society from its colonial origins. So in a societal sense, America is Christian, not secular.

But it is not exclusively Christian. Jews have been part of the fabric of American society since its beginning, albeit in comparatively small numbers. Equally important, but less noted, is the fact that America's social roots are Judeo-Christian because of the Christian Bible's retention of the Jewish Pentateuch, or the Five Books of Moses, and other books of the Old Testament.

Therefore  the phrase "Judeo-Christian heritage" accurately describe our nation's religious foundation. Christianity has a heritage which can legitimately be called Jewish and which can be appropriately applied to America.

First, there is scriptural basis for "Judeo-Christian heritage." Jesus was a Jew. He said, "Think not that I am come to destroy the law, or the prophets; I am not come to destroy but to fulfill" (Matthew 5:17). At his trial, Jesus was asked, "Art thou the King of the Jews?" His answer, although ambiguous, nevertheless accepted use of the term "Jew." He did not say, "I don't understand the question" or "I reject use of the term." That Jesus meant something quite different than Talmudic Phariseeism by "Jew" doesn't negate the term itself. What's in a name? The important aspect is the meaning. The meaning of the phrase indicates an element of spiritual continuity between Christianity and what is popularly called Judaism.

There is also historical basis for "Judeo-Christian heritage" to be used in describing the roots of America. U.S. civil law is largely based on the Ten Commandments—so much so that they are posted in many American courtrooms and a portrait of Moses with the Ten Commandments hangs above the Speaker's chair in the United States Congress. Additionally, personal and place names taken from the Old Testament can be found everywhere in America, and have been present from the time the first English settlers came to this continent. Moreover, the Founders of America were steeped in biblical learning and frequently cited Old Testamental sources. As stated above, some Founders expressed their hope that the new nation would fulfill an ancient longing by many for a New Israel, not a specifically Jewish body politic but a society which was truly moral and God-centered (which was the meaning Jesus brought to the term "Jew").

Although the roots of America are Christian, they contain elements of Judaism, elements which are wholly positive for the American experience, and which justify speaking of America having a Judeo-Christian heritage.

17 With regard to our nation's policies, however, Americans should not automatically assume that God is on our side. Rather, our stance should be that of Abraham Lincoln when someone asked him, during the Civil War, whether God was on the Union side. Lincoln replied, "The question, sir, is not whether God is on our side but whether we are on God's side."

18 While writing this book, a correspondent in Australia who read parts of it accused me of mythmaking, factual misstatements and zealotry which inflated certain events and ignored facts to the contrary. He characterized it as "typical American arrogance," "fundamental dishonesty" and "an ultra-nationalistic diatribe." He told me, "You paint an overly idealized and romanticized, revisionary view of America. The problem I have with your material is that it seeks to glorify America. This is 'the' American trait that so annoys the rest of the world—the tendency to self-inflation." He added that the companion of the inflated image is national hubris. "America," he said, "may have been founded on grand ideals but it has failed miserably to live up to those ideals."

I replied that a person is entitled to be wrong in his opinions but not his facts, so (I said) if I am wrong in any facts, I welcome correction. (We then had a useful exchange which led to several modifications of this chapter.) As for inflation of the image we

Americans may hold of ourselves as a nation, I agree that hubris and self-glorification are wrong. Moreover, I state clearly above that humility should be the quality of Americans because boastfulness and self-aggrandizement are contrary to the qualities which God-realization requires of people.

However, if there is such a thing as the American Spirit—which is the theme of this book—then it is not self-glorification to point out the characteristics and results of it because the American Spirit is a reflection of God's divine plan for humanity. (Critics will object to that statement as well. My correspondent said that "the true American Spirit is about the expansionary lust for riches," including the prolongation of slavery, dispossession of Native Americans and betrayal of treaties, and a foreign policy based on empire-building.") Rather, it is, from my perspective, simply education of Americans about their own past and future, based on the ideals, principles and values espoused by our Founders and by enlightenment traditions. I say that with what I regard as legitimate (i.e., genuinely humble) pride in the positive accomplishments of America. Sadly, there is a significant segment of the American public which rejects our past, finds little to no good in our present, and has a view of our future which is decidedly at odds with that of our Founders. My book is especially intended for them. Moreover, readers will find in the following chapters that I, too, share some of my correspondent's criticism of America for its failure to live up to its promise. To the extent that my critic's litany of America's wrongdoings is true, it is also true that they are totally contrary to the American Spirit. I regard the historical aspects of this book as narrative rather than myth. But note that "myth" is only secondarily a synonym for falsehood or ill-founded belief; the primary meaning of myth is a story of ostensibly historical events which serves to unfold part of the world view of a people—in short, a means of conveying profound spiritual truth.

19 With regard to the possibility of widespread oppression by government itself, not just wrongdoing by an individual, some people, including me, maintain we should add "the cartridge box" to this list, meaning a final resort to arms if all prescribed, lawful and nonviolent efforts fail to correct the wrongdoing. The authority they cite for that is the intent of the Second Amendment to the Constitution and the statement in the Declaration of Independence arising from our War for Independence: "…to secure these rights, Governments are instituted among Men, deriving their just powers from the consent of the governed. …whenever any Form of Government becomes destructive of these ends, it is the Right of the People to alter or to abolish it, and to institute new Government, laying its foundation on such principles and organizing its powers in such form, as to them shall seem most likely to effect their Safety and Happiness." Thus, in America there are four levels of protest against abusive government: the soap box, the ballot box, the jury box and the cartridge box. I hope and pray that American citizens never have to take that last line of defense.

Why? The pen still remains mightier than the sword. Although Thomas Jefferson said the tree of liberty must be refreshed from time to time by the blood of patriots, he meant only when all else fails and government oppression or abuse continues. Even so, anyone who takes up arms against the central government can expect to be put down quickly by the might of its armed forces, both police and military, unless those forces can be convinced not to obey unconstitutional, tyrannical orders. (That is the mission of a new but growing organization called Oath Keepers. They describe themselves on their website www.oathkeepers.org with these words: "Oath Keepers is a non-partisan association of currently serving military, reserves, National Guard, peace officers, and veterans who swore an oath to support and defend the Constitution against all enemies, foreign and domestic … and meant it. Our oath is to the Constitution, not to the politicians, and that oath will be kept. We won't 'just follow orders'." In other words, there is no expiration date on the oath.)

Additionally, anyone who takes up arms against the central government will also be put down by public opinion unless public opinion can be sufficiently drawn into supporting them because enlightened patriots want peaceful resistance, not violence. Tea partiers and other patriots have aroused the American Spirit in the populace against overreaching government. (See Appendix 6.) That will express itself in a variety of lawful, nonviolent means. Most notable will be the process given in Article V of the Constitution by which the states can amend the Constitution. Equally important will be Tenth Amendment nullification by states. In addition to that will be state legislative action to oppose federal overreach; state Attorneys General and private organizations suing to block unconstitutional federal acts; the fully informed jury movement; and an informed, engaged electorate who will remove from office—using the soap box, ballot box and jury box—those officials who fail to support and defend the Constitution and fail to honor America's commitment to liberty, justice and the pursuit of happiness for its citizens.

For a powerful modern example of patriotic Americans taking up arms against a corrupt and abusive government to restore the rule of law, see accounts of the Battle of Athens, Tennessee, including The Patriot Post's at: http://patriotpost.us/alexander/2012/05/03/the-battle-of-athens-tennessee.

In 1946, the Athens city administration—part of a statewide political machine—was rigging elections so blatantly that World War Two veterans trying to restore integrity to the process were met by sheriff's deputies threatening armed force. The veterans took up arms and forced the administration to capitulate. They went on to elect a new sheriff —one of their own—who returned the election process to its proper, lawful operation.

[20] The Supreme Court building in Washington, D.C., has the statement "Equal justice under law" inscribed across the front, below a sculpture of a seated female figure named Liberty. The artist, Robert I. Aitken, described his work as a "sculptural story" with these words: "Liberty enthroned—looking confidently into the Future—across her lap the Scales of Justice—She is surrounded…by two Guardian figures. On her right Order…On her left Authority…Then to the right and left…two figures each represent Council. Then to the right and left…two figures represent Research Past and Present."

[21] My use of the masculine "His" follows longstanding tradition in the English language, but not to denote God as strictly male. God is beyond gender. But insofar as gender is attributable to the Deity, there is also a feminine aspect. For my discussion of the genders of God and the meaning of the Trinity, see Chapter 24, "What Is Spirituality?", in *The Meeting of Science and Spirit.*

[22] After I had finished writing this book, I was pleasantly surprised to learn that Victor Hugo had preceded me by a century and a half in creating the name "The United States of the World." In 1851, writing about the liberation of the entire earth, he used the name, saying, "A day will come when you France, you Russia, you Italy, you England,

you Germany, all you continental nations, without losing your characteristics, your glorious individuality, will intimately dissolve into a superior unity …"

# Sidebar 1

# THE BILL OF RESPONSIBILITIES—
# A COMPANION TO THE BILL OF RIGHTS

Freedoms Foundation is a nonprofit organization dedicated to teaching young people the principles upon which America was founded and the duties of responsible citizenship. It seeks to convey the close link between the rights and the responsibilities of citizens in society. It was established after World War Two by prominent business leaders to honor patriotism and good citizenship. President Dwight D. Eisenhower served as chairman of the Foundation from its founding in 1949 until his death in 1969.

A centerpiece in the foundation's worldwide educational efforts is its "Bill of Responsibilities." It was designed as a corollary to the Bill of Rights and developed in 1985 under the foundation's sponsorship. More than three million copies of this document have been circulated throughout the world.

In addition to educating young Americans, the Foundation educates teachers and volunteers to go out into their communities and teach their fellow Americans what it means to be an American citizen—the rights and responsibilities of being an American.

## BILL OF RESPONSIBILITIES

**Preamble**. Freedom and responsibility are mutual and inseparable; we can ensure enjoyment of the one only by exercising the other. Freedom for all of us depends on responsibility by each of us. To secure and expand our liberties, therefore, we accept these responsibilities as individual members of a free society:

*To be fully responsible for our own actions and for the consequences of those actions.* Freedom to choose carries with it the responsibility for our choices.

*To respect the rights and beliefs of others. In a free society, diversity flourishes.* Courtesy and consideration toward others are measures of a civilized society.

*To give sympathy, understanding and help to others.* As we hope others will help us when we are in need, we should help others when they are in need.

*To do our best to meet our own and our families' needs.* There is no personal freedom without economic freedom. By helping ourselves and those closest to us to become productive members of society, we contribute to the strength of the nation.

*To respect and obey the laws.* Laws are mutually accepted rules by which, together, we maintain a free society. Liberty itself is built on a foundation of law. That foundation provides an orderly process for changing laws. It also depends on our obeying laws once they have been freely adopted.

*To respect the property of others, both private and public.* No one has a right to what is not his or hers. The right to enjoy what is ours depends on our respecting the right of others to enjoy what is theirs.

*To share with others our appreciation of the benefits and obligations of freedom.* Freedom shared is freedom strengthened.

*To participate constructively in the nation's political life.* Democracy depends on an active citizenry. It depends equally on an informed citizenry.

*To help freedom survive by assuming personal responsibility for its defense.* Our nation cannot survive unless we defend it. Its security rests on the individual determination of each of us to help preserve it.

*To respect the rights and to meet the responsibilities on which our liberty rests and our democracy depends.* This is the essence of freedom. Maintaining it requires our common effort, all together and each individually.

## Sidebar 2

# THE PRICE THEY PAID

Have you ever wondered what happened to those men who signed the Declaration of Independence?

Five signers were captured by the British as traitors, and tortured before they died. Twelve had their homes ransacked and burned. Two lost their sons in the Revolutionary Army, another had two sons captured. Nine of the 56 fought and died from wounds or the hardships of the Revolutionary War.

What kind of men were they? Twenty-four were lawyers and jurists. Eleven were merchants, nine were farmers and large plantation owners, men of means, well educated. But they signed the Declaration of Independence knowing full well that the penalty would be death if they were captured.

They signed and they pledged their lives, their fortunes, and their sacred honor.

Carter Braxton of Virginia, a wealthy planter and trader, saw his ships swept from the seas by the British navy. He sold his home and properties to pay his debts, and died in rags.

Thomas McKean was so hounded by the British that he was forced to move his family almost constantly. He served in the Congress without pay, and his family was kept in hiding. His possessions were taken from him, and poverty was his reward.

Vandals or soldiers or both, looted the properties of Ellery, Clymer, Hall, Walton, Gwinnett, Heyward, Ruttledge, and Middleton.

At the Battle of Yorktown, Thomas Nelson Jr., noted that the British General Cornwallis, had taken over the Nelson home for his headquarters. The owner quietly urged General George Washington to open fire, which was done. The home was destroyed, and Nelson died bankrupt.

Francis Lewis had his home and properties destroyed. The enemy jailed his wife, and she died within a few months.

John Hart was driven from his wife's bedside as she was dying. Their 13 children fled for their lives. His fields and his grist mill were laid waste. For more than a year he lived in forests and caves, returning home after the war to find his wife dead, his children vanished. A few weeks later he died from exhaustion and a broken heart.

Norris and Livingston suffered similar fates.

Such were the stories and sacrifices of the American Revolution. These were not wild-eyed, rabble-rousing ruffians. There were soft-spoken men of means and education. They had security, but they valued liberty more. Standing tall, straight, and unwavering, they pledged: "For the support of this declaration, with a firm reliance on the protection of the Divine Providence, we mutually pledge to each other, our lives, our fortunes, and our sacred honor."

They gave us an independent America. Can we keep it?

---

That brief essay—which has been widely reprinted since it first appeared in 1956 —has inspired decades of Americans and touched their souls as the magnitude of our Founders' sacrifice flooded their understanding. I've been moved to tears more than once when reading it.

After I discovered it in the 1980s, I began to expand it with additional information and commentary because its brevity seemed to need fleshing out. Over time, I expanded it to more than twice its length of 433 words. I gave details about the Second Continental Congress, the ages of the members, the £500 reward for the capture of John Hancock, a quotation by John Adams about the significance of the Declaration.

I felt justified in doing so because the many reprint sources I came across never attributed the essay to a specific author and never indicated it was copyrighted. It was described as written by an anonymous patriot and apparently was in the public domain. Eventually I published my expanded version in my home town newspaper.

However, as I was preparing this book, I felt I should look more closely at the claims made in the essay because, over the years, I'd come to doubt bits and pieces of it as other sources indicated things were somewhat different from what was stated. As I looked around on the Internet, I learned to my surprise and pleasure that there is indeed an author. It is the well-known radio commentator, Paul Harvey. According to the internet site of researcher James Elbrecht (http://home.nycap.rr.com/elbrecht/signers/ HARVEY-reb.htm), Harvey published it in his book *The Rest of the Story* (Hanover House, 1956). The copyright was renewed in 1976 when he reprinted just the essay in a small book entitled *Our Lives, Our Fortunes, Our Sacred Honor.*

Elbrecht and other commentators have strongly criticized the historical accuracy of Harvey's essay. This quotation from "Would July to Me?" in the Urban Legends section of snopes.com on the Internet succinctly states the case:

> "One of the major flaws in this…is that the concept of "risk" has been confused with the concept of "sacrifice," as exemplified by the title: "The Price They Paid." The price who paid? The implication of the article is that many of the Declaration's signers were killed, injured, or tortured; suffered serious illness due to mistreatment; or were stripped of their wealth and possessions for having dared to put their names on that famous document. The truth is that only one man, Richard Stockton, came to harm at the hands of the British as a direct result of his having signed the Declaration of Independence, and he isn't even mentioned here. The omission of anything having to do with Stockton is probably deliberate: After he was "dragged from his bed by night" by royalists and imprisoned in New York, he repudiated the Declaration of Independence and swore allegiance to Great Britain, thereby becoming the only one of the signers to violate the promise that appeared just above their signatures, the pledge to support the Declaration and each other with "our Lives, our Fortunes, and our sacred Honor." Stockton was eventually released by the British after he recanted, although the poor treatment he received during his captivity likely shortened his life.
>
> "The signers certainly believed that "the penalty would be death if they were captured," but that didn't prove to be the case. Several signers were captured by the British during the Revolutionary War, and all of them were released alive by the end of the war. Certainly they suffered the ill treatment often afforded to prisoners of war,

but they were not tortured, nor is there any evidence that they were treated more harshly than other wartime prisoners who were not also signatories to the Declaration. Some signers were killed or injured because they took an active part in fighting the war for independence, some of them lost their wealth or their property because they used their assets to support the revolutionary cause, and some of them suffered losses simply because they (or their property) got in the way of a war that was being waged on American soil, but all of this was the result of the fortunes of war, not of their having signed a piece of paper. "

Harvey and those who elaborated on his essay are in the position of Parson Weems, the first biographer of George Washington, who embellished Washington's life with fanciful but false stories about him cutting down a cherry tree and throwing a silver dollar across the Potomac River. The facts about the Signers of the Declaration are enough in themselves to justify our recognition and admiration of their courage and character. They do not need embellishment; the plain, unvarnished truth is the greatest tribute we can give to those Heroes of '76.

In that spirit, I offer my expansion of the essay which, to the best of my knowledge (except for the matter of Richard Stockton's recanting), stands up to scholarly review.

Freedom is not free. The Declaration of Independence marked the birth of America, but it was a painful and costly birth. The 56 courageous men who signed the declaration paid the price for being freedom fighters through hardship, sacrifice and even, for some, death.

What kind of men were they—those founding fathers of a nation who met in Philadelphia during that hot summer of 1776? Their caliber was astounding. They were public-spirited citizens who had for years been important participants in the affairs of their local communities and governments. The most respected doctors, educators and clergymen in the colonies were among them. Two dozen were lawyers or jurists. Eleven were prosperous merchants, nine were wealthy farmers or large plantation owners. Benjamin Franklin, at 70, was the oldest; nineteen were under 40; three were in their 20s. All but two had wives. They were men of means, for the most part, respected in their communities, who enjoyed much ease and luxury in their personal lives. Almost all were men of learning and accomplishment, not wild-eyed rabble-rousers.

The signers of the Declaration of Independence were the elite of 18th century America—but not elitist. They were moral men, mostly religious, and all men of integrity who had been welded together in a common cause. They had security, but they valued liberty more. John Adams said to his wife Abigail, "I am well aware of the toil, and blood, and treasure, that it will cost to maintain this declaration, and support and defend these states; yet, through all the gloom I can see the rays of light and glory. I can see that the end is worth more than all the means."

## Becoming Wanted Men

The men understood well the struggle facing them when they took up arms to win freedom from an oppressive government. Armed rebellion was high treason; the penalty for treason was death by hanging. Every signer became a wanted man. Even before the declaration was published with their names signed below it, the British tracked every member of Congress suspected of having put his name to treason. John Hancock already had a price of £500 on his head. As he signed the declaration, Hancock allegedly declared, "There! His Majesty can now read my name without glasses. And he can double the reward on my head!"

While declaring their independence from England, the Founders of America also declared their dependence upon God as the author of their being and the source of such wisdom and moral leadership as would be needed to create and sustain a new nation. The Declaration of Independence has four clear references to deity. The Founders concluded their statement with these words: "For the support of this declaration, with a firm reliance on the protection of Divine Providence, we mutually pledge to each other our lives, our fortunes and our sacred honor."

## The Fate of the Signers

[This section was the disputed and criticized account of what happened to the Signers.]

## Unwavering for Liberty

For all their hardship, none of the signers ever betrayed his pledged word. There were no defectors; no one changed his mind. They stood straight and unwavering for liberty.

Someone once said, "To be born free is a great privilege; to die free is a great responsibility." When the British tried to seize American arms and munitions in Concord, Massachusetts and in Williamsburg, Virginia—because tyrants fear an armed populace—a conflict began which "fired the shot heard round the world." Our benefactors in that struggle are not only those who took up arms against tyranny in defense of freedom and individual rights, but also those who took up the pen and the podium to give voice to the idea of liberty.

To those who sacrificed to create our country and preserve it for posterity, the end was worth the painful means. Their bold, new vision of freedom gave us a nation which shines for the rest of the world like the beacon held by the Statue of Liberty. Where would we citizens of these United States of America be today if there had not been those who counted the cost of freedom and willingly paid that great price? Can we preserve their legacy? Freedom is not free.

## Sidebar 3

# THE HEART AND SOUL OF THE CONSTITUTION

*The following address by Congressional Representative Sol Bloom was published in* The Story of the Constitution, *a U.S. government document produced in 1937 on the 150th anniversary of the U.S. Constitution. (The Constitution was written in 1787 by the Constitutional Convention and ratified in 1789 by the states.) Bloom, a Representative from New York, was Director General of the United States Constitution Sesquicentennial Commission. The Commission was composed of Representatives, Senators, the President and Vice President, and several scholars appointed by the President.*

In discussing the Constitution of the United States, I wish here to consider it from a new angle. We all agree that as a legal document it establishes a successful system of government. Its precision and brevity are admirable. Millions of words have been devoted to its governmental principles. Great jurists have interpreted the meaning of the Constitution and almost all its parts. As a frame of government it has stood the test of time, war and depression. It is based on truth, and, like truth, it laughs at the assaults of time.

But what I would like to discuss at this time is the heart and soul of the Constitution —its qualities that spring from the human heart, and not merely from the human intellect.

Unless the Constitution satisfies the aspirations of the heart, unless it feeds the human soul, unless it stirs our emotions, it cannot be regarded as a complete expression of the American spirit.

Why was the Constitution formed? Who were its framers? What was the emergency before them? What did they aim to accomplish?

In a nutshell, the Constitution was formed for the purpose of perpetuating American liberty by uniting the states in a firm union. All other aims were subordinate to the safeguarding of the liberty that had been won by the Revolution. It was evident after the Revolution that American liberty would be lost unless States banded themselves together to preserve it.

If you and I believe that life comes from God, and that the Creator endows man with the right of liberty when He breathes life into him, we must agree that the framers of the Constitution were obeying the will of God when they sought a way to perpetuate liberty.

Life and the right to enjoy liberty come from God. The guaranty of the right to enjoy liberty, the power to maintain liberty, must come from the human heart and soul. The Constitution is this guaranty. It enables the American people to exercise their power to maintain their liberty against foreign attack or internal dissension.

The signers of the Declaration of Independence pledged their lives to liberty. Their hearts directed their hands when they sent forth this declaration of war for freedom.

The framers of the Constitution were no less earnest. They saw the light of liberty dying in America as the states quarreled and threatened to disband. It was a new Declaration of Independence which the Constitution-makers prepared for the approval of the people—a declaration that their hard-won liberty should not perish, but should be made perpetual by joining the hearts and souls of the people of all the States in an indestructible Union.

These framers of the Constitution were chosen by their States to meet together. They were soldiers, planters, lawyers, physicians, merchants, and judges. Some of them were rich and others were poor. One of them, a luminous star in the human firmament, had been a penniless printer [Benjamin Franklin]. Another, Roger Sherman, who, with Robert Morris, had the honor of signing the Declaration of Independence, the Articles of Confederation, and the Constitution, had been a poor shoemaker who studied at night to become a lawyer. The university which fitted George Washington to preside over this body of men was the stern school of war.

Being human, these delegates had human failings. They were devoted to State and local interests. Those from large States were bent upon exercising the strength of large States. Those from small States shrank from a Union that might make them the pawns of greater States. The commercial North and the agricultural South had clashing interests. All the States had been disappointed by the failure of such central government as was exercised under the Articles of Confederation. They were suspicious of any proposal for a national government. They feared it would swallow the States and the liberty of the people, or be just another failure like the Confederation.

After many jarring sessions, in which misunderstanding, jealousies and selfish sectional interests bore down their efforts to agree, the delegates were almost in despair. Their hearts cried out for union, but their minds seemed to be overwhelmed. At this crisis, the venerable Benjamin Franklin suggested they they call upon Providence to give them guidance, that their appeal to the Almighty Father might soften their temper, and, drawing strength by relying on Divine Aid, they might go forward together in common sympathy. What their hearts desired their minds discovered. They found a way to make American liberty secure forever.

We've all read the Constitution. We all know, at least in a general sense, how it fulfills the people's will by uniting the States. But have we analyzed the Constitution, to search out its heart and soul? I maintain that, next to the Bible, "that Holy Book by which men live and die," the most precious expression of the human soul is the Constitution. In the Bible man finds solace, refreshment and instruction in the most secret and sacred relation of the soul—its relation to God.

In the Constitution we find solace and security and the next most important thing in life—our liberty. Every American, as he studies the marvelous framework of the Constitution, can say with truth and pride: *"This was made for me. It is my fortress. When danger threatens my life or liberty I can take safe refuge in the Constitution. Into that fortress neither President nor Congress nor armies nor mobs can enter and take away my life or liberty."*

You may ask me, where in the Constitution is there any language that throbs with human heartbeat? Where is the soul of the Constitution? My answer is, in every paragraph. All its parts are mighty links that bind the people in an unbreakable chain of

Union—a chain so beautifully wrought that it reminds us of the mystical golden chain which the poet saw binding earth to God's footstool.

Let us consider the preamble to the Constitution. We do not know from whose brain it came, [1] but we know that it sounds the heartbeat of the framers. It is the majestic voice of the people, giving expression to their soul's desire.

"WE THE PEOPLE OF THE UNITED STATES, IN ORDER TO FORM A MORE PERFECT UNION." For what purpose? To make our liberties secure. For how long? So long as humanity wanders through the wilderness of time. For whom? For every man, woman, and child under the American flag.

"ESTABLISH JUSTICE." What is justice but a guardian of liberty? My rights and immunities made secure against tyranny. Your rights safeguarded against my wrongdoing. Your widow and your child protected when you are gone. Can there be a higher aspiration of the soul than to establish justice? Justice is an attribute of the Almighty Himself; for He said, "I, the Lord thy God, am a just God."

"INSURE DOMESTIC TRANQUILLITY." The people longed for harmony. The framers of the Constitution saw that a central government would bring the States into common accord on all national questions, while removing other vexatious causes of disagreement. The very fact of equality of States was a guarantee of tranquillity. But the Constitution also provided a means whereby the government could protect the people against disturbances of public order and private security. The great charter thereby insured domestic order and peace, both among the states and the people.

"PROVIDE FOR THE COMMON DEFENSE." It was well understood that the separated States were not strong enough to ward off foreign aggression. Divided, they invited invasion and conquest, even from the second-rate foreign powers. United, they constituted a nation capable of defending itself in every part. The framers therefore clothed the common government with power to make war and peace, to raise armies and navies, to use the State militia for common defense, to build arsenals and navy yards. All that a mighty nation can do to defend its people and territory the United States of America can do; and even in its infancy the United States became a powerful nation through union of the States. The protection provided by the Constitution is the protection which a wise father provides for his family. This nation is like a strong fort defended by armed men. And far out at sea, prepared to meet and destroy any assailant, the United States Navy rides the waves in unwearied and vigilant patrol.

"PROMOTE THE GENERAL WELFARE." This provision has a far wider sweep than latter-day commentators accord to it. They seem to think that the government has limited powers in promoting the general welfare. They speak of relief of unemployment, flood control, and drought-control as examples of promoting the general welfare. Those objects may come within the scope of the government's general welfare powers, it is true, but those powers extend far beyond that point. The general welfare is promoted by the unification of the States. They are thus enabled to pool their resources and concentrate their energies. An example of promotion of the general welfare is the establishment of the postal system. Another example is provision for uniform coinage and currency. Still another is the consolidation of defense forces which I have just spoken. Indeed, the promotion of the general welfare by unification of the States is manifest in nearly every paragraph of the Constitution.

And finally, the Preamble declares that the Constitution is established to "SECURE THE BLESSINGS OF LIBERTY TO OURSELVES AND OUR POSTERITY." Who are we but the posterity of the great souls who wrought for our perpetual liberty? Can you agree that the forefathers of America were selfish and heartless men, when this proof is given that 150 years ago they were thinking of us, their posterity and heirs? Are we of this day equally foresighted? Do we give thought to our posterity that will live 150 years from now? If we are ready to pledge our lives, our fortunes, and our sacred honor for our distant posterity, we are worthy of the forefathers who did that much for us.

Summed up, the Preamble declares that our forefathers sought Union, Justice, Tranquility, Safety, Welfare and Liberty. These are the virtues enjoined upon mankind by their Heavenly Father. He who seeks justice is blest with the benediction of God. It is God's wish that mankind should be free. In securing their liberty, the people obey God's will.

We hear it said that the Constitution is faulty because it does not invoke the name of the Deity. I hold that it does more than lean on Divine strength. It strives to do God's will on earth, as it is done in Heaven. Not a line, not a word in the Constitution is in conflict with Divine will. On the contrary, every word and every declaration breathes an ardent desire to pattern the American nation in accordance with God's Holy will.

Can an atheist become President of the United States? I maintain that the spirit of the Constitution forbids it. [2] The Constitution prescribes an oath or affirmation which the President must take in order to qualify for his office. This oath or affirmation in its essence is a covenant with the people which the President pledges himself to keep with the help of Almighty God.

All officers of the United States and of the States, all judges and defenders of the Union must bind themselves to support the Constitution. Whether given by oath or affirmation, this pledge is essentially an appeal for Divine help in keeping inviolate a sacred obligation.

Upon all the coins of the United States appears the inscription "In God We Trust." Every word of the Constitution breathes this trust in God. Read the Preamble again and again. Give wings to your thought, so that you may poise like an eagle over time and the universe, and you will find within those words all the most ardent hopes of the human heart, the holiest aspirations of the human soul.

That this nation is established upon the rock of God's favor and protection will be proved, we devoutly believe, by its indestructibility. Time does not wear down nor eat away the eternal truths of the Constitution. War cannot overturn the temple of liberty so long as American sons are worthy of their forefathers. Instead of fading with age, the glory of the Constitution takes on a new splendor with the passing of the centuries. The faith of the forefathers gave them strength to plan for the ages. May we, with equal faith, guard our birthright and hand it down to OUR posterity as their most precious heirloom —LIBERTY, "the immediate jewel of the soul."

---

**FOOTNOTES**

[1] Gouverneur Morris is regarded as the principal author of the Preamble. He headed the "Committee of Stile and Arrangement" charged by the convention with taking all the articles and clauses agreed upon and putting them into logical order and consistent style.

[2] Rep. Bloom is technically incorrect on this point. There is no religious test for public office in America; the Constitution forbids it. An atheist could indeed become President; he or she would have no obligation to add "so help me God" to the Oath of Office, or to perform any ceremonial action involving words or deeds acknowledging God. But two things bearing on the matter should be pointed out.

First, the Constitution embodies the spirit of the Declaration of Independence, which has four references to deity. As I point out in Chapter 4, upholding the Constitution includes supporting the principles it embodies, including God as the Spirit of Liberty, the source of our freedom. A firm belief in God as the foundation of our nation is necessary to the true spirit of executive, legislative and judicial action in America. Any atheist who cannot, or will not, acknowledge that is either sadly ignorant or willfully hypocritical, and if such a person were to attain the Office of the Presidency, he or she would be false to the Oath of Office and therefore liable to impeachment and removal from office.

Second, and more obviously, because the denial of God is so contrary to the perspective of the vast majority of Americans, an atheist candidate for President would have no chance of winning an election. Only if atheism were embraced by a majority of the American people would an atheist President be possible.

## Chapter 2

# THE HISTORY OF THE PLEDGE OF ALLEGIANCE

It began as an intensive communing with salient points of our national history, from the Declaration of Independence onwards; with the makings of the Constitution...with the meaning of the Civil War; with the aspiration of the people.... The true reason for allegiance to the Flag is the 'Republic for which it stands.' ...And what does that vast thing, the Republic mean? It is the concise political word for the Nation—the One Nation which the Civil War was fought to prove. To make that One Nation idea clear, we must specify that it is indivisible, as Webster and Lincoln used to repeat in their great speeches.

– Francis J. Bellamy

The Pledge of Allegiance was first made public on September 8, 1892, in a magazine called *The Youth's Companion.* The magazine proposed a national celebration of the 400th anniversary of Christopher Columbus's arrival in the New World and the Pledge was to be part of it. The Pledge was only 22 words long. It read, "I pledge allegiance to my Flag and the Republic for which it stands: one Nation indivisible, with Liberty and Justice for all." Although it was just a single sentence, it would become the most repeated statement in American history.

The front page of the September 8 edition began:

**National School Celebration of Columbus Day**
The Official Programme

Let every pupil and friend of the Schools who reads *The Companion,* at once present personally the following programme to the Teachers, Superintendents, School Boards, and Newspapers in the towns and cities in which they reside. Not one School in America should be left out of the Celebration.

In obedience to an Act of Congress, the President on July 21 issued a Proclamation recommending that October 21, the 400th Anniversary of the Discovery of America, be celebrated everywhere in America by suitable exercises in the schools.

A uniform Programme for every school in America, to be used on Columbus Day, simultaneously with the dedicatory exercises of the World Columbian Expedition grounds in Chicago, will give an impressive unity to the popular celebration. Accordingly, when the Superintendents of Education, last February, accepted *The Companion*'s plan for this national Public School celebration, they instructed their Executive Committee to prepare an Official Programme of exercises for the day, uniform for every school.

To enable preparations for the National School Celebration in every community to begin *Immediately,* the Executive Committee now publish through *The Companion.*

THE OFFICIAL PROGRAMME
for the National Columbian Public School Celebration

of October 21, 1892.


The Pledge of Allegiance was first said by schoolchildren on that day. (Columbus Day was established as a national holiday on October 12 only in 1971.) The author of the Pledge was a Freemason, [1] Francis J. Bellamy (1855-1931) of Rome, New York. He was circulation manager of *The Youth's Companion*, which was located in Boston. He wrote the Pledge in the magazine office one evening in August of 1892.

*The Youth's Companion* was the leading family magazine of its day, with a circulation of about 500,000. It was filled with adventure stories and came once a week to homes across the country. Begun in 1825, it was published for more than a century until 1927. Some years before the proposed Columbus Day celebration, the *Companion*, in a spirit of patriotism, began a movement to have flags flown over public buildings and in public places. In 1888, it asked children to help buy American flags for their schools. The project was a success; the children collected enough money to purchase 30,000 flags to fly over their school buildings. [2]

In 1892, the magazine presented another idea for children. James P. Upham of Alden, Massachusetts, who was a partner of the firm publishing the magazine and also a Freemason, proposed a ceremony in all the nation's schools in celebration of the quadricentennial anniversary of Columbus' discovery voyage to the Americas. As Upham envisioned it, the school celebration would be called Columbus Day. Children across America would would begin the ceremony with a "Salute to the Flag" to honor their country. The magazine's owner, Daniel S. Ford, appointed Bellamy as chairman of a national committee to enlist widespread support for the project.

Bellamy traveled to Washington, D.C., to talk with President Benjamin Harrison about the celebration. Harrison liked the idea. He proclaimed Columbus Day a holiday for the nation and called on America to commemorate the anniversary.

Bellamy was also chairman of a committee of state superintendents of education in the National Education Association. He prepared the program for the public schools' celebration of Columbus Day. He structured the program around a flag raising ceremony and a flag salute—his Pledge of Allegiance.

There was already a salute in common use, the Balch Salute, which stated: "We give our heads and our hearts to God and our Country—one country, one language, one flag." Upham discussed this with Bellamy and asked for his help. Here is Bellamy's account of what happened.


Mr. Upham and I spent many hours in considering the revision of this salute. One suggested that the other write a new salute. It was my thought that a vow of loyalty or allegiance to the flag should be the dominant idea. I especially stressed the word "allegiance." So Mr. Upham told me to try it out on that line.

It was a warm evening in August, 1892, in my office in Boston, that I shut myself in my room alone to formulate the actual pledge. Beginning with the new word "allegiance," I first decided that "pledge" was a better school word than "vow" or "swear" and that the first person singular should be used, and that "my" flag was preferable to "the." When those first words, "I pledge allegiance to my flag" looked up at me from the scratch paper, the start appeared promising. Then: should it be "country," "nation," or "Republic"? "Republic" won because it distinguished the form of government chosen by the fathers and established by the Revolution. The true reason for allegiance to the flag is the "Republic for which it stands."

Now how should the vista be widened to teach the national fundamentals? I laid down my pencil and tried to pass our history in review. I took the sayings of Washington, the arguments of Hamilton, the Webster-Hayne debate, the speeches of Seward and Lincoln, the Civil War. After many attempts, all that pictured struggle reduced itself to three words, "One Nation, indivisible."

To reach that compact brevity, conveying the facts of a single nationality and of an indivisibility both of states and of common interests, was as I recall, the most arduous phrase of the task, and the discarded experiments at phrasing overflowed the scrap basket.

But what of the present and future of this indivisible Nation here presented for allegiance? What were the old and fought out issues which always will be issues to be fought for? Especially, what were the basic national doctrines bearing upon the acute questions already agitating the public mind? Here was a temptation to repeat the historic slogan of the French Revolution, imported by Jefferson. "liberty, equality, fraternity." But that was rather quickly rejected as fraternity was too remote of realization, and equality was a dubious word. What doctrines, then, would everybody agree upon as the basis of Americanism? "Liberty and Justice!" were surely basic, were undebatable, and were all that any one Nation could handle. If these were exercised "for all" they involved the spirit of equality and fraternity. So that final line came with a cheering rush. As a clincher, it seemed to assemble the past and to promise the future.

That, I remember, is how the sequence of ideas grew and how the words were found. I called for Mr. Upham and repeated it to him with full emphasis.

The Pledge of Allegiance as Bellamy originally wrote it said "to my flag and the Republic" and did not have the phrase "under God." That was a curious oversight because among his various roles in life, Bellamy was Reverend Bellamy, a Baptist minister. A graduate of Rochester Theological Seminary, he had been ordained in 1879 at the Baptist Church in Little Falls, New York. However, he was without a congregation. (He had been forced to leave his Boston church a year earlier because of his views supporting equality for women and African-Americans.) He considered adding the word "equality" to the line "with liberty and justice for all" but decided against it because he knew that many members of his committee opposed the idea. In early October he added the word "to" before "the republic," bringing it to 23 words.

*I pledge allegiance to my Flag and to the Republic for which it stands—one Nation, indivisible—with liberty and justice for all.*

Thousands of leaflets with the Pledge were sent to public schools across the country, proposing that it be said on Columbus Day. Patriotic fervor swept the nation over the idea for an appropriate prayer filled with reverence and love of country. On October 21, 1892, more than 12 million children recited the Pledge of Allegiance, thus beginning a school-day ritual which is now used in most American schools, public and private. Bellamy himself heard 6,000 children say the "Salute to the Flag" in Boston that day.

Years after its composition, a controversy arose concerning the authorship of the Pledge. Claims were made on behalf of Upham. In 1939, a committee of the U.S. Flag Association settled the dispute; it accepted Bellamy's claims and ruled in his favor. A detailed report was issued by the U.S. Library of Congress in 1957 supporting the committee's ruling.

## The First National Flag Conference

At the first National Flag Conference in Washington, D.C., convened by various patriotic and civic groups on June 14, 1923, for the purpose of regulating flag etiquette (see Chapter 9 and Appendix 1 for greater details), a change was made to the Pledge. There was increasing concern that the continually arriving immigrant population might not understand the Pledge properly. It was thought that some foreign-born children and adults, when saying the Pledge, might construe the words "my flag" to mean the flag of their native land. For clarity, the words "the Flag of the United States" replaced "my flag"—despite Bellamy's protests. The Pledge was now 27 words.

*I pledge allegiance to the Flag of the United States and to the Republic for which it stands, one Nation indivisible, with Liberty and Justice for all.*

A year later, at the Second National Flag Conference, the words "of America" were added after "the United States," bringing it to 29 words.

*I pledge allegiance to the Flag of the United States of America, and to the Republic for which it stands, one Nation indivisible, with Liberty and Justice for all.*

In the following years various other changes were suggested but were never formally adopted except for one, described below.

Although the Pledge was originally in the public domain in terms of ownership, in 1942, shortly after America entered World War II, the Pledge received official recognition by Congress in an Act approved June 22, 1942, outlining rules pertaining to the use and display of the flag. The Pledge became the official property of the United States of America. It was the 50th anniversary year of the creation of the Pledge. In 1945, Bellamy himself received official recognition by Congress in Public Law 287, which designated his work as "the Pledge of Allegiance to the Flag." However, Bellamy was not present to enjoy the recognition; he had died on August 28, 1931.

## The Barnette Case and the Supreme Court

Patriotic fervor of the times had led several states to pass laws requiring children to begin each school day by saluting the flag and reciting the Pledge of Allegiance. In 1942, West Virginia's Board of Education had mandated a daily flag salute and recitation of the Pledge to "teach, foster and perpetuate the ideals, principles and spirit of Americanism." Students who did not conform could be expelled from school and threatened with commitment to reformatories; some parents were actually prosecuted for contributing to their children's delinquency.

Some people disagreed with this on religious grounds. Others disagreed on grounds of freedom of speech. (More recently, some Americans, including descendants of slaves, have refused to recite the Pledge because they feel America has not lived up to its ideal of liberty and justice for all. [3] Another group of Americans—atheists—have refused to recite the Pledge because of its reference to God. Some libertarians and states' rights advocates declare that states should have the right to secede from the Union and therefore "indivisible" is unacceptable in the Pledge; for that reason they, too, choose not to say the Pledge.)

A group of Jehovah's Witnesses who disagreed with the West Virginia's mandate went to court to challenge it. Walter Barnette, one of several Witness parents, objected on religious grounds. He and the other parents said they were willing to "pledge allegiance and obedience to all the laws of the United States that are consistent with God's law, as set forth in the Bible." However, they argued that saluting the flag violated the Bible, which for them was the Word of God, the supreme authority for their conduct. Specifically, the Witnesses said, the Board of Education's mandate violated the commandments "Thou shalt not make unto thee any graven image" and "Thou shalt not bow down to [a graven image]" given in Exodus, chapter 20, verse 4. They considered the flag to be an "image" within the meaning of that commandment.

The Barnette group was successful. In June 1943, the Supreme Court ruled in "West Virginia State Board of Education v. Barnette et al" that school children could not be compelled to recite the Pledge of Allegiance. It said:

> We think the action of the local authorities in compelling the flag salute and pledge transcends constitutional limitations on their power and invades the sphere of intellect and spirit which it is the purpose of the First Amendment to our Constitution to reserve from all official control.

(Speaking personally, I agree with that decision, but I disagree with the reasons— political, religious, philosophic or social—which lead some Americans to refuse to say the Pledge. I try to show why throughout this book.) The Court added:

> If there is any fixed star in our constitutional constellation, it is that no official, high or petty, can prescribe what shall be orthodox in politics, nationalism, religion, or other matter of opinion or force citizens to confess by word or act their faith therein.

Today only half of our 50 states have laws which encourage the recitation of the Pledge in the classroom.

## The Final Version of the Pledge

In 1945, Congress decreed that the official salute for reciting the Pledge of Allegiance was to place the right hand over the heart. The Balch salute had long since been succeeded by what was known as the Bellamy Salute: the right fist was placed against the chest with the knuckles facing the left side of the body, and then the arm was extended straight out at the beginning of the recitation of the Pledge. When Adolf Hitler rose to power in Germany, the innocuous Bellamy Salute suddenly resembled the Nazi "Heil Hitler" salute, so it was changed. Also in 1945, the Pledge was formally titled "The Pledge of Allegiance" and added to the United States Flag Code (see Appendix 1).

In 1951, concern about the Korean War prompted the Knights of Columbus, a fraternal Roman Catholic organization, to put Abraham Lincoln's phrasing "this nation, under God" from the Gettysburg Address into the Pledge. The Knights began urging modification of the Pledge; their state and national meetings adopted resolutions calling for the words "under God" to be inserted after "one nation."

In 1953, they sent copies of their resolution to the President, Vice President and each member of Congress. That generated 17 congressional resolutions in favor of it.

The resolution introduced by Representative Louis C. Rabaut of Michigan [4] was adopted by both Houses of Congress.

Then, in February 1954, Rev. George Docherty, pastor at the New York Avenue Presbyterian Church in Washington, D.C., preached a sermon attended by President Dwight D. Eisenhower and the national press corps. Docherty, who had arrived in the U.S. from Scotland in 1950, wrote a sermon to amend the Pledge of Allegiance. Afterward, he asked Eisenhower, who was sitting in the front pew, what he thought. Eisenhower said, "I agree." The news story flashed across the nation. Senator Homer Ferguson (R-Mich.) sponsored a bill and it was approved as a joint resolution on June 8, 1954.

On Flag Day, 1954, the version of the Pledge as we know it today was made official. The phrase "under God" was added to the Pledge by an act of Congress. The Pledge is stated in full in Section 7 of the Flag Code. Section 8 says the Pledge cannot be altered, modified or deleted without the consent of the President.

Congress, in adding "under God" to the Pledge, explained that it intended to make clear that America stood in total opposition to the godless Communist movement threatening the world. It said:

> At this moment in our history the principles underlying our American Government and the American way of life are under attack by a system whose philosophy is at direct odds with our own. Our American Government is founded on the concept of the individuality and the dignity of the human being. Underlying this concept is the belief that the human person is important because he was created by God and endowed by Him with certain unalienable rights which no civil authority may usurp. The inclusion of God in our pledge therefore would further acknowledge the dependence of our people and our Government upon the moral directions of the Creator. At the same time it would serve to deny the atheistic and materialist concepts of communism with its attendant subservience of the individual. [5]

When signing the bill into law, President Eisenhower said, "In this way we are reaffirming the transcendence of religious faith in America's heritage and future; in this way we shall constantly strengthen those spiritual weapons which forever will be our country's most powerful resource in peace and war." [6]

Thus the Pledge of Allegiance was brought to 31 words—the best-known and most-recited 31 words in American history.

*I pledge allegiance to the flag*
*of the United States of America*
*and to the Republic*

*for which it stands,*
*one Nation under God,*
*indivisible,*
*with liberty and justice for all.*

---

## FOOTNOTES

[1] I call attention to this fact because Freemasons have played a highly significant but little-noted role in the founding of America. It is no accident that the first syllable of Freemasonry is "free." Among the better-known Masons who helped to win our national independence are George Washington (see Sidebar 3), Benjamin Franklin, Paul Revere, John Hancock and John Paul Jones. Many of the signers of the Declaration of Independence were Masons. As for the formulation of our national constitution, 13 of the signers were Masons. Freemasonry stands squarely for the Constitution and all the fundamental freedoms bequeathed to us by the writers of that great document. In fact, Freemasonry had its own constitution written half a century before America's and it is believed by some scholars that the idea of our written national constitution—the first in world history—and various state constitutions was derived, at least in part, from that Masonic tradition.

Freemasons have also played significant roles in establishing the patriotic traditions of America. In addition to Bellamy's creation of the Pledge of Allegiance, consider these Masons: Francis Hopkinson, a signer of the Declaration of Independence, designed our first national flag (see Chapter 10); Francis Scott Key wrote our national anthem and set the words to a tune, "Anacreon in Heaven," composed by John Stafford Smith (1750-1838), an English Mason; John Philip Sousa wrote our national march, "The Stars and Stripes Forever" (see Appendix 3); and Benjamin Franklin was a member of the first Congressional committee (with John Adams and Thomas Jefferson) which began designing the Great Seal of the United States (although Franklin's contribution was not used in the final design).

A passage from Gordon L. Anderson's *Philosophy of the United States* (Paragon House: St. Paul, MN, 2004, p. 88) succinctly describes the role of Freemasonry in the founding and formation of America:

> It has been said that George Washington would not trust any officer under his command who was not a Mason. Masons had to undergo tests of moral integrity intended to make them socially responsible citizens. Masons, as Masons, also remained neutral with respect to religious denomination or political party. Freemasonry has been described as "the religion of the American Revolution." The list of members of early American Masonry reads like a *Who's Who* of American founders, and the American presidents, judges and military leaders of the nineteenth century also were frequently Masons. Masonry also included freethinkers and rationalists as well as Christian pastors and church elders.

2 Displaying the American flag inside schools began only in the 20th century. However, flying the American flag outside a school was begun in the 19th century. According to Wayne Whipple in *The Story of the American Flag* (Henry Altemus Co., Philadelphia, 1910), the first flag ever flown over a schoolhouse in the United States was unfurled in May of 1812 above a small log building on Catamount Hill in the town of Colrain, Massachusetts, in the Berkshire Mountains. However, that was performed by adults in honor of the men who went to war—the War of 1812—from Catamount Hill. The first instance of a flagraising over a grammar school as a patriotic practice for students was done on May 11, 1861 by Sylvander Hutchinson, principal of the Fifth Street Grammar School in New Bedford, Massachusetts. His example was soon followed by other towns in Massachusetts, New Hampshire, New York and elsewhere in the Northeast. After the Civil War, the practice became general. By the time *The Youth's Companion* advocated it and the Pledge of Allegiance, millions of children were saluting a flag at school.

3 For example, some years ago a black member of the Chicago City Council objected to starting the council meeting with the Pledge of Allegiance. He said African-Americans owed no allegiance to the nation which had enslaved them and considered them only three-fifths of a person. He added that he personally considered it an insult even to suggest that blacks should be expected to salute the American flag. For a counterview of the disdain which the councilman demonstrated, see *Up From Slavery* by Roger Wilkins (Beacon Press: Boston, 2002), a nephew of black civil rights activist Roy Wilkins.

4 At the request of Rep. Rabaut, the Pledge of Allegiance was set to music in 1955 as a song, "The Pledge of Allegiance to the Flag." It was composed by Irving Caesar and sung on the floor of the House of Representatives on Flag Day, June 14, 1955 by the official Air Force choral group, the "Singing Sergeants," in special Flag Day ceremonies.

5 Bellamy was also a socialist. Like his cousin, the utopian novelist Edward Bellamy, he believed in an American socialist utopia in which the government would run a peacetime economy and the people would live with political, social and economic equality. According to Dr. John W. Baer, author of *The Pledge of Allegiance: A Centennial History—1892-1992,* Bellamy wanted the Pledge to serve as "an international peace pledge" of universal brotherhood so that all the republics of the world "on their peace day, would put a white border around their flag, and recite it as a pledge." Bellamy, a person of high-minded ideals, co-founded the Society for Christian Socialists. Socialism, with its emphasis on the individual subordinated to the Total State, is the antithesis of American freedom. Bellamy's ideals were therefore naively misplaced in socialism, as the bloody history of the Union of Soviet Socialist Republics demonstrated the true character of the Total State to be totalitarian dictatorship and tyranny. According to William Norman Grigg ("One Nation Under the State?," *The New American*, 29 July 2002), Bellamy intended the Pledge to advance socialism via the classroom, but the phrase "under God" which was added by Congress in 1954 "detoxified" the Pledge and gave it meaning "exactly the opposite of what its author intended." In its present wording, our Founders would certainly have approved of the Pledge.

<sup>6</sup> President Eisenhower also said in a letter dated August 17, 1954, to the Knights of Columbus, recognizing their initiative in originating and sponsoring the amendment to the Pledge of Allegiance, "These words ["under God"] will remind Americans that despite our great physical strength we must remain humble. They will help us to keep constantly in our minds and hearts the spiritual and moral principles which alone give dignity to man, and upon which our way of life is founded."

In his 1955 State of the Union address he made this statement which further clarified the nature of America and its difference from atheistic Communism:

Ours is not a struggle merely of economic theories or of forms of government, or of military power. At issue is the true nature of man. Either man is the creature whom the Psalmist describes as "a little lower than the angels," or man is a soulless, animated machine..

# Chapter 3

# AND TO THE REPUBLIC FOR WHICH IT STANDS

At no time, at no place, in solemn convention assembled, through no chosen agents, had the American people officially proclaimed the United States to be a democracy. The Constitution did not contain the word or any word lending countenance to it, except possibly the mention of "We, the people," in the preamble… When the Constitution was framed no respectable person called himself or herself a democrat.

– Charles Austin Beard and Mary Ritter Beard,
*America in Midpassage*, 1939

In 1787, when the delegates to the Constitutional Convention in Philadelphia had finally agreed upon our form of government, a woman asked Benjamin Franklin, "What kind of a country have you given us, Mr. Franklin?" He replied, "A republic, madame, if you can keep it."

In 2001, according to *The American Legion* magazine ("The Misunderstood Constitution," May 2002, p. 26), Sen. Tom Daschle (D-South Dakota) began addressing an audience of students at Harvard Law School by recalling the famous story about Franklin. In Daschle's version, however, Franklin informed the woman that the country decided upon by the delegates would be "a democracy, if you can keep it."

Like Daschle, many citizens mistakenly think our government is a democracy. It is not; America is a republic. We pledge allegiance to the republic, not to "the democracy." The two are not the same. We are a democratic *society* but have a republican form of *government*. That is a critical distinction, poorly understood nowadays, but its ramifications are profound.

There are two primary aspects to the American experiment in living: our society and our government. They are based on different principles and should not be confused. Our society is based on freedom for all; our government is based on restraint of power to prevent abuse of that freedom. (See chapter 5.) So America is a democratic republic.

In a democracy, the people decide; in a republic, the people decide who decides. Democracy is actually an approach to governing—participation by all or most citizens. As a type of government rather than a particular form of government, democracy is different from autocracy, monarchy and oligarchy. However, as *The American Legion* article pointed out, democracies abound around the globe and they produce political systems as different in form as India and Switzerland. America has a democratic approach to governing, but even that is not pure democracy; rather, it is limited democracy because only certain citizens, not all, can vote and hold public office.

"Democracy" is derived from the Greek words *demos* and *kratein*, meaning "the people to rule." A democracy is direct rule by the people, especially the majority. Democracy functions via mass meetings, and as the population grows, such meetings become increasingly unwieldy and inefficient. A democracy is direct rule by the electorate.

"Republic" comes from the Latin *res* and *publica*, meaning "the public thing(s)," "of interest to the public" or more simply, "the law(s)." A republic is rule by a government in which supreme power resides in a body of citizens entitled to vote and is exercised by elected officers and representatives responsible to them and governing according to law. A republic can expand indefinitely as its size or population grows, yet still function efficiently and effectively. A republic is indirect rule by the electorate through representative government.

James Madison, the "Father of the Constitution," contrasted the two approaches to governing—direct rule vs. representative rule—with these words in The Federalist Papers, No. 10:

> Democracies have ever been spectacles of turbulence and contention; have ever been found incompatible with personal security or the rights of property; and have in general been as short in their lives as they have been violent in their deaths...
>
> A Republic, by which I mean a government in which the scheme of representation takes place, opens a different prospect and promises the cure for which we are seeking.

Likewise, Gouverneur Morris, the author of the Preamble to the Constitution and the key member of the Committee on Style who made most of the stylistic improvements to the Constitution, rejected unbridled democracy for America. "History, the parent of political science," Morris wrote of the Founders at the Constitutional Convention, "had told them that it was almost as vain to expect permanency from a democracy as to construct a palace on the surface of the sea."

Edmund Randolph of Virginia, describing the effort his contemporaries had in dealing with the issue at the Constitutional Convention, wrote, "The general object was to produce a cure for the evils under which the United States labored; that in tracing these evils to their origins, every man had found it in the turbulence and follies of democracy."

John Adams said plainly, "Remember, democracy never lasts long. It soon wastes, exhausts, and murders itself. There never was a democracy yet that did not commit suicide."

Benjamin Rush, a signer of the Declaration of Independence, was equally plain: "A simple democracy...is one of the greatest of evils."

John Witherspoon, another signer, said, "Pure democracy cannot subsist long nor be carried far into the departments of state, it is very subject to caprice and the madness of popular rage."

Benjamin Franklin wittily explained, "Democracy is two wolves and a lamb voting on what to have for lunch." (1)

In simplest terms, the difference between a democracy and a republic is this: the tyrannical rule of man vs. the enlightened rule of law. As John Adams put it, America functions as "a government of laws, not of men."

Unlike a democracy, in a republic the individual is sovereign. In the American republic, the rule of law protects individual life, personal liberty and personal property, even against majority demands. The minority, even when it is a minority of one, is protected against the whims and passions of the majority.

Neither the Declaration of Independence nor the Constitution mention democracy, and for a good reason. (Nor do any of the constitutions of the 50 states.) The Founders of our nation were skeptical of pure democracy because it is unchecked power. They recognized that pure democracy is unbridled individualism which tends toward anarchy, that "the many" cannot govern directly and that the passions of the electorate can be manipulated by demagogues, factions and cabals. To the Founders, democracy meant centralized power, controlled by majority opinion, which was up for grabs and therefore completely arbitrary. They had the opportunity to establish America as a democracy, but chose not to and made clear that we were never to become one. They wisely created a representative government of deliberative bodies via a Constitution which decentralized power and is difficult to change. When change is made, it is made only through a carefully devised system of deliberation among all the states representing "we the people." As Thomas Jefferson declared, "The republican is the only form of government which is not eternally at open or secret war with the rights of mankind." (2)

Moreover, since we the people have inalienable rights from God and simply delegate power to the government, ***under the Constitution our government cannot have rights which we the people do not have***. Understanding that is fundamental to the maintenance of good government in America. It assures freedom and keeps government subordinate to us.

The Founders formed a check-and-balance system to limit federal power by dividing government into three branches: the executive, the legislative and the judicial. They regarded that as the first line of defense of liberty. No. 51 of *The Federalist Papers* warned, "But what is government itself but the greatest of all reflections on human nature? If men were angels, no government would be necessary." Likewise, George Washington solemnly warned in his 1796 Farewell Address, "The spirit of encroachment tends to consolidate the powers of all the departments into one, and thus create, whatever the form of government, a real despotism." The delegated powers of those branches are strictly enumerated, and all else is left, as the Tenth Amendment puts it, "to the states respectively, or to the people." (In other words, the Founders wanted to make it absolutely clear that the states and the people had *even more* rights, even if they were not explicitly listed in the Constitution. If the Constitution does not explicitly set forth a delegated power, the federal government does not have it.) The Founders also limited the terms of office for elected officials to conduct the people's business so there would not be "career" or "lifetime" politicians running the country. And unlike many countries, the brilliance of the Constitution assures the peaceful transition of power in Congress following each election, so that the winning party is not challenged by a military dictator or a citizens' revolution.

## Democracy vs. the Constitution

The brilliance of the Constitution is why the disputed 2000 presidential election was settled through the rule of constitutional procedure and law. When the race between George Bush and Al Gore became too close to be certain who the winner of the popular vote was, voter recount was used. Charges of voter fraud were handled by public officials and the courts.

Then the institution of the Electoral College entered the picture, as required by the Constitution. Many Americans do not realize that the president is not elected democratically; he is elected by the delegates to the Electoral College. A voter's ballot is cast not for a candidate but for a party's slate of electors. That is yet another safeguard which our Founders devised to protect our freedom against the flaws of democracy. In presidential elections the winner in each state receives the state's electors (and even then, electors are free to vote otherwise). When one candidate has a majority, the electors cast their votes in the Electoral College, thereby choosing the next chief executive of the nation.

The Founders created the Electoral College because they trusted neither politicians nor the direct vote method. They felt Congress shouldn't elect the President because he would then owe those politicians favors. They also felt that voting directly for the President might give the most populated states an unfair advantage and could lead to mob rule. Thus, after weeks of debate at the Constitutional Convention, the Electoral College was created. It has worked well in handling presidential elections. The 2000 election, although highly disputed and litigated, was not a constitutional crisis; rather, the Constitution worked well, as it has for more than two centuries. It remains the oldest national constitution on Earth because of its brilliance.

Note that the Constitution states in Article 4, Section 4, "The United States shall guarantee to every State in this Union a republican form of government." So each state of the Union is a republic as well.

## Democratic Society, Republican Government

Yes, we are a democratic society in the sense of being open, classless and assuring equal rights and protection for all under the rule of law, and also by extending the voting franchise widely in the citizenry, but we have a republican form of government which uses voters to elect representative officials to serve us in that function. Some people, using a phrase which combines those two aspects of our nation, call America a representative democracy. However, that term, while technically correct, directs attention away from our republican form of government which alone enables democracy to work—and work fairly.

Now, it is true that our Founders had the democratic principle in mind when they established our nation. The concept of equality under the law is a democratic one; there can be no aristocracy or legally privileged class in America. In a democracy such as America, the saying "every man is king" means every citizen is sovereign, just as a king or queen is sovereign, not a subject. American citizens have no ruler except their own self-rule (that is, self-control or self-government) and the external government which they authorize to act on their behalf. Citizens are free to pursue all areas of life, without restrictions of rank or class.

It is also true that democracy as a specific form of government is in the American tradition because many towns and villages have long used the direct vote in deciding local issues; the town meeting of all voters is an important instrument for self-government and local control. In fact, the principle of decentralized government (as distinguished from monolithic government, whether by monarchism or totalitarian collectivism) and local control was fundamental to the thinking of our Founders, and is embodied in the Constitution through the three-part structure of the federal government and the bicameral structure of Congress. Decentralized government is a principle form of check-and-balance against usurpation of power.

Additionally, some states have the initiative, referendum and recall, which are democratic direct-vote procedures. The initiative allows citizens to initiate a proposal which is then placed on an election ballot; electors vote for or against it, and if it "wins," it goes into law. (California's famous Proposition 13, which froze property taxes in the 1980s, is an example of the initiative.) Thomas Jefferson himself suggested the democratic procedure called referendum, which allows the electorate to directly vote "yes" or "no" (i.e., retain or repeal) on legislation already passed and to recall a legislator (i.e., remove the person from office) if the majority of the electorate are dissatisfied with him or her.

However, Alexis de Tocqueville's classic 1835 book *Democracy in America* is not so much about our government as it is about our society, our nongovernmental institutions, our egalitarian (nonaristocratic, classless) way of life as a people. (The distinction between the government of our nation and the society of our nation is critical to resolving the issue of separation of church and state. See the next chapter.)

In a democracy, the rule of law can change to whatever the majority wants at any moment; 51% of the voters can overrule the rights of the other 49%. In a republic, the rule of law is removed from direct control by the electorate; this makes for more thoughtful and deliberative consideration of all lawmaking. The republican method safeguards against tyranny, not only from rule by despots and classes, but also from tyranny by the masses. Those masses have, at times, "democratically" become lynch mobs, depriving individuals of due process of law, even when the "crime" is nothing more than challenging the status quo. That's neither liberty nor justice; that's mobocracy. In mobocracy, the majority rules directly and the only dissenting vote comes from the person at the end of the rope.

As John F. McManus, former publisher of *The New American,* put it (October 6, 2003, p. 44), our Founders abhorred democracy because it is unbridled majority rule, and majority rule is not always right or righteous. Our Founders, he pointed out, showed their contempt for rule by unrestricted popular opinion with their decision to have senators appointed by state legislators and presidents chosen by electors. "They understood that popular sentiment should never replace independent thought, good judgment, and courageous adherence to principles." [3] (With regard to senators, that safeguard was changed in 1913 by the 17th Amendment, which authorized their direct election by the people of each state. The intent of our Founders was to have Senators allied to state legislatures, unlike representatives who were elected directly by the voters of their district. That way, our Founders thought, states' rights would be better protected when national affairs were subjected to legislation.)

## The Danger of Unchecked Democracy

Unchecked democracy can be unjust, as when Socrates was condemned to death by his fellow Athenians—the very men who first articulated the concept of democracy—simply because he asked discomforting philosophic questions. [4] To guard against such democratic tyranny, our Founders took an additional step. They amended our Constitution with a Bill of Rights which guarantees individual liberties, no matter what the group in power may say. In the American republic, under the rule of law articulated by the Constitution and the Bill of Rights, majority rule, executive order and judicial decree can never override individual rights because, as the Declaration states, they are conferred upon us by God and are therefore inherent and inalienable.

Unlike Socrates, Americans can raise questions which challenge the status quo, thanks to our constitutional freedom of speech and the press. Unlike the Puritans who were driven from 17th century England for their religious beliefs which differed from the established Church of England (see the next chapter for details), Americans can worship as they want, thanks to our constitutional freedom of religion. In a democracy, that might not be the case.

In a democracy, nothing is off-limits to a vote which can overrule the previous condition. Democracy does not support the doctrine of inalienable rights which is essential for a free society. In our American republic, the will of the majority can never override our God-given rights because they are held to exist in us prior to government, and government itself is instituted to protect them against people, whether inside and outside our borders, who would override our rights by stealth, coercion or naked force. *The Constitution does not grant rights; it only guarantees rights which are already ours, even before the Constitution was written, by virtue of our spiritual nature*. In a democracy, however, where the majority makes the rules, whatever rights a citizen may have are bestowed by the government and can be taken away by the government if popular opinion so dictates.

Note this well: *in America, there are only individual rights*. The idea of collective, class or group rights is totally contrary to the theory of American government. God created all people equal; He did not create some with special privileges. If each individual American is sovereign and protected, all are sovereign and protected; if a class or group of people are given special rights or privileges, aristocracy will arise, followed by despotism and tyranny from a ruling class. Collective rights lead only to collective authority and then to rampant collectivism, which is another name for totalitarianism and tyranny.

This principle of individual rights is expressed in a wide variety of ways which uphold personal freedom: freedom of conscience, the secret ballot, the idea that a man's home is his castle (safe from spying and government invasion), the privacy of the mail, the privacy of a person's financial, medical and educational records, the confidentiality of client-attorney communications, the judicial concept of presumed innocence until proven guilty, and so forth. Either everyone's rights are protected or no one's rights will be protected. Thomas Paine put it simply: "He that would make his own liberty secure must guard even his enemy from oppression."

In our American republic, the primary duty of government is to safeguard our freedom; in a democracy, no one's freedom is safe. Americans need to understand that clearly. Without such understanding, we will fall prey to demagogues preaching democracy as a pretext for tyranny.

The words "democratic" and "republic" appear in the names of many countries, but without justification. For example, the People's Republic of China and the Republic of Iran clearly are not republican in their government, and the Democratic Republic of Vietnam and the Democratic Republic of Uganda are neither democratic nor republican. In fact, Communist countries call themselves "people's democracies" but in those cases, "democracy" is a synonym for "Communism." There is no pluralism, that is, no rights for minorities, let alone individuals. There is one-party rule by the dictator who maintains power through military might and suppression of all dissent. So naming something democratic does not make it so. America lives up to the words. Therefore, *if the word democracy is used in describing American government, let it be "democratic constitutional republic."*

---

## FOOTNOTES

[1] Franklin's complete statement was "Democracy is two wolves and a lamb voting on what to have for lunch. Liberty is a well-armed lamb contesting the vote."

John Adams described the evils of democracy at greater length: "[D]emocracy will soon degenerate into an anarchy, such an anarchy that every man will do what is right in his own eyes and no man's life or property or reputation or liberty will be secure, and every one of these will soon mould itself into a system of subordination of all the moral virtues and intellectual abilities, all the powers of wealth, beauty, wit and science, to the wanton pleasures, the capricious will, and the execrable cruelty of one or a very few."

[2] Rush Limbaugh elaborated on this point in an essay entitled "Whatever Happened to Limited Government?" (*The Limbaugh Letter*, August 2003, p. 2). Smaller government is arguably the single most significant idea, the core principle which explains the success of America, he said. Protecting the individual from the power of government by limiting the reach of government is the foremost accomplishment of the Constitution. Our Founders recognized that throughout history, government has been the biggest obstacle to the individual pursuit of happiness.

> The Founders realized that it is overreaching government power which…robs human beings of their God-given birthright: freedom. They knew it is government which impinges on liberty. It is government which shackles and thwarts and stifles human imagination and human potential the world over, and has throughout mankind's experience.
> The secret [to overcoming that evil]? Government power must be divided, checked, limited.

[3] McManus's essay is entitled "How Polls Can Destroy America." He points out the dangerous trend in polling which announces what the majority supposedly thinks and then drives politicians toward making that national policy. The logic behind it is: If the majority wants something, the government has a duty to provide it. Yet pollsters themselves may have an agenda which drives them to shape public opinion, rather than

objectively reporting it, by skewing questions toward the results they want. They may even falsify results altogether. "More and more in America," McManus writes, "the opinion of the majority is what counts. But majorities are often incorrect. If we Americans continue to allow ourselves to be influenced by polls, we might as well tear up the Constitution, abolish Congress, and ask a pollster to discover what we should do about everything."

[4] In ancient Greece, women could not vote. Moreover, there was no such thing as a secret ballot; the men voted publicly by voice or by show of hands. In addition, votes were weighted according to the age and wealth of the voter; the oldest and the richest counted for more in a voting situation.

## Chapter 4

# "ONE NATION UNDER GOD"

...it is the first duty of all nations to acknowledge the providence of almighty God, to obey His will, to be grateful for His benefits, and to humbly implore His protection and favor in holy fear....Now, therefore I do recommend and assign Thursday, the 26th day of November next to be devoted by the People of these States...that we may then all unite in rendering...our sincere and humble thanks.
— George Washington, First Presidential Thanksgiving Proclamation
October 3, 1789

It has seemed to me fit and proper that the blessings to America should be reverently, solemnly, and gratefully acknowledged, as with one heart and voice, by the whole American people. I do, therefore, invite my fellow citizens in every part of the United States, and also those who are at sea, and those who are sojourning in foreign lands, to set apart and observe the last Thursday of November next as a day of thanksgiving and prayer to our beneficent Father who dwelleth in the heavens. And I recommend to them that, while offering up the ascriptions justly due to Him for such singular deliverances and blessings, they do also, with humble penitence for our national perverseness and disobedience, commend to His tender care all those who have become widows, orphans, mourners, or sufferers in the lamentable civil strife in which we are unavoidably engaged, and fervently implore the interposition of the Almighty hand to heal the wounds of the nation, and to restore it, as soon as may be consistent with divine purposes, to the full enjoyment of peace, harmony, tranquility, and union.

— Abraham Lincoln, Thanksgiving Proclamation, 1863

During the 2000 presidential election campaign, former Sen. Joseph Lieberman (D-Connecticut), the running mate of Vice President Al Gore, began referring to God in his political speeches. Lieberman is an Orthodox Jew; on Sabbaths when Congress was in session, he walked to the Capitol because it is against his religious principles to drive a vehicle then.

Shortly after Lieberman's references to deity began, a fellow Jew, Abraham Foxman, head of the Anti-Defamation League, criticized Lieberman about them. On national television during the evening news, Foxman said that religious talk has no place in political life and should be kept strictly private. He claimed that was the intent of the "wall of separation between church and state" erected by the Framers of our Constitution via the First Amendment.

No reporters questioned Foxman's stance, but they should have because he was completely and utterly wrong. His comment was based on ignorance—a sadly widespread ignorance which, ironically, is becoming destructive of the very freedom which supporters of that view claim to uphold.

The decision in 2002 by the Ninth Circuit Court of Appeals to prohibit the Pledge of Allegiance because God is mentioned exemplifies that. It was likewise completely and utterly wrong—a gross distortion and pathetic reversal of the truth. So was the 2003 vote of the court confirming its previous decision. The court's decision is totally contrary to the original intent of our Founders and the Framers of the Constitution. It stands the First Amendment on its head and demonstrates an appalling ignorance of our religious heritage.

The First Amendment does not prohibit religious expression in public settings; it does not require the public to be protected or insulated from things which may have religious significance or origin. It most certainly does not compel hostility to religion. Rather, it prohibits (1) establishment of a national religion and (2) government interference in the free expression of religion. Thus it provides no grounds whatsoever for barring the Pledge of Allegiance or even just the two words "under God." (It also prohibits federal funding of religious establishments; the nation may not formally support or favor any religious body as an institution.) In short, the First Amendment guarantees that the federal government cannot abridge the freedom we naturally have. Freedom of religion (or of anything else, such as speech, assembly, the press, etc.) is not *granted* by the Constitution. That freedom is inherent in us, prior to all government being established. The Constitution simply *protects* our God-given freedom—including our freedom of conscience and freedom to worship—by limiting the powers of the government.

## Secular Government, Religious Society

The so-called "wall of separation" is not mentioned in the Constitution, the Declaration of Independence or any other document upon which American government is founded. However, God is. [1] Moreover, our Founders not only mentioned God repeatedly, they also publicly prayed for God's guidance and help, and called on all citizens to do likewise. Our Founders did *not* intend for America to have a rigidly secular public society in which religious "God-talk" was prohibited in the public square. For example, when independence from Great Britain was being debated, Patrick Henry declared, "An appeal to arms and to the God of hosts is all that is left us!" Likewise, when Congress first met, the delegates began with public prayer. (See Sidebar 4.) For yet another example, when Congress approved the Declaration of Independence, John Adams declared that the Fourth of July "ought to be commemorated as the day of deliverance by solemn acts of devotion to God Almighty." And a final example: In 1777 the Continental Congress ordered a day of thanksgiving and praise. It urged that the people "join the penitent confession of their manifold sins...[that the day, through] their humble and earnest supplication...may please God, through the merits of Jesus Christ..."

Thus, Lieberman's campaign references to God were aligned with one of the noblest of America's political traditions: public piety by civic officials.

The phrase "wall of separation between church and state" was first stated by Thomas Jefferson in January, 1802, when he was President, in a personal letter he wrote replying to a question by the Baptist Association in Danbury, Connecticut, about a rumor that a national religion was to be established. He told the Baptists that the First Amendment built "a wall of separation between church and State" because it is the "expression of the supreme will of the nation *in behalf of the rights of conscience*" [emphasis added]. The wall keeps government from controlling religion and from "prohibiting the free expression thereof."

In other words, **the First Amendment erects a wall of separation between organized religion and political authority in order to keep political authority from interfering with organized religion—precisely the opposite of what is happening today across America by people intent on driving God out of the public square**. Jefferson continued:

> Believing with you that religion is a matter which lies solely between man and his God, that he owes account to none other for his faith or his worship, that the legislative powers of government reach actions only, and not opinions, I contemplate with sovereign reverence that act of the whole American People which declared that their legislature should "make no law respecting an establishment of religion, or prohibiting the free exercise thereof," thus building a wall of separation between church and state.

Jefferson concluded his letter to the Danbury Baptists by saying, "I reciprocate your kind prayers for the protection and blessing of the common Father and Creator of man..."

America has a secular *government*, but we are, and always have been, a religious *society*. Our republican government is strictly prohibited from endorsing religion or interfering with the free expression of religion, but our democratic society, rooted in religion, is free to express itself religiously in the public square at all levels, including presidential debates. Religion has been a major influence in the affairs of our country from the time of the first English settlements.

The charter for Virginia, written in 1606, stated that one reason, among others, for establishing the Jamestown colony was to propagate Christianity to the Native Americans who "live yet in Darkness and miserable Ignorance of the true Knowledge and Worship of God."

The Mayflower Compact, written in 1620 by the Pilgrim Fathers to express their agreement upon rules for self-government of "the Lord's free people," begins, "In the Name of God, Amen."

Some say the American Revolution itself started in our churches. That means more than just ideologically. Remember that Paul Revere's ride began when a lantern was hung in the belfry of the North Church. Clergy were among the signers of the founding documents of the United States. [2]

Our Founders were not neutral on the question of whether there is a God and what that means for human conduct, both public and private. To understand how important religion was to them, ask yourself what the very first freedom enumerated in the Bill of Rights is. Answer: freedom of religion. The First Amendment begins, "Congress shall make no law respecting an establishment of religion, or prohibiting the free exercise thereof..." Thomas Jefferson called religious liberty "the most inalienable and sacred of all human rights." It is no exaggeration to say that, just as the Pilgrims landed at Plymouth Rock in search of religious liberty, America itself is founded on the rock of free exercise of religion to worship our Creator, without interference or oppression from the state. Religious pluralism—i.e., freedom of religion and conscience—is one of the pillars on which our national unity stands. Consider, for example, John Adams' words in his 1776 essay "Thoughts on Government":

> It is the duty of all men in society, publicly, and at stated seasons, to worship the SUPREME BEING, the great Creator and Preserver of the universe. And no subject shall be hurt, molested, or restrained, in his person, liberty, or estate, for worshipping GOD in the manner most agreeable to the dictates of his own conscience; or for his religious profession or sentiments; provided he doth not disturb the public peace, or obstruct others in their religious worship.

Those are the words of our second president. Our sixth president, his son, John Quincy Adams, echoed his father in this thoughtful statement:

> Our political way of life is by the Laws of Nature and of Nature's God, and of course presupposes the existence of God, the moral ruler of the universe, and a rule of right and wrong, of just and unjust, binding upon man, preceding all institutions of human society and government.

## Separation of Church and State, Not God and State

The Founders of America believed in the separation of church and state, but not in the separation of God and state. [3] The founding idea of our republic, Terence Jeffrey comments (*Human Events*, 10 March 2003, p. 8) is that our elected representatives will seek through constitutionally limited government to honor God's law in our own. The Founders deliberately built America upon religious principles, even while excluding the possibility of a national religion, because they understood that if we refuse to recognize God's sovereignty and authority over America, we would be forced to recognize someone else's, such as a king or a military dictator. They never intended to exclude and divorce all religious expression and exercise of faith from public life, let alone suppress it as some Americans are now trying to do.

On the contrary, the Founders did not hesitate to demonstrate religious piety when in civic office. They called the populace to observe days of fasting and days of giving thanks to God. (The quotations from George Washington and Abraham Lincoln at the head of this chapter are two of hundreds of similar quotes which could be cited from nearly every president, state governor and other public officials throughout the history of our nation.) They called in public prayer for wisdom and guidance from God, and Congress even held worship services in the Capitol itself. [4] (See Sidebar 4.) Why? It was fundamental to their view of good government and good society. It was self-evident to them that God is the foundation of America. ***Belief in Man's divine origin, and in the supreme dignity and value of the individual because of his or her spiritual nature, are the twin principles which control the relationship of us citizens with our government and our society. We are "one Nation under God."***

The Framers did indeed erect a wall of separation between church and state in the First Amendment—and also in Article VI, which prohibits any religious test for civic officials—but only to protect religion from the state, not the state from religion. As Stephen L. Carter, Professor of Law at Yale University, says in *The Culture of Disbelief*, the purpose of the wall is to assure maximum freedom for religion.

Through the First Amendment's "separation" clause, the Framers intended to keep the nation from establishing an official religion such as Great Britain had with the Church of England, and from controlling religious matters. There would be no merging of political and ecclesiastical organizations. That was to assure Americans freedom of religious practice and freedom from religious domination. In England, where the monarch was head of both church and state, if you did not belong to the established Church, you could not vote, own property, go to college or sit in Parliament, but you nevertheless had to pay taxes to support the Church—e.g., for construction and maintenance of buildings and for ministers' salaries. English law required everyone to attend the Church's services. Worst of all, if you worshipped in unapproved ways or refused to attend Church of England services, you could be punished by fines, imprisonment, hanging or even burning at the stake. Religious intolerance and persecution resulted in the deaths of thousands, all because of differences in belief. Precisely that was why the Pilgrims sailed to Massachusetts.

In no way did the Founders want to keep religio-moral thought and behavior out of government—or out of schools. On the contrary, they stated clearly and repeatedly that for a republic such as ours, which functions on self-government, only the moral constraints of religion would keep American liberty from degenerating into libertinism and tyranny. They envisioned a "republic of virtue." James Madison, the Father of the Constitution, said in Federalist 55 of *The Federalist Papers* that citizen virtue is more important in republican regimes, where the people rule, than in nondemocratic forms of government, where autocratic force can be used to control the populace. Even more to the point, Madison said, "We have staked the entire future of the American civilization, not upon the power of government, but on the American people following the Ten Commandments of God." [5]

President Lyndon Johnson made a similar point in this 1961 statement:

We need to remember that the separation of church and state must never mean the separation of religious values from the lives of public servants... If we who serve free men today are to differ from the tyrants of this age, we must balance the powers in our hands with God in our hearts.

For the same reason, President Franklin D. Roosevelt, in announcing that America had been attacked at Pearl Harbor by Japan, prayed aloud publicly with these words: "We humbly ask the blessings of God. May He protect each and every one of you. May He guide me in the days to come."

Political self-government begins with governing ourselves personally, which means morally. For our Founders, moral instruction was to begin in the home and be continued in church and synagogue, in school and through public example of office holders, civic leaders and opinion makers. Religion was vital in all that. The false, inverted interpretation of the separation of church and state doctrine which Foxman, the Ninth Circuit Court and others uphold today actually *separates* morality from political and public life. It separates morality from America's common, daily experience and drives God and godliness from the public square. It is therefore profoundly destructive of the fabric and the very foundation of American society. Our Founders would have roundly condemned such an aberrant misunderstanding of their intent to establish a godly nation.

For example, the Northwest Ordinance passed by Congress in 1787 said, "Religion, morality and knowledge, being necessary to good government and the happiness of mankind, schools and the means of education shall forever be encouraged." In his Farewell Address to the nation in 1796, President George Washington declared that "religion and morality are indispensable supports [for] political prosperity" and warned that we cannot expect "that national morality will prevail in the exclusion of religious principle." Likewise, in 1798, when John Adams was President, he told a group of Massachusetts military officers, "We have no government armed with power capable of contending with human passions unbridled by morality and religion.... Our Constitution was made only for a moral and religious people. It is wholly inadequate for the government of any other." Benjamin Franklin stated, "Only virtuous people are capable of freedom. As nations become more corrupt and vicious, they have more need of masters [dictators]." Samuel Adams declared that "neither the wisest constitution nor the wisest laws will secure the liberty and happiness of a people whose manners are universally corrupt." Similarly, Thomas Jefferson, in *Notes on the State of Virginia*, said, "And can the liberties of a nation be thought secure when we have removed their only firm basis, a conviction in the minds of the people that these liberties are of the gift of God?" And likewise James Madison: "The belief in God All Powerful wise and good, is so essential to the moral order of the World and to the happiness of man, that arguments which enforce it cannot be drawn from too many sources..." All were implicitly echoing the statement by William Penn, founder of Pennsylvania, a century earlier: Unless we are governed by God, we will be governed by tyrants. Benjamin Franklin, another Pennsylvanian, agreed: "Man will ultimately be governed by God or by tyrants."

Prayers at public events and displays of religious symbols such as nativity scenes and menorahs on public property are wholly in line with the intent of the Founders, who understood God and nation to be inseparable. It was self-evident truth. Therefore they sought divine guidance through public and private prayer, study of the Bible, and through instruction via sermonizing by ministers and clerics, both in places of worship and in private discourse. Placing study of our national motto "In God we trust" in school curricula would be unanimously regarded by them not simply as appropriate, but as absolutely necessary to the education of youth. To rephrase Penn, unless we are one nation under God, we will be one nation ungodly—which is to say, we will cease to exist as a free and virtuous democratic republic.

Today, however, Americans who are ignorant of their history and their heritage have secularized society to the point where freedom of religious expression is under assault and Christian worship in particular is subject to persecution. God is being outlawed in our culture. [6] For example, prayer is outlawed at graduations and athletic events, Christmas carols are forbidden in schools, students are suspended from school for saying grace over lunch, nativity scenes are prohibited on public property and student religious clubs cannot meet in classrooms after the school day is over. (Sad joke: Why is it that children can't read a Bible in school but can in prison?) Similarly, politically active clergy who speak out on issues of the day from their pulpits or in the media are threatened by the IRS with loss of tax-exempt status for their church—and some have actually lost it—as if the First Amendment does not apply to houses of worship. [7] The natural and divine foundation of the rights of man is no longer self-evident to all Americans.

That truth and the fundamental distinction between secular government and religious society is being lost to the understanding of our citizenry because organizations such as American Civil Liberties Union, American Atheists, Anti-Defamation League, and Americans United for Separation of Church and State are trying to blur and eventually remove it. Whether that is due to ignorance or something else, their irrational and self-destructive goal is to remove God from America, even though God is fundamental to our country's very existence and to the freedom they seek to preserve. [8]

## God Is the Foundation of America

Why fundamental? Read the Declaration of Independence. It states the basic principles and universal truths upon which the United States of America is founded. The Declaration clearly indicates that our freedom, our sovereignty, our equality, our rights, our justice and our human dignity descend to us from God, not government. As Alexander Hamilton explained in 1775, "The sacred rights of mankind are not to be rummaged for among parchments and musty records. They are written, as with a sun beam, in the whole volume of human nature, by the hand of the divinity itself, and can never be erased or obscured by mortal power." In 1961 Supreme Court Justice William O. Douglas restated that in McGowan vs. Maryland:

> The institutions of our society are founded on the belief that there is an authority higher than the authority of the State; that there is a moral law which the State is powerless to alter; that the individual possesses rights, conferred by the Creator, which government must respect. The Declaration of Independence stated [that] theme.

There are four references to deity in the Declaration. They are "nature's God," "Creator," "Supreme Judge of the world" and "Divine Providence." As mentioned earlier, one signer, John Adams, also described God in his writings as "the Spirit of Liberty." These terms make clear that the Founders believed Man is made in the living image of God, and that the fundamental basis on which our nation stands is acknowledgment of God as the supreme authority for the conduct of our national life and our personal life. The Declaration announced both our independence from foreign authority and our dependence on God for life and the blessings of liberty. The references to deity show that our Founders regarded God as the Creator, Lawgiver, Judge and Source of individual rights. That is the most basic fact of our existence as individuals and as a society. It is the religio-moral, or spiritual, underpinning of the American nation. (See Appendix 3, "The Ten Principles of American Patriotism.")

To be American, therefore, inherently means to live in accordance with the will of the Divine Source of all creation, as expressed in the Declaration of Independence. Freedom, rightly understood, carries a responsibility to honor the source of our freedom, which is the Spirit of Liberty. Respect for everyone's inalienable rights to life, liberty, property and the pursuit of happiness was expected of all Americans because all rights carry the inherent obligation to exercise the right properly—that is, wisely, responsibly, morally. As George Washington put it, happiness and moral duty are inseparably connected. Such conduct is, quite simply, respect for law as a reflection of the Divine Source of life, liberty and law. Such conduct distinguishes liberty from license and is the hallmark of good citizenship. It is the religio-moral, or spiritual, identity of the American people.

## God and the Constitution

Clearly, the Founders did not intend for citizens to be bound to any denominational understanding of God. They themselves had differing conceptions of God, ranging from Roman Catholicism and various forms of Protestantism to the more philosophic views of Theism and Deism. This respect for freedom of thought and worship was reinforced in the Bill of Rights, which assured in the First Amendment that Congress would make no law "respecting an establishment of religion"—i.e., no law giving special status to one denomination above all others, which had been the case in Britain, where the monarch —both temporal and spiritual sovereign of the realm—was head of the Church of England. An oppressive establishment of religion was why the Pilgrims left England, separated from the Church and eventually settled at Plymouth, Massachusetts. [9]

However, a simple acknowledgment of God by government was not regarded as an "establishment of religion." The God referred to in the Declaration of Independence is universal and transcends the particulars of any religion; our Founders deliberately took that stance. (See Sidebar 4, "The First Prayer in Congress.") In fact, to Jefferson's two references to God ("nature's God" and "Creator") in his draft of the Declaration of Independence, the Congress added two more ("Supreme Judge of the world" and "Divine Providence"). Therefore, as I noted above, since the beginning of our nation, it has been customary for public officials, from the federal to the local levels, to swear an oath to God upon taking office, to call upon God for guidance, support and deliverance from difficulties for the American people, and to express gratitude for good fortune (as in Thanksgiving Day proclamations—see Sidebar 6). When Parliament closed the port of Boston in 1774 as a result of the Tea Party, Virginia's House of Burgesses observed a day of fasting, humiliation and prayer. When the British bombarded Boston in 1774, the first act of the Continental Congress was a public prayer. When the Constitutional Convention verged on collapse, Benjamin Franklin suggested that the delegates pray together daily for guidance. His suggestion was adopted and thereafter the convention proceeded successfully to create our Constitution. Franklin's motion for prayer stated:

> I have lived, sir, a long time; and the longer I live, the more convincing proofs I
> see of this truth, that God governs in the affairs of men. And if a sparrow cannot
> fall to the ground without His notice, is it probable that an empire can rise without
> His aid? [10]

Following this rebuke to the convention, David Barton tells us in *America: To Pray or Not to Pray?* (p. 112), the delegates entered a three-day recess, during which they fasted, prayed and invited local ministers to address them and pray for them.

The Father of Our Country, George Washington, demonstrated civic piety repeatedly. Near the beginning of our War for Independence, in the summer of 1776, he rallied his troops, saying, "The time is now near at hand which must  probably determine whether Americans are to be freedmen or slaves….The fate of unborn millions will now depend, under God, on the courage and conduct of the army." Note the phrase "under God."

In 1783, when the Treaty of Paris was about to be signed, marking the official termination of the war, Washington wrote and sent this prayer (known formally as the Circular Address of 1783, but more popularly as Washington's Prayer for the Nation) to the governors of all the states in the name of civic piety.

> I now make it my earnest prayer that God would have you, and the State over which you preside, in His holy protection; that he would incline the hearts of the citizens to cultivate a spirit of subordination and obedience to government; to entertain a brotherly affection and love for one another, for their fellow citizens of the United States at large, and particularly for their brethren who have served in the field; and, finally, that he would most graciously be pleased to dispose us all to do justice, to love mercy, and to demean ourselves with that charity, humility and pacific temper of mind which were the characteristics of the Divine Author of our blessed religion and, without a humble imitation of whose example in these things, we can never hope to be a happy nation.

Washington's "ernest prayer" may not have been well received by freethinkers and atheists—there was no public comment about it either way—but no one, including them, questioned his or anyone else's right to pray publicly on behalf of the nation. Likewise, when Washington was sworn in as President in 1788 with his hand upon a bible, he added the words "so help me God" [11] to the oath of office prescribed by the Constitution, and nearly every president since then has done likewise. (See Sidebar 5.) For the same reason, our coins and currency proclaim "In God We Trust" and Congress begins session with a prayer offered by the Chaplain to Congress. In 1998, the U.S. District Court of Ohio affirmed the practice of civic piety in rejecting a suit by the American Civil Liberties Union to declare unconstitutional  the Ohio state motto, "With God All Things Are Possible." The Court remarked that "this nation was founded on transcendent values which flow from a belief in a Supreme Being." (In Spring 2000, the Sixth Circuit Court of Appeals overturned that decision, but the governor of Ohio pledged to go to the Supreme Court about it. The following year the ACLU withdrew its suit.)

Although God is not explicitly mentioned in the Constitution, it was nevertheless assumed by the Framers that the principles expressed in the Declaration provided the basis on which our laws and policies would be articulated. Equally important, they assumed that government officials would conduct themselves in accordance with that religio-moral view of life. In fact, the American theory of government also has a clear demand for moral behavior by those holding governmental office; it reflects the Founders' understanding that God demands moral behavior of us all as the foundation for growth to deeper understanding of our nature and destiny. Elected officials are required to take an oath or to affirm that they will support the Constitution. Obviously, supporting the Constitution means honoring and upholding the fundamental principles which it embodies. An official who egregiously violates that understanding is subject to impeachment, whether his or her misconduct involves high crimes (violations of law) or misdemeanors (grossly immoral misbehavior). All this reflects the Founders' understanding that an immoral people is incapable of self-government. Any government it may set up will devalue honor, honesty and civility; it will legalize plundering, abridge rights and erode freedom. That is why Jefferson said, "A nation as a society forms a moral person, and every member of it is personally responsible for his society." Morality, of course, is rooted in religion.

***Without public recognition that God is the basis of our government, our social order and our moral character as a people, this nation will not stand.*** And while it is true that America is "a covenant nation" founded primarily by Christians, the God to whom we Americans appealed in the Declaration of Independence is the nondenominational Universal Creator of the world and Man. That God, in America, can never become the exclusive property of any denomination or religion; the First Amendment assures that.

If we are to live successfully as a society dedicated to liberty and justice for all, that fact must be acknowledged and honored by every American. It must again become self-evident. With that understanding and the moral behavior it requires of us, America will continue to lead the way to a better world. Without it, freedom will perish from the earth. The American Legion *Chaplain's Handbook* summarizes the matter clearly (p. 4):

> In the beginning of our Nation's history, when it was still a colony of England, America covenanted with God in a unique sense, and later, when the Republic was born, God was recognized as the source of all fundamental rights. Since its very beginning, America has recognized God and God's purposes as standing above the Nation and the Nation's interests. The highest role a Nation can play is to reflect God's righteousness in national policy and to promote God's purposes in all of life's relationships. The greatest and most significant heritage of our Country has been its spiritual heritage, our religious heritage. Apart from faith in God, American history has no meaning. In this faith our institutions were created, our laws enacted, and our liberties secured. To safeguard America today, that same dynamic force of religion must prevail in our political, social and economic life. Our aim must be the same as that of our Country's Founders, that religion must permeate every phase of living. An individual belongs to God alone; their only purpose in life is to enhance God's glory and do God's will.

## Religious Pluralism, Religious Tolerance

Our Founders, respecting the tradition which began with the Pilgrims who fled England in 1620 to avoid persecution for their religious beliefs, rightly rejected sectarianism in the name of religious liberty and freedom of conscience—not just for Christianity's various denominations but for all religions. Although George Washington was an Episcopalian, he frequently attended the services of other denominations, including Roman Catholic, Jewish, Quaker, Dutch Reformed, Baptist, Methodist and Presbyterian. When he was touring the new nation in 1790, Washington wrote to the Jewish congregation at Touro Synagogue in Newport, Rhode Island (the oldest synagogue in America), that the American republic would give "to bigotry no sanction, to persecution no assistance." Rhode Island, of course, had been established by Roger Williams in 1636 to allow freedom of religious thought and practice, which was harshly forbidden by the dogmatic Puritan leaders of the Massachusetts Bay Colony where he and his followers had lived. [12] Williams declared that religion must not be subject to regulation by the state—that it should be a matter of individual conscience.

Likewise, in a ringing declaration of religious freedom for all Americans, in 1776 Thomas Jefferson wrote and introduced to the Virginia General Assembly "The Bill for Establishing Religious Freedom in Virginia." After long delay and much debate, it was approved in 1785. Jefferson's *Autobiography* tells us:

> The bill for establishing religious freedom, the principles of which had, to a certain degree, been enacted before, I had drawn in all the latitude of reason and right. It still met with opposition, but, with some mutilations in the preamble, it was finally passed; and a singular proposition proved that its protection of opinion was meant to be universal. Where the preamble declares, that coercion is a departure from the plan of the holy author of our religion, an amendment was proposed, by inserting the words "Jesus Christ," so that it should read, "a departure from the plan of Jesus Christ, the holy author of our religion"; the insertion was rejected by a great majority, in proof that they meant to comprehend, with the mantle of its protection, the Jew and the Gentile, the Christian and Mahometan, the Hindoo, and Infidel of every denomination.

In the same spirit of religious freedom for all, George Mason, the father of the Bill of Rights, said, "It cannot be emphasized too strongly or too often that this great nation was founded, not by religionists, but by Christians, not on religions, but on the gospel of Jesus Christ. For this very reason peoples of other faiths have been afforded asylum, prosperity, and freedom of worship here."

## What About School Prayer?

If America contains a multitude of religions, as Jefferson pointed out, then what about school prayer?

It should be obvious that freedom of religion and freedom of conscience mean you cannot force others to worship as you do. Thus, the 1964 Supreme Court decision outlawing the practice of requiring students to recite an official prayer is constitutionally correct. *Requiring* recitation of an official prayer violates the separation of church and state in the true sense and also violates freedom of conscience.

However, the error which followed from that decision—declaring there can be no prayer in school whatsoever—is an illogical, gross misunderstanding and a departure from the foundation principles of our nation. The situation is the same as that pertaining to the Pledge of Allegiance. No student can be required to say the Pledge, but students are nevertheless free to recite the Pledge voluntarily, and the vast majority do so. Likewise, no student can be required to say an official school prayer, but it is constitutionally legitimate for prayers to be recited in school by those who wish to do so. The right of the dissenting individual is protected from religious domination or coercion, but the right of the believing majority to express their religious belief in public is also protected and encouraged, as our Founders declared necessary and proper. Voluntary school prayer is simply another expression of the freedom to which our nation is dedicated.

Prayer in school should therefore be restored, with the understanding that it may not be required of those who dissent, but may be freely expressed by those who believe in God as the Supreme Authority of our nation. The particular form of that prayer should be up to local authorities and the community—including its religious bodies—to determine in true democratic fashion, in accordance with the principle of local control which our Founders upheld. Acceptable interfaith prayers already abound. Here is "A National Prayer" allegedly composed by Thomas Jefferson in 1805 when he was president (although his authorship of it is disputed):

> Almighty God, Who has given us this good land for our heritage, We humbly beseech Thee that we may always prove ourselves a people mindful of Thy favor and glad to do Thy will. Bless our land with honorable ministry, sound learning, and pure manners. Save us from violence, discord, and confusion, from pride and arrogance, and from every evil way. Defend our liberties, and fashion into one united people the multitude brought hither out of many kindreds and tongues. Endow with Thy spirit of wisdom those to whom in Thy Name we entrust the authority of government, that there may be justice and peace at home, and that through obedience to Thy law, we may show forth Thy praise among the nations of the earth. In time of prosperity fill our hearts with thankfulness, and in the day of trouble, suffer not our trust in Thee to fail…

Jefferson closed the prayer with this: "all of which we ask through Jesus Christ our Lord, Amen." Let that closing be noted for the record, so that Christians may adopt it for their own use or delete it if the prayer is to be used for interfaith purposes.

## Our National Motto: "In God We Trust"

Since American government is essentially self-government, we citizens have an obligation to understand the principles which are intended to govern our lives, privately and publicly, as members of American society. Those principles are spiritual. They are the religio-moral compass which keeps us on course to provide the blessings of liberty to ourselves and our posterity. That course points directly to God, the Spirit of Liberty.

United States Code, Title 36, Chapter 10, Patriotic Customs, Section 186, National Motto, states: "The national motto of the United States is declared to be 'In God we trust'." The phrase does not appear in the Bible, but it clearly expresses the idea behind a number of similarly worded scriptural verses declaring that God is the author of our very lives, and that to rightly guide ourselves we must trust in and follow the laws given to us by our Creator. The last verse of our national anthem also says it clearly: "And this be our motto: In God is our trust." That idea is the primary foundation principle enunciated in the Declaration of Independence: God is the source of our liberty and well-being, and the blessings of liberty therefore require—as the Signers put it—"a firm reliance on the protection of Divine Providence." [13] Benjamin Franklin reiterated it at the Constitutional Convention: "All of us who were engaged in the struggle [for independence] have observed instances of a superintending Providence in our favor. To that kind of Providence, we owe this happy opportunity of consulting in peace on the means of establishing our future national felicity." " George Washington did likewise in his first Inaugural address:

> It would be peculiarly improper to omit in this first official act my fervent supplications to that Almighty Being who rules over the universe, who presides in the council of nations, and whose providential aids can supply every human defect, that His benediction may consecrate to the liberties and the happiness of the people of the United States, a government instituted by themselves for these essential purposes, and may enable every instrument employed in its administration to execute with success the functions allotted to his charge.

Prior to 1956, our national motto was *E pluribus unum*, which are the words on the obverse (front) of the Great Seal of the United States. Those words—Latin for "Out of many [states], one [nation]"—were suggested by Thomas Jefferson. He was one of three men appointed by Congress in 1776 to design a seal for the new nation. The others were Benjamin Franklin and John Adams. Congress rejected their design. After various designs by newer committee members were also rejected by Congress, Jefferson's proposal was used as an element of the Great Seal design submitted to Congress in 1782 by Secretary of Congress Charles Thomson and William Barton. They had borrowed from the designs of earlier committees and modified each other's designs. *E pluribus unum* appears on the banner held by the eagle in its mouth. The Great Seal was first officially used on September 16, 1782. [14]

Why was the original motto replaced? At the height of the Cold War with the Soviet Union, Congress was motivated by a desire to differentiate between Communism, which promotes atheistic materialism, and the American perspective on human existence which is so profoundly opposed to the godless perspective of Communism. "In God we trust" perfectly expressed that fundamental distinction.

On July 11, 1955, President Eisenhower signed Public Law 140 making it mandatory that all coinage and paper currency display the motto "In God We Trust." The following year, Public Law 851 was enacted and signed, which officially replaced the national motto "*E pluribus unum*" with "In God We Trust"

Therefore, since 1957, when the U.S. Mint implemented the law, all American currency and coins have included the phrase "In God We Trust."

The motto first appeared on American coinage (but only on a short-lived two-cent piece) in 1864. During the Civil War, various Protestant denominations on the Union side mounted a campaign to add references to God to the U.S. Constitution and other federal documents. Secretary of the Treasury Salmon P. Chase asked James Pollock, Director of the Mint, to prepare suitable wording for a motto to be used on Union coins. Specifically, Chase wrote, there should be a "distinct and unequivocal national recognition of the divine sovereignty" on American coins. Pollock suggested "Our Trust Is In God," "Our God And Our Country," "God And Our Country" and "God Our Trust." Chase decided to have "In God We Trust" used on some of the coins.

Congress passed the Coinage Act of April 22, 1864, which designated that "In God We Trust" be put on coins "when and where sufficient space in the balance of the design" would permit it. The phrase implied the wrongness of slavery and was a subtle reminder that the Union was on the side of God regarding the issue.

"In God We Trust" has been used continuously on the penny since 1909, and on dimes since 1916. Since July 1, 1908, "In God We Trust" has also been stamped on gold coins, silver dollars, quarters and half-dollar coins.

In 1955, as Congress was debating whether to place "In God We Trust" on all U.S. coins and currency, Rep. Charles E. Bennett of Florida declared:

> I sincerely hope that the Senate will give its prompt approval to this proposal. In these days when imperialistic and materialistic communism seeks to attack and destroy freedom, we should continuously look for ways to strengthen the foundations of our freedom. At the base of our freedom is our faith in God and the desire of Americans to live by His will and His guidance. As long as this country trusts in God, it will prevail. To serve as a constant reminder of this truth, it is highly desirable that our currency and coins should bear these inspiring words: "In God We Trust."

I agree. Therefore, as a step toward restoring public understanding of our most fundamental self-evident truth, I propose that our national motto be posted (with an explanatory text) in every schoolroom of America, along with the opening paragraphs of the Declaration of Independence and the Constitution. Doing so would not force religion on students any more than a display case containing trophies forces athletics on them. Rather, it would be a strong reinforcement of the lesson which students should receive throughout their schooling: God is the foundation of the United States of America; we are one nation under God.

--------

# FOOTNOTES

[1] Moreover, God is acknowledged in all 50 state constitutions. The oldest ones are those written by the former colonies—Virginia and Pennsylvania (1776), Georgia and Vermont (1777), South Carolina (1778), etc. On behalf of the people of their states, they declared their gratitude to God for (as Pennsylvania put it) "the blessings of civil and religious liberty" and (Vermont) "other blessings which the Author of Existence has bestowed on man." They established their constitutions "relying upon protection and guidance of Almighty God" (Georgia).

The remaining states did likewise, right up to the most recent members of the Union. The people of Louisiana (1921) stated they were "grateful to Almighty God for the civil, political and religious liberties we enjoy." Missouri (1945) felt "profound reverence for the Supreme Ruler of the Universe, and grateful for His goodness." The people of Alaska (1956) also were "grateful to God" and the people of Hawaii (1959) said they were "Grateful for Divine Guidance."

Author William J. Federer, who compiled this information and published in it 2003 on WorldNetDaily.com, concluded: "After reviewing acknowledgments of God from all 50 state constitutions, one is faced with the prospect that maybe, just maybe, the ACLU and the out-of-control federal courts are wrong."

[2] See Appendix 11, "Congressional Resolution Calling for American Religious History Week."

[3] The Chaplain Corps of the U.S. military predates the founding of our nation. When George Washington took command of the Continental Army in 1775, he began the Chaplain Corps to serve the spiritual needs of his soldiers.

Chaplains have likewise served the spiritual needs of Congress since the founding of America. Sidebar 2 tells of the first prayer in Congress by Rev. Jacob Duché and notes that he later became the first chaplain to Congress, just two days after the Declaration of Independence was signed. Rev. Duché was paid out of the public treasury, as were military chaplains.

When the Constitution was ratified in 1789, both houses of Congress continued the chaplaincy tradition. The Senate elected Samuel Provost as their chaplain and the House of Representatives elected William Lynn as the House Chaplain. The tradition of chaplains to Congress has continued unbroken since then, indicating the religious principles inherent in the founding of America.

[4] That fact has been given concrete form for America as the National Day of Prayer, an annual observance inviting people of all faiths to pray for our nation. It is held on the first Thursday of May. The National Day of Prayer was created in 1952 by a joint resolution of the U.S. Congress, and signed into law by President Harry S. Truman. It is designated by Congress as a day when all Americans, regardless of faith, are asked to come together and pray in their own way for America.

In 1775, the first Continental Congress called for a national day of prayer to assist "in forming a new nation." In 1863, during the Civil War, Abraham Lincoln likewise called for such a day. In 1988, the 1952 law was amended and signed by President Reagan, permanently setting the first Thursday in May as National Day of Prayer. In doing so, President Reagan said:

> Today, prayer is still a powerful force in America, and our faith in God is a mighty source of strength. Our Pledge of Allegiance states that we are "one nation under God," and our currency bears the motto, "'In God We Trust." The morality and values such faith implies are deeply embedded in our national character. Our country embraces those principles by design, and we abandon them at our own peril.

Every year the President signs a proclamation, encouraging all Americans to pray on this day. Likewise, the governors of the states and of several U.S. territories issue a call to prayer as a vital part of our national heritage.

The National Day of Prayer Task Force is a privately funded organization whose purpose is to encourage participation on the National Day of Prayer. According to its Web site (http://www.ndptf.org/home/index.cfm), it exists "to communicate with every individual the need for personal repentance and prayer, to create appropriate materials, and to mobilize the Christian community to intercede for America's leaders and its families. The Task Force represents a Judeo-Christian expression of the national observance, based on our understanding that this country was birthed in prayer and in reverence for the God of the Bible." It adds:

The National Day of Prayer has great significance for us as a nation. It enables us to recall and to teach the way in which our founding fathers sought the wisdom of God when faced with critical decisions. It stands as a call to us to humbly come before God, seeking His guidance for our leaders and His grace upon us as a people.

In addition to the National Day of Prayer, members of Congress have their own weekly prayer breakfast groups. They were initiated in 1942, but in 1952 members of the Senate and the House prayer groups established the first Presidential Prayer Breakfast with President Dwight Eisenhower to seek divine guidance for the national leadership and to reaffirm our country's faith in and dependence upon God. In 1970 the name was changed to The National Prayer Breakfast. The annual event occurs in February after Congress convenes. Leaders in business, labor, education and science from every state in the Union, as well as military leaders from each branch of service join the members from the legislative, judicial and executive branches. Although the political, economic, philosophic and religious viewpoints represented are varied, the result is a fellowship of concerned citizens, dedicated to affirming the moral, ethical and spiritual values upon which American is founded. Since the first National Prayer Breakfast, the sitting president has attended every one. The 2009 National Prayer Breakfast, held at a Washington, D.C. hotel, was attended by some 4,000 people from more than 160 countries.

5 In this stance, our Founders were following the insight of French political philosopher Montesquieu, who taught that the actuating principle of a republic was virtue in the citizenry. Virtue, according to Prof. Forrest McDonald of the University of Alabama, meant manhood and independence and a disinterested devotion to the welfare of the public—"virtue," like "public," deriving from the Latin roots for manliness.

6 See David Limbaugh's *Persecution: How Liberals Are Waging War Against Christianity* (Regnery Publishing, Washington, D.C., 2003). Limbaugh provides details of case after case which demonstrate that anti-Christian forces now controlling significant portions of American society are aggressively targeting public expressions of Christianity for discrimination. Note well: often the decision to oppress Christianity is made judicially under a false interpretation of the First Amendment "establishment" clause, which then becomes in effect government-sanctioned religious persecution.

7 An especially egregious violation by the federal government can be seen in the Internal Revenue Service policies for churches and religious organizations. Because of their tax-exempt status, they are controlled by the IRS in ways which are totally contradictory to the intent of our Founders. A religious leader may not preach from the pulpit on political issues nor offer his views or guidance in church bulletins and paid advertisements. Likewise, that leader may not endorse or criticize a candidate while acting in an official capacity. Specifically, the IRS says in its Publication 1771, that churches and religious groups are "absolutely prohibited from directly or indirectly participating in, or intervening in, any political campaign on behalf of (or in opposition to) any candidate for elective public office." This is a profound violation of the principles of free speech, freedom of religion and the obligation which our Founders saw for religious

leaders to lead—that is, to speak out forcefully on moral and spiritual aspects of political issues and politicians, and especially from the pulpit.

8 The attack on God in America was initiated by atheists and is often fueled by fanatical hatred of the very idea of a deity. Why? The research of Paul C. Vitz, professor of psychology at New York University, in *Faith of the Fatherless: The Psychology of Atheism* (Spence Publishing: Dallas, TX, 1999), offers an interesting explanation. He shows that atheists have the absence of a good father as the source of their intense atheism. Vitz himself was an atheist until his late 30s. He notes that atheism "is a recent and distinctively Western phenomenon and...no other culture has manifested such a widespread public rejection of the divine." He concludes, "Despite its pretensions to cool-headed rationality, modern atheism originated in the irrational, often neurotic, psychological needs of a few powerfully influential thinkers. He adds that "self-avowed atheists tend, to a remarkable degree, to be found in a narrow range of social and economic strata: in the university and intellectual world and in certain professions. Today, as a rule, they make up a significant part of the governing class."

I think Vitz has an important insight, although it seems overstated to attribute atheism solely to bad parenting. Nevertheless, a child's first "gods" are his or her parents; to the young child they appear to have godlike attributes in the sense of power and control over the child's life. If the father's behavior emotionally damages the child, his or her unconscious formulation becomes: "I reject my male parent because of the abuse and shame he placed on me and/or because he was emotionally distant and unloving. If God is the heavenly father of all, and my biological father models for me what is called my heavenly father, then I reject the notion of God altogether."

If an atheist's "bad father" state of mind mellows or is overcome through maturation, the shortcomings of atheism's projection onto the cosmos of bad-father-rejection becomes apparent. The fanatical hatred of "the father" which fueled his or her "religion of atheism" is dissipated, discharged. Then the possibility of what the Christian theologian Paul Tillich calls "the God Beyond God"—a nonanthropomorphic understanding of God—becomes acceptable in that person's worldview. Those who dare to follow where their newly awakened heart-understanding and emotional intelligence lead often find themselves surprised and converted toward some form of theism or sacred tradition.

9 The idea of religious freedom in America did not spring up full-blown, as Roger Williams' experience shows. At the time of the War for Independence, Massachusetts had a state church, Congregationalism. Connecticut's official religion was likewise Congregationalism. Virginia's was the Anglican Church of England (which, after the War for Independence, became the Episcopal Church of America). In fact, most of the thirteen states at one time had their own official churches and five of the thirteen had their own at the time the First Amendment was ratified. When James Madison was writing the Constitution, no mention of a guarantee of religious liberty was at first included because he feared that states such as Massachusetts and Virginia would otherwise not accept the Constitution. However, he was persuaded to include the "no religious test" clause of Article VI. The Bill of Rights, Amendment I, which he later supported, provided the final corrective to the situation. The last of the state religions

was disestablished in 1833. Thy were disestablished not by the Supreme Court but by the states' own free will.

10 The full text of Franklin's remarks are given in James Madison's *Notes of Debates in the Federal Convention of 1787*, which was published in 1787 and reprinted in modern editions. Franklin said:

> In the situation of this Assembly, groping, as it were, in the dark to find political truth, and scarce able to distinguish it when presented to us, how has it happened, Sir, that we have not hitherto once thought of humbly applying to the Father of lights to illuminate our understanding! In the beginning of the contest with Great Britain, when we were sensible of danger, we had daily prayer in this room for the Divine protection. —Our prayers, Sir, were heard, and they were graciously answered. All of us who were engaged in the struggle must have observed frequent instances of a superintending Providence in our favor…And have we now forgotten this powerful Friend? Or do we imagine we no longer need His assistance? I have lived, sir, a long time, and the longer I live, the more convincing proofs I see of this truth—that God governs in the affairs of men. And if a sparrow cannot fall to the ground without His notice, is it probable that an empire can rise without His aid? We have been assured, Sir, in the Sacred Writings, that "except the Lord build the house, they labor in vain that build it." I firmly believe this; and I also believe that without His concurring aid, we shall succeed in this political building no better than the builders of Babel…I therefore beg leave to move—that henceforth prayers imploring the assistance of Heaven, and its blessings on our deliberation, be held in this Assembly every morning before we proceed to business.

Further evidence of Franklin's view on the intimate relation between God and state is shown in this statement by him: "Freedom is not a gift bestowed upon us by other men, but a right that belongs to us by the laws of God and nature."

11 The phrase is Masonic in origin. Washington, a dedicated Freemason, adopted it from rituals used in Masonic lodges. See Sidebar 10, "The President's Inaugural Bible."

12 Specifically, Williams wrote in his 1644 tract *The Bloudy* [Bloody] *Tenent of Persecution:* "…that no civil magistrate, no King, nor Caesar, have any power over the souls or consciences of their subjects, in the matters of God and the crown of Jesus."

13 Jefferson echoed the theme of Divine Providence in his First Inaugural Address. Americans, he said, were "enlightened by a benign religion, professed, indeed, and practiced in various forms, yet all of them including honesty, truth, temperance, gratitude, and the love of man; acknowledging and adoring an overruling Providence."

14 As yet another proof that our Founders recognized God as the ultimate authority for our government and our society, consider the symbolism of the reverse of the Great Seal of the United States. It shows a 13-step pyramid representing the 13 original states, placed under what the designer described as "the Eye of Providence." The Latin words *Annuit Coeptis*, meaning "He [God] has favored our undertakings," float above the scene. The seal was approved after six years of deliberation over various designs. Secretary of Congress Charles Thomson reported to the Congress that "The Eye over & the Motto allude to the many signal interpositions of providence in favour of the

American cause." If the doctrine of separation of church and state had been intended by the Founders to keep God and religion out of government, does it seem reasonable that such direct references to deity would have been approved for the official signature of our nation?

## Sidebar 4

# THE FIRST PRAYER IN CONGRESS

The First Continental Congress of the American colonies convened in September 1774 at Carpenter's Hall in Philadelphia. Twelve of the 13 colonies participated; Georgia did not send any delegates. The purpose of the Congress was to decide upon a unified course of action for dealing with the increasingly intolerable acts of the King of Great Britain and his Parliament. Just a year earlier the Boston Tea Party had demonstrated to them that Americans would not accept taxation without representation in Parliament.

The Congress opened session on September 6, 1774, amid a rumor that the British had shelled Boston, firing on civilians. (The rumor proved false.) John Adams was a member of the Massachusetts delegation. In a letter to his wife Abigail, Adams said that a Mr. Cushing, also representing Massachusetts, made a motion to open the session with prayer. Various delegates from other colonies opposed the idea because, as Adams put it, "we were so divided in religious Sentiments, some Episcopalians, some Quakers, some Anabaptists, some Presbyterians and some Congregationalists, so that we could not join in the same Act of Worship."

Then Samuel Adams of Massachusetts arose to say, as his cousin John's letter reported, "he was no Bigot, and could hear a prayer from a Gentleman of Piety and Virtue, who was at the same Time a Friend to his Country." He added that he had heard of a such a man, the Rector of nearby Christ Church, Rev. Jacob Duché. He moved that Rev. Duché be invited to offer prayers the next morning.

Adams' motion was seconded and passed. Rev. Duché received and accepted the invitation. Next morning, he appeared in his clerical garb and read several prayers, in the established form of the Anglican tradition. Then he read the Collect for the day, the Thirty-fifth Psalm, which begins, "Plead thou my case, O Lord, with them that strive with me, and fight thou against them that fight against me."

The psalm spoke directly to the Congress, which was feeling overwhelmed by tyrannical forces. John told Abigail to remember that this was the morning after the delegates had heard the horrible rumor about a cannonade of Boston. Adams wrote: "I never saw a greater effect upon an Audience. It seemed as if Heaven had ordained that Psalm to be read on that Morning."

Then Rev. Duché spoke extemporaneously. His ten minutes of spontaneous prayer asked God to support the American cause. One delegate said he was "worth riding 100 miles to hear." John Adams told Abigail that Rev. Duché's words "filled the Bosom of every Man present. I must confess I never heard an better Prayer or one so well pronounced."

Here is Rev. Duché's text referred to as The First Prayer in Congress:

Lord, our Heavenly Father, High and Mighty King of Kings, and Lord of Lords, who dost from thy throne behold all the dwellers on earth; and reignest with power supreme and uncontrolled over all the Kingdoms, Empires and Governments; look down in mercy we beseech Thee, on these American States, who have fled to Thee from the rod of the oppressor, and thrown themselves on Thy gracious protection, desiring henceforth to be dependent only on Thee; to Thee, they have appealed for the righteousness of their cause; to Thee do they now look up for that countenance and support which Thou alone canst give; take them therefore, Heavenly Father, under Thy nurturing care; give them wisdom in Council and valor in the field; defeat the malicious designs of our cruel adversaries; convince them of the unrighteousness of their cause; and if they persist in their sanguinary purpose, O, let the voice of Thy own unerring justice, sounding in their hearts, constrain them to drop the weapons of war from their unnerved hands in the day of battle!

Be Thou present, O God of wisdom, and direct the councils of this honorable assembly; enable them to settle things on the best and surest foundation, that the scene of blood may be speedily closed; that order, harmony and peace may be effectually restored, and truth and justice, religion and piety prevail and flourish among Thy people. Preserve the health of their bodies and vigor of their minds; shower down on them and the millions they here represent, such temporal blessings as Thou seest expedient for them in this world, and crown them with everlasting glory in the world to come. All this we ask in the name and through the merits of Jesus Christ, Thy Son, Our Savior. Amen.

After the prayer, a profound and prolonged silence followed, so deep was the sense of responsibility upon each man present.

In July of 1776, two days after the Declaration of Independence was adopted, Rev. Duché was appointed Chaplain of Congress. He officiated every morning at 9 a.m. until September 28, 1776, when he was arrested by the British. While he served Congress he asked that his $150 salary be used for the relief of widows and orphans of Pennsylvania officers.

However, as the Continental Army lost one battle after another, Rev. Duché's enthusiasm for the American cause waned. In October, 1777—with General Howe's army occupying Philadelphia—he wrote to Gen. Washington urging him to surrender. Soon afterward Rev. Duché and his wife sailed home to England.

Nevertheless, his prayer had done its work. One of the principle results of the First Continental Congress was widespread financial support for the City of Boston, which was under British attack in response to the Boston Tea Party. Without Samuel Adams' support for the prayer, it is doubtful that Boston's citizens would have received the help they needed. It is also doubtful that the Congress would have found the harmony of purpose which led them to sign the Declaration of Independence two years later.

Note well that the various religious sects, which at first would not worship together in Congress, found common ground in the concept of a universal God as a primary principle, senior to all secondary doctrinal differences, and that the only value which made that concept politically workable was freedom—specifically, freedom of religion and freedom of conscience. When the Declaration of Independence was written, that primary principle and value were subscribed to by all, including freethinkers, because it alone guaranteed their right to worship or to refrain from worship.

By proposing and supporting this prayer, the Massachusetts delegates created the feeling among the other delegates that "we are all in this together." The Congress was the first test for the quarreling colonies to see if they could work in harmony. The very existence of our country probably depended to a great extent on this one prayer.

Details about The First Prayer in Congress are available on web sites on the Internet, where you can also see the famous 1848 painting by T. H. Matteson entitled "The First Prayer in Congress." It shows Founding Fathers such as George Washington, Samuel Adams, John Rutledge and John Adams in a posture of prayer.

**Sidebar 5**

# THE PRESIDENT'S INAUGURAL BIBLE

When George Washington was elected President of the United States, he consciously sought to invest the Presidency with dignity, formality and honor. He recognized that his acts would set precedents for the conduct of the office which could become traditions. Noting exactly that, he wrote to James Madison, "it is devoutly wished on my part that these precedents may be fixed on true principles."

Ironically—because it happened beyond even his own careful forethought—the very instant he entered the office, he initiated a practice which remains the focal point of each presidential inauguration: taking the Oath of Office upon a bible and adding "So help me God." That act became a custom, then an inaugural tradition. The reverent invocation of the deity is standard for presidential inaugurations and the idea of taking the oath is certainly incomplete without it. Washington acted on "true principles."

The Constitution prescribes the Oath of Office for the President-elect. It is just 35 words long. The last paragraph of Article 2, Section 1 reads:

Before he enter on the execution of his office, he shall take the following oath or affirmation:—"I do solemnly swear (or affirm) that I will faithfully execute the office of President of the United States, and will to the best of my ability, preserve, protect and defend the Constitution of the United States."

No mention is made of a bible so use of one is not obligatory. Nevertheless, since Washington's time, all presidents except John Quincey Adams and Theodore Roosevelt have been sworn in by using a bible. Adams used a legal volume, Roosevelt had no bible. Harry S. Truman used two bibles—his personal one and a Gutenberg Bible—for his first inauguration. John F. Kennedy, a Roman Catholic, used a Catholic version of the bible for his oath in 1961. Barack H. Obama used the same bible as Abraham Lincoln.

More than one president has chosen to affirm his oath rather than swear it. And there have been other modifications to the tradition which Washington established. For example, after he took his oath, Washington kissed the bible. However, that aspect of the tradition ended with Franklin Pierce in 1853; Pierce placed his left hand on the bible but didn't kiss it. (There was an exception in 1944, when Harry Truman, a Mason, was sworn in. He kissed the Bible—his personal one—following Washington's example and Masonic tradition.)

The custom of crossing one's heart in the sign of fidelity, which Washington also initiated, ended at some unrecorded time and ever since, presidents have placed one hand on a bible while raising the other toward the heavens.

Why did Washington elaborate upon the constitutional prescription? In doing so, did he violate the constitutional principle of separation of church and state?

The Father of Our Country was a Freemason. He joined the Masonic fraternity in 1752 at Fredericksburg, Virginia, when he was 20. Then, as now, Masons place their hand upon a Book of Holy Scripture as they take their oath and, afterward, reverently kiss the book to solemnize the event.

Affirming a belief in God is required of all Masons. However, Freemasonry is not a religion and is open to men of all faiths, so the Book of Holy Scripture used in the Masonic Degrees ceremonies is selected by the candidate and reflects his particular religion or, if he has no religious affiliation, his spiritual persuasion or orientation. Christians use the Holy Bible, Jews use the Torah, Hindus use the Bhagavad Gita, Muslims use the Qur'an, Buddhists use The Diamond Sutra or other text, Confucians use the Analects, Taoists use the Tao Te Ching, etc. Washington, an Episcopalian, swore his Masonic oath upon a bible; it would have been unthinkable for him not to. That act would echo through the centuries via the Presidential inaugural tradition.

Freemasonry was profoundly significant for Washington all his life. When he laid the cornerstone for the U.S. Capitol during his second term of office, he did so wearing his Masonic apron and regalia, accompanied by other Masons. He was buried at Mount Vernon with full Masonic honors, at his request, including use of the Bible upon which he had twice taken the presidential oath. In his final years he said, "The Masonic lessons I learned on my admission to Masonry and my contact and conversation with prominent Masons thereafter were of greatest encouragement in after years when I encountered and underwent several trials, especially those of commencement and during the Revolution."

Washington was first inaugurated on April 30, 1789 at Federal Hall in New York City, our nation's capital at the time and the seat of Congress. Now a national memorial administered by the National Park Service, Federal Hall is located at 26 Wall Street, across from the Stock Exchange. (The building is actually a reconstruction because the original one was torn down in 1812.) The Bill of Rights was adopted by Congress there later in 1789.

The Continental Congress had specified March 4 as Inauguration Day, but harsh weather delayed Washington's travel. (The Twentieth Amendment, ratified in 1933, moved Inauguration Day to January 20 in order to speed the changeover of administrations.) The day was clear and cool.

The swearing-in ceremony was held on the second-floor outside balcony in full view of the assembled crowd of townspeople, citizens of other states, foreign ambassadors, statesmen and, of course, the U.S. Congress inside the hall. (A large statue of Washington stands on a pedestal outside the balcony today.) The 57-year-old Washington was dressed in a dark brown suit, white silk stockings and silver shoe buckles; he wore a steel-hilted sword. He was surrounded by a small group of distinguished men. Upon his right was the short, athletic figure of John Adams, the Vice President-elect. Behind them were Connecticut's Roger Sherman and, notably, many Masons such as Baron Friedrich von Steuben, the Prussian General who drilled Washington's troops at Valley Forge, and George Clinton, Governor of New York.

Preparations for the inauguration had been made by Congress with great attention to detail, from the color of the curtains and the arrangement of the furniture, to decisions of who should sit where. Nevertheless, one detail was overlooked: a bible which would validate and publicly demonstrate the solemnity and reverence for God with which the oath was to be taken. Robert Livingston, the Chancellor (Chief Justice) of the State of New York and a Mason, was to administer the oath. At the last minute Livingston and Washington realized there was no bible available for the swearing-in ceremony. Livingston determined judicially that Washington must swear on a bible and that without such, the ceremony would lack legitimacy. That immediately set off a search for one through Federal Hall, but none was found.

A member of the ceremony was Jacob Morton, Master of St. John's Lodge No. 1 of Free and Accepted Masons, the oldest Masonic lodge in New York. St. John's was, and still is, located in lower Manhattan, only a few hundred feet down the block from Federal Hall. Morton rushed to the nearby lodge and returned with its bible.

The large volume of scripture had been printed in London in 1767 and bound in maroon Moroccan leather with silver hasps. It was brought to the colonies three years later. Jonathan Hampton gave it to St. John's Lodge when he became its master. It weighed nine pounds.

The bible was opened at random. (The random selection was Chapter 49 of the Book of Genesis, whose name literally means "the book of new beginnings.") The Secretary of the Senate held the bible while Livingston administered the Oath of Office to Washington. Washington placed his left hand on the bible and his right hand over his heart in the Masonic sign of fidelity. When the oath was completed, Washington leaned over and kissed the sacred volume, just as he had done in the lodge room in Fredericksburg 36 years before.

Then Livingston said, "It is done," turned to the crowd and shouted "Long live George Washington, President of the United States." A salvo of 13 cannons sounded, church bells rang and a joyous noise went up from the crowd. Celebration followed. Meanwhile, Jacob Morton stepped forward, folded down a corner of the open page and inserted a silk cloth into the bible to mark the place where Washington had rested his left hand. Thus he preserved a record of that random bible opening.

Since then, the historic pre-Revolutionary War volume has been known as the Washington Bible. St. John's Lodge has cared for and cherished it. Carefully preserved, it is now kept on public display in a protective plexiglas showcase in Federal Hall. It is in good condition, though its pages are highly fragile. It is open to Genesis 49.

It is the custom of St. John's Lodge to bring the Bible to Washington for any President-elect who wishes to use it. Those who have it used it to date are Warren G. Harding (who was also a Mason), Dwight D. Eisenhower, Jimmy Carter and George Herbert Walker Bush. George W. Bush intended to use it for his first inauguration in 2001, but bad weather caused the lodge officials accompanying it to forego its use at the last hour for fear that rain might damage the pages. Instead, Bush used a family bible; he continued with it at his second inauguration.

As for the concept of church-state separation, note that many men who had personally helped to write the U.S. Constitution and the Bill of Rights which articulated that concept had not the slightest concern that introduction of a bible would violate it. Our Founders and Framers separated church and state, not God and state. (See Chapter 4 for a more full discussion.) How could they? Our nation's founding document, the Declaration of Independence, has four references to deity: "nature's God," "Creator," "Supreme Judge of the world" and "Divine Providence." Altogether, the references make clear that it was self-evident to our Founders that God, not government, is the source of our liberty, our sovereignty, our equality, our rights, our justice and our human dignity. There was no violation of the Constitution but, rather, an affirmation of the bedrock principle of America: we are a nation under God.

## Sidebar 6

# THANKSGIVING AND CIVIC PIETY IN AMERICA

Since our nation's colonial beginning, it has been customary for public officials to call upon God for guidance, support and deliverance from difficulties for the American people, and to express gratitude for good fortune. Making governmental proclamations in the name of civic piety is a long-standing American tradition—perhaps our oldest public tradition. Thanksgiving is, quite simply, a form of worship.

Days or periods of religious thanksgiving have been practiced in many lands since ancient times. Thanksgiving in America developed from that age-old universal practice. Christians adopted it from the Old Testament. The Book of Psalms, for example, exhorts worshipers to "offer unto God thanksgiving" and "come before his presence with thanksgiving" and "enter into his gates with thanksgiving."

The Pilgrims who founded the Plymouth Colony in 1620 established our national tradition of feasting and fellowship called Thanksgiving Day. In 1621, they harvested bountifully at the end of their first—and extremely difficult—year in the New World. They and the local Wampanoag Indians met for three days of feasting. That widely celebrated event established Thanksgiving in America as a harvest festival. [1]

Strictly speaking, however, thanksgiving is an occasion to be observed at any time of the year and for reasons which may have nothing to do with harvesting or feasting. The first permanent English settlement in the New World was Jamestown, Virginia, founded in 1607. Although the records of the Jamestown colony don't note it, there undoubtedly were many occasions of formal thanksgiving there, with or without feasting.

A second colony on the James River was established in 1619 through a patent granted by the King of England to the Virginia Company of London. The patent commanded the colonists to kneel in prayer and give thanks to God upon reaching their destination. They arrived on December 4, 1619 on a ship called the *Margaret* commanded by Capt. John Woodlief and his 38 men. Then, in accordance with their patent orders, the crew and colonists offered thanks. The colonists observed that day every year thereafter as "a holy day of thanksgiving to Almighty God." Their record of that event establishes that the first known Thanksgiving in America in the English language was held in 1619 on the site of what is now the Berkeley Plantation in Charles City, Virginia. There was no feasting; there were simply prayers of thanks for safe passage across the sea.

There probably also were occasions of official thanksgiving at the "Lost Colony" established at Roanoke, North Carolina in 1587. The colony lasted three years and then mysteriously vanished into the wilderness. However, it was English-speaking and, because of the religious character of the time, it undoubtedly followed the tradition of giving thanks to God for various blessings.

Europeans speaking other languages were in the New World well before even Roanoke. The French established colonies in Canada prior to Plymouth and, being a Christian people, they undoubtedly held thanksgiving events—some within the territory of what is now the United States. So did the Dutch.

The Spanish were also Christian, and when they explored Florida, California and the Southwest in the early 1500s, they, too, had occasions of thanksgiving. The earliest record of a thanksgiving in America is 1541 by Spanish explorer Francisco Vasquez do Coronado at Palo Duro Canyon in the vicinity of what is now Dallas, Texas; a Catholic Mass was celebrated. Some Texans say that qualifies as America's first Thanksgiving. In 1565, Pedro Menendez de Aviles led an expedition of 800 Spanish settlers to found St. Augustine, Florida. Later that same year, Menendez de Aviles and the settlers shared a communal meal with the Timucuan Indians.

On November 1, 1777, the Continental Congress issued the first proclamation of thanksgiving extending to all the colonies-become-states:

> Forasmuch as it is the indispensable duty of all men to adore the superintending Providence of Almighty God; to acknowledge with gratitude their obligation to Him for benefits received and to implore such further blessings as they stand in need of... to smile upon us as in the prosecution of a just and necessary war for the defense and establishment of our unalienable rights and liberties...set apart Thursday, the eighteenth of December next, for SOLEMN THANKSGIVING and PRAISE. That with one heart and one voice the good people may express the grateful feelings of their hearts, and consecrate themselves to the service of their Divine Benefactor and together with their sincere acknowledgments and offerings, may join the penitent confession of their manifold sins...and to prosper the means of religion for the promotion and enlargement of that kingdom which consisteth "in righteousness, peace and joy in the Holy Ghost."

George Washington was the first president to proclaim a national day of thanksgiving. On October 3, 1789, Washington issued a Presidential Order—requested by both houses of Congress—proclaiming a Thanksgiving Day for the United States of America. The proclamation designated Thursday, November 26, 1789 as a "day of public thanksgiving and prayer" honoring our new constitution. Thus, Thanksgiving Day was established as a national holiday or holy day—that is, a time of prayer and solemn reflection on the sacred source from which all blessings flow. God and nation were understood to be inseparable; it was self-evident. Washington stated:

> ...it is the first duty of all nations to acknowledge the providence of almighty God, to obey His will, to be grateful for His benefits, and to humbly implore His protection and favor in holy fear.

During the Civil War, Abraham Lincoln proclaimed Thanksgiving Day for the Union in his 1863 Presidential Order:

> It has seemed to me fit and proper that they [the blessings to America for that year] should be reverently, solemnly, and gratefully acknowledged, as with

one heart and voice, by the whole American people. I do, therefore, invite my fellow citizens in every part of the United States, and also those who are at sea, and those who are sojourning in foreign lands, to set apart and observe the last Thursday of November next as a day of thanksgiving and prayer to our beneficent Father who dwelleth in the heavens.

Thanksgiving, therefore, is a time for gratefully acknowledging God's providence. (The Eye of Providence watches over America on the back of the Great Seal of the United States.) That's what Thanksgiving at Plymouth was really all about; the feasting was secondary. Thanksgiving is also a time for celebrating America's Judeo-Christian heritage; without it, there would have been no Thanksgiving and, later, no America.

That fact of history doesn't slight any American. Nor, when the President and state governors make Thanksgiving Day proclamations, does it preclude proclamations celebrating the heritage and contributions of other faiths. (Such proclamations can and should be made.) Some politically correct citizens, including some Christians, have called for an abolition of Thanksgiving because, they say, it is offensive to non-Christians and Native Americans. However, proclaiming a day of public thanksgiving in the name of civic piety does not violate the separation of church and state, and it should not be offensive to anyone who upholds our national values of religious freedom and unity-in-diversity. It is a noble tradition and part of the moral foundation of our nation. Non-Christians—whether they belong to other faiths, to no faith or are antifaith—can enjoy a turkey dinner on that day of rest and reflection, and be thankful for the blessings of liberty which they enjoy as citizens of this nation. They may not support the idea that American liberty is founded in God, but they can nevertheless appreciate the idea of liberty itself and all which flows from it. In that sense, Thanksgiving is indeed for all Americans.

————————

## FOOTNOTES

[1] An event from that time gives indication of "the hand of Providence" guiding humanity to help establish a godly society in the New World. (See Chapter 5, "George Washington and the Hand of God," for further examples.) According to A. L. Rouse in *The Elizabethans and America* (Harper & Row, 1959), a 1605 voyage to the Massachusetts mainland sponsored by Sir Ferdinando Gorges, an Englishman with an interest in exploration and trade, brought back some kidnapped Indians.

One was a Patuxet Indian named Tisquantum. The Patuxet lived primarily in and around the area of what would become Plymouth, Massachusetts. They were part of the Wampanoag confederation of tribes, headed by the Grand Sachem, Massasoit. Tisquantum was sold into slavery in Spain, where a group of Catholic monks taught him Christianity in preparation to send him back to America as a missionary among his tribe. After the monks completed his Christian education, Tisquantum went to England, where he continued learning the English language and way of life he'd begun acquiring aboard ship. In 1619, after various adventures, Tisquantum was able to return to his homeland. He was set ashore, only to find that all his people were dead, decimated by a disease—

possibly bubonic plague—caught from European fishermen. Tisquantum then attached himself to the Wampanoag tribe living near the area where the Pilgrims would land. He was the last of the Patuxet people.

When the Pilgrims arrived at what they called New Plimouth, they were astonished to find an Indian who spoke fluent English. Without his assistance that first terrible year in the wilderness, the Pilgrims likely would have perished altogether. (As it was, half of them died of various causes the first winter.) The Pilgrims anglicized Tisquantum's name to Squanto. He famously showed them how to plant corn, beans and squash, and fertilize the kernals with a fish, and further increase their food production through hunting and fishing. Less known is the fact that, acting for Massasoit, he provided food, advice, interpreter service, guidance through the territory to locations where they could obtain commodities and seafood, and showed them how to build warm houses. He also provided hope in the face of terrible adversity. Last of all, he helped the Pilgrims establish a peace treaty with the local tribes which would last nearly half a century.

The Pilgrims considered Squanto "a special instrument of God for their good beyond their expectation," as Governor Bradford wrote in his *History of Plymouth Plantation, 1620-1647.* Squanto died during the second winter of the colony, succumbing to smallpox. Bradford noted that he died

> desiring the Governor to pray for him that he might go to the Englishmen's God in heaven, and bequeathed sundry of his things to sundry of his English friends, as remembrances of his love; of whom they had a great loss.

Rowse comments: "It is hard to see how the Pilgrims could have got through their first two years without him."

## Chapter 5

# GEORGE WASHINGTON AND THE HAND OF GOD

No people can be bound to acknowledge and adore the invisible hand, which conducts the Affairs of men, more than the People of the United States. Every step, by which they have advanced to the character of an independent nation, seems to have been distinguished by some token of providential agency.
- George Washington (First Inaugural Address, 30 April 1789)

The Founders of America were men who saw God working in human affairs to bless or to punish, depending upon whether people behaved righteously or otherwise. [1] Many times they spoke and wrote of Divine Providence intervening on behalf of the colonies in their struggle for independence. Their view was derived from the Bible—the experiences of the Hebrews coming out of Egypt, the prophets of the Old Testament trying to correct erring Israel and, of course, the teaching of Jesus Christ. All sources pointed toward the presence of God in our lives, and his favor for those whose thoughts and actions honored Him by aligning with his will.

That is why the signers of the Declaration of Independence appealed to "the Supreme Judge of the world" in declaring their political stance.

That is why the Great Seal of the United States, designed by the Continental Congress, shows the Eye of Providence watching over the unfinished 13-tier pyramid symbolizing America.

That is why the Great Seal proclaims *Annuit Coeptis,* "He [God] favors our undertaking."

That is why Charles Thomson, Secretary of the Continental Congress, described the Eye of Providence as alluding to "the many signal interpositions of providence in favour of the American cause."

That is why Patrick Henry, in his speech declaring "give me liberty or give me death," said, "There is a just God who presides over the destinies of nations."

That is why Samuel Adams, in his August 1776 oration on American Independence, said, "The hand of Heaven seems to have led us on to be, perhaps, humble instruments and means in the great Providential dispensation which is completing."

That is why Benjamin Franklin declared at the Constitutional Convention, "All of us who were engaged in the struggle must have observed frequent instances of superintending providence in our favor. To that kind providence we owe this happy opportunity of consulting in peace on the means of establishing our future national felicity. And have we now forgotten that powerful friend? Or do we imagine that we no longer need his assistance? I have lived, Sir, a long time, and the longer I live, the more convincing proofs I see of this truth—that God governs in the affairs of men. And if a sparrow cannot fall to the Ground without his Notice, is it probable that an Empire can rise without his Aid?"

That is why the Father of the Constitution, James Madison, said of its creation in Federalist No. 37, "It is impossible for the man of pious reflection not to perceive in it a finger of that Almighty hand which has been so frequently and signally extended to our relief in the critical stages of the revolution."

The hand of God was notably evident in the life of the Father of Our Country. George Washington was indispensable to the American Revolution and to the first years of our fledgling republic. Instance after instance was attested to by him and others of what they recognized as divine intervention to protect him for a purpose: the creation of a new nation and a godly society. For example, in a letter to his wife Martha, written after the Continental Congress selected him to lead the Continental Army, he said, "I shall rely, therefore, confidently on that Providence which has heretofore preserved and been bountiful to me, not doubting but that I shall return safe to you…" A young officer who observed Washington in combat at the Battle of Princeton wrote, "…I saw him brave all the dangers of the field…with a thousand deaths flying around him." The sight of his commander-in-chief, he said, set an example of courage such as he had never seen. Although he placed himself in harm's way many times throughout his extensive military career, Washington was never wounded in battle.

Thomas Jefferson, who knew Washington intimately, described him with these words:

> He was incapable of fear, meeting personal dangers with the calmest unconcern. Perhaps the strongest feature in his character was prudence, never acting until every circumstance, every consideration, was maturely weighed; refraining if he saw a doubt, but, when once decided going through with his purpose, whatever obstacles opposed. His integrity was most pure, his justice the most inflexible I have ever known, no motives of interest or consanguinity, of friendship or hatred, being able to bias his decision. He was, indeed, in every sense of the words, a wise, a good, and a great man…

George Washington should be much better known to Americans today than just the fanciful, untrue stories about him chopping down a cherry tree and throwing a silver dollar across the Potomac River. His portrait no longer hangs in American schoolrooms; school children no longer celebrate his birthday with classroom ceremonies. They don't learn of him as a role model for the conduct of their lives. Yet his character and courage demonstrate human goodness and greatness at their finest. Like all people, he had flaws, notably a hot temper. Yet even his enemy, King George III, called him "the greatest man in the world" when he learned that Washington had voluntarily given up power after the Revolutionary War. (King George realized Washington could have been the uncrowned king of our new nation by popular acclaim.) After the war, Washington's officers formed the Society of the Cincinnati to honor their fellowship with him. They named their organization after Lucius Quinctius Cincinnatus, the Roman general who was recalled by the Senate from civilian life to lead the defense of Rome against threatening barbarian tribes about 450 B.C. After achieving victory, Cincinnatus could have been proclaimed permanent Dictator of Rome, but instead chose to return to his farm and the life of an ordinary citizen of the republic. Like Cincinnatus, Washington could have had absolute power, but refused it.

Washington is a hero for the ages and a figure whose life should be studied, especially by young people. America, if it is to survive, needs citizens who understand and respect that function of The Father of Our Country. [2]

However, according to James C. Rees, former Executive Director of Mount Vernon, a recent survey of college seniors showed that only thirty-four percent could identify George Washington as the commanding general of the American forces at Yorktown—the battle which assured America's independence. He writes:

> How sad for these young Americans that they don't know about the Father
> of Our Country's inspirational leadership or appreciate the heroic sacrifices made
> for their freedom by his soldiers shivering in the winter cold at Valley Forge.
> What kind of citizens do you think they will make?

Washington secured the freedoms we Americans enjoy today. But it was not military skill alone which achieved that. Without his character, patriotism, leadership and service, we probably would not be an independent nation. Here are some vivid instances of Divine Providence at work in the life of George Washington, a man, if ever there was one, chosen by God and raised up to lead his country as an example to all the world.

## Escaping Death...

In 1755, at the age of 23, George Washington, acting as a volunteer aide-de-camp to General Edward Braddock, left Williamsburg with an expedition of 2,100 British regulars and 500 Virginia militiamen. Their mission: to expel the French encroaching on the western lands claimed by England. Their target: Fort Duquesne, at the fork of the Allegheny and Monongahela Rivers, near present-day Pittsburgh.

Washington's mother, concerned for his safety, tried to dissuade him. Washington replied, "The God to whom you commended me, madam, when I set out upon a more perilous errand, defended me from all harm, and I trust He will do so now." (The "perilous errand" was a military venture against the French on the western frontier the previous year in which he and his men were defeated but allowed to return home.)

The army set out in late Spring with its artillery, 150 wagons of provisions and equipment pulled by four horses each, about 260 pack and saddle horses, cattle for slaughtering as food along the way, and three companies of Virginia militiamen. An advance party of several hundred soldiers and axmen cut a 12-foot-wide path through the wilderness for the army to follow. The army itself stretched out in a thin column nearly four miles long.

Braddock was unfamiliar with the style of warfare used by the Indian allies of the French. Washington warned him of Indian ambushes, but the haughty British general ignored the warning, feeling certain his experienced troops would be more than a match for a bunch of savages.

By July, Braddock was within a few miles of Fort Duquesne. The French, aware of his presence via reports from Indian allies, set a trap. The number of French and Indian warriors was less than half that of the British, but the ambush would give them victory. They chose a ravine in which to attack the British from cover of trees and rocks. As Braddock's troops entered the narrow opening, their concealed enemy commenced firing. Gunsmoke came from the trees, but not a man was seen by the British, who were totally surprised by the guerrilla warfare.

Unable to do more than return feeble fire at the invisible enemy, the advance party retreated in utter confusion. Braddock, farther back, hurried toward the sound of battle. He busied himself in forming his men into ranks and, unable to think past European battle tactics where men advanced upon other men across open fields in precise formations, ordered his men not to hide behind trees. Their bright red coats made perfect targets. French and Indian musket balls dropped the British by the hundreds.

The pandemonium lasted two hours. Braddock had five horses shot from under him and finally was shot in the right side and sank to the ground. He had been a special target, along with all his other mounted officers. The army was practically annihilated. More than 700 British soldiers were killed or wounded. The colonials accounted for another 300 dead. The French and Indians had only 30 wounded, none killed. Braddock was taken from the field and died three days later.

What was Washington doing in all this slaughter? At first, being the only unwounded aide of Braddock, he rode over every part of the battlefield, carrying the general's orders to subordinates. According to religious historian David Barton in his 1990 book *The Bulletproof George Washington* (WallBuilders Press, Box 397, Aledo, TX 76008), one survivor who saw Washington undaunted in the midst of battle later reported, "I expected every moment to see him fall. Nothing but the superintending care of Providence could have saved him" (p. 42).

Upon Braddock's fall, everything was abandoned to the enemy. The regular troops fled in confusion; the battle became a rout. Braddock had placed the Virginia militia in the rear because of his contempt for them as soldiers. Scarcely 30 were left alive. Washington organized them to defend the fleeing British. But the abandoned booty on the battlefield was more appealing to the Indians than taking still more scalps. They did not pursue the survivors, who returned to Williamsburg.

Washington later wrote of the battle and matter-of-factly said about himself: "…by the all-powerful dispensations of Providence I have been protected beyond all human probability of expectations, for I had four bullets through my coat and two horses shot under me, yet escaped unhurt, although death was leveling my companions on every side of me!"

Fifteen years later, in 1770, Washington learned who had fired at him. While traveling with a friend in the western territories, a band of Indians approached them, led by an old, respected Indian chief. The chief had heard of Washington's presence in the area. A council fire was kindled and, through an interpreter, he addressed Washington about the battle at Fort Duquesne, where he had fought. Barton quotes an old account of the chief's speech:

> It was on the day when the white man's blood mixed with the streams of our forest that I first beheld this chief [Washington]. I called to my young men and said, mark yon tall and daring warrior? He is not of the red-coat tribe—he hath an Indian's wisdom, and his warriors fight as we do—himself is alone exposed.

Quick, let your aim be certain, and he dies. Our rifles were leveled, rifles which, but for you, knew not how to miss—'twas all in vain; a power mightier far than we shielded you. Seeing you were under the special guardianship of the Great Spirit, we immediately ceased to fire at you....Listen! The Great Spirit protects that man [pointing at Washington], and guides his destinies—he will become the chief of nations, and a people yet unborn will hail him as the founder of a mighty empire. I am come to pay homage to the man who is the particular favorite of Heaven and who can never die in battle.

Barton notes that this incident was well known in the early days of our republic and was confirmed by dozens of historical texts. Indians testified afterward that they had specifically singled out Washington and repeatedly shot at him, but without effect.

Mary Draper Ingels, who was kidnapped by Shawnee Indians in 1755, escaped and wrote an account of her experience. Included was an incident in which French and Indians met in council after the battle of Fort Duquesne and talked animatedly about Washington, whom Ingels knew. She listened carefully and later asked questions. The Frenchmen told of a chief named Red Hawk who shot at Washington 11 times without killing him. At that point, because he had never missed before, Red Hawk stopped firing at him, being convinced that the Great Spirit protected Washington.

Rev. Samuel Davies, who later became president of Princeton University, praised Washington in a sermon and noted his remarkable escape from numerous perils.

In September 1777, at the Battle of Brandywine, outside Philadelphia, Washington again escaped certain death because of circumstances which defy conventional thinking. A few days before he engaged the British, Washington and an aide rode out of camp to scout the terrain. During this reconnoitering in the vicinity of Chadd's Ford on the Brandywine River, Washington encountered an English soldier named Patrick Ferguson—a man who might have single-handedly won the war for Britain.

British Army infantry officer Captain Patrick Ferguson was the designer and patent holder of the Ferguson rifle. His breech-loading flintlock rifle was far superior to the Brown Bess, the standard-issue weapon for British infantry. The Brown Bess was a muzzleloader; its most rapid rate of fire, in the hands of an experienced shooter, was four rounds per minute. Its accuracy was good to about 80 yards. By contrast, the Ferguson rifle could fire six rounds per minute and was accurate up to 300 yards. It weighed about half as much as a Brown Bess.

in the summer of 1776 Ferguson demonstrated his rifle's capabilities to the British senior generals and King George III. He proved that his gun could fire rapidly in rain or high wind or during an advance. A sharpshooter, he shot bulls eyes at 300 yards while standing and at 100 yards while lying on his back. The shooting exhibition so impressed the king that Ferguson's rifle was adopted as the British army's first breech-loading firearm. Ferguson was sent to North America with orders for Sir William Howe, commander-in-chief of the British forces, to establish a Sharp Shooters Corps—snipers —headed by Ferguson. The Corps had 100 men, all with Ferguson rifles. Ferguson, with the most advanced rifle on earth and the most experience and skill with it, was therefore the best and most dangerous marksman in the entire British army.

On September 7, 1777, Ferguson and three of his Sharp Shooters went out to scout the American lines. Washington was likewise scouting. When Ferguson got a glimpse of two horsemen approaching in the distance, he instructed his men to hide in the bushes. Ferguson later wrote, "We had not lain long when a rebel officer passed within a hundred yards of my right flank." The officer was riding a huge bay horse, wearing the traditional blue and buff uniform of an American general officer and had on "a remarkably large cocked hat." Ferguson noted that the officer was of "exceptional distinction."

Washington was roughly six feet three inches tall and weighed about 200 pounds. The typical Continental Army soldier was almost eight inches shorter. So size alone was an indication that the officer was Washington; his uniform and hat added to the identification of the man whom Ferguson knew was in the area. Furthermore, printed likenesses of Washington were publicly posted by admirers. But by Ferguson's own admission, he did not recognize Washington! Only days later, when he was in a field hospital for a wound in his right arm, did he learn who the man was.

At the time of the encounter, Ferguson's first thought was to shoot down the two riders, so he ordered his men to "steal near to them and fire at them." Then he changed his mind and rescinded the order because his first impulse was, he later wrote, "disgusting." He was a man of honor; shooting down enemy officers in cold blood was regarded as dishonorable. He stepped out from concealment and ordered the first rider, Washington's aide, to get down. The aide shouted an alarm. Ferguson decided to take Washington prisoner.

> I advanced from the woods towards him. He stopped, but after looking at me, proceeded. I again drew his attention and made signs for him to stop, but he proceeded on his way.

Washington turned his horse and the two officers rode off, apparently without a sense of great danger because they were, after all, at what they knew to be the limits of a Brown Bess and were on horseback, while Ferguson and his men were on foot. Their retreat was deliberate, not frantic. Had they only known...

Ferguson recounted what happened next.

> As I was within the distance, at which in the quickest firing, I could have lodged a half dozen balls in or about him before he was out of my reach, I had only to determine, but it was not pleasant to fire at the back of an unoffending individual who was acquitting himself coolly of his duty, and so I let him alone.

Would Ferguson have fired if he knew his easy target was the commander-in-chief of the Continental Army, whose death would quickly lead the American forces to ruin? It is a matter for debate. A 19th Century historian, Lyman Draper, observed:

> Had Washington fallen, it is difficult to calculate its probable effect upon the result of the struggle of the American people. How slight, oftentimes, are the incidents which, in the course of human events, seem to give direction to the most momentous concerns of the human race. This singular impulse of Ferguson

illustrates, in a forcible manner, the over-ruling hand of Providence in directing the operation of a man's mind when he himself is least aware of it.

The Battle of Brandywine was the only battle in which Ferguson rifles were used in America. While Ferguson recuperated from his arm wound, his unit was disbanded and his rifles replaced with Brown Bess muskets. Over the ensuing years Ferguson was promoted to Major, then Lieutenant Colonel. In the Battle of Kings Mountain, 1780, Lt. Col. Patrick Ferguson was killed while fighting gallantly, and was buried there.

## ...and Defeat

The Battle of Brooklyn demonstrates "providential intervention" to an extraordinary degree. In late August 1776, Washington's troops on Long Island had been outfought and hemmed in at Brooklyn, with their backs to the East River, by Gen. William Howe's soldiers. Defeat and capture of Washington's 9,000 soldiers seemed imminent. If that happened, the war would be lost.

Washington had to retreat. There was no choice so he gave the order. But to cross the river, he had to get hundreds of boats, which he didn't have, and favorable weather conditions. Moreover, the British could sail ships up the river to block escape. The American army was trapped and a disaster was in the making.

On August 29 bad weather—and bad judgment—kept Lord Howe from advancing his troops across the mile and a half of open terrain separating the two lines. A violent storm broke out. Howe decided to put off the attack until morning. The storm brought a northeast wind so strong that the British ships could not sail upriver. That was a mixed blessing for the Americans because, while it deterred the British ships, it also made the river so rough that small boats, heavily laden with soldiers, could not cross the mile-wide river.

One of Washington's generals in Manhattan commandeered sufficient small boats for the retreat but the weather prevented their use. About eleven o'clock, according to David McCullough in *1776*, "as if by design, the northeast wind died down. Then the wind shifted to the southwest and a small armada of boats...started over the river from New York..." (page 187).

All night long the army retreated across the East River, boatload by boatload, aided by darkness and the deception which Washington ordered: leave campfires burning to give the appearance of our troops remaining in place. But with daylight, the deception would be exposed! And the river was open to British ships. McCullough tells us (page 191):

> Incredibly, yet again, circumstance—fate, luck, Providence, the hand of God, as would be said so often—intervened.
> Just at daybreak a heavy fog settled in over the whole of Brooklyn, concealing everything no less than had the night.

The fog was so thick that one man could scarcely see another six yards away. Yet even with the sun up, McCullough notes, the fog remained as dense as ever, while on the New York side of the river there was no fog at all. The "heavens" assisted the American cause. The entire army escaped without a single loss of life. When the British attacked that morning, the first redcoats to reach the river saw only the fog and heard only the oars of boats taking the last soldiers across. By 7 a.m. Washington and his army were safe in New York with their horses, field artillery, baggage and equipment. It was a miracle on the order of the Hebrews, pursued by Pharaoh's army, crossing the Red Sea.

Miraculous weather played a role in the end of the war, as well as the beginning. At Yorktown in 1781, the tables were turned. The British were encircled with their backs to the York River. Washington's American troops and Rochambeau's French troops were tightening the noose around Lord Cornwallis and his redcoats.

Like Washington at Brooklyn, Cornwallis sought to escape by boat to the farther shore rather than surrender. At 10 p.m. on October 16, he began sending his troops by boat across the river. However, he later reported to commander-in-chief Sir Henry Clinton:

> With the utmost secrecy the light infantry, greater part of the guards, and part of the Twenty-third regiment landed at Gloucester; but at this critical moment, the weather, from being moderate and calm, changed to a most violent storm of wind and rain, and drove all of the boats...down the river.

Cornwallis was nearly out of gunpowder and "could not fire a single gun," he told Clinton. "I therefore proposed to capitulate." On October 17 he sent a message to Washington proposing that terms of surrender be agreed upon. Washington accepted, and they were written up the next day. On October 19, 1781, the Articles of Surrender were signed. Cornwallis's men, numbering nearly 8,000, marched onto the Field of Surrender between two rows of soldiers, Americans on one side, French on the other, and laid down their arms under Washington's gaze. Cornwallis himself was not present. He was, his second-in-command reported, too ill to attend.

After the surrender, Washington sent the prisoners of war to prison camps in Virginia and Maryland, beyond the reach of the British forces remaining in America. He also issued the following order:

> Divine service is to be performed to-morrow in the several brigades and divisions. The Commander-in-chief earnestly recommends that the troops, not on duty, should universally attend, with that seriousness of deportment and gratitude of heart which the recognition of such reiterated and astonishing interpositions of Providence demand of us.

When Lord North, the British Prime Minister, heard the news of Yorktown, he cried, "Oh God! It is all over." There were continued hostilities for a short time—but nothing significant—until the news of Cornwallis's surrender reached the rest of the British forces. Although the British army remained armed and ready for more fighting, the British government forbade further offensive movements and began peace negotiations. However, it would be another two years before the Treaty of Paris formalized the cessation of hostilities and restored peaceful relations between Great Britain and its newly independent American offspring.

Washington commented later, "It will not be believed that such a force as Great Britain has employed for eight years in this country could be baffled in the plan of subjugating it, by numbers infinitely less, composed of men oftentimes half starved, always in rags, without pay, and experiencing every species of distress which human nature is capable of undergoing."

## Washington's Prayer for the United States of America

In September 1783, the Treaty of Paris was signed, marking the official termination of America's War for Independence. In June of that year, when it was clear that the treaty was near completion, Washington wrote a letter at his headquarters in Newburgh, New York, to mark his upcoming resignation as general of the Continental Army and sent it to the governors of all the states. (It became known as his "Circular Address or circular letter" because it was intended to circulate.) Before commenting on a number of issues facing the nation, he mentioned "the glorious events which Heaven has been pleased to produce in our favor." He ended his letter with a statement which clearly summarizes his attitude toward God, Jesus Christ and the role of religion in American society. He wrote:

> I now make it my earnest prayer that God would have you, and the State over which you preside, in his holy protection; that he would incline the hearts of the citizens to cultivate a spirit of subordination and obedience to government; to entertain a brotherly affection and love for one another, for their fellow citizens of the United States at large, and particularly for their brethren who have served in the field; and, finally, that he would most graciously be pleased to dispose us all to do justice, to love mercy, and to demean ourselves with that charity, humility and pacific temper of mind which were the characteristics of the Divine Author of our blessed religion and, without a humble imitation of whose example in these things, we can never hope to be a happy nation.

When Washington resigned his commission on December 23, 1783 at Annapolis, Maryland, where Congress was meeting, he told the assembly, "I consider it an indispensable duty to close this last solemn act of my official life by commending the interests of our dearest country to the protection of Almighty God and those who have the superintendence of them into His holy keeping." Historian Thomas Fleming called Washington's resignation the single most important moment in American history. Because of it, we would never be subjects of a monarch or autocrat.

## The Death of Washington

When Washington died December 14, 1799, the country mourned. His friend, Gen. Richard Henry Lee, eulogized him as "first in war, first in peace, and first in the hearts of his countrymen." (Lee delivered the eulogy but it was written by John Marshall.) John Adams likewise praised him: "Washington's example is complete; and it will teach wisdom and virtue to Magistrates, Citizens, and Men, not only in the present age, but in future generations." One London newspaper reported, "His fame, bounded by no country, will be confined to no age." In Amsterdam, funeral music filled the air. In France, Napoleon, upon learning of Washington's death, ordered a ten-day requiem. Years later, deep in exile, he commented in tribute that the citizens of France "expected me to be another Washington"—i.e., to willingly give up power. Decades later, Abraham Lincoln added his praise: "Washington is the mightiest name on earth.... To add brightness to the sun or glory to the name of Washington is alike impossible. Let none attempt it. In solemn awe pronounce the name, and in its naked deathless splendor leave it shining on."

Washington is deservedly a national icon. It is appropriate that the Rotunda of our nation's Capitol has a fresco entitled "The Apotheosis of Washington." It shows Washington ascending to heaven in glory, surrounded by figures symbolizing ideals such as Liberty and Victory. (Apotheosis means literally raising a person to the rank of a god, or the glorification of a person as an ideal.) It is likewise appropriate that on July 4, 1976, during America's bicentennial year, Congress appointed George Washington, posthumously, to the five-star rank of General of the Armies of the United States. Previously there had been a handful of officers who had attained five-star rank (as General of the Army, General of the Air Force and Fleet Admiral), but Washington was elevated to the highest rank possible and given unique status as the most senior military officer in American history for his role in the founding of America. In America's military, no one can ever outrank George Washington. His name in enshrined as the name of our nation's capital city and in hundreds of other places such as towns, streets, schools, colleges, monuments, mountains, counties and a state. May it also be enshrined in your heart.

---

## FOOTNOTES

[1] Roger Williams, founder of the colony which would become Rhode Island, was driven out of the Massachusetts Bay Colony and into the wilderness in the middle of winter for being a religious dissenter. The settlement he and a handful of followers established was named Providence. "[Having] a sense of God's merciful providence unto me in my distress," said Williams, "[I] called the place Providence."

[2] Although Washington is rightly called The Father of Our Country and was unanimously elected our first President under the Constitution, the United States did not begin with the Constitution being written and ratified. It began, of course, with the Declaration of Independence in 1776. There were two representative bodies and three documents preceding our present Constitution which served as instruments of government or deliberative national bodies for what we now call our country. Each document established the office of a president of the American body politic.

The First Continental Congress of the United Colonies of America was convened in 1774 in Philadelphia and elected Peyton Randolph of Virginia as its president. That same year it authorized the Articles of Association to promote unity among the colonies against British trade restrictions. The first president under the Articles of Association, which was the first central government of America, was Samuel Huntington of Connecticut. The Second Continental Congress, which produced the Declaration of Independence, had John Hancock as its president. (The presidents of Congress were heads of government but not heads of state.)

In 1777, Congress produced the Articles of Confederation, which were ratified in 1781. The first president under the Articles of Confederation was John Hanson. The

Articles allowed a President to serve only a one-year term during any three-year period. Seven other presidents were elected after Hanson; one was John Hancock.

Altogether, thirteen men served as president of what can be loosely termed "our country" under one or another of the federated governments established to unify the colonies/states. Some of them served more than once; some were elected but did not serve for long and therefore were replaced by acting presidents.

Thus, George Washington was not our first president. Depending on how you count the men involved, he was anywhere from our 11th president to the 14th. This point is perhaps more of interest to historians and scholars than to school children, but it is nonetheless interesting to consider. However, in no way does it detract from the glory and honor which are rightly attributed to George Washington.

## Chapter 6

# "INDIVISIBLE": WHAT HOLDS AMERICA TOGETHER?

Then join hand in hand, brave Americans all—
By uniting we stand, by dividing we fall!
John Dickinson, "Liberty Song"
*Boston Gazette*, 18 July 1768

Indivisible means "cannot be divided." What holds America together as one nation? What makes us the *united* states?

Since there are two primary aspects to our nation—the society and the government—we need to examine both to answer that question.

During the American Revolution, George Washington, the Father of Our Country, said that before he was a Virginian, he was an American. And in a 1794 letter to John Adams, he noted that immigrants, "by an intermixture with our people, they, or their descendants, get assimilated to our customs, measures and laws: in a word, soon become one people."

The America of Washington's ideals, and ours, is united as one people politically and culturally. "Politically" refers to our form of government; "culturally" refers to our form of society. Our national unity arises from our shared sense of identity, which is founded on respect for both those aspects of the body politic. To repeat what I said in Chapter 1, our national identity consists of the ideals, principles and values which flow from the metaphysical to the physical, from God to the nation, where they are embodied in the institutions, customs, laws and practices of our civil and political life. That is what unites us—a geographically, racially, ethnically and religiously diverse people—into one nation. If either aspect should change, America would be susceptible to division and disunion.

Let's first examine the governmental aspect of our national unity.

## Our Political Unity

The word "indivisible" was inserted into the Pledge of Allegiance because, as noted in Chapter 2, Francis Bellamy saw America as "a single nationality and of an indivisibility both of states and of common interests." He was referring to what was then a recent event, The Civil War (also known in the South as The War Between the States and The War for Southern Independence). Secession by the South had disunited the Union for four years. Secession is the act of withdrawing or separating from an organization, union or political entity. (That is how America itself began—by seceding from Great Britain over irreconcilable differences.) The South was defeated by the North for attempting that and, as Bellamy saw it, the issue of secession was thereafter settled for all time.

"A house divided against itself cannot stand," said Abraham Lincoln in 1858, quoting the Bible (Mark 3:25). Someone from the South might have replied, "Of course it can. It's called a duplex—a two-family house."

Should there have been a war between the Union and the Confederacy? Abraham Lincoln has saintly stature in the popular mind because, it is widely believed, he fought to end slavery. He is known as the Great Emancipator. His actions brought an end to two centuries of bondage in America.

However, that was not what the Civil War was all about, as Lincoln saw it.

As vile an institution as slavery is—the worst wholesale violation of human rights short of genocide—and as central to the Civil War as it was, by his own admission, Lincoln did not go to war to end slavery. In his First Inaugural Address in 1860, he told America, "I have no purpose, directly or indirectly, to interfere with the institution of slavery in the states where it now exists. I believe I have no lawful right to do so, and I have no inclination to do so." After Fort Sumter was fired on in 1861, he enlarged upon that view with these words from his Letter to Horace Greeley: "My paramount objective is to save the Union, and it is *not* either to save or destroy slavery. If I could save the Union without freeing any slave, I would do so." [1]

## Lincoln Chose War

Lincoln chose war when he could have done otherwise. The South desired to secede peaceably, and there was considerable sentiment in the North which favored "letting the erring sisters go in peace." The Constitution, the South argued, created the federal government only because of the authority *delegated* to it by the states. The federal government was created to serve the states and the people, not the other way around. There is nothing in the Constitution which prohibits secession. The Constitution is a compact among sovereign and equal states, and it was the view of the seceding states that, like marriage, they had a right to divorce their partner states and live separately. There was no thought of conquering the North to assert their freedom. "All we ask is to be left alone," said Jefferson Davis at his inauguration after being elected President of the Confederate States of America.

The "house" to be divided was the Union, and Lincoln believed deeply in the indivisibility of it. "I hold that the union of these states is perpetual," he declared. But was he correct in that belief? Was he justified in declaring war—a war which resulted in the death of more than 600,000 Americans—more recent estimates go as high as 750,000—and the severe disabling of more than 400,000 others, cities burned, farms destroyed and homes leveled? (Remember that the South had renamed itself by changing only one word in "United States of America" and Southerners believed themselves to be as truly American as citizens of the North. After all, Virginia was the first of the original 13 colonies.)

In 1863, Lincoln said, "If I had my way, this war would have never been commenced. If I had been allowed my way, this war would have ended before this [time]."

But Lincoln *did* have his way from the very outset! It was he who chose armed force over negotiation (against the advice of his Cabinet). Using his executive power to wage war, he initiated the armed conflict without approval from Congress (which was not in session at the time). The opening shots of the war were fired by South Carolina in retaliation for Lincoln's order to resupply Fort Sumter. Rather than resupply the fort, Lincoln could have ordered it to be abandoned to South Carolina. It was, after all, on their soil. Moreover, his own general-in-chief, Winfield Scott, advised him to surrender the fort rather than reprovision it.

As for the institution of slavery, [2] Lincoln could have offered to purchase all the slaves in a businesslike manner, compensating their owners, and then releasing them as freed men and women. To his credit, Lincoln did try exactly that. His strategy was a gradual compensated emancipation; it had been employed successfully in other countries where slavery was legal. Slaveholders were paid for releasing their slaves, and the institution was gradually phased out.

On March 6, 1862, Lincoln proposed to the Senate and the House of Representatives that Congress adopt a joint resolution favoring his plan for gradual compensated emancipation. It would state that the federal government had no right to interfere with slavery within the states but would offer financial compensation for the emancipation of slaves in any state which accepted the offer.

Lincoln "tested the waters" in a letter to Illinois Senator James A. McDougall, dated March 14, 1862. The small state of Delaware had 1,798 slaves listed in the 1860 census. Lincoln proposed to pay slaveholders $400 for each slave. He told McDougall it would be less than half the $2 million which each day of the war was costing. But the idea never took root with Delaware. It scornfully dismissed the idea as an "abolition bribe."

Congress, however, favored the resolution and took a further step. It passed a bill freeing slaves in the District of Columbia upon payment to their owners of $300 for each slave. Lincoln signed the bill on April 16, 1862. Thus Congress was pledged to Lincoln's concept of the government buying all slaves and freeing them. But as with Delaware, the idea was nevertheless strongly rejected by both Southern and Northern states.

Some historians argue that Lincoln could have simply let the South go its own way because industrial mechanization of farming was making slavery unnecessary. [3] It would have been easier and more productive to pick cotton with a machine than with people who had to be clothed, housed and fed. The institution of slavery was dying, the argument goes, and when it did in a few decades, the South would be ready to return to the Union, voluntarily. The "Great Divorce" would have ended because the benefits of belonging to the union, once the issue of slavery was settled, would have prompted a return. Historian Sam Dickson, writing about Lincoln in *The Barnes Review* (January/ February 2006, p. 10) points out:

> The union had existed half slave and half free from its inception. There appears
> no logical reason why it could not continue to have existed in that fashion, given
> responsible leadership and good will on both sides, until slavery was gradually
> and peacefully eliminated by the progress of technology.

So why did Lincoln choose war? Did he act constitutionally in fighting to preserve the Union when the Constitution never ruled out secession?

In his Gettysburg Address, Lincoln called for the preservation of government of the people, by the people and for the people. Ironically, that was what the South was fighting for—self-determination and government by consent of the governed, as stated in the Declaration of Independence—with Lincoln opposing it. Lincoln, it is now widely acknowledged, acted unilaterally, in dictatorial fashion, during the war. He closed down nearly 300 newspapers because they criticized him or his policies; he had thousands of people arrested as traitors for the same reasons, and he suspended the right of habeas corpus when their attorneys appealed to judges to release the prisoners being held without charge. He created the military draft—something which had never existed before on the national level. In 1864, referring to the Emancipation Proclamation, Lincoln boldly declared, "I conceive that I may in an emergency do things on military grounds which cannot be done constitutionally by Congress." He did not mention that he himself had created the emergency. Even General Ulysses S. Grant, in his 1883 *Personal Memoirs*, noted of the Constitution: "While it did not authorize rebellion it made no provision against it." (Volume II, p. 506, original edition) Grant, like Lincoln, insisted on characterizing the southern stance as rebellion rather than peaceful withdrawal but, unlike Lincoln, he nevertheless acknowledged that the Constitution did not forbid secession.

## Lincoln Exceeded His Authority

All that action by Lincoln can be described as unconstitutional. It is also described by some historians and political commentators as expanding the power of the federal government at the expense of the states and of the people, while trampling their rights. Furthermore, it is seen as the start of the destructive and unconstitutional process, now woefully evident, of power being consolidated in Washington, D.C., so that the federal government is fast becoming a national government. Before the Civil War, America was generally thought of as *these* United States, a federal republic; afterward, it became *the* United States, a monolithic nation governed from Washington, D.C. In fact, before the Constitution and the Articles of Confederation, America was, as the Declaration of Independence phrased it, composed of "Free and Independent States."

Lincoln believed his actions were necessary to quell what he saw as rebellion against the Union because his Oath of Office required it. In his First Inaugural Address he declared:

> In *your* hands, my dissatisfied fellow countrymen, and not in *mine*, is the momentous issue of civil war. The government will not assail *you*. You can have no conflict, without being yourselves the aggressors. *You* have no oath registered in Heaven to destroy the government, while I shall have the most solemn one to "preserve, protect and defend" it.

The trouble with Lincoln's stance is this: the oath calls for the President to preserve, protect and defend the Constitution, not the Union. Nor is secession the same thing as destroying the government. It can be argued, and has been, that Lincoln exceeded his Constitutional authority in using armed might to force his will upon the South when their secession was no threat to the government or to the Union. There still would have been a United States of America if the South had been able to maintain its secession. They were not "the aggressors." The United States of America was 34 states large at that time, and although 11 states joined together to form the Confederate States of America, the United States was still the United States, even though reduced in size. Constitutional federalism would still have been possible for the remaining states because the Constitution is not written for a specific number of states. How could it have been when originally there were only 13? Since the Civil War another 16 states have been added and, in theory, it is possible for all the nations of the world to become states of the Union. (I will argue for exactly that in the last chapter.) In short, Lincoln chose to enforce the *geographic form* of the Union by warfare rather than the spirit of the Union by following the Constitution and the principles expressed in the Declaration of Independence.

## Force Rather Than Freedom

Lincoln forced civil war on the South not in the name of freedom for all (a pillar of the Constitution), and not for states' rights (another pillar of the Constitution), but to keep states in the Union against their will—a violation of two fundamental values in the American theory of government. In other words, he chose form over substance and force over freedom. [4]

Lincoln once said he never had "a feeling, politically, that did not spring from the sentiments embodied in the Declaration of Independence." He also said, "Let reverence for the laws...become the political religion of the nation." It is sadly ironic that the criticism leveled against him by some contemporary historians and political commentators should include his violation of those very words by his unconstitutional acts. And it is the greatest irony of all that his violation went on to contradict his expressed hope in the Gettysburg Address for "a new birth of freedom." In seceding, the South did not violate any law or anyone's freedom (slaves, of course, were already unfree); in suppressing the South, Lincoln did both. The South's intention was to live peaceably side-by-side with the North, going their separate ways, of course, but without interfering in the other's manner of living.

Walter E. Williams, a professor of economics at George Mason University and a syndicated columnist, summarized the situation with these words:

> The War Between the States settled by force whether states could secede. Once it was established that states cannot secede, the federal government, abetted by a Supreme Court unwilling to hold it to its constitutional restraints, was able to run amok over states' rights, so much so that the protections of the Ninth and Tenth Amendments mean little or nothing today. Not only did the war lay the foundation for eventual nullification or weakening of basic constitutional protections against central government abuses, but it also laid to rest the great principle enunciated in the Declaration of Independence that "Governments are instituted among Men, deriving their just powers from the consent of the governed."

The Declaration of Independence established a nation founded on the highest, most universal value: freedom. The Constitution established a form of government for America which guaranteed that freedom for its citizens (slaves excepted—and I've already discussed that in Chapter 1. Slaves were not legally citizens and would remain so until the 14th Amendment was ratified). [5] It is the principles of government and the form of that government—a constitutional federal republic—which are most important to America, not the actual number of states. Lincoln spoke words which were contradicted by his actions. In the name of freedom and the Constitution, he led the nation into the worst bloodbath in our history.

Was that necessary in order to establish that our union of states is indivisible? If one argues in favor of that, America must be prepared to go to war internally whenever another secession movement emerges on the national or federal level. Let's see what that means.

## How to Respond to Secession

At the local level, secession occurs fairly often, such as when part of a town or municipality separates from its original body and becomes independent. For example, in recent years the city of Palo Alto, California, saw its eastern section become the city of East Palo Alto. It was achieved peacefully through political discourse and due process of law.

At the state level, there have been a significant number of attempts to generate secessionist support for such projects as making the Upper Peninsula of Michigan a state and for Staten Island breaking away from New York City. Such efforts are lawful and depend for their success on friendly persuasion and political support of the people involved.

However, all that has nothing to do the U.S. Constitution and the effect of such secessions does not change the borders of America. What about the very recent movement in Vermont to turn the state into an independent nation, The Republic of Vermont? The same sentiment exists in Texas, where some Texans declare their state is The Republic of Texas. Neither of these endeavors has gotten much popular support, so not much has become of them, although the Vermont organizers created a public entity called The Middlebury Institute (http://middleburyinstitute.org), which sponsored two North American Secessionist Movement Conventions. A handful of delegates attended and issued declarations of intent to secede, stating their reasons for it. Their reasons accuse the federal government of acting dishonorably, becoming abusive and corrupt, departing from Constitutional principles and generally turning our republic into a global empire for the financial and commercial interests of Wall Street. Their rationale for secession is the Declaration of Independence's statement about the right of people to alter or abolish the government and to create a new form of government congenial to their interests, including political and economic freedom. Their method of accomplishing that is described as separating themselves "by peaceful and well-established legal and constitutional means." One statement notes, "Recourse to the right of separation, or secession, is the very antithesis of armed revolution." That, of course, was the same general stance which the South took toward the North.

What is the solution for remaining undivided when a mood of state or regional secession grows in part of the nation? The answer is clear and simple: work out differences nonviolently and honorably, [6] with good will, through patient diplomatic negotiation, legislative redress of legitimate grievances and an humble, brotherly attitude toward the aggrieved parties. Take a civil and restrained stance in all discourse. Keep alive the hope of reconciliation. That, of course, was the same general stance which the colonies took toward England—until it became clear that the King and Parliament would not budge, making armed rebellion unavoidable. The League of the South (http://dixienet.org/New%20Site/index.shtml), a secessionist organization wishing to restore the Confederacy and its way of life as an independent Southern republic—but without slavery—calls for "education, recruitment, and organization" as the primary means of establishing sufficient "mass base" for success. It notes on its web site:

> Q: Is secession not illegal, unconstitutional, and discredited?
>
> A: By no means. Most of those who wrote and ratified the constitution recognized secession as a legitimate, legal, and constitutional measure of protection against the possibility that the national government might in the future consolidate and centralise power, violate the terms of the constitution, and usurp the rights and liberties of the people of the sovereign States. Secession is a right of a truly free people and the cornerstone of confederalism. What has been tried, failed, and discredited is centralism—by unitary government that reneged on its original compact as an agent of the States, usurped their sovereignty, and opted instead to hold the 'Union' together by brute force.

So long as the ideals, principles and values which guided the establishment and growth of America remain intact, our national unity will remain intact. What are they? As given in Chapter 1: the proclamation of liberty for all, individual sovereignty, self-determination, inalienable rights, equality of opportunity, justice under the rule of law, and human dignity for all, derived from God and guaranteed through constitutional republican government of the people, by the people and for the people—all for the purpose of enabling us to find individual and collective happiness. But if our nation departs from them, as is happening today, disunity and widespread secessionist sentiment will surely follow.

The Preamble to the Constitution says one purpose of the document is to form a more perfect union. The motto on the Great Seal declares "out of many [states], one [nation]." The indivisibility of America is predicated on voluntary unity, not imposed federal government.

## Our Cultural Unity

In addition to our political unity, America needs to maintain its cultural unity if we are to remain one nation, indivisible. So now let's examine that aspect.

There are two things essential for U.S. citizenship: learning English and learning civics. That goes for native-born and immigrant alike. Without the ability to speak, read and write English, we cannot have a national culture and an informed citizenry. Without understanding the principles and practices of local, state and federal government, we cannot have the responsible, engaged electorate necessary for a society based on self-government. Without those essentials, it's good-bye America.

Civics is discussed in Chapter 7, so I will disregard it here and focus on the need to learn English, our common tongue.

The indivisibility of America depends in great part on having a single, common language. It is vital for the preservation of the American way of life. A nation of many tongues will not remain a nation; it will degenerate into a people divided by language and by culture. The "melting pot" of multiethnic America has always unofficially had English as its common tongue and immigrants learned English in order to enter the mainstream of American society. And until recently, the written test to be passed in qualifying for citizenship was in English only.

Today, however, America is undergoing a great societal transformation with regard to English as a unifying force for our nation. Sadly, in a stark reversal of the past, our federal government is accommodating other languages in the name of "diversity."

According to U.S. English, a nonprofit lobbying organization in Washington, D.C. (web site: www.usenglish.org), more than 300 languages are spoken in America and more than 20 million U.S. residents speak very limited English or none at all.

First, changes in law over the last few decades have eroded the need to learn English. Dozens of languages are being used for such things as drivers' license testing, voter ballots, IRS instructions and citizenship ceremonies.

Second, the need to learn English for cultural assimilation is being undercut by government welfare programs, thereby giving immigrants less incentive to find a job. Hundreds of thousands of foreigners collect SSI benefits from the Social Security Administration without having to work in America for even one day. They also are eligible for Medicare.

There is even a plan in Washington which would expand this outrageously. Top officials at the State Department and Social Security Administration want to give away as much as $345 billion from Social Security trust funds to Mexicans who worked illegally in the U.S. for fewer than the required years and then returned to Mexico. The scheme would allow them to collect full Social Security benefits for the rest of their lives while living in Mexico!

Likewise, state and local welfare (such as food stamps, medical benefits and housing assistance) increase the disincentive to work; this amounts to billions of dollars a year. Furthermore, all government agencies are required by Executive Order 13166, issued by President Clinton in 2000, to print all documents in foreign languages and provide translators for people who don't speak English or have very limited ability to speak in English. (The cost to taxpayers for full government compliance is billions of dollars; in 2004 the Congressional Budget Office estimated the cost of implementation in the health care sector alone at $267 million.)

Third, various blocs of citizens are elevating their racial, ethnic and national origins above that of their present nationality, American. [7] They are placing their past ahead of their future. According to *The American Legion Magazine* (June 2008, p. 13), only 40 percent of the foreign-born population is naturalized; the figure for 1950 was 78 percent. As economist and social commentator Dr. Thomas Sowell observed, "In the past, people came here to become Americans, not remain foreigners." Those foreigners who refuse to learn English are reversing the meaning of "E pluribus unum" and breaking up American unity into subgroups claiming superiority to all others or seeking separation from all others. The result of all that "identity politics" will be the balkanization of our country into linguistic ghettos and the creation of the Disunited States of America.

Fourth, bilingual and multilingual education in schools has been shown to be costly, ineffective and against the wishes of the majority of taxpayers and immigrant parents of non-English speaking schoolchildren, yet teachers and administrators force continuation of such programs.

## Make English Our Official Language

For the good of the nation, English should be made the official language of the United States. All business of the government of the United States, from local to federal, should be conducted in English except for Department of Defense operations and State Department diplomatic communications which might require otherwise. That includes voting ballots and traffic signs. What language people use at home, at work, in the market, in school, at worship or in the streets should be their choice or the choice of their employers or their administrators, but for the business of government, one and only one language should be used: English, the tongue in which our Founders wrote those magnificent documents which gave birth to America. No one should entitled to government services in another language.

There is a global dimension to the situation as well. According to U.S. English, 92 percent of the world's countries have at least one official language, so America would not be setting a precedent. English is the sole official language in 31 nations and has an official status in 20 others, including India, Singapore, the Philippines, Samoa and Nigeria. As Mauro E. Mujica, head of U.S. English, said (*Human Events*, 28 July 2003, p. 24), "English is the global language of business, communications, higher education, diplomacy, aviation, the Internet, science, popular music, entertainment and international travel. Immigrants who don't know English not only lose out in the American economy, but also in the global economy."

The most important aspect of all this is stated clearly in *Common Sense on Mass Migration* by John H. Tanton, M.D., Editor (The Social Contract Press, 445 E. Mitchell Street, Petosky, MI 49770-2623, 2004, p. 16):

> ...the Constitution alone cannot guarantee that we will remain free. Freedom requires that Americans share a common loyalty to the principles of the Constitution. If we don't embrace these principles as a society, they will pass away—despite what any document says. The excessive levels of immigration we now have [both legal and illegal] are overwhelming our ability to assimilate the newcomers to our culture.

Happily, there is a growing recognition of this danger to our nation and our heritage. More than 30 states have passed or preserved Official English legislation, and many other states now have bills pending in their state legislatures to either establish English as their official language or strengthen existing laws.

However, there is still resistance to the idea in Washington, where the pro-immigrant lobby is a powerful force affecting Congress. Even though surveys show that more than 80 percent of the American public believe English should be the official language of our nation, [8] some legislators continue to drag their feet and cater to anti-Official English groups who want them to provide costly and inefficient foreign language programs on demand.

The only sane and sensible answer to this problem is Official English—and encouraging immigrants to learn English. It is part of our "melting pot" tradition, and is part of the solution to the politically correct idea of mandatory diversity. It is one thing to be tolerant and welcoming to "the huddled masses yearning to breathe free," as Emma Lazarus described them in her poem about the Statue of Liberty; it is quite another thing to demand that diversity of race and ethnicity be officially required on juries, government boards, college campuses, boards of directors, and so forth. The former generates national unity and organic wholeness; the latter disrupts that and generates adversarial enclaves.

I think it fitting to end this discussion with the words of President Theodore Roosevelt, who said this in 1907 about immigrants and being an American:

> In the first place, we should insist that if the immigrant who comes here in good faith becomes an American and assimilates himself to us, he shall be treated on an exact equality with everyone else, for it is an outrage to discriminate against any such man because of creed, or birthplace, or origin. But this is predicated upon the person's becoming in every facet an American, and nothing but an American... There can be no divided allegiance here. Any man who says he is an American, but something else also, isn't an American at all. We have room for but one flag, the American flag... We have room for but one language here, and that is the English language... and we have room for but one sole loyalty and that is a loyalty to the American people.

---

## FOOTNOTES

[1] At Christmas of 1860, before Lincoln left Illinois for Washington, D.C., he wrote a letter to the vice president of the Confederacy, Alexander Hamilton Stephens, whom Lincoln knew and liked from their days together in Congress. The letter was marked "For Your Eyes Only" and promised that his administration would not interfere with slavery. He subsequently changed his mind and refused to meet with Stephens when he (Stephens) led a delegation seeking to negotiate an end to the crisis.

[2] Although the first Africans arrived in America in 1619 at Jamestown, Virginia, it is not clear from historical records whether they were slaves or indentured servants. Probably there were both. In any case, slaves could buy their freedom and could also gain freedom by converting to Christianity. Indentured servants were granted 50 acres of land when freed from their term of indenture.

According to the document-rich archives on slavery posted on the Public Broadcasting System website (www.pbs.com), the imposition of *permanent* slave status on a person in America did not occur until 1640. At Jamestown, an African named John Punch, who had been declared a slave, was ordered by the court "to serve his said master or his assigns for the time of his natural life." This is the first judicial record of involuntary servitude except as punishment for a crime. Ironically, Punch's master was also black, the first-generation son of an African who was part of the first group to arrive in America. Thus the first lifelong slave in America was owned by a black man.

In 1650, there were only 400 negroes in Virginia, about two percent of an estimated 19,000 settlers. They were not slaves any more than the approximately 4,000 indentured servants working out their loans for passage money to Virginia. In one county, at least 20 African men and women were free, and 13 owned their own homes. One of them, Anthony Johnson of Northampton, Virginia, had purchased his first property in 1640. He married an African servant named Mary, who also became free, and they had four children. By the 1650s, their estate had grown to 250 acres. They raised cattle and in 1651 imported five indentured servants of their own.

There were cases in colonial America of free black women owning their husbands, free black parents selling their children into slavery to white owners, and absentee free black slave owners who leased their slaves to plantation owners. *Free Negro Owners of Slaves in the United States 1830* by the black historian Carter C. Woodson lists the names and addresses of free blacks who owned slaves.

In Africa, where the slave trade began long before North America was settled by Europeans, we learn from Hugh Thomas in *The Slave Trade : The Story of the Atlantic Slave Trade: 1440-1870* (Touchstone Books: New York, 1999, p.561) that the confusion after the abolition of the slave trade by Britain and the U.S. was considerable. In 1820, the King of Ashanti asked a British official named Dupuis why the Christians did not want to buy slaves any more. Was their God not the same as that of the Muslims, who continued to buy, kidnap and sell slaves just as they had always done? Since the Qur'an accepted slavery, some Muslims even persuaded themselves that the new Christian behavior was an attack on Islam.

There were more slaves in Africa in 1807 than in the Americas, although there were also more gradations of enslavement in the former. Slaves probably constituted three-quarters of the West African exports in the 18th century. "The slave trade has been at all times popular and is now," commented an English businessman, John Hughes, after a visit to Cacheu-Bissau, or Portuguese Guinea, in 1828. He added, "I believe that every native African…would indulge in the slave trade if allowed to do so." Historian Thomas Sowell notes in *Race and Culture* that while a total of 11 million Africans were shipped to the Americas, 14 million were sent East, mostly to the Arab world.

American teachers using an Afrocentric perspective when teaching American history are doing a disservice to their students unless they tell the whole story, including facts such as these. It is indeed important for black children to learn of their racial and ethnic roots and to develop a healthy respect for their ancestral heritage. However, those children are American, not African. Their culture is Western, not African. Their skin may be black, but In the melting pot of America, the only colors which matter are red, white and blue. Those colors stand for God-given liberty, individual sovereignty, inalienable rights and human dignity in a democratic constitutional republic based on the rule of law which gives equal opportunity to all. That should be at the center of an American teacher's perspective.

[3] Lincoln himself once held that view. When he was elected to Congress in 1846, he expressed his belief that slavery was wrong but would eventually be righted so long as the Northern States forbade slavery and it was barred from new western territories north of the Missouri Compromise line of 1820. Slavery was a vexing but "minor question," Lincoln said, "on its way to extinction."

[4] Even Lincoln's famous "Letter to Mrs. Bixby" maintains his stance that the departure of the Confederate states equals the end of the republic and the death of freedom. In offering condolences to the Boston mother who lost five sons in the war, he expresses "the thanks of the republic they died to save" and describes their deaths as

"a sacrifice upon the altar of freedom." But neither the republic nor freedom was threatened. The deaths of the five brothers were unnecessary.

[5] The Amistad Affair (1839-1842) was little known in American history until Steven Spielberg's 1998 film *Amistad*. I learned of it well before then, in part because the Amistad captives were jailed in New Haven, Connecticut, and were transported by barge through my home town of Cheshire, on the Farmington Canal, en route to trial in Hartford. In this poem, written in 1995, I sought to recreate the kind of atmosphere found in 19th century poetry which inspired patriotic feeling in readers; I wanted to honor the Amistad prisoners' struggle for freedom and the eventual triumph of justice and brotherhood. The Committee mentioned in it is the Amistad Committee, formed by abolitionists to support the Amistad prisoners in their quest for liberty. Singbe is the African name of Singbe Piet, better known as Cinque, the leader of the Amistads.

## SINGBE'S DREAM

"To be born free is a great privilege; to die free is a great responsibility."
–Anonymous

They crossed the wild Atlantic sea
Enchained in ships of slavery,
Stripped of their humanity
    And, most of all, their freedom.

Captured as chattel through tribal strife,
Then auctioned off and sold for life—
Child from mother, husband from wife
    And each from precious freedom.

Then forced to labor in the field
Of those to whom the Africans kneeled.
But one man, Singbe, would not yield
    The distant dream of freedom.

In self-defense, he rose to fight
Against the cruel, tyrannical might
Of laws and commerce which lost sight
    Of Man's inherent freedom.

To court and conscience Singbe spoke,
Assisted by Committee folk
Whose righteous action then awoke
    A just regard for freedom.

The Amistads then won the day,
But lonely months would pass ere they

Could board a ship and sail away —
    Away to home and freedom.

'Twas thus a brave and hardy band
Returned, without bound foot and hand,
To walk again their native land
    And savor fragile freedom.

So Singbe's dream at last came true.
America had forged anew
A statement of the sacred view
    That God gave all men freedom.

But other suffering does not end,
Nor shall the heart begin to mend
Till all men call each other friend
    And all men honor freedom.

6 Our Founders saw America as a "republic of virtue." Honor is a virtue. Honor is fundamental to good character, good citizenship and good government. It means "a keen sense of ethical conduct" and is synonymous with "integrity." Without honor, there is no honesty. Its meaning is illustrated dramatically in this story from the Civil War.

Three days after General Robert E. Lee had surrendered to General Ulysses S. Grant at Appomattox, the Confederate troops, led by Major General John B. Gordon, a Mason, were marching in columns toward the Federal troops at Appomattox, who were standing in formation waiting for the Confederates to stack arms and fold their flags. Suddenly a shifting of arms was heard. Gordon, who had been riding with a heavy spirit and a downcast face, looked up with alarm but quickly saw there was nothing to fear. Brigadier General Joshua L. Chamberlain, also a Mason, had ordered his troops to assume the position of salute. Gordon, catching the meaning, personally returned the salute to Chamberlain and then ordered his troops to likewise render a salute as they passed Chamberlain. It was, in Chamberlain's words, "honor answering honor." It was also one of the first acts to begin healing the wounds of civil war. (Grant's agreement to Lee's request at Appomattox to let his men keep their arms and horses, which would be necessary for them to hunt and farm upon their return home, was the first.)

Chamberlain, the hero of Little Round Top at the Battle of Gettysburg, was awarded the Medal of Honor for his combat actions. He was from Portland, Maine. After the war, he was four times elected Governor of Maine (1866-1871) and later became President of Bowdoin College (1871-83). Nearly killed in battle, he died in 1914 from complications of his wartime wounds. His Confederate counterpart is described in Willard M. Wallace's biography of Chamberlain, *Soul of the Lion* (Stan Clark Military Books: Gettysburg, PA, 1988, p. 188) thus:

Gordon was riding erect, but with his chin on his chest and his eyes on the ground. As he heard the call and the machine-like shift of arms [from Chamberlain's order to his troops to change position from "order arms" to "carry arms"], he looked up, startled. Then he caught the significance of the movement, and his whole attitude changed. Wheeling his horse toward Chamberlain, he touched the animal slightly with the spur so that it reared, and as the horse's head came down in a graceful bow, Gordon brought his sword-point down to his boot-toe. Then wheeling back to his own column, he gave the command to carry arms. The two armies thus accorded each other the final recognition of gallant opponents.

Gordon became a popular public speaker after the war, and often alluded to Chamberlain in the highest terms: "One of the knightliest soldiers of the Federal army"—a man of honor.

[7] For example, according to Tom DeWeese in *The DeWeese Report* (September 2007, p. 6), the Chicano Student Movement of Aztlan believes that Aztlan is the legendary homeland of the Aztecs (a large portion of the American Southwest) and it is theirs to "reconquest." The movement states: "Chicano is our identity…it rejects the notion that we…should assimilate into the Anglo-American melting pot."

[8] Interestingly, one poll taken recently in Los Angeles showed radically different statistics. The poll asked respondents whether illegal aliens were a problem for the country. Thirty-five percent said yes; the other sixty-five percent said, "No está una problema." (Joke!)

## Chapter 7

# THE MEANING OF AMERICAN CITIZENSHIP

Now more than ever before, the people are responsible for the character of their Congress. If that body be ignorant, reckless and corrupt, it is because the people tolerate ignorance, recklessness and corruption. If it be intelligent, brave and pure, it is because the people demand these high qualities to represent them in the national legislature.... If the next centennial does not find us a great nation... it will be because those who represent the enterprise, the culture, and the morality of the nation do not aid in controlling the political forces.
— President James A. Garfield, 1877

Governments do not make ideals, but ideals make governments. This is both historically and logically true. Of course the government can help to sustain ideals and can create institutions through which they can be better observed, but their source by their very nature is in the people
— President Calvin Coolidge, 1937

The people have to bear their own responsibilities. There is no method by which that burden can be shifted to the government. It is not the enactment, but the observance of laws, that creates the character of a nation.

In the first chapter, I described the American Spirit as the essence of our nation. I'm sorry to say, however, that our embrace of the American Spirit appears to be waning. Many things are wrong in our land, all the way from Main Street to the highest offices of government. America seems to be losing its spiritual compass. Civility, morality and patriotism—markers of health in the body politic—are declining noticeably. The greatest threat facing America is not war, terrorism or weapons of mass destruction. As bad as those are, **the greatest threat to America is the ignorance and apathy of our own citizens**. As Abraham Lincoln said, "America will never be destroyed from the outside. If we falter and lose our freedoms, it will be because we destroyed ourselves."

If America is to remain free and strong, we as a people must thoroughly understand the fundamentals on which our nation is founded. We must relearn the basics. Why? Sadly, over the last six decades or so the fundamentals have, to a significant degree, passed out of public awareness and out of the curriculum of many schools (see Chapter 8). They are not being adequately transmitted to succeeding generations. They are being lost to America. Consequently, America is in danger of being lost. As President Reagan warned:

Freedom is never more than one generation from extinction. We did not pass it to our children in the bloodstream. It must be fought for, protected, and handed on for them to do the same, or one day we will spend our sunset years telling our children and our children's children what it was once like in the United States where men were free.

Therefore, in order to make further progress toward what the Preamble to the Constitution calls "a more perfect union," we must first reeducate ourselves in the basics of our national experience and recommit ourselves to that. We must thoroughly understand fundamentals here at home and thereby perform a much-needed "course correction" for America before we're ready to move ahead in the world community.

By reeducation, I do not mean a simple "return to the past." That is both impossible and undesirable. (Would you select a whale oil lamp over electric lights or quill-and-ink over ballpoint pen and e-mail?) Rather, I mean a reawakening to the timeless truth which is the spiritual foundation of America. I mean reawakening to the ideals, principles and values which have supported the creation of the most wondrous nation on Earth—the freest, most prosperous society in history. Those ideals, principles and values are not old-fashioned. Rather, they are eternal, sacred wisdom which will apply to the course of human events far, far into the future. They are the basis on which we can build a true global society. However, if they are not strongly intact, the foundation will eventually collapse, bringing down the entire edifice of America—and with it, the hopes of people everywhere for the blessings of liberty which we Americans enjoy in abundance.

In short, and as I noted in the Introduction, we must revive the American Spirit across our land so that the best of our nation's heritage is publicly recognized and reasserted as the basis of our local, state and national life and our international relations.

## The Practice of American Government

In previous chapters I have stated the fundamentals of the *theory* of American government. (Also see "A Vision for Americans" in Chapter 13.) Now let's look at the fundamentals of the *practice* of American government.

First and foremost is this fact: ***We the people of America are the source of all governmental power***. Our Founders established a federal government having three branches—the Legislative, the Executive and the Judicial—all of which derive their limited constitutional authority from us. The Preamble to the Constitution says the citizens of America—"we the people"—are the primary authority. We the people, through our delegates in convention, framed and ratified the Constitution. We delegated the power which government utilizes. We are the roots and trunk of the tree of government; the branches are secondary and subordinate to us. As Thomas Jefferson put it, "The people...are the only sure reliance for the preservation of our liberty." John Adams was even more specific: "As the happiness of the people is the sole end of the government, so the consent of the people is the only foundation of it..." *Our Constitution and Government: Federal Textbook on Citizenship*, which was published by the U.S. Government Printing Office in 1940 for use in public schools by candidates for citizenship, said it clearly: "...our Federal government does not have unlimited power but can only exercise such powers as are given to it by the people, through the Constitution" (p. 322).

Because we the people created our government, the government cannot claim any rights or powers unto itself unless we the people grant those rights and powers to it via the Constitution. When government imposes its will on the people without the people giving it the right to do so, it no longer represents the people, but becomes tyrannical in its actions.

To further underscore the supremacy of we the people, consider this statement by Gene Owens in a letter to *The New American* (13 September 2010, p. 5):

> The Supremacy Clause found in Article VI Clause 2 clearly makes the Constitution the Supreme Law of the land, not any so-called federal government, because all laws and treaties must be made pursuant to the Constitution.
>
> When our Founders instituted our Republic, they created a federal system, not a federal government. This federal system is a compound form of government consisting of a general legislature and state legislatures, and supreme power is not vested in either of them but in the Constitution.

In short, **our Founders made the state subordinate to society and politics subordinate to culture**.

To be a U.S. citizen therefore means you are an owner of this country and personally responsible for its well-being. If you are old enough to vote, you are responsible at this very moment for the operation of our government, from the local to the federal, via those representatives you elect to work as your employees and whom you are obligated to oversee. If you are not old enough to vote, you are nevertheless responsible for learning how to run the country you will "inherit" when you attain legal age, and in the meantime, you, like your elders, have civic duties to perform.

In America today, however, many owners have become derelict in performing their civic duties and supervisory responsibilities and in teaching the young about them. Their sense of civic involvement is fading; their ownership obligations are being disregarded, even abdicated. Those responsibilities and obligations are, in simplest terms, (1) to understand the principles of our government and our society, (2) to inform ourselves about the issues pertaining to them, and (3) to vote for what our conscience tells us is best for our country and best for ourselves—because they are one and the same. Then we must (4) follow up by communicating with our elected officials about legislative matters, directly and through the organizations to which we belong. If those officials are unresponsive or unrepresentative of our views, we must vote them out of office—i.e., fire them from being our employees—or, if their behavior deserves it, impeach them. The same applies to appointed officials, such as judges who adjudicate improperly, legislate from the bench or otherwise sully their position.

Our basic obligation as owners of the country is loyalty to the Constitution rather than to the government. So long as the two are one, all is well. But if the government becomes unconstitutional or proposes unconstitutional action, it is up to us, the citizen-owners of America, to prevent it or correct it. Remember the two primary aspects of the American nation—the society and the government—and the profound difference between them. Our Founders' experiment in self-governance installed the people—the society—as the ultimate authority of the nation and made the government subordinate to the people. It is the people who oversee and govern the government.

That is an awesome responsibility! If it is not upheld, if it is not performed well, the result for America will be a decline and fall into tyranny. So **American patriotism can be defined as loyalty to the Constitution.**

## Freedom or Slavery?

In *Animal Farm,* George Orwell's satire on totalitarianism, the dictator of the barnyard is Napoleon the pig—an appropriate a choice of animals for that role. Why so? The answer is simple. Government is a pig which feeds on your liberty, your property and your privacy. [1] It has an insatiable appetite for running your life, controlling your property, spending your money and invading your privacy.

***Government is the greatest enemy of freedom***. When government expands, freedom contracts. All government officials are potential tyrants. Today's benevolent government is tomorrow's tyranny because the natural course of unchecked power is totalitarianism by those who govern and slavery for those who are governed. The ultimate purpose of government, and the only justification for granting it a monopoly on legalized force, is *the protection of individual rights*. But more often than not, government itself has been the greatest violator of rights, turning the power entrusted to it against the very people it is supposed to protect.

The Founders of America understood that well. They knew that humanity's struggle for personal freedom was always primarily a struggle against government. They knew it is the nature of government to expand and to live by the creation of privileges for groups or classes, beginning with itself, while exploiting others. They knew that injustice and arbitrariness are two characteristics of government, regardless of the form of government, and that those characteristics resulted in rampant interference with the personal lives and happiness of people. [2] They knew, as John Adams put it, that the state tends to turn every contingency into an excuse for expanding itself. They knew, as James Madison put it, "Since the general civilization of mankind, I believe there are more instances of the abridgment of the freedom of people by gradual and silent encroachments of those in power than by violent and sudden usurpations." They had seen it "up close and personal" enough to drive them to fight against oppression and for independence from Great Britain. They had seen clearly that government can never be rational without a principled system firmly rooted in liberty.

John Locke, the English political philosopher whose thought laid the groundwork for our War for Independence, had written almost a century earlier in his 1690 classic, *Second Treatise on Government*:

> The natural liberty of man is to be free from any superior power on earth, and not to be under the will or legislative authority of man, but to have only the law of nature for his rule. The liberty of man in society is to be under no other legislative power, but that established by consent in the commonwealth; nor under the dominion of any will or constraint of any law, but what that legislative power shall enact according to the trust put in it....
>
> However it may be mistaken, the end of law is not to abolish or restrain, but to preserve and enlarge freedom.

After the war, George Washington said the same thing in plainest language:

Government is not reason. It is not eloquence. It is force. Like fire, it is a dangerous servant, and a fearful master.

Similarly, James Madison, in a speech in the Virginia constitutional convention in December 1829, said:

The essence of Government is power; and power, lodged as it must be in human hands, will ever be liable to abuse.

Since government is simply organized force—that is, force made legal—the less government there is, the less force and control over your liberty there is. Woodrow Wilson wrote in 1912, "The history of liberty is the history of the limitations placed upon governmental power." Thomas Jefferson said the best government is the one which governs least. He summed up the relationship between the American people and government in his 1801 inaugural address:

Still one thing more, fellow citizens, to make us a happy and prosperous people: A wise and frugal government which shall restrain men from injuring one another, which shall leave them otherwise free to regulate their own pursuits of industry and improvement and shall not take from the mouth of labor the bread it has earned... Equal and exact justice to all men... Economy in the public expense, that labor may be lightly burdened; the honest payment of our debts and the sacred preservation of public faith; encouragement of agriculture and of commerce in its handmaid; the diffusion of public information and the arraignment of all abuses at the bar of public reason; freedom of religion, freedom of the press; ...these principles form the brightest constellation which has gone before us... They should be the creed of our political faith, the text of civil instruction, the touchstone by which to try the services of those we trust.

## Governing the Government

All that is why our Founders wisely limited the powers of the federal government to those delegated and enumerated in the Constitution, and reserved all other powers to the states and to the people (as stated in the Tenth Amendment). That is also why they amended the Constitution with the Bill of Rights, which specifies the inalienable rights of each citizen, no matter what the government or a majority of the population might want to do otherwise. They wanted *freedom from* government, not *dependence on* government. (That is the simple distinction between our Founders' view of welfare and our freeloaders' view of welfare. The proper role of government, our Founders believed, is to protect, not to provide. The Preamble to the Constitution says the people wrote it to *promote* the general welfare, not provide welfare programs.) Through the Constitution and the Bill of Rights—with their safeguards such as constitutional limitations on term of office, separation of powers, local control and other legal barriers to tyranny—the revolutionaries' hard-won liberty and rights were to be preserved for them and their posterity against the self-aggrandizing tendency of those wielding power. Through the Constitution and the Bill of Rights, the federal government was to remain forever a servant of the people, not become their master.

The Constitution and the Bill of Rights are, in simplest terms, *a carefully devised system to govern the government,* not the people and not the states. They were not written to limit and restrict the citizens of America; they were written to limit and restrict the government—in its scope, its power and its reach—and thereby protect our inherent God-given liberty and rights. (Most of the first ten amendments to the Constiutution state clearly that Congress "shall *not...*".) They would, as Jefferson put it, bind down with chains those who govern to keep them from mischief. To quote Patrick Henry: "The Constitution is not an instrument for government to restrain the people; it is an instrument for the people to restrain the government—lest it come to dominate our lives and our interests." In a similar vein, James Madison noted in a 1792 letter to Edmund Pendleton: "If Congress can do whatever in their discretion can be done by money, and will promote the general welfare, the government is no longer a limited one possessing enumerated powers, but an indefinite one subject to particular exceptions."

Everything the government is allowed to do is only done with explicit permission from the people or the Constitution. The people are to remain free and self-governing, and to the extent that government is needed to protect people against aggressive and unscrupulous behavior by others, it would be primarily the local government of town and state, since there was no standing national army in the Founders' time.

Incidentally, insofar as the federal government is charged with punishing crime, the only crime defined in the Constitution is treason, yet how many other crimes have been federalized since then, thereby unconstitutionally expanding the power of the federal government over our lives! The Founders clearly saw routine law enforcement activities—devising criminal codes and apprehending, trying, convicting and punishing criminals—as a function of state and local government. Economist and syndicated columnist Walter Williams observed in a 2009 column:

> Most of what [the Founders] understood as legitimate powers of the federal government are enumerated in Article 1, Section 8. Congress is authorized there to do 21 things, and as much as three-quarters of what Congress taxes us and spends our money for today is nowhere to be found on that list.

The price of freedom is eternal vigilance against those who would steal our liberty, our property and our privacy, whether by direct force, by coercion or by stealthy means. That is the second fundamental of the practice of American government. ***Our liberty, our sovereignty, our equality, our rights, our property, our justice and our human dignity can only be preserved by an informed, alert electorate who cares***. Thomas Jefferson gave this warning:

> We have the greatest opportunity the world has ever seen, as long as we remain honest—which will be as long as we can keep the attention of our people alive. If they once become inattentive to public affairs, you and I, and Congress and Assemblies, judges and governors would all become wolves.

Vigilance to safeguard liberty is the primary obligation of all citizens of the American republic. That is loyalty to the Constitution in action. We the people are the owners of America, so we have the responsibilities which every owner of an enterprise has. We have to supervise the operation of our country and we have to elect or appoint stewards to represent us in performing the activities necessary to operate the enterprise —i.e., govern our country. The Constitution is the only thing which stands between us and total government tyranny and despotism. However, the Constitution does not defend itself. That is the responsibility of we the people. [3] That is why some vehicles carry a bumper sticker which reads "I love my country but I fear my government." What could say it more plainly?

## Signs of Public Ignorance and Apathy

I'm sorry to say that many Americans today—young people and adults alike—show little or no sense of the deepest significance of this nation and how to honor it and protect it. They seem unappreciative of our precious national heritage and the great price which so many paid for it. They seem ignorant of the spiritual foundations of our nation and the principles of American government. They seem unconcerned about our eroding liberties and the growing assaults upon the Constitution as government at all levels of society expands its power, extends its tentacles and intrudes into every aspect of our lives with ever-increasing regulation and taxation. They seem unaware of the growing threat to American sovereignty and independence as our nation is brought into a web of international agreements and global organizations managed by unelected bureaucrats who are not subject to control by American law or by the American electorate. They seem oblivious to the truth of the saying: "To be born free is a great privilege; to die free is a great responsibility." And likewise: "Any government big enough to give you everything is big enough to take away everything."

There are many other signs of ignorance in our society. Some people think rights are called entitlements and come from Congress. They think the government owes them a living. They have little knowledge of American history and civics. They don't exercise the privilege of voting or become informed about political and social issues. They don't know simple etiquette for saluting the flag when it passes by in a parade. They don't know to stand at attention, become silent, uncover their head, cross their heart and face the flag when the national anthem is played. And, sadly, some people clap after "Taps" is played at a ceremony honoring deceased soldiers, sailors, airmen, Marines and Coast Guardsmen, as if the music were entertainment rather than a tribute to fallen heroes.

That ignorance seems especially true of many young Americans, who have not known great hardship or imminent danger to their freedom. Youth is twenty percent of the population but one hundred percent of the future. If the youth of America don't have a vital understanding of what this nation is all about, in a few generations there will not be an America. It is as simple and sad as that.

It has been said that liberty does not descend to the people; the people must ascend to it. That explains why, in the face of increasing assaults upon our liberty and our rights from internal and external sources, the American Spirit must be nurtured carefully in all Americans. Without that, our hard-won independence and the cultural wisdom which made our nation the greatest on Earth will be lost due to ignorance, apathy, irresponsibility, disrespect for law and legitimate authority, and so many other social ills besetting America and fomenting disharmony and disunity. [4]

Our Founders understood that an educated, moral, self-governing people was absolutely necessary for a democratic constitutional republic dedicated to freedom. George Washington, addressing the need for an educated and moral electorate, said in his 1796 Farewell Address, "In proportion as the structure of a government gives force to public opinion, it is essential that public opinion should be enlightened." His successor, John Adams, addressed the need with these words:

> The only foundation of a free Constitution is pure virtue, and if this cannot be inspired into our people in a greater measure than they have it now, they may change their rulers and the forms of government, but they will not obtain a lasting liberty.

Without an informed and involved electorate who understand that a moral government can only come from a moral people, the American political experiment will fail. Therefore, indifference is not an option, complacence is not a choice. This is a point which needs to be stated loud and clear: We get exactly the government we deserve! If we citizens are ignorant and apathetic, if we don't take responsibility for running our country, if we don't apply conscientious judgment in selecting those who will perform the day-to-day operations of the body politic, sooner or later we will get exactly the kind of government which ignorant, lazy, irresponsible, immoral fools deserve: a totalitarian tyranny. The quotation by President James Garfield at the head of this chapter says it so well that it bears repeating:

> Now more than ever before, the people are responsible for the character of their Congress. If that body be ignorant, reckless and corrupt, it is because the people tolerate ignorance, recklessness and corruption. If it be intelligent, brave and pure, it is because the people demand these high qualities to represent them in the national legislature.... If the next centennial does not find us a great nation...it will be because those who represent the enterprise, the culture, and the morality of the nation do not aid in controlling the political forces.

## Patriotism Is Citizenship-Plus

Most Americans say they are patriotic, but are they truly so? Patriotism is love of country, but as I showed in the first chapter, it is intelligent love of our country. It is informed and knowledgeable appreciation and respect for our country's past, present and future. It is best shown by responsible citizenship.

What is responsible citizenship? It can be defined as (1) honorable conduct of your daily affairs, (2) understanding and reverence for the principles of our government, (3) participation in the political process and the life of our communities, (4) service on juries and in the armed forces, if called, (5) dignified public display of pride in our national heritage, and (6) vigilant action to preserve American freedom. (Sidebar 1, "The Bill of Responsibilities," enlarges upon the meaning of responsible citizenship.)

There is a big difference between being an American citizen and being an American patriot. America has some citizens who are anything but patriots; their actions are detrimental, even destructive, to the well-being of our nation. The most notable example are spies and traitors who wish to harm America's national security for ideological reasons or simple greed. There are other citizens, such as thieves, rapists, drug pushers, child molesters, white-collar criminals and welfare cheats, whose behavior undermines the safety and integrity of American society. Still other citizens act within the law, but without civility or a sense of public decency, and they debase American society by their vulgar, degenerate behavior. The land of the free and the home of the brave is becoming the land of the freeloaders and the home of the depraved, the land of the me and the home of the knave. Our national story is changing from simple revolution to simply revolting.

Citizenship, whether by birth or naturalization, is the most basic expression of our nation's ideals, principles and values. The requirements for American citizenship do not consider skin color, ethnic background, religious affiliation or national origin. Rather, they are concerned with a person's knowledge and behavior, and the only colors which matter are red, white and blue. To be a citizen means to possess basic understanding of America's history, political system, national culture and the English language [5]; it also means to abide by the laws of our nation and to perform the civic duties which Americans have, such as voting and serving on a jury. Failure to live within the law is grounds for suspending or revoking the benefits of citizenship—i.e., loss of life (capital punishment), liberty (via imprisonment or capital punishment) or property (such as fines and monetary judgments), loss of rights (such as no voting or gun possession by convicted felons) and, if the person is not native-born, loss of citizenship itself (deportation).

Each year, hundreds of thousands of immigrants complete the naturalization application process and take part in naturalization ceremonies across the country. These naturalization ceremonies may be conducted by a Federal court or by a local Citizenship and Immigration Services office; they may involve a handful of people at a local courthouse or several thousand at a sports arena. Regardless of a ceremony's size or venue, the applicants for naturalization share a common experience as they take an oath of allegiance, declaring their fidelity and loyalty to the United States, its Constitution and laws. They are required to renounce all fealty to their former land and to pledge their allegiance to America by saying the United States of America Oath of Allegiance. The Oath, like the Pledge of Allegiance, states the requirements for citizenship:

> I, _(name)_, hereby swear on oath that I absolutely and entirely renounce and abjure all allegiance to any foreign prince, potentate, state or sovereignty of whom or which I have heretofore been a subject or citizen; that I will support and defend the Constitution and laws of the United States of America against all enemies, foreign and domestic; that I will bear true faith and allegiance to the same; that I will bear arms on behalf of the United States when required by law; that I will perform non-combatant service in the armed forces of the United States when required by law; that I will perform work of national importance under civilian direction when required by law; and that I take this obligation freely and without any mental reservation or purpose of evasion. So help me God.

Actually, the requirements of citizenship are simple and minimal. Basically, they are: obey the law, pay your taxes, perform your civic obligations and respect the rights of others. However, the requirements of patriotism go beyond that. Patriotism carries a moral responsibility to contribute to the betterment of our communities and to serve America, on the basis of enlightened self-interest, with whatever talents and resources we have. Since we citizens own America and since we citizens are self-governing, doing it for America is ultimately doing it for ourselves on the basis of The Golden Rule. The result is mutual gain, which is a win-win situation for everyone. As Thomas Jefferson said, "That government is the strongest of which every man feels himself a part."

## Citizenship Day

Did you know there is a time of national observance related to citizenship itself?

Citizenship Day is observed annually on September 17, celebrating the day the U.S. Constitution was signed in 1787. (See Sidebar 7, "A Patriot's Calendar.") It is an important reminder of the rights and responsibilities associated with U.S. citizenship. In addition, it provides an opportunity to honor those people who have become U.S. citizens. To highlight the occasion, on that day naturalization ceremonies are held around the nation in a high-profile manner.

Citizenship Day has been celebrated in some form since 1940, when Congress designated the third Sunday in May as "I Am an American Day." In 1952, President Harry Truman signed a bill formalizing the celebration of Citizenship Day on September 17. Each year the President signs a proclamation declaring September 17 as Citizenship Day and the start of Constitution Week. The proclamation calls upon all U.S. citizens, by birth or naturalization, to reflect on the enduring importance of this great document known as the Constitution and to rededicate themselves to their country and the ideals, principles and values upon which it was founded.

Citizenship requires good behavior; patriotism requires good character. Together, they produce a good society. Without that, America will fade from history as a noble experiment which was not upheld by its people. [6]

Patriotism honors America in thought, word and deed. Patriots understand that freedom is not free, and that rights are always accompanied by responsibilities. Patriots are therefore responsible, law-abiding members of society who uphold the principles of American government and honor our national heritage. "For God and country" was once a common expression because we are one nation under God. Unless citizens have a clear understanding of the theory and practice of American government, this nation will not endure. But with the proper understanding, our way of life can transform the world because no nation has done so much for the common people as America, this wonderful land of freedom and opportunity. And it can do still more, far more! (The last chapter enlarges on that.)

## The American's Creed

The Pledge of Allegiance is a short, simple guide to the fundamentals of American citizenship. There is another guide which was once well known but has, in recent decades, fallen into obscurity. It is called The American's Creed and it deserves to be revived for public edification. Here is its story. (See Sidebar 7 for more about it.)

As America was being drawn into World War I, patriotism held sway in the hearts of citizens. The spirit of the times breathed love of country and a deepened fellowship of Americans working together in harmony. The time was therefore right to state an American creed—the country's ideals, principles and values—which were showing forth daily in the service and sacrifice of Americans on behalf of the freedom and democratic society they appreciated so well.

To capture that sense of national unity, a countrywide contest was sponsored by the press and informally approved by President Woodrow Wilson. The contest was the idea of Henry Sterling Chapin, Commissioner of Education for the state of New York. The City of Baltimore offered a prize of $1,000 for the best creed of patriotic faith submitted, and it appointed celebrated authors, governors of states, United States senators, and other national and state officials to act as committees to receive manuscripts, decide on awards, and to advise concerning matters related to the contest. For a year, 1916-1917, contestants submitted material. More than 3,000 entries were received.

Finally, of the many splendid entries, that of William Tyler Page was selected the winner. His entry entitled "The American's Creed" was adjudged to be the best brief summary of the political faith of the United States of America. This is The American's Creed:

> I believe in the United States of America as a Government of the people, by the people, for the people; whose just powers are derived from the consent of the governed; a democracy in a Republic; a sovereign Nation of many sovereign States; a perfect Union, one and inseparable; established upon those principles of freedom, equality, justice, and humanity for which American patriots sacrificed their lives and fortunes.
>
> I therefore believe it is my duty to my Country to love it; to support its Constitution; to obey its laws; to respect its flag; and to defend it against all enemies.

Page's statement used passages and phrases ranging from the Declaration of Independence and the Preamble to the Constitution, through Lincoln's Gettysburg Address and a speech by Daniel Webster, to the United States Oath of Allegiance and a then-recent War Department circular. As an expression of our national faith and purpose, The American's Creed therefore represents, like the Pledge of Allegiance, an "official" definition of patriotism. It is more expansive and specific than the Pledge. Its 100 words are worthy of study and reflection by every American.

The Speaker of the House of Representatives and the Commissioner of Education for the state of New York accepted the Creed on behalf of the people of the United States, and the proceedings relating to the award were printed in the Congressional Record of April 13, 1918. It was a time when patriotic sentiments were very much in vogue. The United States had been a participant in World War I only a little more than a year at the time the Creed was adopted.

Page, who lived in Friendship Heights, Maryland, had a career in government. He began it in 1881 at the age of 13 as a Capitol page boy. Later he became an employee of the Capitol building and served in that capacity for almost 61 years. In 1919 he was elected Clerk of the House of Representatives and held that position until 1931. Then, when the Democrats again became a majority party, they created for Page the office of Emeritus Minority Clerk of the House of Representatives. He held this position for the remainder of his life. He died on October 20, 1942.

Page was a descendant of John Page, who came to America in 1650 and settled in Williamsburg, Virginia. Another ancestor, Carter Braxton, had signed the Declaration of Independence. Still another ancestor, John Tyler, was the tenth president of the United States.

Referring to the Creed, Page said: "It is the summary of the fundamental principles of the American political faith as set forth in its greatest documents, its worthiest traditions, and its greatest leaders." (See Sidebar 3 for his statement about how he wrote the Creed.) Here is the key to The American's Creed:

I believe in the United States of America [1] as a Government of the people, by the people, for the people; [2] whose just powers are derived from the consent of the governed; [3] a democracy in a Republic; [4] a sovereign Nation of many sovereign States; [5] a perfect Union, one and inseparable; [6] established upon those principles of freedom, equality, justice, and humanity for which American patriots sacrificed their lives and fortunes. [7]

I therefore believe it is my duty to my Country to love it; [8] to support its Constitution; [9] to obey its laws; [10] to respect its flag; [11] and to defend it against all enemies. [12]

1. The closing words of the Preamble to the U.S. Constitution. 2. Lincoln's Gettysburg Address. 3. The Declaration of Independence. 4. William Tyler Page. 5. Daniel Webster 's reply to Robert Y. Hayne in the Senate in 1830. 6. The Preamble to the Constitution. 7. Adapted by Page from the closing words of the Declaration of Independence. 8. A speech by John Hancock. 9. The U.S. Oath of Allegiance. 10. George Washington's Farewell Address. 11. A War Department circular dated April 14, 1917. 12. The U.S. Oath of Allegiance. **[INSERT SIDEBAR 7 HERE]**

## Self-Reliance and Rugged Individualism: Key American Virtues

Although our Founders intended the federal government primarily to protect us from external and internal threat to our life, liberty and property, and secondarily to perform a few limited functions—such as creating a postal system, a monetary system and conducting a census—government, whether local, state or federal, was seen as playing a relatively small role in the operation of America for this basic reason: *The American nation is much more than just the American government!* It is a way of life based on personal, economic, social, religious and political freedom. Government doesn't provide that freedom; it simply protects it from encroachment by forces hostile to freedom. Aside from that, it is supposed to have a minimal role in our lives.

American society is "we the people" in the full range of our activities. American society is the daily functioning of individuals and families and communities in ways which have little or nothing to do with government—at least it was originally intended that way by our Founders. Religious worship, child-rearing, education, the transportation and sale of food and other goods, public communications such as newspapers and magazines, expression of the arts and sciences, holiday recreation—all these and more are aspects of American society which contribute to our quality of life and which are independent of government. We are not dependent upon government in those activities and we do not look to government to perform the activities for us. We simply want government to assure freedom for us—protection from force and fraud—as we pursue our activities.

America is not the American government; patriotism does not mean working for the benefit of the state. That was well understood for a long time—until the welfare state arose in the 20th century and the federal government began changing into a national government. In earlier times, people expected government to *protect* life, liberty and the pursuit of happiness. Today they expect government to *provide* life, liberty and the pursuit of happiness. A something-for-nothing mentality is enveloping America and people are increasingly trying to live at the expense of others. It is turning the traditional American Dream into a societal nightmare.

But while America was a young and growing nation, citizens did not look to the government for support. (That "support" can only be given by taking wealth away from productive wage-earners, depriving them of their private property. See Appendix 4.) Two of the primary qualities of those citizens who built our society were self-reliance and self-responsibility. Ralph Waldo Emerson extolled the former in his famous essay, "Self-Reliance." It means essentially "standing on your own two feet" without external aid rather than looking to others to do it for you. The so-called Protestant work ethic is included in the concept of self-reliance.

As for self-responsibility, everyone who was able to care for themselves regarded it as simply what was necessary and right for Americans. As President Theodore Roosevelt put it, "The first requisite of a good citizen in this Republic of ours is that he shall be able and willing to pull his weight." In a similar vein, Benjamin Franklin commented, "The Constitution only gives people the right to pursue happiness. You have to catch it yourself."

Sadly, that is not so today for many Americans. Instead, they look to government for services and income, and complain they are being oppressed or marginalized or "underserved", and their rights violated, if they don't get their way. The characteristic American virtues of self-reliance and rugged individualism are fading away. The thought of doing it for themselves, the thought of taking responsibility for their lives is apparently out of the question. The idea of standing on their own two feet without whining about being "victims" doesn't seem to enter their consciousness. Their only use of the political system is to seek more entitlements; their only use of the legal system is to sue for alleged damages. They have a slave mentality which looks to Washington, D.C. for everything, as if the federal government were "Massa" of the plantation. If they were told their lives depended on crossing the Atlantic in a small wooden ship which would take more than two months to reach the New World in the middle of winter, as the Pilgrims did, and if they were told they would then have to carve a living out of the wilderness, build their own homes and furniture, weave their own cloth, grow and hunt their own food, and provide for themselves or else die, they wouldn't have the slightest understanding or inclination to do what generations of their forebears did. [7]

Friedrich A. Hayek, author of the 1945 classic *The Road to Serfdom* which championed free market capitalism, criticized the socialist/welfare state with this penetrating observation. The real threat to individual liberty by extensive government control is subtle, he said. The most important change which it produces is "a psychological change, an alteration in the character of the people." He cited a warning from the French aristocrat-scholar Alexis de Tocqueville's 1835 *Democracy in America*:

> Democratic despotism covers the surface of society with a network of small complicated rules, minute and uniform, through which the most original minds and the most energetic character cannot penetrate... The will of man is not shattered but softened, bent and guided; men are seldom forced to act, but they are constantly restrained from acting. Such a power does not destroy, but it prevents existence; it does not tyrannize, but it compresses, enervates, extinguishes, and stupefies a people, till each nation is reduced to nothing better than a flock of timid and industrial animals, of which government is the shepherd.

As self-reliance has given way to dependence on government, as personal liberty has been traded for governmentally provided "security," a host of societal ills have arisen which are directly attributable to that loss of moral fiber. The moral fiber of individuals collectively becomes the social fabric of a nation. America's social fabric is being rent asunder; family and social bonds are weakening. Think of some signs of social decay: Increasing divorce and broken homes. Increasing out-of-wedlock births and single-parent families. Deadbeat dads. Multigenerational welfare families. Children graduating from high school barely able to read, write and perform elementary mathematics. Increasing high school dropout rate. Drug abuse, the illegal drug trade and its associated violence. School shootings. Gangsta rap and other forms of vulgar pop culture. Public profanity and the decline in civility, courtesy and public decorum. (See Sidebar 5.)

Is this what America was built for? Will the heretofore invincible American Spirit fade away due to public ignorance, apathy, immorality and incivility?

## Volunteerism, the Third Virtue

Although the virtues of self-reliance and rugged individualism have played a huge role in building America, there is a third virtue which is equally important. Self-reliance and rugged individualism alone will produce only strong but solitary people. However, we humans are much more than that. We are gregarious and sociable; we gather together to live as communities, to enjoy the company of others and to share our mutual burdens. In the American experience, that human trait has produced a society deeply conscious of the general welfare. It is the proverbial third leg of the stool which produces balance and stability for our nation.

Volunteerism is the most important tool we Americans have for making good things happen and for improving society. It's what makes America great. It's inherent in the American Spirit: free, responsible, involved citizens with a can-do attitude making democratic society work for all. (Remember that the last four letters of American spell "I can.") We "secure the blessings of liberty" for ourselves and our posterity by giving of our time, our talent and our effort to ever so many things. Without that behavioral expression of our ideals, principles and values, our country would be at least undistinguished, and possibly nonexistent. A volunteer military protects us externally. Volunteer local government and an extraordinary array of volunteer, community-based civic, social and health services—such as voting poll staffs, fire departments (originally in all communities, but now only in the smaller ones) and various charitable programs—nurture us internally. Americans are the most socially responsible people in the world.

It was thus from the beginning of our nation. America at the founding was a communitarian society, an extended community, an extended family, a society of people who understood their obligations to each other. This sense of community, this recognition of the transcendent value of the common good—the Golden Rule in action—has kept America strong and healthy. It is a moral underpinning of our society. We pull together for the general welfare, the common good. The American way is to do it ourselves on the basis of mutual benefit and to include the concerns of the poor, the disadvantaged and the hopeless in our plans, our work, our personal and corporate budgets, our personal and social agendas. Caring citizens throughout our country contribute countless hours and dollars in community service and to numerous charities. The well-off voluntarily act to reduce the burden of the less fortunate. Because of that, the poorest of the poor and the neediest of the needy in America are a hundred times better off than their counterparts in most other countries, which don't have our tradition of organized human caring and sharing to provide safety net upon safety net. Charity and volunteerism are the primary social expressions of love. That's authentic altruism.

De Tocqueville, who came to the United States in 1831 and observed our political and social institutions, declared that equality was basic to the American way of life. For nearly a year, the 25-year-old man traveled thousands of miles through 17 of the 24 states existing then, from New Orleans to Michigan. After observing our civil society based on the free consent of equals, he wrote, "This equality of condition is the fundamental fact from which all others seem to be derived, and the central point at which all my observations constantly terminated." He further noted that voluntarism—the spirit of neighbor helping neighbor—was a typical American trait. "I have often seen Americans make large and genuine sacrifices to the public good and I have noted on countless occasions that when necessary they almost never fail to lend one another a helping hand." He added:

> Americans of all ages, all conditions, and all dispositions, constantly form associations. They have not only commercial and manufacturing companies, in which all take part, but associations of a thousand other kinds—religious, moral, serious, futile, general or restricted, enormous or diminutive. Americans make associations to give entertainments, found seminaries, build inns, construct churches, distribute books, and send missionaries to the antipodes ["ends of the earth"]; they found in this manner hospitals, prisons, and schools. I have come across several types of associations in America of which, I confess, I had not previously the slightest conception, and I have often admired the extreme skill they show in proposing a common object for the exertions of very many and in inducing them voluntarily to pursue it.

De Tocqueville saw deeply into the American character and its relationship to the religio-moral basis of our self-governing nation. Equality is one of the primary attributes derived from our understanding that God is the author of our being and the moral authority for our laws and behavior. Another attribute is charity. Together with volunteerism or social engagement to improve the general welfare, we have built the most wondrous nation on earth. De Tocqueville said of us:

> I sought for the greatness and genius of America in her commodious harbors and her ample rivers, and it was not there; in her fertile fields and boundless prairies and it was not there. Not until I went to the churches of America and heard her pulpits aflame with righteousness did I understand the secret of her genius and power. America is great because she is good and if America ever ceases to be good America will cease to be great.

According to Independent Sector (which describes itself as a coalition of leading nonprofits, foundation and corporations strengthening not-for-profit initiatives, philanthropy and citizen action; Web site: independent sector.org) in 2001, 44% of the U.S. population over 21—nearly 90 million people nationwide—volunteered 15.5 billion hours of their time to numerous community service organizations and projects. The value of that donated time totaled more than $239 billion.

In addition to volunteerism, Americans donate directly to U.S. charities. Giving USA Foundation of Glenview, Illinois, finds Americans to be extraordinarily generous. Even when you factor out one-time events such as America's disaster-relief rally for Hurricane Katrina victims in 2005 and billionaire Warren Buffet's gift of $35 billion to the Bill and Melinda Gates Foundation in 2006, charitable giving made up about 2.2% of the U.S. gross domestic product, a level of giving which sustained itself from the previous year. In actual dollars, giving by Americans rose in 2007 to nearly $314 billion—a record high.

Most recently, in an astounding act of philanthropy, Warren Buffet, Bill Gates and Melinda Gates organized more than 40 American billionaires to give the majority of their wealth to charity. They publicly pledged to give away at least half of their riches during their lifetimes or after their deaths. The organizing trio said they will also approach Chinese and Indian billionaires to do the same thing.

The impact which private citizens can make on a problem through voluntary action is simply amazing to the rest of the world, but it's routine for Americans. It is the the spirit of voluntary association and voluntary effort for the common good which so impressed de Tocqueville. Just look at the following diverse list of helping programs and services available in almost every community to make them better places to live; you'll find that most are charitable grassroots organizations sustained by citizen interest and enthusiasm—i.e., private funding and volunteer staffing.

## An Endless List of Charities

There's the United Way/Combined Health Appeal, Red Cross blood banks and disaster relief, Rotary, Kiwanis, Lions, Exchange Club, Big Brothers/Big Sisters, Gray Ladies, PTA/PTO, recycled clothing centers, pregnancy counseling, Better Business Bureau, Easter Seals, orphanages, Farm Aid, AmeriCare, neighborhood crime watches, animal shelters, Foster Grandparents, food banks, Retired & Senior Volunteer Program, Volunteers in Community Service, AA and other self-help recovery groups, Literacy Volunteers, Habitat for Humanity, the Audubon Society, the Humane Society, Guardian Angels, National Runaway Hotline, legal services, community car pooling, health services and help for people with physical and mental handicaps, illness mutual-support groups for almost any disease you can name, neighborhood cleanups, Day of Caring, garden clubs to beautify our towns and cities, private job training programs, suicide hotlines, Coast Guard Auxiliary and Power Squadron, veterans groups such as American Legion, Veterans of Foreign Wars and Disabled American Veterans, sports coaching by men and women for their school and community teams, Adopt-a-Highway for litter removal, Shriners Hospitals for children, Make-A-Wish Foundation, college scholarship programs, organ donation, neighborhood block watches, hospice volunteers, local fundraisers for social problems and civic improvement—the list is almost endless.

Americans roll up our sleeves and pitch in. We get involved voluntarily for civic improvement and the general betterment of society. That's our social capital, and we're the biggest spenders around. Individually and through businesses, churches/synagogues/temples/mosques, charities, civic and social organizations, veterans groups, unions, clubs, ethnic associations, fraternal/sororal societies, neighborhood leagues, and a hundred other venues for volunteerism, we make deep personal commitment to those involvements. We take on tough problems such as hunger, homelessness, drugs, disease, disability, battered women, abused children, environmental cleanup and hazardous waste disposal. We come up with unique, innovative ways to get things done—by ourselves. Motivated by neighborly concern and community-mindedness, we demonstrate spontaneous leadership to initiate the effort—and then we demonstrate dedicated followership to carry on the effort. This community effort for social, economic and civic progress and vitality is the American way.

Americans care for each other and act on that. We serve the public interest, which is to build a more provident nation, a kinder society, a better world. That makes sound business sense, sound economic sense and sound social sense. We don't sit passively, waiting for the government to do it. We are the government—people helping people and caring for the common good. Our civic and patriotic responsibilities are performed in ways which are personally fulfilling and which keep our communities and our society strong and healthy. Whether motivated by civic duty or a big heart, we honor the foundation-ideals, principles and values of our nation by working on the basis of enlightened self-interest for community and country. We understand that the pursuit of happiness cannot be done on a solitary basis. Only in community, only in national unity of spirit—the American Spirit—is true and enduring happiness to be found.

## America Helps the World Community

Americans also help to strengthen the world community. Our nation is, in fact, the most generous on Earth. When there's a misfortune or disaster, we're the first to send public and private aid. When there's a tragedy in our midst nationally or among our neighbors internationally, it always is followed by spontaneous outpouring of contributions—money, goods and services—to help the unfortunate parties. The trillions of dollars which we've given away since World War Two are unmatched by any other nation and, so far as I'm aware, none comes anywhere near that figure. The former Soviet Union would probably be second, although 95% percent of its amount would be military aid to its Communist satellites. Yes, America's total also includes a huge amount of military aid, but even when that is factored out, the donation of food, emergency assistance, technical expertise, Peace Corps workers and other humanitarian and reconstruction aid is still far greater than any other nation's. Moreover, all that is simply the governmental sector's contribution. The private sector has also contributed greatly — again, far more than any other nation. Just think of the food, tents, blankets, medical supplies and personnel, and other emergency items and building materials from American charities which are sent all over the world whenever there is a famine, earthquake, flood, hurricane or epidemic.

Moreover, none of that government and private aid includes the hundreds of billions of U.S. dollars in direct financial aid to nations made through the World Bank, International Monetary Fund, Export-Import Bank and various federal giveaway programs. Although the aid is described as a loan to be repaid, much of it is uncollectable and is foreseen to be so. It never would have been loaned in the first place if the transaction were a normal, nongovernmental business loan because the debtor couldn't possibly repay it. But when countries default on such loans, the debts are restructured for easier repayment and even simply forgiven without repayment at all. One can debate the wisdom and constitutionality of such financial actions, but credit for producing the wealth itself must be given to the hardworking, taxpaying citizens of this nation which has done so much for the poor and the needy of Earth.

The magnitude of that charity is awesome to contemplate, and it would not be possible except for the basic goodness — including the Work Ethic — of the American people. Our character is ingrained with nobility of spirit which reflects the spiritual foundations of America. Our caring for others, our charitable deeds at home and abroad exhibit a deep recognition of the benevolence of our Creator and a wish to share it with others because, paradoxically, a good thing gets better as you share it. Divine Providence has blessed America with enormous good fortune, spiritually and materially, and, on the basis of freely embraced civic and patriotic duty, we have shared that in a loving way. As President Franklin Delano Roosevelt said, "The creed of our democracy is that liberty is acquired and kept by men and women who are strong and self-reliant, and possessed of such wisdom as God gives mankind — men and women who are just, and understanding, and generous to others — men and women who are capable of disciplining themselves. For they are the rulers and must rule themselves."

*America! America!*
*God mend thine every flaw,*
*Confirm thy soul in self-control,*
*Thy liberty in law!*

What is the meaning of American citizenship? It is this: recognizing the blessings of liberty and our opportunity to share in them by embracing our freedom and the responsibility which goes hand in hand with it in the personal, economic, political and civic dimensions of society, and then living our lives in accordance with the independence, sovereignty and moral equality which have been lovingly granted to us by God, the Spirit of Liberty. Nothing less than that will preserve those blessings for ourselves and our posterity. Are you doing your part?

———————

# FOOTNOTES

[1] Other synonyms for the self-serving, oppressive nature of government which begin with the letter *p* are: panderer, parasite, prevaricator, pickpocket, plunderer, poll-watcher, predator and prostitute. These unflattering terms collectively explain why our Founders placed strict limits on the federal government's authority and further restrained it through strong checks and balances, while emphasizing local control of governmental action. They also explain why opinion polls consistently rank lawyers and legislators appallingly low in the public's respect for them. *The American Heritage Dictionary of the English Language* lists two definitions of politician. First is "one who is actively involved in politics, skilled in government"; second is "a schemer who tries to gain advantage in sly or underhanded ways." Similarly, *Roget's Thesaurus* lists these synonyms for politician: office seeker, demagogue and sycophant. A crude joke exemplifies the public's perception: "Politicians are like baby diapers. They ought to be changed often and for the same reason." Similarly, politics has been humorously defined as a combination of two words: *poli*, which means "many" and *tics*, which are "bloodsucking parasites." I hope this book helps to change the situation so that the only p-word which accurately and appropriately describes politicians is: patriot.

[2] Government has another feature which is equally bad: inefficiency. Government never works as efficiently and productively as private organizations performing the same tasks. Why should it? It has no incentive to do so since government employees essentially live off the wealth produced by others (known as taxpayers). In the marketplace of free enterprise, a company can achieve savings and improve productivity by doing something on a larger scale—generating electricity, for instance, or manufacturing cars. These savings and improvements are called efficiencies of scale, and generally lead to lower prices and greater shareholder earnings.

Government works just the opposite way. The larger government gets, the more costly and less efficient it becomes. Bigger government results in *inefficiencies* of scale. A joke puts it plainly: If pro is the opposite of con, what is the opposite of progress? Congress.

The following anonymous piece of internet humor captures the absurdity of why government should not be relied upon to do anything beyond the minimum and strictly limited functions which—in the case of America—we the people authorize it to do for us because, in the wisdom of our Founders, that was seen as the best means to accomplish such functions.

## NEW ELEMENT DISCOVERED

A major research institution recently announced the discovery of the heaviest chemical element known to science. The new element has been named governmentium.

Governmentium has 1 neutron, 12 assistant neutrons, 75 deputy neutrons, and 224 assistant deputy neutrons, giving it an atomic mass of 312. These 312 particles are held together by forces called morons, which are surrounded by vast quantities of lepton-like particles called peons.

Since governmentium has no electrons, it is inert. However, it can be detected because it impedes every reaction with which it comes in contact.

A minute amount of governmentium causes one reaction to take more than four days to complete when it would normally take less than a second.

Governmentium has a normal half-life of three years. It does not decay, but instead undergoes a reorganization in which a portion of the assistant neutrons and deputy neutrons exchange places. In fact, governmentium's mass will actually increase over time, since each reorganization will cause some morons to become neutrons, forming isodopes.

This characteristic of moron-promotion leads some scientists to speculate that governmentium is formed whenever morons reach a certain quantity in concentration. This hypothetical quantity is referred to as critical morass.

When catalyzed with money, governmentium becomes administratium, an element which radiates just as much energy as governmentium since it has half as many peons but twice as many morons.

3 We the people are assisted in overseeing the conduct of our federal government by the Office of Government Ethics, which was authorized June 27, 1980 by Congress and signed into law by the President on July 3, 1980. It requires government agencies to have a designated ethics official and it requires posting of the Code of Ethics for Government Service. The code declares (I quote verbatim):

**ANY PERSON IN GOVERNMENT SERVICE SHOULD**

I. Put loyalty to the highest moral principles and to country above loyalty to persons, party, or Government department.

II. Uphold the Constitution, laws, and regulations of the United States and of all governments therein and never be a party to their evasion.

III. Give a full day's labor for a full day's pay; giving earnest effort and best thought to the performance of duties.

IV. Seek to find and employ more efficient and economical ways of getting tasks accomplished.

V. Never discriminate unfairly by the dispensing of special favors or privileges to anyone, whether for remuneration or not; and never accept, for himself or herself or for family members, favors or benefits under circumstances which might be construed by reasonable persons as influencing the performance of governmental duties.

VI. Make no private promises of any kind binding upon the duties of office, since a Government employee has no private word which can be binding on public duty.

VII. Engage in no business with the Government, either directly or indirectly, which is inconsistent with conscientious performance of governmental duties.

VIII. Never use any information gained confidentially in the performance of governmental duties as a means of making private profit.

IX. Expose corruption wherever discovered.

X. Uphold these principles, ever conscious that public office is a public trust.

4 This op-ed which I published in a local paper addresses yet another aspect of the health of America:

## GOVERNMENT FAT IS A NATIONAL EPIDEMIC

There is a hue and cry about fat citizens constituting a national health epidemic. However, there is an even worse national health problem: government fat. Porked-up Americans do that to themselves by choice. However wrong their choices may be, it is their right to be fat. It doesn't hurt me if someone else is fat, so long as I don't have to pay for his or her medications and weight-reduction regimen. However, government pork is not chosen by taxpayers; it is forced on us by legislators and bureaucrats.

What is government pork? It is any expense to taxpayers not constitutionally justified by the federal constitution or state constitutions. Government is a pig which feeds on your liberty, your property and your privacy, growing ever fatter. The federal government especially has assumed powers and functions which are unconstitutional, so the cost of all that is nothing but pure pork-barrel.

Our government is so bloated and fat that the political, economic and social health of the nation is at risk. It is time for America to put the body politic on a diet and fitness program.

This national crisis is aggravated by lazy Americans who do not "work out" by performing their obligation as owners of this country to oversee government. The owner's manual for America prescribes some important citizen workout routines:

1. Study the candidates and issues. (This will get us intellectually fit.)

2. Exercise your right to vote and then vote in accordance with constitution and conscience.

3. Rein in spending and bureaucracy until they are scaled back to constitutional limits.

4. Strengthen yourself by resisting all power grabs. (This is true resistance training—resistance to tyranny.)

5. Feed yourself on information about individual liberty and threats to it. (This adds nutritional supplements to your diet for greater intellectual fitness—supplements such as individual liberty, free market economy, property rights and freedom of conscience.)

Through this program, and with dedicated practice in working out, we can lose the fat, cut the pork, restore health to the body politic, and feel good again about ourselves as Americans. Equally important, it will improve the way the rest of the world sees us.


5 In 2002, Congress passed the Homeland Security Act which authorized the Department of Homeland Security. The Act eliminated the old Immigration and

Naturalization Service, merging its functions into the new department and phasing out INS. In 2003, DHS Secretary Tom Ridge created two new Bureaus within the Border and Transportation Security Directorate to receive the INS's traditional functions. Immigration enforcement functions were placed within the Bureau of Customs and Border Protection; immigrant service functions were placed within the Bureau of Citizenship and Immigration Services. CIS is charged with fundamentally transforming and improving the delivery of immigration and citizenship services, while enhancing the integrity of our nation's security.

Within CIS is a new office, the Office of Citizenship (OC). The mission of the Office of Citizenship is to promote instruction and training on citizenship responsibilities for immigrants interested in becoming citizens, including the development of educational materials. According to a statement on the OC web site, it will "reach out to legal immigrants from the time they reach our borders to support their integration into American civil culture and to encourage their efforts to become American citizens." In carrying out this mission, the Office promotes initiatives and activities to:

• Revive and emphasize the common civic identity and shared values that are essential to citizenship.

• Raise awareness about the benefits and responsibilities associated with U.S. citizenship.

• Enhance educational opportunities in English, Civics and History for legal immigrants of all ages to assist their integration.

The Office of Citizenship has two components, program development and outreach, and includes both headquarters and field locations.

Program Development focuses on developing mission-related initiatives, which are executed in collaboration with internal and external partners. It will:

• Partner with other agencies and entities to design educational materials and programs focusing on History, Civics, and English.

• Develop resources and enhance overall educational opportunities to support legal immigrants' integration into American civic culture.

• Identify opportunities to enhance the meaning and stature of CIS citizenship-related ceremonies and events.

• Provide input regarding CIS citizenship and naturalization policies.

Outreach focuses on creating mechanisms to support mission-related program delivery and community outreach in a variety of ways. It will:

• Promote national and local dialogue about a common civic identity by coordinating forums, community meetings, and other special events.

• Partner with information delivery sources reaching immigrant communities to promote programs and initiatives related to citizenship and immigration services.

• Engage a strong network of key stakeholders, including federal, state, and local agencies as well as community-based and civic education organizations in promoting programs and initiatives related to citizenship and immigration services, soliciting feedback from immigrant communities, and identifying appropriate delivery channels.

For more information, go to the OC web site: www.immigration.gov/graphics/citizenship/index.htm.

6 The growing trend toward dual citizenship is, in my opinion, a dangerous one for America. Although it was once banned, a series of U.S. Supreme Court decisions in the latter half of the 20th century has upheld the concept. Americans can legally acquire a second citizenship in nations which offer it, and nearly 100 nations do so.

There are various reasons behind the trend. Some Americans want to carry more than one passport to honor their ancestry and show pride in their family's homeland. Others want dual nationality in order to reduce the problems and delay of going through Customs. Still others want the financial advantages offered by nations with lower taxes and stronger financial privacy laws. And lately, some Americans want the safety of a non-American passport to show if confronted by terrorists.

All these motives are legitimate and understandable. Nevertheless, the trend is one which may grow into a problem for America. Why? The answer is simple. As two Bible verses put it: "A man cannot serve two masters." "A house divided against itself cannot stand." These biblical maxims speak to the question of loyalty and fidelity to the United States. If an American has dual citizenship, will that weaken his or her support for the fundamentals of our nation in favor of another nation's? And if so, will that lead to further disunity here?

The subject of dual citizenship deserves reconsideration by Congress.

7 An anonymous wit parodied the Twenty-Third Psalm to express this very point:

The Government is my shepherd, I shall not work.
It encourageth me to lie down on a good job;
It leadeth me beside the still factories.
It destroyeth my initiative and confiscateth my earnings.
It leadeth me in the path of a parasite for politics' sake.
Yea, though I walk through the valley of deficit spending,
I will fear no evil, for the Government is with me;
Its entitlements and welfare checks they comfort me.
It promiseth an economic Utopia, and appropriateth the earnings of my grandchildren.
It filleth my head with the false security of a dream world
Until my inefficiency runneth over.
Surely the Government will care for me, all the days of my life,
And I shall dwell in a fool's paradise forever.

## Sidebar 7

# THE BACKGROUND OF THE AMERICAN'S CREED

*The following statement, in William Tyler Page's own words, tells how he came to write The American's Creed.*

I first learned of a National Creed contest in May, 1917. It then had been in progress for some time. I was simply told about it by one of the contestants but did not see the rules of the contest until later. This contestant showed me a copy of his own manuscript and said, "Why don't you write one?" I thought he meant he wanted me to write one for him because he said the rules permitted a contestant to send in more than one manuscript. I thought nothing more about it until the next day, Sunday, a beautiful May day, while walking home from church. At church I had just recited the Apostles' Creed. The thought came to me as I walked along that a secular creed should be fashioned in form on the lines of the Christian Creed, and should be subordinate to it in length.

Knowing the Apostles' Creed to have been a compilation expressing the Apostles' doctrine and principles, which they practiced long before the Creed was formulated, and that the source of its articles were the books of the New Testament, I resolved at once to write a civic creed of like form but of course of different substance. But where was I to find a secular bible, so to speak? Then the thought came to me: My sources of information must come from recognized, authoritative, historical documents. I did not want to use my own words. No creed worthy the name could be written in the words of any one man which could express the belief or the faith of many others. A creed, it seemed to me, should contain those things to which its subscribers had believed all along, but which never had been brought together concretely. It must be a composite and so readily recognized as to be accepted without much, if any, controversy.

It has been my custom for a long time, in fact ever since the Fourth of July, 1898, just following our glorious victories in the Spanish-American War, to spend Independence Day in my library reading our American fundamental documents—the Declaration of Independence, the Articles of Confederation, the Constitution of the United States, the Mayflower Compact, speeches of great Americans, such as Webster's and Hayne's; such as Lincoln's and Douglas's, and Lincoln's Gettysburg address. Thus I was fairly familiar with those great fountains of patriotic literature which I called my American Bible. I thought over these things on my way home that day and upon reaching home went right to work to formulate a civic creed out of my head off-hand.

First, I reexamined the Apostles' Creed and found it to contain one hundred and nine words. The National Creed must be shorter, I argued to myself, but my first effort at brevity was a failure, for, to my dismay, the initial draft contained one hundred and thirty-seven words, much too many. To make sure of my phraseology I resorted to the documents comprising my American Bible, and my second attempt that day brought me within striking distance of my own limitation. But still I did not get below one hundred and nine words.

I really did not intend to pursue the matter any further, having found considerable pleasure in this brief experience. But the next day I took what I had formulated to my friend who had acquainted me with the contest and actually offered to give him the manuscript. He read it cursorily and handed it back to me with faint praise. It was easy to see that he did not appraise it very highly and that he did not want it. Then day by day I whittled away, reshaping the language, here a little, there a little, line upon line, precept upon precept, twisting it about, improving the rhythm, aiming all the while at brevity, until the following August, when the product was as nearly satisfactory as I could hope to make it. Meanwhile, I had learned the rules of the contest and was satisfied that my plan was what the originators of the contest desired.

To the Creed I added a key showing the sources of the various sentences. This, I thought, would stimulate research and the reading of our fundamental literature. My manuscript, sealed according to directions, was sent to the Committee on Manuscripts the latter part of August, 1917. The last date for their reception was the anniversary of the writing of The Star-Spangled Banner, September 14.

As time passed and I heard nothing further about the matter it became almost a memory, and nothing more, until one day in March, 1918, I received notice from the Committee on Award that I was the successful competitor. The award of one thousand dollars offered by the City of Baltimore was presented to me by the Mayor of that city, Honorable James D. Preston, on April 3, 1918. The award proceedings were held in the House of Representatives Office Building, Washington, D.C., and the Creed was accepted on the part of the United States by the Commissioner of Education and by the Speaker of the House of Representatives, Honorable Champ Clark, who happened at that time to be the highest ranking officer of the government in the City of Washington. Honorable Joseph G. Cannon, the former Speaker of the House, also participated in the proceedings. A few days later the Chairman of the Committee on Education of the House of Representatives, Honorable William J. Sears, of Florida, caused the award proceedings to be printed in the Congressional Record of April 13, 1918. On April 6, three days after the award, I bought the first of the Liberty Bonds in the Third Liberty drive on the front steps of the Capitol Building.

## Sidebar 8

## THE U.S. CITIZENSHIP TEST

Do you have adequate basic knowledge of what it takes to be an American citizen? The U.S. Citizenship and Immigration Services (formerly the Immigration and Naturalization Service) offers a test entitled Civics (History and Government) Questions for the Naturalization Test. It is available on the internet and in books to prepare immigrants for citizenship. It consists of 100 questions; the answers follow each question. On the Internet, go to the U.S. Citizenship and Immigration Services web site at https://www.uscis.gov/sites/default/files/USCIS/Office%20of%20Citizenship/ Citizenship%20Resource%20Center%20Site/Publications/100q.pdf.

However, I think there is serious flaw in the test, apparent in the very first line, which reads "Principles of American Democracy." Chapter 3 of this book discusses why that is an ignorant and misleading statement, but to be brief in my critique: America is a republic, not a democracy.

Here is my own quiz on fundamentals of American history, government and patriotic customs.

## TEST YOUR KNOWLEDGE OF AMERICA

1. <u>True or false</u>: America was the first nation in history to be founded on spiritual principles.

2. Where are the basic principles of American government stated?

3. Who wrote the statement?

4. Who authorized it?

5. When did it become official?

6. What national holiday celebrates that event?

7. In the American theory of government, what is the source of our liberty, our sovereignty, our equality, our rights, our justice and our human dignity?

8. Where is that stated?

9. <u>True or false</u>: America was the first nation in history to have a written constitution.

10. What is the supreme law of the land in America?

11. Who wrote the Constitution?

12. When was it written?

13. What form of government does America have?

14. Who owns America?

15. Where is that stated?

16. Who are the owners' employees?

17. In the American theory of government, what is the primary purpose of government?

18. What are the first ten amendments to the Constitution called?

19. When were those amendments made?

20. Which right in the Bill of Rights is "the first among equals" on which all the others depend?

21. Why is it regarded that way?

22. <u>True or false</u>: The phrase "a wall of separation between church and state" is in the Constitution.

23. <u>True or false</u>: The purpose of the "wall of separation" is to keep religion and morality out of government.

24. <u>True or false</u>: The U.S. Congress is authorized to make any law it wants.

25. <u>True or false</u>: The function of the Supreme Court of the United States is to interpret the Constitution.

26. Who may abridge or eliminate our rights?

27. What is the only crime defined in the U.S. Constitution?

28. Who wrote America's national anthem?

29. When was it written?

30. What should you do when the national anthem is played?

31. When was the American flag created?

32. What day celebrates that event?

32. What do the colors of the American flag stand for?

33. When viewing a parade, what should you do when the American flag passes by in a color guard?

34. Who wrote the Pledge of Allegiance?

35. When was it written?

36. Why was it written?

37. <u>True or false</u>: In America, our personal, political, economic and social freedom are inextricably linked.

38. All the powers and responsibilities given to the President can be covered in three titles which name his primary capacities. What are they?

39. What are the five civil rights stated in the First Amendment of the Constitution?

40. Where do all bills to raise revenue for the federal government have to start for that bill to become a law?

41. What was the initial purpose of the gathering in Philadelphia which we call the Constitutional Convention?

42. When and where is the complete U.S. Constitution displayed?

43. Where in the Constitution are local governments mentioned?

44. Where in the Constitution is democracy mentioned?

45. What battle in the War for Independence brought victory for the American cause?

46. How often must Congress meet?

47. What is the maximum number of states Congress may admit to the Union?

48. <u>True or false</u>. Congress may pass a law to punish people for a crime already committed.

49. What happens if a Senate vote is tied?

50. <u>True or false</u>. The Constitution guarantees that every state has a republican form of government.

# ANSWERS

1. True.

2. In the Declaration of Independence.

3. Thomas Jefferson drafted the Declaration of Independence for a committee of five people appointed by the Second Continental Congress. The committee members were Thomas Jefferson of Virginia, John Adams of Massachusetts, Benjamin Franklin of Pennsylvania, Roger Sherman of Connecticut and Robert R. Livingston of New York. Franklin and Adams made a few changes to the draft. Then the committee submitted it to the Congress, where it was debated and, after many amendments, ratified.

4. The people of the 13 colonies through their representatives to the Second Continental Congress.

5. July 4, 1776.

6. Independence Day, the birthday of America, which is observed annually on the Fourth of July.

7. God, our Creator and author of the laws of nature.

8. In the opening lines of the Declaration of Independence. ("We hold these truths to be self-evident, that all men are created equal, that they are endowed by their Creator with certain unalienable rights, that among these are life, liberty, and the pursuit of happiness.") There are four distinct references to God in the Declaration. They are "nature's God," "Creator," "Supreme Judge of the world" and "Divine Providence."

9. True. Our constitution is the oldest, most enduring national constitution in the world.

10. The Constitution.

11. The 13 united colonies-become-states of America, through their delegates to the Constitutional Convention assembled in Philadelphia. James Madison was the principal author of the document. He was knowledgeable about the history of republics and had the "Virginia plan" of his home state as a model for constitutional government. He participated in the debates more than any other delegate and also persuasively discussed issues outside the convention. Last of all, after the Constitution was written, he was effective via his role in the authorship of The Federalist Papers in gaining ratification of it by the states. Madison is therefore known as the "Father of the Constitution."

12. May to September 1787.

13. A constitutional federal republic.

14. We the people of the United States.

15. In the Preamble to the Constitution. The Constitution is the supreme law of the land. ("We the people of the United States, in order to form a more perfect union, establish justice, insure domestic tranquility, provide for the common defense,

promote the general welfare, and secure the blessings of liberty to ourselves and our posterity, do ordain and establish this Constitution for the United States of America.")

16. All government officials, whether elected or appointed.

17. To protect individual freedom and rights, and thereby "secure the blessings of liberty to ourselves and our posterity."

18. The Bill of Rights.

19. The Bill of Rights was ratified in 1791.

20. The Second Amendment.

21. Government and the military cannot subjugate an armed citizenry willing to fight to protect their lives, their liberty, their property and their rights. ("A well regulated militia, being necessary to the security of a free state, the right of the people to keep and bear arms, shall not be infringed.")

22. False. The phrase comes from a letter written by Thomas Jefferson in 1802 when he was President. Replying to a question by the Baptist Association in Danbury, Connecticut, he said that the First Amendment built "a wall of separation between church and State" because it is the "expression of the supreme will of the nation in behalf of the rights of conscience." The wall keeps the government from controlling religion and also from "prohibiting the free expression thereof."

23. False: The purpose of the wall is to keep the state out of the affairs of churches and religious matters. However, religion and morality were regarded as necessary elements of a school curriculum in order to develop electors and government officials who would uphold the spiritual principles of American society. That is why, for example, Congress has a chaplain and courts have the Ten Commandments on their walls.

24. False. The powers of Congress are strictly enumerated and narrowly defined in the Constitution. Many aspects of American society are off limits to Congress and are left to the states or to the individual citizens. For example, there is no delegation of power to create a federal Department of Education, Department of Housing and Urban Development, or organizations such as the National Foundation for the Arts and the National Foundation for the Humanities.

25. False. Its purpose is to defend the Constitution—that is, to be final authority in all cases arising under the Constitution to assure strict conformity with the original intent of the Constitution, and to invalidate those which do not conform. It is unconstitutional for the Supreme Court to create new laws by judicial fiat (i.e., legislating from the bench) or to find new powers in the Constitution to expand the federal government (i.e., interpreting the "general welfare" clause of the Preamble to justify unspecified federal functions such as the Department of Health, Education and Welfare). Supreme Court justices are not supposed to amend the Constitution, read public opinion polls into it, or make it conform to "international law."

26. No one except "we the people" through amendment to the Constitution.

27. Treason, which is bearing arms against America or giving aid and comfort to an enemy of America.

28. Francis Scott Key, a young attorney from Washington, D.C.

29. On September 14, 1814, during and after the bombardment of Fort McHenry in Baltimore Harbor by the British in the War of 1812.

30. Stop talking, stand at attention, face the flag and place your right hand over your heart until the music has stopped. If you are a man wearing a headdress, remove it with your right hand and place it against your left shoulder so that your right hand is over your heart. Hold this position until the last note. People in military uniform should salute at the first note of the anthem and retain this position until the last note. When the national anthem is played and the flag is not displayed, all present should stand, face toward the music and act in the same manner they would if the flag were displayed there.

31. On June 14, 1777, by an act of Congress.

32. Flag Day, the birthday of the American flag, which is observed annually on June 14.

32. The meaning of our flag's colors was first stated in the description of the Great Seal of the United States, made in 1782 by the congressional committee charged with designing the seal. Their report says the seal's escutcheon has the same colors and meaning as those of the flag. Red stands for hardiness and courage, white stands for purity and innocence, and blue stands for vigilance, perseverance and justice. Today it is more broadly said that red stands for the courage, heroism and sacrifices of the 44,000,000 men and women who have served in the armed forces of our country; white stands for hope and the purity of our high ideals; and blue, the color of the heavens, connotes the justice, strength, loyalty and unity of all our states.

33. Stand up, stop talking, face the flag and place your right hand over your heart when the flag passes by. If you are a man wearing a hat, remove it with your right hand and place it against your left shoulder so that your right hand is over your heart.

34. Francis J. Bellamy, an employee of the magazine *The Youth's Companion*.

35. In August of 1892. It was published in the September 8 edition of *The Youth's Companion*.

36. To have school children honor the flag of our nation on the 400th anniversary of Columbus' discovery of America and in morning exercises thereafter.

37. True.

38. Chief Executive, Chief of State, Commander in Chief.

39. Freedom of religion, freedom of speech, freedom of the press, freedom of assembly and the right to petition the government for a redress of grievances.

40. The House of Representatives.

41. The purpose was to amend the Articles of Confederation.

42. It is displayed in the National Archives in Washington, D.C., but only one page at a time throughout the year except on September 17, Constitution Day, when all four pages are displayed.

43. They are not mentioned at all.

44, It is not mentioned at all.

45. The Battle of Yorktown, Virginia in 1781. The Continental Army, commanded by George Washington and assisted by French troops under General Rochambeau, defeated General Cornwallis, who surrendered. That essentially ended the war, although hostilities continued until the Treaty of Paris was signed in 1783.

46. At least once a year.

47. Congress may admit as many new states as desired.

48. False.

49. The President of the Senate (the Vice President) casts a vote.
50. True.

## Chapter 8

# HOW TO RECITE THE PLEDGE OF ALLEGIANCE

I pledge allegiance to the Flag
of the United States of America
and to the Republic
for which it stands,
One Nation under God,
indivisible,
With liberty and justice for all.

The federal law governing the Pledge of Allegiance is United States Code, Title 36, Chapter 10, Patriotic Customs, Section 172, titled "Pledge of allegiance to the flag; manner of delivery." It states:

The Pledge of Allegiance to the Flag, "I pledge allegiance to the Flag of the United States of America, and to the Republic for which it stands, one Nation under God, indivisible, with liberty and justice for all.", should be rendered by standing at attention facing the flag with the right hand over the heart. When not in uniform men should remove their headdress with their right hand and hold it at the left shoulder, the hand being over the heart. Persons in uniform should remain silent, face the flag, and render the military salute.

Some amplification of that official but brief description can be helpful, so here are the details.

When the Pledge of Allegiance is recited, you should stand erect at attention and face the flag. This applies to all Americans, whether you are a civilian or in the military. Civilians speak the Pledge aloud; military personnel in uniform remain silent throughout the Pledge.

If you are a civilian, place your right hand over your heart in the ancient sign of fidelity. Hold it there until the conclusion of the Pledge. If you are wearing gloves, remove the one on your right hand. If you are a male wearing a hat or other headdress, remove it with your right hand. This applies to both men and boys. If you are holding a hat, it should then be at your left shoulder, with the palm of your hand over your heart. That is the civilian way of saluting the flag. In any case, uncover your head when reciting the Pledge; to remain covered is disrespectful, even if not intended so by the person.

Members of the armed forces in uniform should face the flag and render the military salute. Veterans may render the military salute even if they are in civilian clothing. [1] Hold the salute throughout the Pledge. After the words "justice for all," lower your arm to your side.

Others in uniform, such as Boy Scouts, Girl Scouts, police and fire department members, should render respect to the flag in accordance with the traditions of their organization.

Notice there is no comma in "one Nation under God." Therefore, in order to properly convey the meaning, it should be spoken without pause or hesitation as one continuous phrase.

This protocol also applies to the playing or singing of the National Anthem. As with the Pledge, the person should face the flag if one is present. Otherwise, the salute should be toward the source of the music. Military salutes and civilian hand-over-heart salutes should begin at the first note of the anthem and be held until the final note.

No one should engage in talking, walking around or other movement during either the recitation of the Pledge of Allegiance or the playing of the National Anthem.

## Advice for Dissenters

Thanks to the First Amendment, no one is, or can be, required to say the Pledge. As the Supreme Court has stated, the public expression of patriotism cannot be coerced. So if you choose not to recite the Pledge for religious, political or personal reasons, you should nevertheless stand up and remain at attention until the Pledge is completed. That is simply being courteous. Citizens of other nations display this courtesy to the Pledge of Allegiance and the Star-Spangled Banner, notably when foreign sports teams competing in the U.S. are seen on television. During the Pledge of Allegiance or the playing of the National Anthem, they stand politely at attention, stop talking, and although they do not cover their heart with their hand, they face in the direction of the flag, if one is present, or in the direction of the music if our National Anthem is played. I urge dissenters to the Pledge of Allegiance to likewise show common courtesy and respect for those who pledge their allegiance. Reciting the Pledge takes about 15 seconds. That is not too long a time for basic manners.

These instructions are simple and easy for all Americans to follow, but they serve a profound purpose. They describe how to display the courtesy and respect due to our national flag and what it stands for. They also offer a means of publicly expressing the gratitude which patriotic Americans feel for the blessings of liberty so abundantly ours.

---

## FOOTNOTES

[1] In January 2008 President George W. Bush signed into law a bill which contains the following text which allows military veterans not in uniform to nevertheless render the military salute:

SEC. 594. CONDUCT BY MEMBERS OF THE ARMED FORCES AND VETERANS OUT OF UNIFORM DURING HOISTING, LOWERING, OR PASSING OF UNITED STATES FLAG.

Section 9 of title 4, United States Code, is amended by striking "all persons present" and all that follows through the end of the section and inserting the following: "all persons present in uniform should render the military salute. Members of the Armed Forces and veterans who are present but not in uniform may render the military salute. All other persons present should face the flag and stand at attention with their right hand over the heart, or if applicable, remove their headdress with their right hand and hold it at the left shoulder, the hand being over the heart. Citizens of other countries present should stand at attention. All such conduct toward the flag in a moving column should be rendered at the moment the flag passes."

## Chapter 9

# EXPLAINING THE PLEDGE OF ALLEGIANCE
# TO YOUNG CHILDREN

The Fourth of July was approaching so the nursery school teacher took the opportunity to tell her class about patriotism and the Pledge of Allegiance. "We live in a great country," she said. "One of the things we should be happy about is that in this country, we are all free."

A little boy walked up to her with a slight scowl on his face. He stood with his hands on his hips and said, "I'm not free. I'm four."

A little girl said to her teacher, "I know what a vegetable stand is, but what's a widget stand?"

The teacher looked puzzled. She replied, "I don't know, honey. Where did you hear that? Can you use it in a sentence?"

"Sure," said the girl. "We say it in the Pledge of Allegiance: and to the republic for widget stands."


When my first grandchild, Brandon, was two, I taught him the Pledge of Allegiance. During a visit to Grandma and Grandpa one summer, I'd take him to the front porch each morning and "raise the Colors." I'd let him carry the flag outside and help unfurl it from its staff. Next I'd insert the flag staff in its bracket on the porch column. Then we'd stand at attention and say the Pledge. I'd place Brandon's hand over his heart in that tiny little chest and we'd recite the words. I'd begin by saying a phrase, then I'd pause for him to say it while I repeated it with him. When he had spoken the words in his two-year-old's speech, we'd proceed to the next phrase. In that way, we saluted the flag each morning. By the end of the visit a week later, he'd made a good start toward memorizing the Pledge of Allegiance.

Did he understand the Pledge at that age? No. Did he comprehend concepts such as allegiance, republic, indivisible and liberty? No. Was the meaning of the event clear to him? Of course not. Like the children in the jokes above, his grasp of the words was extremely limited. But did he enjoy saying the Pledge with his grandfather? Yes. Did he like raising the Colors each morning? Yes.

As I mentioned earlier, patriotism is not inborn—it is learned. Just as little children begin to understand their parents' religious practice by going to Sunday School or its equivalent, and later to catechism class or its equivalent, so, too, the sentiment of patriotism is instilled in children one step at a time.

Brandon was just beginning to learn patriotism, and I wanted to make it fun for him. The concepts in the Pledge were beyond his intellectual capacity then, but rote learning of words was not. He is now in his 20s and has known the Pledge of Allegiance by heart since he was three.. When he was three, four and five, he said it several times a week at the beginning of his nursery school and kindergarten sessions. When he was in elementary school, he recited it daily. His understanding deepened over time through his ongoing experience of school, reading, watching television and movies, through the examples he saw among adults and through the instruction he received from leaders in groups he was involved with, from uncovering his head and crossing his heart for the National Anthem before a soccer or baseball game to the morning exercise of saluting the flag at YMCA and Boy Scout camps. I'm pleased and proud to say he served in the special Boy Scout Honor Guard for his district, carrying the flag in precision drill style. The only time he wasn't part of the Honor Guard was when the Colors were presented at his own Eagle Scout rank ceremony. His younger brother Sean, now also an Eagle Scout, was also part of the Honor Guard.

The rest of this chapter is intended for reading aloud to young children, at home and in school. I've explained the pledge, phrase by phrase, in language for youngsters who can't read or are just beginning. I suggest that you precede the reading with simple explanation and demonstration of how to say the Pledge of Allegiance. (Review the preceding chapter for details.) Show your child how to stand at attention and face the flag. Show your child how to cross his or her heart with the right hand. Demonstrate that the fingers are held together out straight with the thumb also in line, like a military salute, rather than splayed apart or dangling at the wrist. Demonstrate how to lower your arm at the conclusion of the Pledge, so that it drops smartly to the side rather than lingers or strays upward to the neck or head.

When your child has completed saying the Pledge, reward him or her with a compliment. Patriotism should be associated with love and respect for elders, not fear or dislike of them. As *Focus on the Family* magazine (September 2002, p. 14) notes:

> More than ever, children need to be taught to cherish the inspiring ideals set forth in the Pledge of Allegiance, including why it is important to be one nation under God. People will not defend what they do not cherish, and they will not cherish what they do not understand.

According to the U.S. Department of Education, the *Focus* article says, on a national civics test 34% of the fourth grade students did not know what the Pledge of Allegiance meant. How sad! And how dangerous for our freedom! Youth is 20% of the population but 100% of the future. Today's children are tomorrow's society and leaders. Unless citizens, especially young people, have a clear understanding of America, this nation will not endure. Tyranny is always only a generation or two away, ready to prey on the ignorant. It's as simple as that. Therefore, teach your children well the lesson of Americanism embodied in the Pledge of Allegiance. You can summarize it with words from the American Legion's educational comic book for children entitled *I Pledge Allegiance*:

> When we pledge allegiance to our flag, we promise to be loyal to our country. When you're loyal to a friend, you always want to help and support them. So when we pledge allegiance, we agree to always help and support our country.

**I pledge...**

A pledge is a promise. When you promise something, you are saying you give your word to do something and you'll keep it. You'll be true to it. You are saying you'll do that, no matter what happens.

### allegiance …
"Allegiance" means being faithful or loyal. It means staying together like a family. So when we pledge allegiance, we are saying that we promise to be faithful, loyal and true to our country, just like it was our family.

### to the Flag of the United States of America…
The flag stands for our country. It is a symbol of America. The 13 stripes represent the original 13 colonies and the 50 stars represent all the states today. The colors of the flag have meaning, also. Red is the color of blood; red stands for courage and heroism, such as when soldiers and sailors had to fight in war to protect America and keep us free. White stands for innocence and purity; white means the ideals and principles of America are pure and holy. Blue is the color of the sky; blue stands for justice, which comes to us from God in heaven through the way we've set up our country to be fair to everyone because God created everyone equal.

### and to the Republic for which it stands…
America is a republic. That is the kind of government we have. In a republic, citizens vote in elections for the people they want to run the government and make the laws. But the elected people are the servants or employees of the citizens. We, the people of the United States, own America. Our government works for us, not the other way around. It is government of the people, by the people and for the people.

### one Nation…
"One Nation" means all 50 states are joined together to make one country, the United States of America. The United States started in 1776 when the original 13 colonies joined together. That happened on July 4, 1776, when the Declaration of Independence was signed. That was more than two hundred years ago.

### under God…
The special thing about America is this: We say that God, not government, gives us our freedom, our sovereignty, our equality, our rights, our justice and our human dignity. The Declaration of Independence says all people are created equal by our Creator, God. It also says that God gives everyone the right to life, liberty and the pursuit of happiness, and that the main purpose of government is simply to make sure our freedom and rights are not violated or hurt by anyone.

### indivisible…
"Indivisible" means the country cannot be split apart by war or groups of people. From 1861-1865 we had a Civil War because some states in the South tried to leave the country and start their own. America was then divided into two groups, the Union in the North and the Confederacy in the South. They fought each other. A lot of people were

killed and wounded. The Union won the war, and ever since then, America has been reunited as one nation.

**with liberty...**
"Liberty" means being free. All Americans have the same freedoms, such as freedom of speech, freedom of religion, freedom to get together and freedom to travel around the country. No American can have his or her freedom taken away unless that person is punished for breaking the law. Punishment can take away some of your freedom by sending you to prison.

**and justice...**
"Justice" means getting fair and equal treatment under the law. Even if you are poor, you should be treated the same as a rich person or a famous person when you go to court or when you want something done by the government.

**for all.**
This means the laws in America are the same for everyone. All citizens are entitled to freedom and should be treated fairly. There are equal rights for all but special rights for none.

**Sidebar 9**

# RED SKELTON'S COMMENTARY ON THE PLEDGE OF ALLEGIANCE

The following commentary on the Pledge of Allegiance was written by Richard Bernard ("Red") Skelton (1913-1997). He was known to generations of Americans as a great comedian who went from vaudeville to starring on radio, television and in the movies with his classic characters such as Freddy the Freeloader, Clem Kadiddlehopper and Deadeye. He was also deeply patriotic. When he was a boy, one of Red's teachers explained the words and meaning of the Pledge of Allegiance to his class. The teacher, Mr. Lasswell, felt his students had come to think of the Pledge of Allegiance as merely something to recite in class each day. Red later wrote down, and eventually recorded, his recollection of that lecture. He intended it for reading to young children. It is followed by an observation of his own which he made on national television in 1969.

Mr. Lasswell said, "I've been listening to you boys and girls recite the Pledge of Allegiance all semester and it seems as though it is becoming monotonous to you. If I may, may I recite it and try to explain to you the meaning of each word?"

**I**—Me; an individual; a committee of one.

**Pledge**—Dedicate all of my worldly goods to give without self pity.

**Allegiance**—My love and my devotion.

**To the Flag**—Our standard, Old Glory, a symbol of freedom. Wherever she waves there is respect, because your loyalty has given her a dignity that shouts, "Freedom is everybody's job."

**Of the United**—That means that we have all come together.

**States**—Individual communities that have united into 48 great states, 48 individual communities with pride and dignity and purpose, all divided with imaginary boundaries, yet united to a common purpose, and that is love for country.

**Of America**—[Red did not comment on this phrase.]

**And to the Republic**—Republic—a state in which sovereign power is invested in representatives chosen by the people to govern; and government is the people, and it's from the people to the leaders, not from the leaders to the people.

**For which it stands**—[Red did not comment on this phrase.]

**One Nation**—The nation, meaning "so blessed by God."

**Indivisible**—Incapable of being divided.

**With Liberty**—Which is Freedom; the right of power to live one's own life, without threats, fear, or some sort of retaliation.

**And Justice**—The principle or quality of dealing fairly with others.

**For All**—Which means it's as much your country as it is mine.

And now, boys and girls, let me hear you recite the Pledge of Allegiance:

*I pledge allegiance to the Flag of the United States of America, and to the Republic, for which it stands, one Nation indivisible, with liberty and justice for all.*

Since I was a small boy, two states have been added to our country, and two words have been added to the Pledge of Allegiance: *under God.* Wouldn't it be a pity if someone said that is a prayer, and that it would be eliminated from schools, too?

## Chapter 10

# WHAT EVER HAPPENED TO CIVICS?

It will be worthy of a free, enlightened, and, at no distant period, a great nation, to give to mankind the magnanimous and too novel example of a people always guided by an exalted justice and benevolence.

– President George Washington

Children should be educated and instructed in the principles of freedom.

– President John Adams

We live in an age of science and of abounding accumulation of material things. These did not create our Declaration. Our Declaration created them. The things of the spirit come first. Unless we cling to that, all our material prosperity, overwhelming though it may appear, will turn to a barren sceptre in our grasp. If we are to maintain the great heritage which has been bequeathed to us, we must be like-minded as the fathers who created it.

– President Calvin Coolidge

The only sure bulwark of continuing liberty is a government strong enough to protect the interests of the people, and a people strong enough and well enough informed to maintain its sovereign control over its government.

– President Franklin Delano Roosevelt

An America that is militarily and economically strong is not enough. The world must see an America that is morally strong with a creed and a vision. This is what has led us to dare and achieve. For us, values count.

– President Ronald Reagan, 1983

At the memorial service for a deceased person in my home town, a large crowd of friends and acquaintances attended. Marilyn had been deeply involved in the life of our community. My wife and I knew her through Girl Scouts, where she had been a long-time troop leader.

After the service, everyone gathered in the parish hall to offer condolences to her family and to have refreshments. There was a display board of photos and documents from events in Marilyn's life. One particularly caught my attention. It was her third grade report card for the school year 1939-40. The report card was just a small piece of paper about 8" x 8", folded in half. On one side of the paper was the name of the school system, the student, the grade, the teacher and a message to parents which read in part: "This report concerning your child is sent to you five times during the school year. It is an attempt to give you an idea of how your child is doing in his studies and the teacher's judgment as to the citizenship traits he is developing."

The other side containing the actual grades for the marking periods struck me forcefully. It had two columns. One was headed Scholarship Progress and Reading Level. The other column—fully half of the grading section—was Citizenship Progress. An explanation under the heading said: "The child's attitude and behavior are of great importance. Education is not just a matter of book learning. It also includes learning to get on well with people, doing one's best, facing facts, and doing the right thing in each situation."

Specific subheads made clear what that meant. They included: Health and Posture, Orderliness, Thrift, Promptness, Clear Thinking, Initiative and Self-Reliance, Self-Control and Obedience, Perseverance, Honesty and Trustworthiness, Fair Play and Sportsmanship, Civic Responsibility, Courtesy and Consideration, and Cooperativeness. Each topic had a number of very specific statements on which the child was graded as having strength or weakness, and whether the child needed to improve a trait or was improving. Civic Responsibility, for example, read: "Supports the right and opposes the wrong." "Performs well the duties of any office to which he is elected." "Takes pride in appearance of school property and does his share to keep it in good order."

That was for a third grade child! Good citizenship traits were instilled and developed to prepare the child not just to exist but to participate positively in the life of his or her community and the nation. The teacher and the school system inculcated honesty and morality along with scholarship, a sense of civic duty along with reading progress, courtesy and consideration along with penmanship, self-control and fair play along with spelling and language, an attitude of self-reliance equal in importance to learning arithmetic.

What ever happened to Citizen Progress? Whatever happened to civics?

## The Dumbing Down of America

In the late 19th and early 20th centuries, the study of citizenship and government in schools was called civics. Notice that *both* aspects of our nation were included—the society and the government. According to my 1961 edition of *The Encyclopedia Britannica*, the term "civics" included materials derived from sociology, economics, geography, social psychology, international affairs, social ethics and the study of occupations. Today, however, the *Britannica* noted, these areas of study, along with history, are known in secondary education as the social studies or the social sciences. Among the social studies still may be found courses devoted specifically to the organization and processes of governments and the rights and duties of citizens. Such courses may be called civics or they may be called government or citizenship or some yet different name.

Wikipedia, the on-line encyclopedia, likewise tells us: "Civics is the science of comparative government and means of administering public trusts—the theory of governance as applied to state institutions. It is usually considered a branch of applied ethics and is certainly part of politics."

That narrowing of the meaning, it seems to me, is part of what has been called "the dumbing down of America"—not just intellectually but also civically and morally. Civics today is not the same thing as civic education. Civics should again become more than merely the study of government because there is so much more to America than that.

The word "civics" is derived from the Latin *civitas*, meaning "the city." Civic means "of or related to a citizen, city, citizenship or civil affairs." That definition comes from *Our Constitution and Government*, published in 1940 by the U.S. Government Printing Office. It gives this summary sentence of the meaning of civics: "Interested in the good of a city or a community."

A city often has a civic center for business and commerce, a civic arena for sports, a civic auditorium for entertainment, lectures and other public events—none of which are governmental entities per se. But they *are* central to the life of the community and hence have to do with the society. Moreover, they can be sources of what is called "civic pride," or positive feeling toward one's city or community. And, again, that has nothing to do with government per se.

Perhaps the most obvious form of civics are neighborhood groups called civic associations. They are formed by local people to protect and advance the quality of life in their neighborhood. Civic associations are grassroot expressions of concern for "the city." They are local demonstrations of citizen involvement in the life of their part of the city in general and their local piece of it, the neighborhood. They display citizen pride and responsibility and volunteerism—all of which are not dependent on, or even connected with, government per se.

Civics, then, in its broad and best sense deals with the rights and responsibilities of citizens of the American republic, both locally and nationally. In America, one's citizenship training begins at home via the family. It continues at the local or community level via schooling and other activities involving young people such as religious training, Scouting, Demolay, Rainbow Girls, etc.

Civil means "of or related to citizens." **The purpose of civics is to teach civility.** **Civility is the basis of civil-ization.**

Turning once more to the 1940 GPO pamphlet, we find this important statement:

> Civility means "courtesy, politeness" but it is much more than an expression of manners. An older meaning is "training in the humanities." That training refers to education in a broader sense. It includes formal, academic studies, but more broadly, it means education in the higher realms of human thought which provides the basis of civilization. The civility of all the individuals of a society supports or detracts from the quality of civilization. A civilized person is one who understands and supports the principles of his or her society. Included in that is civil law and civil liberty.

**Education begins at home; so does civics.** Let's look at some of the elements of civility which are largely absent from current-day teaching of civics.

In a self-governing society such as ours, the basic safeguard against crime and social breakdown is, quite simply, morality and religious values. Those are first learned at home in the process of parents rearing their children. The higher levels of government—the city, the state and the nation—come much later into the lives of young people learning to function in society. That is why **the home is the first level of**

***government in America***; it is where children first learn to govern themselves. Laws don't prevent crime and social breakdown; they merely define the limits of acceptable social behavior and punishment for those who don't conform through moral living and internal control.

The home, as a two-parent, marriage-based family, is where young people first see role models for good citizens, with all the rights and responsibilities to oversee the governing of our nation. There is where they learn self-control, morality, the work ethic, respect for others, respect for private property, respect for law and duly constituted authority, love of learning for lifelong education, respect for our history and heroes, and other civic virtues which have built our nation, such as self-reliance, rugged individualism, thriftiness, charitable giving, community volunteerism and exercising the right to vote. The schools, churches, temples and mosques reinforce what is learned in the home—or at least should. Without proper upbringing in a stable home and local community, young people become dysfunctional and lost to society. All too often they end up as incarcerated criminals or dead-end derelicts.

> "You have often read that in a democracy like ours the people get the kind of government they ask for. If they give all their time to their own affairs, try to avoid the obligations of citizenship, pay no attention to politics, and don't bother to vote on election day, they are asking for corrupt and inefficient government—and they usually get it. If they take an active interest in politics, try to have their parties nominate honest, capable men, and work hard to elect them, their town and state will usually have honest and efficient government. What this means to the average person is that the town and the state will be a better place to live in." *Connecticut—The State and Its Government* (secondary school text book) by William E. Buckley and Charles E. Perry (Oxford Book Company, New York, 1954).

As I've said before, young people are twenty percent of the population but one hundred percent of the future. Therefore, if the youth of America do not have a vital understanding of what this nation is all about, in a few generations there will not be an America. It is as simple, and sad, as that.

Somehow, over the last half century, the curriculum of America's public schools has lost touch with many of the elements which developed the sentiment of patriotism in children. Why? The curriculum has room for sex education, drug awareness and AIDS prevention, but not for simple exercises such as memorizing the Preamble to the Constitution. Why?

Education is fundamental to all life, and with regard to our national life (and its preservation), patriotism must be taught—and taught far better than it is at present. Patriotism, like charity, begins at home.

How is patriotism inculcated in young people? To recap Chapter 1: Patriotism is a sentiment, not an instinct. It results from a process which, over time, unites head, hand and heart into a clear vision of what America is all about. In other words, patriotism is not inborn; it is learned. And it is learned as much by example as by speech. It is learned from parents, teachers, public figures and others in positions of authority and influence who demonstrate patriotism in their words and their lives. It is absorbed from the culture, directly and indirectly, in the process of becoming responsible citizens. Native-born children learn it growing up; immigrants learn it by assimilating into mainstream America.

American patriotism is understanding and appreciating the fundamental ideas, principles, values, events, traditions, goals and dreams which have built our nation. Without that, America will decline and eventually vanish into history—a future history of tyranny and oppression horrible to contemplate because of forces in the world hostile to freedom. American patriotism, therefore, is intelligent love of our country—informed and grateful love of our country's past, present and future.

Patriotism begins in the home. "The hand that rocks the cradle rules the world." And it continues growing through a child's schooling. As the poem "The Schoolhouse Stands by the Flag" states:

> 'Tis the schoolhouse that stands by the flag,
> Let the nation stand by the school;
> 'Tis the school bell that rings for our liberty old,
> 'Tis the schoolboy whose ballot shall rule.

Likewise, a child's religious and social training is part of the educational process of inculcating the sentiment of patriotism. Starting athletic events with the National Anthem and hearing patriotic invocations by clergy at the beginning of public events are examples of that.

Another educational resource for teaching patriotism is literature. As a child, I loved stories of heroism and gallantry, whether the stories were in prose or poetry, in books, movies or on radio or TV. Patriotic poems and songs especially had a profoundly formative effect on my character and on my appreciation of America. Young people today are not being exposed to the literature of patriotism the way I was as a boy. The tales about colonial America, Valley Forge, the USS *Constitution* (better known as "Old Ironsides"), the Alamo, the Westward movement of pioneers—the entire epic of America —gave me an inspiring sense of what it means to be a citizen of this nation. It was deepened by rote memorization of key passages from documents such as the Declaration of Independence and the Constitution, from speeches by various Founding Fathers ("Give me liberty or give me death!", "I only regret that I have but one life to give for my country."), and by opening exercises in school. My training as a Boy Scout also contributed greatly. (I have collected the words and lyrics to many patriotic poems and songs in a reader intended for school children I titled it *Celebrating America in Poem and Song*.)

Because of that, I propose that the elementary school curriculum should embrace the following topics. Moreover, the present curriculum should be reviewed for opportunities to enhance patriotism and civics. The curriculum should:

1. Discuss the meaning of patriotism, The Pledge of Allegiance, the national anthem, Independence Day, Flag Day, Memorial Day and Veterans Day.

2. Memorize the Pledge of Allegiance, the national anthem, the national motto, the Preamble to the Constitution and the opening two paragraphs of the Declaration of Independence.

3. Teach how to show respect for the flag and how to show proper etiquette for it; how to display the flag in public; how to show respect when the national anthem and "Taps" are played; include a brief history of the flag (from Betsy Ross to Ft. McHenry to now).

4. Study symbols of American liberty: The Great Seal of the United States, Independence Hall, the Liberty Bell, Washington Crossing the Delaware, Lincoln at Gettysburg, the Statue of Liberty, raising the flag on Mt. Suribachi at Iwo Jima, etc.

5. Discuss what makes America unique among all nations and why it stands out so favorably (especially our Declaration of Independence, which says all people are equal and have inalienable rights derived from God, not any government body; and our Constitution, which guarantees those rights for everyone while establishing a government which is the servant of "we the people").

6. Discuss why the United States is a democratic republic, not a pure democracy, and what the difference is between the two. Compare a republic with other forms of government (monarchy, oligarchy, democracy, socialism, fascism, totalitarianism, statism, etc.) Discuss the two aspects of any nation: the society and the government, and why both are necessary.

7. Contain a unit on the military structure and history of the United States. The unit should cover the branches of the armed forces; the chain of command from the President, through officers, to enlisted people; the Medal of Honor and the Purple Heart; and the nation's military academies (West Point, Annapolis, Air Force Academy, Coast Guard Academy and King's Point for Merchant Marine).

8. Contain a unit on what a veteran is and what they do after military service when they join the American Legion, Veterans of Foreign Wars, Disabled American Veterans, etc.

Thomas Jefferson provided the greatest short lesson on civics when he said in his First Inaugural Address (1801):

> The essentials principles of our Government…form the bright constellation which has gone before us and guided our steps through an age of revolution and reformation. The wisdom of our sages and the blood of our heroes have been devoted to their attainment. They should be the creed of our political faith, the text of civic instruction, the touchstone by which to try the services of those we trust; and should we wander from them in moments of error or of alarm, let us hasten to retrace our steps and to regain the road which alone leads to peace, liberty and safety.

## Sidebar 10

# THE WORLD'S SMALLEST POLITICAL QUIZ

Don't understand political philosophies very well? A brief on-line quiz can help.

To see where you fit on the political landscape, the Advocates for Self-Government in Cartersville, Georgia—a libertarian group—has you answer ten questions about personal and economic issues. The questions are:

## Personal Issues
(Choose A if you agree, M for Maybe, D if you disagree.)

1. Government should not censor speech, press, media or Internet.
2. Military service should be voluntary. There should be no draft.
3. There should be no laws regarding sex for consenting adults.
4. Repeal laws prohibiting adult possession and use of drugs.
5. There should be no National ID card.

## Economic Issues
(Choose A if you agree, M for Maybe, D if you disagree.)

1. End "corporate welfare." No government handouts to business.
2. End government barriers to international free trade.
3. Let people control their own retirement; privatize Social Security.
4. Replace government welfare with private charity.
5. Cut taxes and government spending by 50% or more.

You score yourself, but the scoring can only be done on-line at the Advocates for Self-Government web site (http://www.theadvocates.org). The score places a red dot showing you where you fit on the political map devised by the Advocates for Self-Government. The map is a square with a grid inside. At each corner is one of four political philosophies: Left (Liberal), Right (Conservative), Statist and Libertarian. A fifth political philosophy, Centrist, is in the middle of the square. Your score will show where you are on the political landscape and give a summary of the philosophy behind that position.

The five political philosophies are defined by the Advocates as follow:

**Left (Liberal/Progressive).** Liberals usually embrace freedom of choice in personal matters, but tend to support significant government control of the economy. They generally support a government-funded "safety net" to help the disadvantaged, and advocate strict regulation of business. Liberals tend to favor environmental regulations, defend civil liberties and free expression, support government action to promote equality, and tolerate diverse lifestyles.

**Right (Conservative).** Conservatives tend to favor economic freedom, but frequently support laws to restrict personal behavior that violates "traditional values." They oppose excessive government control of business, while endorsing government action to defend morality and the traditional family structure. Conservatives usually support a strong military, oppose bureaucracy and high taxes, favor a free-market economy, and endorse strong law enforcement.

**Statist.** Statists want government to have a great deal of power over the economy and individual behavior. They frequently doubt whether economic liberty and individual freedom are practical options in today's world. Statists tend to distrust the free market, support high taxes and centralized planning of the economy, oppose diverse lifestyles, and question the importance of civil liberties.

**Libertarian.** Libertarians support maximum liberty in both personal and economic matters. They advocate a much smaller government; one that is limited to protecting individuals from coercion and violence. Libertarians tend to embrace individual responsibility, oppose government bureaucracy and taxes, promote private charity, tolerate diverse lifestyles, support the free market, and defend civil liberties

**Centrist.** Centrists espouse a "middle ground" regarding government control of the economy and personal behavior. Depending on the issue, they sometimes favor government intervention and sometimes support individual freedom of choice. Centrists pride themselves on keeping an open mind, tend to oppose "political extremes," and emphasize what they describe as "practical" solutions to problems.

*This quiz is reprinted by the kind permission of Sharon Harris, President of Advocates for Self-Government.*

**Sidebar 11**

# CHECKLIST FOR VOTERS

Since citizens—we the people—are the owners of America, a candidate for public office should be considered as if you were a business owner hiring a CEO to run a business for you. You want the very best person for the position.

An election is not a beauty contest or a popularity contest. Good looks or a pleasing personality are not enough. Nor are charisma and oratorical skill. (Hitler had both.) High visibility in the media does not necessarily mean trustworthiness. There are more important concerns which should be examined thoroughly before deciding whether a person is qualified for the job and deserves your vote. In other words, what is the candidate's resumé?

Here is a checklist of a dozen significant topics to examine about people seeking your vote. Cast your vote on the basis of thoughtful consideration of them rather than hasty, superficial judgment or warm, but vague, fuzzy feelings. The future of America to some extent depends on that.

1. **PRINCIPLES, IDEALS AND VALUES.** What are the candidate's publicly declared principles, ideals and values? Are they based on the Declaration of Independence and the Constitution? Or does the candidate espouse principles, ideals and values which are contrary to them, such as socialism, communism, fascism, benevolent dictatorship, monarchy or other forms of government which place the state above the citizen and disregard the liberty and rights of the individual? Has he or she been consistent in espousing those ideals, principles and values or has he changed over time? If he has changed, why—and what does that tell you about the person? Does he place principles before party? Is she loyal to a party or to the country and the Constitution? In short, what does the candidate stand for? And is that the same as what the candidate *says* he or she stands for?

2. **VOTING RECORD.** If the candidate has held office, what is his or her voting record? Does it support his public declarations? What legislation has he supported? What legislation has he introduced? What are his top priorities if elected? What position(s) has he taken on various issues such as taxes, spending and fiscal policy, welfare, monetary policy, the Federal Reserve System, foreign aid, military strength, the national debt, health care, abortion, same-sex marriage, etc.? Has he been consistent in his position or has he changed his position on issues, and if so, why? Does he cite the Constitution as the basis for his votes in office? How do various organizations rate the candidate? Does he believe that your property and wealth belong to you or to the state? Does he favor bigger government and more spending, or reduced government and lower spending? Does he want more taxes or debt to pay for more spending or

does he want to reduce taxes and debt? What promises has he made to voters? Has he followed through on his promises? If not, why not?

3. **ACCOMPLISHMENTS.** What is the candidate's record of accomplishment? What has he done during his term(s) of office? What has he attempted? Accomplished? How have those accomplishments been regarded by various political, business and social organizations?

4. **VISION FOR AMERICA.** What does the candidate say about the past, present and future of America? Does he have a vision for the future? Is it a future you want for America? Do his actions support his words? What are his top priorities if elected?

5. **POLITICAL SKILLS.** Has the candidate demonstrated leadership? What type of leadership: bold and courageous or quiet and diplomatic? Was it appropriate and effective for each situation? Does he or she show good organizational skills, with a clear understanding of how to administer or manage and how to rally public support? Does he show good communication skills in speaking, writing and media appearances?

6. **WORK EXPERIENCE AND PUBLIC SERVICE.** What is the candidate's experience outside the office he holds or seeks? Has he or she worked in private industry? In what capacity? Has he started a business or run one? If so, how successfully? Does he support free enterprise and capitalism or government control of markets and pricing? Does he support any philanthropic or charitable organizations, and if so, for how much and how long? Does he or she volunteer in any civic or community capacity, and if so, how long has he been involved?

7. **LICENSES AND CERTIFICATIONS.** Does the candidate have any licenses or certifications which indicate special skill and accomplishments? Are they relevant to the office being sought by the candidate? For example, is he or she licensed to practice law? Does he have certification as a public accountant or other profession immediately relevant to holding political office?

8. **EDUCATION.** What is the candidate's education, both formal and informal? What is his academic performance, grades and class standing? Does he or she hold any academic honors? Is his academic record appropriate for the office he seeks? If it is not directly related, how has the candidate schooled himself for political office?

9. **CHARACTER.** How do you evaluate the candidate's character? The Founders said very clearly that our republic is made only for a moral people. An immoral people will devalue honor, honesty, justice, fair play and the rule of law. Only people of good character were intended to serve in public office; that is why there is the process of impeachment for high crimes (violations of law) and misdemeanors (grossly immoral behavior). Do you believe the candidate is honest? Do you trust him or her to keep his promises? Will he live up to the oath of office which requires him to preserve, protect and defend the Constitution? Is he what you regard as a mature person and a moral person?

10. **BACKGROUND.** Is there anything in the candidate's background to recommend him, discredit him or raise a caution sign, such as organization memberships or crime convictions? Is the candidate married? If married, what do you know about his or her spouse? His immediate family background? Does he or she have children? Does he have a religious upbringing and/or practice a faith? Does he have military service? If so, what kind, and was it honorable? Is he decorated for combat bravery or other military excellence? Where did he grow up? Is he native born or

naturalized? Has he published anything which bears on his qualifications? Is there any scandal in his life or hint of it? Are his business associates upstanding? Are his political associates known as honest and patriotic?

11. **FAMILY AND RELATIVES.** Who are the candidate's parents and close relatives? Are they well-known public figures or unknowns? If any are public figures, what are they known for? Do they have significant accomplishments or personal scandals? Are they well-rated for public service or do they have unsavory reputations? Do they offer guidance and support for the candidate, either directly or indirectly? Does the candidate appear to be utilizing them because of their notoriety? Is the candidate running as successor to a "political dynasty" or on his own merits?

12. **REFERENCES.** Who recommends the candidate? Is he or she supported by people and organizations you know and trust? Are there any special interests or lobbies behind him, such as a church, veterans groups, civic and fraternal organizations, labor unions, financial companies, medical groups, etc.? If so, how do you regard them?

When casting your vote, remember the words of Samuel Adams, who said to the *Boston Gazette* in 1781:

> Let each citizen remember at the moment he is offering his vote that he is not making a present or a compliment to please an individual — or at least that he ought not so to do; but that he is executing one of the most solemn trusts in human society for which he is accountable to God and his country.

## Sidebar 12

# THE DYSFUNCTION OF THE BLACK COMMUNITY

Black Americans have been debating the comments of entertainer-activist-philanthropist Bill Cosby, who has criticized the black community for failing to raise their children properly. He blames bad parenting for:

- the high rate of crime in the black community
- the high rate of incarcerated black men
- the high dropout rate of black high school students
- the high rate of unwed mothers and one-parent households
- the coarse behavior and vulgar speech of black youth
- the failure of many blacks to move up the socioeconomic ladder

Cosby declared that parents are primarily responsible for this—not their slave heritage and not white oppression—and therefore they must change their parenting behavior to provide moral guidance and socioeconomic instruction for their children.

I agree with Cosby. In response to a story in the *New Haven* [Connecticut] *Register* about the Greater New Haven NAACP sponsoring a conference on crime in the community, I said that the high rate of young black men killing other young black men and fathering children whom they don't raise is a sign of near-complete breakdown of traditional community mores. But, I added, the problem is even larger. Describing the dysfunction of the black community is only the most visible aspect of the national situation. America itself has been declining in civility, morality and patriotism for decades.

It seems to me that the black community is nearly dysfunctional except for the religious institutions such as churches and mosques where there is insistence on moral behavior and self-restraint.

The root cause of crime and social decay in America is the breakdown of the two-parent, marriage-based family which takes responsibility for socializing their children and teaching them morality, personal responsibility and respect for law and order. That is true, regardless of race or color.

In a self-governing society such as ours, the basic safeguard against crime and social breakdown is, quite simply, morality and religious values. Those are first learned at home in the process of parents rearing their children. The higher levels of government—the city, the state and the nation—come much later into the lives of young people learning to function in society. That is why **the home is the first level of government in America**; it is where children first learn to govern themselves. Laws don't prevent crime and social breakdown; they merely prescribe social behavior and punishment for those who don't control themselves through moral living and internal control. Blaming institutional racism, as some do, is a copout. The high rate of young black men in prison is due to their criminal behavior and getting caught—period.

There's more to it than that, however. It's also due to their parents' absence in their lives as a moral influence when they were young children, so they didn't get a healthy role modeling, especially the boys whose fathers are absent. It's due to the welfare system which destroys human dignity, self-reliance and community caring for one another, and drives the father out of the family residence while subsidizing poverty and promiscuity. (The welfare system perpetuates slave mentality; it substitutes Washington, D.C. for "Massa in de big house" while placing golden shackles on welfare recipients.) It's due to drugs and sexual promiscuity because parents didn't instill moral training in their kids. It's due to kids not being taught to respect duly constituted authority, whether that authority is a cop or a teacher or a preacher. It's due to kids not being taught basic principles of American society, such as respect for private property, the work ethic and respecting public decorum. It's due to kids not being taught to appreciate education, to strive for academic success and to understand that education is what allows a person to advance in life. It's due to kids not learning to respect the simple truth of the Declaration of Independence when it says all men, meaning all people, are born with the inalienable right to life, liberty and the pursuit of happiness, and the simple truth of the Constitution which says you must likewise respect the rights of others and not look to government to deliver happiness.

The days of Jim Crow are long gone. When a Colin Powell, Michael Jordan, Oprah Winfrey, Denzel Washington, Clarence Thomas, Ben Carson, Aretha Franklin, Thomas Sowell or Condoleezza Rice can say that they achieved success by earning it the old fashioned way—meaning hard, honest work—there is no excuse for young blacks to hang out on street corners or run in gangs or turn to crime. Nothing is stopping them from similar achievement and success except their disrespectful attitude and their lazy or lawless behavior. Despite its flaws and shortcomings, America is still a land of opportunity, and the only colors that really count are red, white and blue.

## Chapter 11

# EIGHT BASIC REASONS FOR
# THE COLUMBINE HIGH SCHOOL MASSACRE

There is no institution more vital to our nation's survival than the American family. Here the seeds of personal character are planted, the roots of public virtue first nourished. Through love and instruction, discipline, guidance and example, we learn from our mothers and fathers the values that will shape our private lives and our public citizenship.

– President Ronald Reagan, 1981

When I was a teenager in the 1950s, I had a single-shot .22 rifle—my very first gun (if you don't count the Daisy Red Ryder BB gun I got when I was 10). I carried it around town with me openly when I rode my bike to shoot at targets in an abandoned quarry or at squirrels in the woods. Nobody worried about it—not my parents, my neighbors or the police. That's the way it was then.

I bought the rifle by myself when I was 14. I just went into the local hardware store and paid for it and the ammunition with money I'd earned by delivering newspapers and mowing lawns. The clerk knew me and simply handed it over. No questions were asked, no forms had to be filled out, no fears or suspicions were raised. My father, who'd been on his college rifle team, had taught me to shoot and handle a gun safely and properly. That's the way it was then.

Many young people had guns in that era. We kids had a shooting club (run by adults, of course) and a shooting range in the basement of an elementary school. (It's still there, structurally speaking, but has been closed for a long time.) My friend Bill, his sister and his father were avid target shooters who went annually to compete in national matches at Camp Perry, Ohio. Shooting was a family sport and a healthy activity for youngsters. [1]

Kids of that era had much greater access to guns than they do now, but there was none of the violence and killing such as the 1999 Columbine High School massacre in Colorado and others since then. Why? Because, as trite as this may seem, our culture didn't allow it. Cultural factors of that time collectively established a strong moral barrier to violence and killing by young people. Since then, those factors have weakened profoundly or disappeared altogether, so that now they are failing to prevent gun violence by young people, despite increasing legal barriers in the form of more laws and regulations.

The Roman historian-philosopher Seneca (who was also a legislator in the Roman Senate) wrote, "The more corrupt a people, the more numerous its laws." That succinctly states the case today. As I said earlier, America is declining in civility, morality and patriotism. Those are three primary indicators of health or sickness in the body politic. They are the elements of good citizenship. When internalized by each citizen, they provide a solid basis for self-control, self-respect and respect for others, making external factors such as laws and the threat of punishment unnecessary for self-rule. When they are strong, the body politic is healthy; when they decline, the body politic weakens and grows ill.

Over the last half of the 20th Century, American culture underwent a sea-change, a fundamental shift in personal and public regard for those factors which keep society law-abiding and peaceful. That process continues today. More and more laws have become necessary to maintain order in America because the internal controls are disappearing from the mental or psychosocial makeup of citizens. More laws require more police to enforce them. The logical conclusion to the process I'm pointing out is: America will become a police state. If that happens, you can say good-bye to your liberty, your sovereignty, your equality, your rights, your justice and your human dignity. A new Dark Ages will have arrived.

Here are what I see as the eight basic factors of our culture which used to prevent gun violence in America.

## The Eight Basic Reasons for Columbine

First and foremost, there were two-parent, marriage-based families who raised their children, socialized their children, and taught their children personal responsibility and accountability for their actions. They understood that in a society such as ours, which is based on self-government, *the family is the first level of government*, so it is responsible for teaching children how to govern themselves. They understood that an immoral people cannot be a self-governing people, so they taught morality—a clear and simple sense of right-and-wrong, such as you find in the Ten Commandments. They taught respect for law and duly constituted authority. They sat down together at meal time and discussed family problems, school activities, and whatever else seemed necessary for "growing up". They sent their kids to Sunday school or Sabbath school and to other forms of moral instruction. Every kid as young as six knew it was wrong to shoot someone. They were taught respect for life and property. They were educated about guns and gun safety, and about the severe penalty they'd have to pay for misusing a gun. They also understood that their misbehavior would bring public shame on them and their family, and they feared doing that because they were subject to parental authority and the governance of the family. [2]

There were circumstances when it was okay to shoot someone, but those circumstances were also well understood by children. You shot the Bad Guys, the criminals, the lawbreakers who committed violence and inflicted abuse on law-abiding people. That's what the police did. That's what the cowboy movies, gangster movies and war movies were all about. There were heroes in the movies who always stood up for law and order and for the defenseless, the helpless, the weak. There was no moral relativity in the worldview of that time, and certainly no glamorizing of violence. (Even James Cagney, the tough-guy gangster in *Angels with Dirty Faces* who was unafraid of death, pretended to be afraid of the electric chair at the end of the film so that his gang of admiring boys wouldn't regard him as a role model.) The worldview simply did not permit the mayhem and killing we see in the news today.

Second, there was a strong sense of community and concern for the neighborhood. Mothers stayed home and watched not just their own kids but also the neighbors' kids as they played outside. Moreover, the mothers didn't hesitate to correct children, whether their own or their neighbors, if they saw misbehavior. No one claimed child abuse for using a hairbrush or a belt across a youngster's backside or a ruler across the hand. Was there abuse? Undoubtedly, but it was the rare exception, not the rule. Discipline by parents and adults included appropriate punishment. As a kid, I once got smacked by a neighborhood mother, who then took my hand, marched me home and reported my misbehavior to my own mother. I don't remember what I did wrong, but I haven't forgotten that my mother thanked the neighbor, then spanked me a second time! I don't feel I was abused. (At dinner, she told my father, who further admonished me for misbehavior.)

Third, school teachers were respected and had authority to correct students if they misbehaved. If a student was sent to the principal's office, that was a fearful experience! And when the student got home, he or she would probably get more punishment from the parents. The idea of parents even questioning a principal's decision, let alone hiring a lawyer to contest it, as often happens today, was unthinkable. The principal's decision was backed up by the parents and the community. So kids toed the line in the home, in the community and in school. (Parents saw to it that their children did their homework, dressed properly and got to school each day.) By contrast, some years ago in Boston, there was public debate over the charge made in a newspaper by a teacher that unruly, disruptive kids are running—and ruining—classrooms, right down to the kindergarten level, and that the Superintendent of Schools was too cowardly or too politically correct to do anything about it.

Fourth, public officials and opinion makers clearly stood up for civility, civic responsibility, patriotism and public decorum. They may not always have lived up to it in private, but the public sense of proper behavior was strong, and it flowed into the young people of the era. Kids said the Pledge of Allegiance every morning in school, along with a prayer and a patriotic song such as "My Country, 'Tis of Thee." They said "Yes, ma'am" and "Yes, sir." They would never address their elders as "You guys" the way young people do today. When the flag passed by in a parade, everyone stood up and crossed their hearts; men uncovered if they were wearing a hat. No one would ever think of leaving their hat on at that moment, or when the national anthem was played, let alone think of wearing their hat in school or restaurants and even when visiting in someone's home, as happens today. It was regarded as bad manners, uncouth, almost unpatriotic, as if disrespecting America.

Fifth, the news media did not glamorize violence and vulgarity. Nor was it selected on the basis of "entertainment" value by finely coiffured and fashionably dressed talking heads who pass for journalists today. And the ghastly obscenity of gangsta rap music would not have been tolerated in homes, let alone celebrated and imitated by young kids dressing in the "grunge" look; parents would have confiscated the records/tapes/CDs from their kids and would have enforced a dress code which drew the line at slovenliness. The same goes for violent video games which kids play today.

Sixth, there was no governmentally funded permanent welfare class. The "War on Poverty" has been one of the greatest social-political failures in U.S. history—and probably the costliest. (I've seen estimates as high as $21 trillion.) It has led directly to the breakup of families and to driving fathers out of the home, so that young people grow up without a male role model/authority figure immediately in their lives. The welfare rules first encourage unwed motherhood and then encourage unwed mothers to have more children to get more welfare money. (That's subsidizing promiscuity! No wonder promiscuity spreads.) They also penalize the mother if there is a male (wage-earner or not) in the household by reducing welfare payments. As a result, kids are running in the streets, getting into drugs and crime. In a socially destructive spiral, babies are having babies, and poorly educated and poorly socialized children are having children who are then even more poorly educated and socialized—all at the expense of the taxpayer. (That's subsidizing poverty! No wonder poverty spreads.) Moreover, when the children's parents are derelict in their responsibility, the government steps in to make the children wards of the state, as if this were the former Soviet Union, rather than relatives or private charity taking responsibility. The state becomes the authority/father figure as provider and protector. It's impossible to bond to that kind of Dad, but you sure can get addicted to the welfare payments and state-provided benefits. (Oh, did I mention that when I was a child, families sat down together for meals at regular times?)

Seventh, taxes were much lower, so that both parents in the typical family didn't have to work. The father's paycheck covered necessities. Today, according to various taxpayer organizations, local, state and federal taxes of all kinds—from income taxes to "hidden" taxes on your utility bills—take 50 cents out of every dollar earned by the typical American worker. For many families, the cost of living is so great that both parents have to work to support the household and its necessities. As a result, many children have become latchkey kids or are raised by grandparents or daycare centers which, however nice they may be, are a poor substitute for a solid family life.

Eighth and last, God was present in the schools. There is a sad joke about Columbine which goes like this. One of the murdered students, upon entering heaven, said, "God, you told me that if I placed my faith and trust in you, you would take care of me. Why did you allow me to be killed?" God shrugged His shoulders and replied, "Don't blame me. I wasn't allowed in school."

Since the 1963 U.S. Supreme Court decision banning prayer in school, the moral fabric of America has been coming unraveled at an accelerating rate. If the moral Source is absent, the moral force is also. It is no coincidence that since the ban on school prayer, which has been expanded into a ban on religious expression in general, our schools have been declining educationally and socially. Soaring statistics about sex crimes and violence, divorce, abortion and children born out of wedlock, sexually transmitted diseases, declining educational standards and performance, increasing use of profanity and vulgar language in public, disrespect for school authority, police and civil magistrates—all of this is directly traceable to the removal of moral, civic and patriotic influence on children which was inculcated through morning prayer, school exercises and curriculum which taught the idea that God is fundamental to the character of our nation and ourselves. As a bumper sticker puts it: *No God, no peace. Know God, know peace.*

## This Is Not a Simplistic Picture

Senior citizens can probably add a lot more to this picture of "the good old days." What I've just sketched is a simple picture, but it is not simplistic. Because America is declining in civility, morality and patriotism, our culture and our self-governance are degenerating, right down to the level of the basic social unit, the family, and that is why there is gun violence. Glamorous high-tech gadgets and shiny new SUVs for those who can afford them don't add up to moral improvement or to strengthening the fabric of society.

There are hopeful countervailing trends, of course. I've written about some of them in *The Meeting of Science and Spirit* and *Enlightenment 101*. I believe they herald the eventual emergence of a New Age or New Aeon—which I define as a higher form of humanity and its societal expression as a God-centered global culture founded on love and wisdom, reflecting heaven on earth.

However, at the level of popular culture today, our society is pretty sick. When a vulgar and violent athlete is idolized as a hero, when a foul-mouthed shock jock is listened to avidly on radio and TV, when a president shows absolutely no sense of shame, guilt or embarrassment over defiling his office by disgraceful, criminal misbehavior, the problem is not the athlete, the shock jock or the president. They are merely symptoms. The problem is the people who glamorize them and elect them and publicly support them, even when their wrongdoing is blatant and obviously destructive of a healthy, wholesome society.

The basic problem in America is an ignorant, apathetic citizenry. The problem is people who are complacent, irresponsible and morally numbed. The problem is people who care more about having 140 cable channels or 1,000 satellite channels coming into their living room than they care about educating their children in habits of good citizenship and getting involved in community service and civic improvement. (Sad joke: Pollster: "Sir, what do you think about the problem of citizen ignorance and apathy?" Citizen: "I don't know and I don't care.") The problem is people who look to government to do everything for them rather than being responsible for themselves.

## What Must Be Done?

This sad state of affairs has been developing for five decades or more, so it won't be fixed overnight. You can expect to see things continue downhill for a while, and there's no guarantee that America will survive—at least not the America which did more to raise the standard of living and quality of life for the common person than any other political or social experiment in history by creating a land of liberty, prosperity and opportunity.

However, since God is the inner director of human affairs—as our Founders stated in the Declaration of Independence—sooner or later we errants will learn to listen to conscience, which is the still, small voice of the Divine within us whispering eternally that which is true and right and good for us, and we will construct our lives, our communities and our civilization upon that, ushering in a new epoch in human history.

But we have the free will to ignore our conscience. So until then, you can expect to see more violence, vulgarity, venality and villainy, more disrespect, destruction and death. Don't give in to it, though; don't let it get you down. It's better to light one candle than to curse the darkness. God is still in charge of the universe and in His great love for His creations, God constantly offers us forgiveness and opportunity to change our ways. The question is whether we can recognize that and accept it—with humility, gratitude and true repentance—before the suffering and sorrow generated by our own misdeeds overwhelm us.

If America is to lead Earth toward a truly free, peaceful and prosperous world, with liberty and justice for all—which I believe it can and should do—we Americans must relearn the fundamentals which brought our country to global preeminence and our society to unprecedented freedom and prosperity. Those fundamentals can be stated simply. (See Appendix 2, "The One-Minute Patriot," for a more detailed statement of this.)

1. ***God is the author of our being—the source of our freedom, our sovereignty, our equality, our rights, our justice and our human dignity—and the moral authority for our laws***. That's what the Declaration of Independence and the Constitution are all about. Together, they offer the theory and practice of enlightened government and a free, morally sound society. That is what distinguishes America from all other nations and what places it at the leading edge of human and cultural development on this planet. The future of America is the future of the world. If America fails and falls, there will be global tyranny and a new Dark Ages more terrible than any before.

2. ***Since our nation functions on the principle of self-government, we must begin that government with ourselves because freedom always carries responsibility to use it properly***. Each person must govern her/himself personally in thought, word and deed, and see that those who don't or are too young to understand are brought within the circle of civility and social responsibility. That means behaving lawfully and decently, with a sense of respect for others which guides us in terms of honesty and public decorum. It means being independent and self-reliant, not looking to government for handouts. It means being responsible for our actions and taking the consequences when those actions are discovered to be unlawful or unethical, rather than whining about being victims or copping a legalistic but unjustified plea. It means being honorable and living with integrity.

3. ***We must be actively involved in the social and governmental functions of our nation because, as citizens, we are owners of the country and are therefore responsible for managing it***. That means relearning the principles of civil society and republican government, and applying them at the grassroots level. That means thinking globally while acting locally, and in community, to repair our own small piece of the social fabric. The strong moral fiber of individual citizens is what produces a strong social fabric.

4. ***The inculcation of morality and civility into children is what produces law-abiding adults who understand and uphold the ideals, principles and values which form society***. Law is the final resort for establishing standards of behavior and is, in reality, only an last-step measure for controlling behavior. It is necessary only to the extent that we do not govern ourselves morally and wisely. The first level of government—the family—is where a moral, civil society begins.

Nowadays, the Declaration of Independence and the Constitution, and the ideals, principles and values they embody, are under severe attack. Our national motto is "In

God we trust," but many Americans have so misunderstood our national heritage—and even deliberately twisted it—that they are attacking the very foundations of American government and American society. Morality is the first line of defense of civilization against both anarchy and tyranny, but they and their supporters are trying to de-moralize and secularize America. They are literally acting in an ungodly manner which is self-destructive. They don't understand that the Founders wanted to keep church and state separate, not God and state. Without a clear and public sense of God as the foundation of America—which was self-evident to those who wrote the Declaration of Independence and the Constitution—our downward spiral into a degenerate society will continue. As things are right now, we're in a race to the bottom.

We need a course-correction urgently. We need to restore a common sense of civility, morality and patriotism to America. Without that, the result is clearly foreseeable: the ruin of the republic and the creation of a totalitarian police state which will extend around the globe.

---

## FOOTNOTES

[1] There is an even deeper aspect to the situation. G. Gordon Liddy explains in *When I Was a Kid, This Was a Free Country* (Regnery: Washington, D.C., 2002, pp. 19-20):

> The Founding Fathers [and] the Framers of our Constitution...understood that the right of the individual to keep and bear arms is a God-given right—a *moral obligation*, in fact, because God, having given us our lives and blessed the unions that resulted in our families, holds us accountable for preserving those lives....All of the Framers of the Constitution understood, therefore, that the right of individuals to keep and bear arms preexisted, and existed independently of, any government they could or would create....

> Thus, Richard Henry Lee, a driving force behind the Bill of Rights, said, "To preserve liberty, it is essential that the whole body of the people always possess arms, and be taught alike, especially when young, how to use them." Patrick Henry of Virginia, he of "give me liberty or give me death" fame...said, "The great object is, that every man be armed....Everyone who is able may have a gun." James Madison, in *The Federalist* No. 46, excoriated the European governments that were "afraid to trust the people with arms" and stressed "the advantage of being armed, which the Americans possess over the people of almost every other nation."

***The issue, therefore, is not gun control but crime control***. Guns are simply another piece of technology which can be used for good (national defense, police protection) or evil (robbery and murder). As someone who understands the situation well put it: "My pistol and rifle are only tools. I am the weapon." The capacity for misuse is not inherent in guns themselves; it depends on the intentions and actions of the people using them. Immoral or irresponsible people will use guns immorally or irresponsibly.

Therefore, until we have a society of none but moral citizens who use their freedom responsibly, there will be a need for weapons to oppose the violence which some sick individuals will try to inflict on innocent, peaceful, law-abiding people. And if the violence is being aimed at you by a crazy shooter, wouldn't you want "a fighting chance" by having access to a gun for use in defending yourself? A gun in the hand is better than a cop on the phone. (Cautionary words from a cop: "When seconds count, we're only minutes away.")

In an enlightened society, there will be no intentional killing of people by guns. Presently, however, muggers, robbers, rapists, psychopaths, terrorists and murderers abound, threatening us with violence. In such a situation, there's usually not a policeman around when you need one, so protecting yourself from harm is your personal responsibility and, as Liddy notes above, your moral obligation. Everyone has to be his or her own first line of defense. I extol the wisdom of our Founders that the Second Amendment guarantees every law-abiding citizen the right to keep and bear arms. A well-armed populace deters muggers, robbers, rapists, psychopaths, terrorists and murderers; violent crime goes down as more people are armed and have the right to carry a concealed weapon, as Prof. John Lott shows in his book *More Guns, Less Crime.* In America, there are more than 20,000 gun laws and the most stringent are in New York City and Washington, D.C. Now guess which two cities are the most violent in the nation. In fact, Washington, D.C., is the murder capital of the nation.

My wife and I sent our four children through the National Rifle Association handgun training course so that (1) they're not afraid of guns or of being around guns, (2) they know how to use guns safely and properly, (3) they understand, up close and personal, that guns are lethal and should never be used carelessly or for any illegal purpose, and (4) they understand that the decision to carry a gun must include a firm answer to the question, "Am I willing to shoot to kill?" (Unless you can take that last step, you probably should not carry a gun because it might be taken away from you by an attacker and used against you. People high on drugs are often insensitive to pain; merely wounding them may not stop them.) And understand this: you don't shoot to kill; you shoot to stay alive. Importantly, according to the NRA, an estimated 17 million American women own or carry guns for self-defense (*America's First Freedom,* May 2001, p. 20).

In 1999, the Libertarian Party released the suppressed findings of a 1993-1995 study of kids and guns conducted by the U.S. Department of Justice's Office of Juvenile Justice and Delinquency Prevention. According to the government's own report, children who get guns from their parents are less likely to commit any kind of street crime (14 percent) than children who have no gun in the house (24 percent)—and are significantly less likely to do so than children who acquire an illegal gun (74 percent). Steve Dasbach, the Libertarian Party national director then, commented on the study, "The evidence is in: The simplest way to reduce firearm-related violence among children is to buy them a gun and teach them how to use it responsibly."

Likewise, the Justice Department's research arm, the Bureau of Justice Statistics, reported in October 2000 (as noted by the *Wall Street Journal* on 12/11/2000) that gun-related deaths and woundings dropped 33 percent from 1993 to 1997, yet during that same time, according to statistics from the Bureau of Alcohol, Tobacco and Firearms, the number of firearms in circulation in the U.S. rose nearly 10 percent. In other words, there is no direct correlation between the proliferation of firearms in the U.S. and gun violence. More guns, less crime.

Furthermore, in 2003 the Centers for Disease Control and Prevention (CDC), another agency of the federal government, reported that a sweeping, three-year review of the nation's gun control laws—including mandatory waiting periods and bans on certain weapons—found no proof such measures reduce firearm violence.

Last of all, in 2004 the U.S. Department of Justice's Office of Legal counsel of the United States addressed the question of "whether the right secured by the Second amendment belongs only to the states, only to persons serving in state-organized militia units like the National guard, or to individuals generally." In a memorandum it stated definitively: "The Second Amendment secures a right of individuals generally, not a right of states or a right restricted to persons serving in militias." The 102-page memorandum posted on the DoJ's website makes clear that the right to keep and bear arms is an individual right for the purpose of self-defense of one's person, property, home and family.

Since those facts are inarguable and are clearly known to those in and out of government who are advocating gun control, their stance is hypocritical and probably designed as part of a policy of incrementalism intended to eventually confiscate all guns and totally disarm America. Those who love liberty should question and challenge that stance; it is a sinister one. The Second Amendment does not read, "A well-regulated population being necessary to the security of a police state, the right of the Government to seize and destroy arms shall not be infringed." Gun control isn't about guns; it's about control. An armed person is a citizen; an unarmed person is a subject. When you remove the people's right to keep and bear arms, you create slaves. So remember: Gun control works—just ask Hitler, Stalin, Mao Zedong, Saddam Hussein and Fidel Castro. (And that's why I'm a life member of the NRA; I put freedom first.)

The following letter to the editor of a local newspaper is a more recent and succinct statement of the argument for crime control, not gun control:

The raging debate about gun violence is clouded by ignorance, misinformation, illogical thinking and irrational fears. For example, a recent Heritage Foundation report on Parkland High School-style shootings notes that firearm deaths on school campuses are incredibly rare.

…the gun-control advocacy group Everytown for Gun Safety makes the dramatic claim that 18 school shootings occurred during the first six weeks of 2018.

But Everytown uses an extremely broad definition of the term "school shooting" and includes all incidents in which "a firearm was discharged inside a school building or on school or campus grounds."

They include accidental discharges, suicides, incidents that did not result in injury, and shootings that took place outside of school hours involving persons unaffiliated with the school.

The "18 school shootings" include an incident that occurred between nonstudents in a high school parking lot at 8 p.m., well after school hours, in which no one was injured.

Everytown also counts an incident in which a 31-year-old man shot himself in the parking lot of a closed-down elementary school.

In other words, the "18 school shootings" claim, while certainly attention-grabbing, is misleading…

While none of this is meant to underestimate the tragedies that have occurred or the urgent need to address them, America's primary and secondary schools are safer than they have been in decades, and violent deaths of any kind rarely occur on school property.

Four times as many children were killed in schools in the early 1990s than are killed today, and the number of shooting incidents involving students has been declining steadily for the past 30 years. (https://www.heritage.org/homeland-security/commentary/parkland-style-shootings-are-devastating-highly-unusual)

Guns don't kill people; guns don't shoot themselves. People kill people. More specifically, terrorists, mentally deranged people and criminally minded people kill people. Law-abiding, responsible people do not cause gun violence. You could place a firearm in their hands and be safe from harm by it for a thousand years. But threaten their life or the life of their loved ones and they are likely to use their firearm to protect themselves and their families—as they should and are legally allowed to do.

People who want to abolish the Second Amendment don't understand that it is the first among equals in the Bill of Rights because without it, none of the other rights can be guaranteed.

The issue isn't gun control; the issue is *crime* control. Gun control is like trying to reduce drunk driving by making it tougher for sober people to own cars. Gun control isn't about guns; it's about control—of you and me. Does gun control work? Just ask Hitler, Stalin, Mao and Castro.

In a free society such as ours, people have access to guns because we have an inherent right to life and self-defense. A gun is a tool which can be used for good or evil; the user makes the choice. But if guns are outlawed, only outlaws will have guns.

As for so-called assault weapons, they do not exist outside of the military and properly authorized groups such as SWAT teams, the Secret Service and licensed firing ranges. All others are obtained illegally by theft or design modification. The AR-15 rifle fires just one bullet per trigger pull, the same as any hunting rifle or pistol. Applying the term "assault" to an ordinary rifle, however much it may look like a military rifle, is sheer propaganda and lies.

As for crime control, here are the facts:

1. Assault is a behavior, not a device.

2. A gun in the hand is better than a cop on the phone. (As one police officer put it, "When seconds count, we're only minutes away.")

3. The best gun control is a steady aim.

4. You don't shoot to kill; you shoot to stay alive.

5. The only person who can stop a bad guy with a gun is a good guy with a gun (as a school resource officer showed recently in the Great Mills, Maryland high school).

6. Research shows that more armed law-abiding citizens equals less crime.

7. Research also shows that stronger punishment for crimes involving guns reduces crime.

Crime control begins at home by teaching children respect for life and property, respect for police and teachers, respect for law and duly constituted authority, and respect for guns and gun safety. It is reinforced in school, places of worship and by public figures who understand and uphold the need for a moral society to keep America free and secure.

2 This unattributed piece of childrearing wisdom from the internet speaks directly to a related problem in America—the rampant use of illegal drugs. As a libertarian, I think the federal War on Drugs is profoundly misguided and a waste of taxpayer money. Legalization of illicit drugs—the same as alcohol—would stop drug trafficking practically overnight, bring drugs under rational control and pour tax money into state coffers, while emptying overcrowded prisons. It would also dry up a major source of terrorist funding. Nevertheless, the point here is parental care and control of children, and it is a point well made in clear, simple language.

## THE DRUG PROBLEM IN AMERICA

The other day, someone at a store in our town read that a methamphetamine lab had been found in an old farmhouse in the adjoining county, and he asked me a question: "Why didn't we have a drug problem when you and I were growing up?"

I replied that I did indeed have a drug problem when I was young.

I was drug to church on Sunday morning.

I was drug to church for weddings and funerals.

I was drug to family reunions and community socials, no matter the weather.

I was drug by my ears when I was disrespectful to adults.

I was also drug to the woodshed when I disobeyed my parents, told a lie, brought home a bad report card, did not speak with respect, spoke ill of the teacher or the preacher, or if I didn't put forth my best effort in everything that was asked of me.

I was drug to the kitchen sink to have my mouth washed out with soap if I uttered a profane four-letter word.

I was drug out to pull weeds in mom's garden and flower beds and cockleburs out of dad's fields.

I was drug to the homes of family, friends and neighbors to help out some poor soul who had no one to mow the yard, repair the clothesline, or chop some firewood; and if my mother had ever known that I took a single dime as a tip for this kindness, she would have drug me back to the woodshed.

Those drugs are still in my veins and they affect my behavior in everything I do, say and think. They are stronger than cocaine, crack or heroin, and if today's children had this kind of drug problem, America would be a better place.

–Author unknown

Sidebar 13

# WHY I'M RUNNING FOR THE BOARD OF EDUCATION

*This is the text of an ad I placed locally at the start of my 2005 campaign to become a member of the Board of Education. I lost the election, coming in fourth of nine candidates running for three seats.*

I am a candidate for the Board of Education. I've never sought elective office before and, quite honestly, I have no wish to do so now. I'd rather be playing with my grandchildren, hiking or reading a good book.

I am not interested in power, fame, fortune, status or any other kind of self-aggrandizement. My life is dedicated to serving God by serving people, so there's no room in it for foolish ego games. I place principles before party. I'm a republican first, then a Republican. My loyalty is to the Constitution and the American republic.

Then why am I a candidate? Simply this: my sense of civic responsibility and community service compels me to run. I'm running because I love America as the country which has done more good for the common person than any other nation in history. I'm running because I love America as the country based on the highest and most universal value: freedom. I'm running because I love America as the land of hope and opportunity. And I'm running because I see America departing from all that.

## My Concerns

*I think America is declining in civility, morality and patriotism.* Those are the key indicators of health or sickness in the body politic. America is declining because we, the first nation in history to be consciously founded on spiritual principles, are departing from those principles and losing our way. (The principles are stated in our founding document, the Declaration of Independence.) We are straying from the fundamentals which built and preserved this great nation. Our culture is degenerating into vulgarity and violence as the standards of civility, morality and patriotism are forgotten or ignored. It is also degenerating from a republic to an empire and from liberty to government control of "we the people."

If America is to remain the land of the free and the home of the brave, rather than become the land of the freeloaders and the home of the depraved, we must return to the fundamentals of our republican form of government and our once-godly society. That means we need to walk the talk ourselves and teach it to our children.

*Youth is 20% of the population but 100% of the future.* If young people don't understand the fundamentals of America and don't appreciate the magnificent heritage left for them by earlier generations, in a few years there won't be an America—at least, not the America I know and love. This nation will descend into depravity and despotism (and it looks like we're in a race to the bottom right now).

When national surveys show that large numbers of high school seniors and college freshmen don't know who their congressional delegates are, and don't know who commanded the American forces at the Battle of Yorktown, something is profoundly wrong with their education. When three CHS graduates who were honor students don't know what D-Day is (this actually happened), something is profoundly wrong with their education. When a CHS student told the Medal of Honor Plaza committee which built the plaza at Bartlem Park, "Oh, I know what the Medal of Honor is. My brother won one in track," something is profoundly wrong with her education. When I march in the Veterans Color Guard in the Memorial Day parade and I see children and their parents fail to stand and salute as the flag goes by, something is profoundly wrong with their education. When I hear young people applaud after "Taps" is played, as if it were a musical performance rather than a tribute to our honored military dead, something is profoundly wrong with their education.

But if young people don't know all that, it's not their fault. It's ours—the parents, teachers, administrators, community leaders and veterans. I'm not blaming the students; I'm simply pointing out major deficiencies in their learning. But they are dangerous deficiencies. They bear on the very existence of America.

## My Objectives

That's why I'm running for the Board of Education. I want to improve the intellectual, civic and moral education of students, so they become responsible, patriotic citizens. Beyond that, I want to restore authority and local control to the school system itself by getting the state and federal government off the backs of teachers and administrators, who have to spend far too much time complying with bureaucratic regulations imposed on them by Hartford and Washington. I want teachers to be free to teach, not worrying about some politically correct mandate to which they must submit. I want administrators to be free to administer as the senior educators in the school system rather than drowning in the paperwork flooding them from state and federal educrats.

Most of all, I want to place before students, via the curriculum, an inspiring vision of what life can be for them personally and for America as global society draws evermore closely together. I want to educate them in the most fundamental sense of the word, which comes from the Latin *educere*. It means to draw out that which is within, that which is potential in them, that which is their highest and best, that which is most satisfying to them personally, in head, hand and heart. I want to offer them education for enlightenment.

## My Qualifications

Am I an idealistic dreamer? Yes. Does that mean I'm naive and impractical? No.

I know education from all sides. I've been a student and a teacher at Cheshire High School. I've taught English and journalism there and on the college level at Quinnipiac, Gateway and Southern Connecticut State. I have a bachelor of arts degree from Dartmouth (which I attended on an NROTC scholarship) and a master of education degree from Yale (which I attended on the GI Bill). I've served as chief administrator of a small private school for adult education and I've worked in private industry (I'm retired from Northeast Utilities). I've been a freelance writer who's published 15 books and had my writing appear in the *New York Times, Reader's Digest, Esquire, Omni* and *Woman's Day.* (For me, writing is an extension of the classroom.) I've worked as

Director of Education for an astronaut doing scientific research on psychic phenomena and the powers of the mind.

I've also been a rebel and a pain in the you-know-what to earlier Boards of Education here in town because I thought things could be done better to educate students, and I wouldn't stop calling for excellence in education. (So they fired me. But that was a blessing in disguise, and later I thanked them for it. Yet in my heart of hearts, I'm always a teacher and always in the classroom with young people.) Some may remember me challenging authority during the Vietnam War when I accused the President of giving false information to Congress about the Gulf of Tonkin events which led our nation to war. Because I'd been a nuclear weapons officer in the Pacific at that time and read classified messages, I knew the true facts, and my sense of patriotism and my conscience compelled me to speak out.

My wife and I met in CHS nearly 50 years ago. We've sent our four children through the Cheshire school system and I've struggled to pay my taxes in support of that. I'm now a senior citizen living on fixed income, so I know the strain which the school system places on the elderly of Cheshire who helped to build this town into a beautiful, thriving community and now feel themselves being squeezed out because of the high cost of living.

## My Campaign

If I'm elected to the Board of Education, I'll bring all that to the table. I'm thinking globally but acting locally to return America to a position of righteous world leadership, safe streets and neighborhoods, and a refuge for those who want to come here legally, as my ancestors did. I want to restore a public sense of the self-evident truth which led our Founders to pledge their lives, their fortunes and their sacred honor to construct a nation in which self-government begins with each citizen governing himself civilly and morally.

**My campaign platform is the Pledge of Allegiance, my campaign logo is the American flag, my campaign song is "The Star-Spangled Banner" and my campaign slogan is "One Nation Under God."**

Please consider this and then *vote your conscience.*

*Paid for by **John White for BOE Committee**. Barbara White, Treasurer.*
*This campaign is self-funded. No contributions will be sought or accepted.*

# Part II

# THE STAR-SPANGLED BANNER

## Chapter 12

# THE FLAG OF OUR NATION

A thoughtful mind when it sees a nation's flag, sees not the flag, but the nation itself. And whatever may be its symbols, its insignia, he reads chiefly in the flag, the government, the principles, the truths, the history that belongs to the nation that sets it forth. The American flag has been a symbol of Liberty and men rejoiced in it.

– Henry Ward Beecher, "The American Flag,"
written at the start of the Civil War

There is no better symbol of our country's values and traditions than the Flag of the United States of America. Chosen by the Continental Congress in 1777, it continues to exemplify the profound commitment to freedom, equality, and opportunity made by our founders more than two centuries ago. Our flag's proud stars and stripes have long inspired our people, and its beautiful red, white, and blue design is known around the world as a beacon of liberty and justice.

– President William J. Clinton, Proclamation of Flag Day
and National Flag Week, June 7, 1996

Our flag is a symbol of the United States in all its aspects: historical, societal, philosophical, metaphysical. It represents the total experience of America and the American people from the founding of our nation to the present. It also represents our philosophy of government—a recognition that life, liberty, personal sovereignty, individual rights, equality, justice, human dignity and the opportunity to pursue happiness are given to us by God because that is the only basis which can guarantee those blessings for everyone. Last of all, it represents our great traditions, institutions and ideals: national sovereignty, representative democracy in a constitutional federal republic, the rule of law, and people of diverse backgrounds living and working together as free citizens. It is an honored symbol of America's unity, achievements, glory and high resolve. In short, the flag represents our country in its fullness. Just as patriotism was defined by a simple formula in Chapter 1, so can our flag be defined: ***The American flag stands for faith + family + freedom.***

To create a nation based on liberty and justice for all, our flag has been drenched in human sorrows and consecrated by American blood. It is the symbol of the most enduring free people who have ever lived. And although it is a symbol, it is also considered to be a living thing. President Woodrow Wilson said, "Though silent, it speaks to us—speaks to us of the past; of the men and women who went before us and of the record they wrote into it."

In the American Legion's *Americanism Manual* (p. 34), our flag has been described with these words:

> It embodies the essence of patriotism. Its spirit is the spirit of the American Nation. Its history is the history of the American people. Emblazoned upon its folds in letters of living light are the names and fame of our heroic dead, the Fathers of the Republic who devoted upon its altars their lives, their fortunes and their sacred honor. Twice-told tales of National honor and glory cluster thickly about it. Ever victorious, it has emerged triumphant from nine great national conflicts. It bears witness to the immense expansion of our national boundaries, the development of our natural resources, and the splendid structure of our civilization. It prophesies the triumph of popular government, of civic and religious liberty and of National righteousness throughout the world.

In an earlier era, when warriors marched into battle behind their regimental and national colors (and children played "Capture the Flag" knowing what that meant), our flag was regarded by our soldiers as the rallying point of action. It represented everything for which they fought—home, corps and country—and it contained the honor, valor and hopes of every man around it. "Our flag must never falter, touch the ground in defeat or be lowered to an enemy," they silently said, and they guarded it courageously, even unto death. The greatest shame in battle was to surrender one's flag to a victor, but the American flag has been unvanquished.

> *Yes, we'll rally round the flag, boys, we'll rally once again,*
> *Shouting the battle cry of Freedom.*
> – "The Battle Cry of Freedom," George Frederick Root, 1863.

The great American heritage of freedom is the most precious possession of the entire world. Because our flag embodies that glorious achievement and ideal, it is worthy of our honor, our affections, our deepest sacrifices. We revere the flag, not through unquestioning worship but from a deep appreciation of our national heritage and from gratitude for our good fortune to be Americans. What other nation in all of human history has stated, as the Preamble to our Constitution does, that it was founded "in order to form a more perfect union, establish justice, insure domestic tranquility, provide for the common defense, promote the general welfare, and secure the blessings of liberty to ourselves and our posterity"? [1] In our flag we see our nation itself and the proud history upon which it stands.

Equally important is how others see our flag. Floating from the lofty pinnacle of American idealism, it is a beacon of enduring hope to the oppressed of all lands. It floats over an assemblage of people from every race, creed and color whose united hearts constitute an indivisible and invincible force for the defense and aid of the downtrodden. It proclaims liberty and justice for all people.

Sadly but undeniably, the American flag has sometimes been used to excite patriotic feelings and allegiance to government policies and actions which do not accord with the ideals, principles and values on which our Founders created this nation. Those who originated, promoted and endorsed those policies and actions have invariably cloaked them in the American flag. in order to evoke unquestioning loyalty to their schemes or misguided stances, they have drawn the red, white and blue fabric around something which was unconstitutional and contrary to our best interests as Americans.

Such misuse of the flag is something Americans must always look for; it is part of the price of freedom. Vigilance by patriots is necessary to prevent abuse of the Constitution and all else which makes America great. Our heartfelt allegiance must be grounded in understanding and discernment so that our flag always stands for what we say in the Pledge of Allegiance. As I noted in Chapter 5, the Constitution governs the government. If a government policy or action departs from it, no amount of flag-fabric should lead us to accept or condone it. The meaning of the flag must never depart from our Constitution and the foundation principles on which it stands. [2]

## The Name of the Flag

The official name of our nation's flag is "The Flag of the United States of America." It is also referred to as the National Flag, National Ensign, National Color and National Standard. The term "National Flag" is applicable regardless of size or manner of display, but the other terms have certain well-defined usages of long standing within the armed services. "National Ensign" is used by the Navy in a general manner, although it actually indicates the national flag flown by planes, ships and boats. "National Color" pertains to a flag carried by an infantry regiment or by any foot or unmounted unit and the flag is stubbier than the National Ensign. "National Standard" is carried by a cavalry regiment or by any mounted, mechanized and motorized units.

However, as with a good friend, Americans speak of our flag by simple nicknames rather than the full, formal name. The most common names for our flag are Stars and Stripes, Star-Spangled Banner, Old Glory, and the Red, White and Blue. How it got the name Stars and Stripes is unknown, but it dates from the Revolutionary era. Francis Scott Key first called our flag the Star-Spangled Banner in his 1814 poem "The Defense of Fort M'Henry," which became our national anthem. William Driver, a ship captain from Salem, Massachusetts, named our flag Old Glory in 1824 (see Chapter 10).

## The Design of the Flag

The flag of our country has 13 horizontal stripes—seven red and six white, with red stripes on the top and bottom. The stripes remind us of the 13 original colonies which constituted America as a new nation and gained us our liberty. The flag has 50 five-pointed stars arranged in alternating rows of six and five in a blue field in the upper left quadrant. The stars represent the 50 states bound together as one nation. The field of blue is technically called a canton, meaning a square or rectangular area of a flag, on the upper left next to the staff or flagpole. However, with reference to the American flag and its stars symbolizing the states as the Union, the canton is generally called the union or field of stars. According to a booklet about the flag published by the U.S. House of Representatives in 1977, "The star is a symbol of the heavens and the divine goal to which man has aspired from time immemorial; the stripe is symbolic of the rays of light emanating from the sun."

Early American flags were far from standardized in design. Some had more than 13 stripes; others had as few as nine. Their stars were likewise irregular. Some had them arranged in rows, some were in squares or circles.

Similarly, the dimensions of the flag were not standardized prior to the 20th century. On October 29, 1912, President William Howard Taft established the legal dimensions by an executive order. If the hoist (height) is 1 unit, then the fly (length) must be 1.9 the height. The height of the union must be 7/13, the fly of the union must be 0.76, the width of each stripe must be 1/13 and the diameter of each star .0616.

What about gold trim or fringe on the flag? Although it is not an official part of the flag's design, neither is it improper. The gold trim is generally used on ceremonial indoor flags for special services and is believed to have been first used in a military setting. It has no specific significance and its use is in compliance with applicable flag codes and laws. According to the Institute of Heraldry, our nation's official body for that subject, placing a fringe on the flag is optional with the person or organization, and no Act of Congress or Executive Order prohibits the practice. *So Proudly We Hail, The History of the United States Flag* by William R. Furlong and Byron McCandless (Smithsonian Institute Press, Washington, D.C., 1981) notes:

> Fringe is used on indoor flags only, as fringe on flags on outdoor flags would deteriorate rapidly. The fringe on a flag is considered an 'honorable enrichment only,' and its official use by the U.S. Army dates from 1895. A 1925 Attorney General's Opinion states: "...the fringe does not appear to be regarded as an integral part of the Flag and its presence cannot be said to constitute an unauthorized addition to the design prescribed by statute. An external fringe is to be distinguished from letters, words, or emblematic designs printed or superimposed upon the body of the flag itself. Under law, such additions might be open to objection as unauthorized; but the same is not necessarily true of the fringe."

## The Colors of the Flag

When the flag was created in 1777, no records were left to explain the meaning of the flag's colors. However, European heraldic tradition for designing shields or coats of arms for families probably governed the situation. According to that tradition, red meant military fortitude or magnanimity, white meant peace and sincerity, and blue meant loyalty and truth.

The meaning of our flag's colors was first stated in 1782 in a report to Congress by the committee charged with designing the Great Seal of the United States. The resolution authorizing a committee to design a seal was passed on July 4, 1776. It was felt that the new nation needed a seal to reflect the Founders' ideals, principles and values, and the sovereignty of the United States of America. The seal would be the official "signature" of the nation. Several designs were submitted to Congress but rejected. Not until 1782 was a design for the Great Seal accepted and made official.

On June 20, 1782, Charles Thomson, Secretary of the Continental Congress, stated in a report to Congress that the seal's escutcheon has the same colors and meaning as those of the flag. He wrote, "White signifies purity and innocence, Red hardiness & valor, and Blue...signifies vigilance, perseverance & justice."

Today it is more broadly—but unofficially—said that red stands for the courage, heroism and sacrifices of the 44,000,000 men and women who have served in the armed services of our country, and the blood shed to preserve our liberty; white stands for peacefulness and the purity of our high ideals; and blue, the color of the heavens, connotes the justice, strength, loyalty and unity of all our states. [3] The heavens is where God resides and God is the foundation of America—the source of our freedom, our sovereignty, our equality, our rights, our justice and our human dignity.

## The U.S. Flag Code

The display of our flag is governed by law to assure that it is treated with the respect due the flag of a great nation. The U.S. Flag Code prescribes proper display of and respect for the Flag of the United States. It is a guide for all handling and display of the flag. It is established by U.S. Code Title 36, Patriotic Societies and Observances, Chapter 10, "Patriotic Customs." (See Appendix 1 for the text of the Flag Code.)

Previous to Flag Day, June 14, 1923, there were no federal or state regulations governing display of the United States Flag. At that time the American Legion called for a National Flag Conference to draft a code of flag etiquette for civilians. Representatives of the Army and Navy, which had evolved their own procedures, and 71 private organizations met in Washington, D.C. Their purpose was to provide guidance based on Army and Navy procedures relating to display and associated questions about the U.S. flag.

President Warren G. Harding, in addressing the conference, said, "I hope that you will succeed in formulating a code that will be welcomed by all Americans, and that every patriotic and educational society in the Republic will commit itself to the endorsement and observance and purposes of the code that you adopt here today."

The resulting National Flag Code was adopted by all organizations in attendance, although it had no official government sanction. Nevertheless, it represented the authoritative opinion of the principal patriotic bodies of the nation, both civilian and military. A few minor changes were made a year later during the Flag Day 1924 Conference. Over time, the National Flag Code became widely accepted.

However, it was not until June 22, 1942, that Congress passed a joint resolution on the subject. The resolution was amended and on December 22, 1942, with some changes, was made the law of our land. Its precise title is Public Law 829; Chapter 806, 77th Congress, 2nd session. Exact rules for use and display of the flag (36 U.S.C. 173-178) as well as associated sections (36 U.S.C. 171), Conduct during Playing of the National Anthem, (36 U.S.C. 172) the Pledge of Allegiance to the Flag, and Manner of Delivery were included.

A joint resolution of the Senate and House of Representatives, Public Law 94-344, was enacted by the 94th Congress on July 7, 1976, to amend the Code. The Code does not impose penalties for misuse of the flag. That is left to the states and to the federal government of the District of Columbia. Each state has its own flag law.

Promotion of respect for the flag and knowledge about it is required in most states, usually through flag exercises, programs or instruction. However, in 1943 the U.S. Supreme Court ruled (in the case of *West Virginia State Board of Education v. Barnette et al*) it unconstitutional for state boards of education or local school boards to make the flag salute compulsory. (See Chapter 2 for details.)

## Flag Etiquette

The fundamental rule of flag etiquette is: Treat the Stars and Stripes with respect and common sense.

The flag is flown at full-staff to indicate joy—the joy of being American. It is flown at half-staff to indicate mourning. In either case, it should always be aloft and free. Likewise, a flagpole should be freestanding, with no guide wires supporting it. When raising the flag to half-staff, raise it briskly to the top of the flagpole for a moment before lowering it. When taking it down for the night, raise it to the top of the flagpole again and then lower it to the bottom.

The flag should be flown daily from sunrise to sunset in good weather from public buildings, schools, permanent staffs in the open and near polling places on election days. An all-weather flag may also be flown in bad weather. When a patriotic effect is desired, the flag may be displayed twenty-four hours a day if properly illuminated during the hours of darkness.

The flag should always be flown on national and state holidays and on those occasions proclaimed by the President (see Sidebar 9). On Memorial Day, the flag should be displayed at half-staff until noon.

The flag should be hoisted briskly and lowered ceremoniously. It should never be dipped to any person or thing, nor should it ever be displayed with the union down except as a signal of dire distress. When lowered, it should be received by waiting hands and arms, and should not touch the ground.

To store the flag, ceremoniously fold it lengthwise in half, then repeat with the blue field on the outside. Finally, while one person holds it by the blue field, another them makes a triangular fold in the opposite end, continuing to fold it in triangles until only the blue field shows. (See Sidebar 8 for full instructions.)

The flag should never be allowed to touch anything beneath it, nor should it ever be carried flat or horizontally.

The flag should never be used as drapery or decoration, for carrying or holding anything, or stored in such a manner that it will be damaged or soiled.

When draped across a wall or building, or hung across a street, the union should be in the upper left corner as viewed by pedestrians.

The flag should never be used for advertising purposes in any manner whatsoever, nor should any picture, drawing, insignia or other decoration be placed upon or attached to the flag, its staff or halyard. The flag should not be embroidered on personal items nor printed on anything designed for temporary use and then discarded.

No flag or pennant may be flown above the flag or, if on the same level, to the right of the flag, except during church services conducted by naval chaplains at sea, when the church pennant may be flown above the flag during church services for the personnel of the Navy.

Never throw away a flag! When a flag is no longer of dignified appearance and cannot be repaired, or when a flag is so worn or soiled that it is no longer suitable for display, it should be destroyed in a dignified manner, preferably by burning (see Chapter 11).

When the American flag passes by in a color guard, stop talking, stand at attention and, when it is six paces away, cross your heart with your right hand until it is six paces past you. Men and boys should remove their hats. People in uniform should salute in the manner prescribed by their organization. According to a recent change in the U.S. Flag Code (see Appendix 1), veterans also may salute in military fashion, even if in civilian clothes. If the flag is simply part of a float or is being carried in some way other than in a color guard, no action is necessary.

The National salute to the flag is 21 guns. The salute is not fired on Sunday unless required by international courtesy.

Although the flag of our nation has undergone many changes throughout our history, none of the earlier ones are considered to be obsolete (see Chapter 10). They are simply representative of a previous era. They may be flown as "legal" and are entitled to the same respect as our current-day flag.

## Military Funeral Honors

Rendering final honors to someone who served in the military is an age-old worldwide custom. In America, the primary objective of all military funeral honors is to provide the deceased's family with a reverent, respectful and professional service befitting a citizen who served in our armed forces.

Congress has long directed that upon request of the next of kin, all eligible veterans must receive military honors when they pass on. It is considered a sacred duty on behalf of a grateful nation.

The ceremonial paying of respect and gratitude to those who have faithfully served and defended our nation must include the sounding of Taps, the ceremonial folding of the American flag which covers the casket or urn, and presentation of the flag to the next of kin by the military funeral honors detail leader. A firing party to fire three volleys over the grave of the deceased is optional, depending upon availability. Military pallbearers are likewise optional.

The order of events in the military funeral honors portion of the funeral ceremony begins with the sounding of Taps, followed by the folding of the flag and the presentation of the flag. If a firing party is present, the volleys are fired before the sounding of Taps. The sounding itself may be done by a bugler (military or civilian) or, if no bugler is available, by playing a recording of Taps. Mourners are asked by the funeral director to stand for the rendering of honors. Upon completion of Taps, the funeral director will request that the mourners be seated. Then the flag is folded and presented by the military funeral honors detail leader, who speaks to the next of kin with words of gratitude on behalf of the President and the nation. The detail leader also offers condolences.

## Interesting Facts about the U.S. Flag

• The U.S. flag is the fourth oldest national flag in the world (after Denmark, Sweden and the Netherlands).

• The only time it is appropriate to fly the United States flag upside down is in an emergency. An upside down flag is a universal distress signal.

• The length of time the flag is flown at half-staff as a sign of mourning depends on the office the person held. The time is thirty days after the death of a president or former president; ten days after the death of a vice president, the chief justice or a retired chief justice of the Supreme Court, or the speaker of the House of Representatives; until the burial of an associate justice of the Supreme Court, secretary of a military department, a former vice president, or the governor of a state, territory or possession; on the day of and the day after a member of Congress; and on Memorial Day until noon.

• During the manufacturing process of the American flag, the leftover material of which the flags are made is never allowed to fall to the floor. Containers are always placed around the cutting tables and the material falls into them.

• The only person who has ever been honored for cutting an American flag into pieces was explorer Robert Peary. Upon his arrival at the North Pole in 1909, Peary cut up a flag and left pieces scattered all over the area.

• The U.S. flag was the first flag to be flown on the moon. The flag which the Apollo 11 astronauts Neil Armstrong and Edwin "Buzz" Aldrin raised on the moon on July 20, 1969 is made of nylon and framed in an extended position in an aluminum frame.

• The ball at the top of official flagpoles is called a "truck." By custom and tradition, inside the truck on flagpoles on official government installations is a .45 caliber bullet, a .38 caliber bullet and a bullet for an M-16 rifle. If the truck should happen to fall and hit the ground, it is constructed in such a manner that it will break into 13 pieces, each piece representing one of the original colonies.

• According to tradition, at the base of every flagpole on an official government installation is a box buried in concrete. This box contains one saber, a .38 caliber pistol and a book of matches. In the event an enemy overtakes the last government installation, the survivor is to defend the flag with the saber and pistol, and burn the flag with the matches so the enemy cannot capture the flag.

• The largest American flag is 255 feet wide by 505 feet long. Suspended horizontally, the "Superflag" was unfurled for display on Flag Day, June 14, 1998, at Moffett Field Air Station in California. Its stars are 17 feet across and its stripes are almost 20 feet wide. It weighs 3,000 pounds. It was commissioned by Thomas Demski of Long Beach, California, who is now deceased. The flag travels in its own motor home, touring the country on display.

• The smallest American flag measures only five microns. (A human hair is 100 microns thick.) It is on a computer chip made by Integrated Device Technology company.

• The highest American flag is the one on the moon placed there by Apollo 11 astronauts in 1969.

• There are now six American flags on the moon.

• The deepest American flag is at the bottom of the Marianas Trench, 210 miles southwest of Guam. It was placed there by Navy Lt. Don Walsh and Swiss scientist Jacques Picard in the bathyscaphe *Trieste* when it descended to a record depth—the floor of the Challenger Deep in the Mariana Trench, nearly 36,000 feet below sea level —in 1960.

• When the President is not in Washington, D.C., the flag outside the White House does not fly.

• There is always a flag displayed outside polling places on election days.

• By Presidential proclamation, the Stars and Stripes is flown around the clock, 365 days a year, at the following locations: Fort McHenry National Monument and Historic Shrine, Baltimore, Maryland; Flag House Square, Albemarle and Pratt Streets, Baltimore, Maryland (the home of Mary Pickersgill, who made the flag for Fort McHenry); United States Marine Corps Iwo Jima Memorial, Arlington, Virginia; on the Green of the Town of Lexington, Massachusetts; The White House, Washington, DC;

The Washington Monument, Washington, DC; all United States Customs ports of entry which are open 24 hours; and the grounds of the National Memorial Arch in Valley Forge State Park, Valley Forge, Pennsylvania.

• "The Stars and Stripes Forever," composed by John Philip Sousa in 1897, was designated our national march by Congress in 1987 (see Appendix 4).

• Since 1834, the U.S. flag has flown continuously next to the grave of the Revolutionary War hero, the Marquis de Lafayette, near Paris, France.

---

# FOOTNOTES

[1] When the Southern states seceded from the Union and established the Confederacy, they did not disavow that great political achievement and heritage which preceded it. The Constitution of the Confederate States begins: "We, the people of the Confederate States, each State acting in its sovereign and independent character, in order to form a permanent federal government, establish justice, insure domestic tranquility, and secure the blessings of liberty to ourselves and our posterity—invoking the favor and guidance of Almighty God—do ordain and establish this Constitution for the Confederate States of America. " Their Constitution was remarkably similar to the original one, often a word-for-word duplication.

[2] Someone who saw part of this text before publication responded with a revision of the Pledge of Allegiance in order to clarify the meaning of the flag. Richard Shinn wrote (and I agree):

> I pledge allegiance to the Constitution of the United States of America. And to the republic for which it stands, as one nation of individual states. United in liberty under God, with justice, freedom and God-given rights protected for all.

[3] In a 1910 book, *The Story of the American Flag* by Wayne Whipple, the generalized meaning of the colors is applied to the lives of individuals in the form of advice about character development and citizenship. Whipple writes, "Its colors—the Red, White, and Blue—sing a beautiful song together." He continues:

> Red sings: "Be brave!—brave!—brave!"
> White says: "Be pure!—be clean!—be pure!"
> And Blue sings: "Be true!—true!—true-blue!"

## Sidebar 14

# HOW TO FOLD THE U.S. FLAG

As an Army and Navy custom, the flag is lowered daily at the last note of Retreat. Special care should be taken that no part of the flag touches the ground. The Flag is then carefully folded into the shape of a tri-cornered hat, emblematic of the hats worn by colonial soldiers during the War for Independence. In the folding, the red and white stripes are finally wrapped into the blue, as the light of day vanishes into the darkness of night.

This custom of special folding is reserved for the United States Flag alone. Here are the official seven steps of folding the flag, from the Uniformed Services Flag-Folding Ceremony.

## The Flag Folding Ceremony

### Step 1
To properly fold the Flag, begin by holding it waist-high with another person so that its surface is parallel to the ground.

### Step 2
Fold the lower half of the stripe section lengthwise over the field of stars, holding the bottom and top edges securely.

### Step 3
Fold the flag again lengthwise with the blue field on the outside.

### Step 4
Make a triangular fold by bringing the striped corner of the folded edge to meet the open (top) edge of the flag.

### Step 5
Turn the outer (end) point inward, parallel to the open edge, to form a second triangle.

### Step 6
The triangular folding is continued until the entire length of the flag is folded in this manner.

### Step 7

When the flag is completely folded, only a triangular blue field of stars should be visible.

## The Meaning of the Flag Folding Ceremony

The flag folding ceremony described by the *Uniformed Services Almanac* is a dramatic and uplifting way to honor the flag on special days, such as Memorial Day or Veterans Day. It is sometimes used at military retirement ceremonies and at the funeral of a member of the Uniformed Services or a veteran. If an Honor Guard is present at the burial, the flag which covers the coffin is removed and folded according to the sequence above. Here is a typical sequence of the reading:

*Begin reading as Honor Guard or Flag Detail is coming forward.*

The flag folding ceremony represents the same religious principles on which our country was originally founded. The portion of the flag denoting honor is the canton of blue containing the stars representing the states our veterans served in uniform. The canton field of blue dresses from left to right and is inverted when draped as a pall on a casket of a veteran who has served our country in uniform.

In the Armed Forces of the United States, at the ceremony of Retreat the flag is lowered, folded in a triangle fold and kept under watch throughout the night as a tribute to our nation's honored dead. The next morning it is brought out and, at the ceremony of Reveille, run aloft as a symbol of our belief in the resurrection of the body.

Wait for the Honor Guard or Flag Detail to fold the flag into a quarter fold. Resume reading when the Honor Guard is standing ready. The following narrative is *not* official; it is a widely used but unofficial statement about the meaning of the flag as perceived by Americas over the years.

The first fold of our flag is a symbol of life.

The second fold is a symbol of our belief in the eternal life.

The third fold is made in honor and remembrance of the veteran departing our ranks who gave a portion of life for the defense of our country to attain a peace throughout the world.

The fourth fold represents our weaker nature, for as American citizens trusting in God, it is to Him we turn in times of peace as well as in times of war for His divine guidance.

The fifth fold is a tribute to our country, for in the words of Stephen Decatur, "Our country, in dealing with other countries, may she always be right; but it is still our country, right or wrong."

The sixth fold is for where our hearts lie. It is with our heart that we pledge allegiance to the flag of the United States of America, and to the republic for which it stands, one nation under God, indivisible, with liberty and justice for all.

The seventh fold is a tribute to our Armed Forces, for it is through the Armed Forces that we protect our country and our flag against all her enemies, whether they be found within or without the boundaries of our republic.

The eighth fold is a tribute to the one who entered in to the valley of the shadow of death, that we might see the light of day, and to honor mother, for whom it flies on Mother's Day.

The ninth fold is a tribute to womanhood; for it has been through their faith, love, loyalty and devotion that the character of the men and women who have made this country great have been molded.

The tenth fold is a tribute to father, for he, too, has given his sons and daughters for the defense of our country since they were first born.

The eleventh fold, in the eyes of a Jewish citizen, represents the lower portion of the seal of King David and King Solomon, and glorifies, in their eyes, the God of Abraham, Isaac and Jacob.

The twelfth fold, in the eyes of a Christian citizen, represents an emblem of eternity and glorifies, in their eyes, God the Father, the Son and the Holy Spirit.

When the flag is completely folded, the stars are uppermost, reminding us of our national motto, "In God we trust."

*Wait for the Honor Guard or Flag Detail to inspect the flag. After the inspection, resume reading.*

After the flag is completely folded and tucked in, it takes on the appearance of a cocked hat, ever reminding us of the soldiers who served under General George Washington and the sailors and marines who served under Captain John Paul Jones, who were followed by their comrades and shipmates in the Armed Forces of the United States, preserving for us the rights, privileges and freedoms we enjoy today.

**Chapter 13**

# THE HISTORY OF OUR FLAG

The Flag of the United States was "born" on June 14, 1777, when Congress authorized it. That date makes it the fourth oldest national flag in the world. It is older than the Union Jack of Great Britain and the Tricolor of France. Only the flags of Denmark (1219), Sweden (1495) and the Netherlands (1643) are older.

On that day Congress passed the following resolution proposed by John Adams of Massachusetts to establish our official national flag: "Resolved that The Flag of the thirteen United States be thirteen stripes, alternate red and white; that the Union be thirteen stars, white on a blue field, representing a new constellation." The thirteen stars were probably arranged in a circle, as if they formed a constellation, and to show that every colony was equal and that their confederation would be a "union without end." (Some scholars believe the stars were arranged in rows rather than a circle—see "The Stars and the States" below.)

We observe Flag Day annually on June 14 to commemorate this event. It is the official birthday of the Stars and Stripes. That June 14, 1777 decision by Congress marks the first time in history that a flag was chosen by representatives of a country's people rather than by a ruler.

This was the flag which cheered the brave patriots at Valley Forge the next winter; it was the flag which waved over Yorktown and shared in the rejoicings at the close of the war. Its first display by the Continental Army was when it was hoisted over Fort Stanwix, New York (on the site of the present city of Rome), on August 3, 1777. It was first under fire three days later in the battle of Oriskany, August 6, 1777. It was first carried in the battle of Brandywine, September 11, 1777. The first foreign salute to it was rendered by the French Admiral LaMotte Piquet when his vessels saluted John Paul Jones' ship *Ranger* on February 17, 1778 at Quiberon Bay, France.

The design of the flag lasted 18 years, until Congress changed it in 1795 to recognize two more states. Therefore George Washington was the only President to serve under our original flag. (The second flag design would become known as "The Star-Spangled Banner"—see below.)

## The First Flags to Fly over America

The first flags to fly over various parts of America were the banner of the Norsemen, the flags of Spain, France, Holland and Sweden, and the flag carried by British explorers in 1497, the Cross of St. George. At Jamestown and Plymouth, the settlers' flag was the King's Colors or the British Union Jack. This was a blue ensign with the juxtaposition of the red cross of St. George of England with the white cross of St. Andrew of Scotland covering its entire surface. The Queen Anne Flag waved over the thirteen colonies from 1707 to the Revolution. This was the merchant flag of England—a red ensign with a union of the crosses of St. George and St. Andrew in the canton (upper left corner).

At the start of the Revolutionary War, the colonists fought under many flags. Most reflected their struggles with the wilderness of the New World. Beavers, pine trees, rattlesnakes, anchors and similar insignia were affixed to the different banners, with mottoes such as "Hope," "Liberty," "An Appeal to Heaven" or "Don't Tread on Me."

The flag which the Minutemen unfurled to April's breeze at Lexington and Concord was the Bedford Flag, a red flag which showed a mailed arm clasping a sword and extending from a cloud, surrounded by a scroll bearing the words "Vince Aut Morire" (Conquer or Die). It was the first flag of the American Revolution. At the Battle of Bunker Hill, the Pine Tree Flag was used. It was a blue English ensign with a pine tree added to the upper left-hand corner.

A flag in use by many of the southern colonies to indicate American solidarity against British oppression was the Rattlesnake Flag or the Gadsden Flag. It had a rattlesnake on a yellow background and the words "Don't Tread on Me." The rattlesnake emblem was adopted at the suggestion of Colonel Christopher Gadsden of South Carolina, a prominent patriot, who spoke of American independence as early as 1764 under the "Liberty Tree" at Charleston. Benjamin Franklin had suggested in his newspaper, *The Pennsylvania Gazette*, that the rattles of the snake cannot make a sound singly, but when united they produce an alarm sufficient to warn the boldest man alive. On December 3, 1775, the Rattlesnake Flag was hoisted at the main mast of the *Alfred*, the flagship of Commodore Esek Hopkins, the commander-in-chief of the Continental Navy, and on the other first ships of our then-very-small fleet.

In general, however, the flags of the colonists expressed protest against unjust rule by England and expressed demand for their rights as Englishmen. Unlike most flags until then in world history, they were not the personal standard of a monarch or other powerful ruler. Rather, they symbolized an abstract idea—liberty and justice—and stood for an entire people. Spiritual hope was also articulated in the coats of arms used on the flags of some colonies. An early motto of Massachusetts (not its present one) was "An appeal to Heaven." Connecticut's coat of arms bore (and still does) the Latin motto *Qui transulit sustinet*, meaning "He who brought us [the colonists] over [the ocean] will sustain us." This motto was often used on flags adopted by many regiments of New England troops.

## The First American Flag

The Grand Union Flag was the first true flag of the United States. It was authorized by the Second Continental Congress late in 1775. Also called the Continental Colors, the Congress Colors, the First Navy Ensign and the Cambridge Flag, it was the flag of the 13 united colonies when they declared independence from England on July 4, 1776 (as "the unanimous Declaration of the thirteen united States of America"), and it remained so throughout the first year of the American Revolution. Its design consisted of 13 alternating red and white stripes representing the colonies, with a blue field in the upper left-hand corner bearing the Union Jack. It was first flown by the ships of the Colonial Fleet on the Delaware River. On December 3, 1775, it was raised aboard Captain Esek Hopkin's flagship *Alfred* by John Paul Jones, then a Navy lieutenant. It was probably this flag which was raised by Jones on his own vessel, the *Serapis*, and carried by the American fleet which sailed out of Philadelphia in February, 1776.

Why was the Grand Union Flag created? When Gen. George Washington attacked the British troops besieging Boston in 1775, the need for a flag for the Continental Army became evident. Congress appointed a committee to decide upon a national flag, with Benjamin Franklin as chairman. The committee, after consulting with General Washington, decided in favor of the Grand Union Flag and the Congress adopted it. Essentially the Queen Anne Flag, the red field was broken into seven red stripes by six white ones to represent the thirteen colonies and colonial unity. The canton contained the Union Jack to signify loyalty to England. At that time, political independence from Britain was not seriously considered by most colonists, even while they resisted oppression by some of Britain's laws and policies. (It wasn't until Thomas Paine's best-selling *Common Sense* was published in January of 1776 that public sentiment was finally mobilized for full independence.) In fact, George Washington drank a New Year's toast to the king on January 1, 1776, while at his Cambridge, Massachusetts headquarters with the Continental Army. (The name "Continental Colors," therefore, was derived from its representation of the Continental Army, and "Cambridge Flag" from the location when it was first flown.)

There is nothing to show who was the maker of the Grand Union Flag, but it was first displayed on January 2, 1776, over General Washington's headquarters at Cambridge, Massachusetts. Washington later said, "We hoisted the Union flag in compliment to the united colonies, and saluted it with thirteen guns."

The final breach between the colonies and Great Britain brought about the removal of the British Union from the canton and the substitution of stars on a blue field.

## The Legend of Betsy Ross and the Flag

General Washington was in Philadelphia at the request of Congress from May 22 to June 5, 1776. According to legend, while he was there, a committee consisting of wealthy landowner Robert Morris, Colonel George Ross and Washington asked a Philadelphia seamstress, the 24-year-old widow Elizabeth Griscom "Betsy" Ross, to sew a flag for use by the Continental Army, and Washington pencil-sketched the design. (Col. Ross was the uncle of Betsy's recently deceased husband.)

Betsy had sewn flags for ships through the upholstery business she and her husband had started before he was fatally injured in an ammunition dump explosion. She agreed to perform the task, the legend asserts, but suggested the five-pointed star —the French rule or molet—rather than the six-pointed star—the English rule or estoile —because they were easier to make. Her suggestion was accepted and thus was born the Stars and Stripes.

The story of Betsy Ross was based on affidavits from some of her descendants —daughters, nieces, granddaughters and others—who said that she told them how she had partly designed the first American flag. Her descendants claimed for her the honor of designing and assembling the first flag. However, the *Journal of Congress* shows no mention of an assignment to Washington, Morris and Ross to have the flag created.

It is true that records of the Pennsylvania State Navy Board for May 29, 1777 show payment "to Elizabeth Ross for making ships colours, 14 pounds, 12 shillings and two pence." However, this was more than two weeks before the Second Continental Congress approved the new national flag. Even more important, the "Betsy Ross" flag, according to the legend, was created a full year before that. These anachronisms make clear that the Ross family's claim is ambiguous at best and false at worst. What is true, however, is that for the next half century, until her death in 1836, Mrs. Betsy Ross' little upholstery shop at 239 Arch Street produced and sold flags.

Today the house is open to the public and is visited by more than a quarter of a million people each year. The Betsy Ross Memorial Association acquired the house in 1898 and established it as a national shrine. In 1937 the Association donated the house to the city of Philadelphia. Betsy and her third husband, John Claypoole, are buried in the house's courtyard.

## The Real Designer of the American Flag?

So the romantic legend of Betsy Ross is unproven and discredited; few historians believe that Betsy Ross made the first flag. As *Our Flag*, a 1973 U.S. Marine Corps publication, notes, "there is no proof that she made the first Stars and Stripes" (U.S. Government Printing Office in 1989, p. 2). John Winthrop Adams explains in *Stars and Stripes Forever* (Smithmark Publishers: New York, 1992, p. 18):

> The journals of the Continental Congress make no mention of the meeting [with General Washington] and, although Washington was a voluminous letter writer and kept very detailed diaries, none of these writings mention any connection he may have had with a matter as interesting and as important as the designing and making of the first United States Flag.

Historical research indicates that Francis Hopkinson may have been the person who designed the first Stars and Stripes. He was a popular patriot, a Congressman from New Jersey, a signer of the Declaration of Independence, a member of the Great Seal design committee, a distinguished civil servant and an accomplished artist. He was appointed to the Continental Navy Board in November 1776. While serving on the Board, he turned his attention to designing a flag for the United States. In a letter to the Board of Admiralty in 1780 Hopkinson asserted that he had designed "the flag of the United States of America" as well as the seals of the boards of Admiralty and Treasury, and the Great Seal of the United States.

There is no dispute about his work in designing the seals. However, the journals of the Continental Congress do not show that he designed the flag, so Hopkinson's claim is unproven. In fact, when he submitted a formal bill to Congress for his work, a congressional committee examined his claim. Their finding stated that "the report relative to the fancywork of F. Hopkinson ought not to be acted upon."

Thus, the person or persons who actual designed the first flag of the United States of America is unknown.

It is clearly established that from July 4, 1776, until June 4, 1777, the national emblem was composed of thirteen stripes, red and white, with a rattlesnake with thirteen rattles across it, and underneath it the motto "Don't tread on me." There is nothing to show, however, that the General Congress wished this form of flag.

## The Design of Our Flag

Why were stars and stripes used as design elements of our national flag? *Our Flag* states that the pattern of the Stars and Stripes arose from several origins back in the mists of antiquity. "The star is a symbol of the heavens and the divine goal to which man has aspired from time immemorial; the stripe is symbolic of the rays of light emanating from the sun. Both themes have long been represented on the standards of nations..." (p. 1)

Some historians claim the stripes were inspired by the Rattlesnake Flag flown on the *Alfred* of the newly commissioned continental fleet. Others claimed the striped banner of the Sons of Liberty was the source. Most agree that the stars were taken from the military banner of colonial Rhode Island.

It was thought at one time that a new stripe as well as a new star should be added for each new state admitted to the Union. Indeed, in 1794, Congress passed an act to the effect that on and after May 1, 1795, "The Flag of the United States be fifteen stripes, alternate red and white; and that the Union be fifteen stars, white in a field of blue." When Vermont and Kentucky entered the Union in 1791 and 1792, new stripes and new stars were added. Thus, a fifteen-striped flag with fifteen stars flew over Fort McHenry in Baltimore Harbor on that historic night of September 13, 1814 when the British fired upon the city, as described in our national anthem. This flag continued to be the official flag until 1818, although five more states had come into the Union. By then it had become apparent that a stripe added for every new state would soon render the flag unwieldy and unsymmetrical, so on April 4, 1818, a bill was signed by President James Monroe restoring the design of the flag to the original thirteen stripes, but one star for each state.

However, from 1777 to 1912, the proportions of the flag and other details were not standardized by Congress and had never been published. The result was a diversity of flags; some had stars with only four points, while others had five-, six-, seven- and even eight-pointed stars arranged in many different designs varying from circles to squares. The Great Star Flag of 1818 had 20 stars arranged in the form of a five-pointed star. In some instances when a new state entered the Union, the Army and Navy worked out the new designs for the stars. But in other cases, no official action was taken.

One of the most unusual U.S. flags has 16 stripes and 16 stars. The only one known to exist still is in Stonington, Connecticut. The 16th state, Tennessee, entered the Union in 1796. The Stonington flag, measuring 11' x 18', was flown above Stonington during the War of 1812. In August 1814, the British attacked the town, but after two days of stout resistance by the townspeople, the British left and the townspeople proclaimed their victory in the Battle of Stonington. The flag, cherished and preserved, is in fragile condition and therefore not on public display. However, the Stonington Historical Society commissioned a replica which is proudly displayed on occasion.

On June 24, 1912, President William H. Taft signed an Executive Order prescribing the official proportions of the flag, the arrangement of the stars, and the relative sizes of the stars and stripes. The proportions specified were given in units to the scale of 1 unit to 1.9 units. Therefore, whatever the actual size of a flag, its form and proportions will conform to the ideal stated by President Taft.

## The Stars and the States

There have been 27 versions of the Flag of the United States of America. Differing arrangements of stars identify succeeding versions of the flag.

The first flag (1777-1795) had 13 stars arranged in a circle on the union. However, some historians think it had a "spread star" pattern devised by Francis

Hopkinson with three rows of three stars alternating with two rows of two stars. This sophisticated pattern is called quincuncial because of its use of groups of five stars. The pattern yields both vertical and diagonal crosses reminiscent of the crosses of St. George and St. Andrew in the Union Jack, although it is not known whether this was intended by Hopkinson or simply coincidental.

The second flag (1795-1818) had 15 stars staggered in five rows and 15 stripes because two more states, Vermont and Kentucky, had joined the Union in 1791 and 1792, but the flag's design had not become standardized as it is today. In fact, by 1814, when this version of the flag flew over Fort McHenry (see below), there were 18 states in the Union, but flag design had not caught up to the number.

The third flag (1818) had four rows of five stars for a total of 20. The arrangement continued to change to accommodate new stars for new states of the Union. Union troops fought under a 33-star flag for the first three months of the Civil War, then a 34-star flag until 1863, and a 35-star flag until the war's end. The last time the flag design changed was in 1960, when Hawaii joined the Union. By law, whenever a star is added to the flag, it is done so on the Fourth of July following the admission of a state to the Union.

The current 50-star flag design was created in 1958 by Robert G. Heft, a 17-year-old Ohio high school student. When he learned that Alaska and Hawaii were to become states, he spent a weekend arranging stars on a blue field for a high school project. He obtained them by cutting up the family flag, which left his mother aghast when she learned of it.

Heft got a B-minus on the project from his teacher, Stanley Pratt, who said the flag lacked originality. However, Pratt added, he would raise the grade if the government approved Heft's design. So Heft sent the design to his congressman, Representative Walter Moeller, who submitted it to the committee in charge of flag design. To everyone's surprise, Heft's design actually got approved! It was chosen over thousands of others.

Richard H. Schneider, in his wonderful recent history of the American flag, *Stars & Stripes Forever* (William Morrow: New York, 2003, p. 61), tells what happened next. "On July 4, 1960, amid the din of military bands, young Robert Heft stood at attention by the side of President Dwight D. Eisenhower and Congressman Moeller as he watched his handmade flag being raised over the U.S. Capitol dome."

Heft later became mayor of Napoleon, Ohio. He now works with youth in Saginaw, Michigan, and travels throughout the country to speak to interested groups about the American flag.

If the United States adds a 51st state, it is likely that the 51-star flag will have six rows of stars, beginning with a row of nine and alternated by rows of eight stars, to total 51. This layout was also created by Heft a few weeks after his 50-star design was approved. The design is currently in the possession of Republican Congressman Clarence Miller of Ohio.

By law, a star is now added to the American flag of the 4th of July following the admission of a state to the Union. There is no legal or official designation of stars in the Flag as representing certain states. However, by tradition, there is a correlation. Starting in the upper left-hand corner of the union, and reading each row from left to right, gives the stars of each state in order of the state's ratification of the Constitution and admission to the Union. They are as follows:

First Row: 1, Delaware (1787); 2, Pennsylvania (1787); 3, New Jersey (1787); 4, Georgia (1788); 5, Connecticut (1788); 6, Massachusetts (1788).

Second Row: 7, Maryland (1788); 8, South Carolina (1788); 9, New Hampshire (1788); 10, Virginia (1788); 11, New York (1788).

Third Row: 12, North Carolina (1789); 13, Rhode Island (1790); 14, Vermont (1791); 15, Kentucky (1792); 16, Tennessee (1796); 17, Ohio (1803).

Fourth Row: 18, Louisiana (1812); 19, Indiana (1816); 20, Mississippi (1817); 21, Illinois (1818); 22, Alabama (1819).

Fifth Row: 23, Maine  (1820); 24, Missouri (1821); 25, Arkansas (1836); 26, Michigan (1837); 27, Florida (1845); 28, Texas (1845).

Sixth Row: 29, Iowa (1846); 30, Wisconsin (1848); 31, California (1850); 32, Minnesota (1858); 33, Oregon (1859).

Seventh Row: 34, Kansas (1861); 35, West Virginia (1863); 36, Nevada (1864); 37, Nebraska (1867); 38, Colorado (1876); 39, North Dakota (1889).

Eighth Row: 40, South Dakota (1889); 41, Montana (1889); 42, Washington (1889); 43, Idaho (1890); 44, Wyoming (1890).

Ninth Row: 45, Utah (1896); 46, Oklahoma (1907); 47, New Mexico (1912); 48, Arizona (1912); 49, Alaska (1959); 50, Hawaii (1959).

## The Story of "The Star-Spangled Banner"

The flag which inspired our national anthem, "The Star-Spangled Banner," is a national treasure on display at the Smithsonian Institution in Washington, D.C. It flew over Fort McHenry in Baltimore Harbor during the War of 1812 when the British bombarded the fort through the day and night of September 13-14, 1814, a few weeks after they burned down Washington, D.C. Since the design of our flag had not been standardized as it is today, the flag had 15 stripes and 15 stars (in five staggered rows of three stars each), recognizing two more states which had entered the Union.

The lyrics of the anthem [1] were written by Francis Scott Key (1779-1843) immediately after the attack on Fort McHenry. (See Sidebar 14 for the complete verses of our national anthem.) The fort is a star-shaped structure of red brick located on Whetstone Point at the mouth of the Patapsco River. It was named for James McHenry, an Irish-born surgeon and son of Maryland who served in the Revolutionary War on Washington's staff and later as a member of the Continental Congress and the Constitutional Convention. Still later he served as Secretary of War for George Washington and John Adams.

Key, who was a native of Frederick, Maryland, was a 35-year-old lawyer and poet who had served for nearly a year in the Georgetown Light Field Artillery. He had been sent to the British by President James Madison, along with Colonel John Skinner, the U.S. Commissioner-General of Prisoners, to negotiate the release of a physician and friend of Key, Dr. William Beanes, who was held prisoner after being captured after the sack of Washington, D.C. The British had a fleet of 16 warships under Vice Admiral Alexander Cockrane and a land force of 5,000 soldiers commanded by Major General Robert Ross. The two joint commanders received Key aboard the flagship, the H.M.S. *Tonnant*, where Dr. Beanes was, and negotiated an agreement to release him.

However, in order to keep Key and Skinner from disclosing their attack plans, they were held captive for several days until the battle was over.

Baltimore was defended by a force of about 13,000 regulars and militia under Gen. Samuel Smith. A fixed force of about 1,000 manned Fort McHenry. A line of 24 sunken hulks barred enemy vessels from the harbor, so the British ships had to fire from long range. When the British soldiers advanced on Baltimore, after disembarking from their ships about 14 miles southeast of the city, they were strongly opposed and slowed down by the American forces, who fell back after inflicting severe casualties on the British. Their advance was halted at the formidable defense works prepared on the Baltimore heights. Likewise, the British fleet's bombardment would prove unsuccessful.

The bombardment began at 6 a.m. when the ships moved into position. About 2 p.m., a heavy rain began. The British fired some 700 rockets and 1,500 bombshells at Fort McHenry, which was then flying a storm flag of moderate size. (This action was "the rockets' red glare, the bombs bursting in air...") The rockets, designed by William Congreve in 1804, were primitive and nonspinning. The 190-pound cast-iron bombshells were designed to explode upon landing, flinging shrapnel with deadly force. However, they were frequently defective and blew up in the air. Key's phrasing drew attention to that fact. The British guns had a two-mile range; Fort McHenry's had only a mile and a half. The British ships stayed outside the fort's range. The Americans could do little more than hunker down and endure the shelling.

Throughout the battle, Key watched anxiously from the deck. His heart was full of concern for his countrymen. Pacing the deck and peering through the darkness with a telescope, he could see occasionally by the illumination of an explosion that the American flag above the fort was still flying. (Although Key wrote that the explosions' brief illumination "gave proof through the night that our flag was still there," some historians maintain that he could not have seen it because of poor visibility caused by the distance, the rain, the darkness and the gun smoke in the air).

The rain stopped just before dawn; the bombardment ended at 7 a.m. on September 14—a 25-hour onslaught. Fort McHenry's commandant, Major George Armistead, had the storm flag which had flown during the night lowered from the fort's 90-foot flagpole. In its place he flew a huge 30 x 42-foot flag as a gesture of defiance. He had ordered both flags a year earlier from a Baltimore seamstress, Mrs. Mary Pickersgill, who designed, sewed and sold flags of many kinds for the military and for merchant ships.

As the firing ceased and the smoke cleared, Key peered to see whether the British or American flag was aloft. In the dawn's early light Key saw the Stars and Stripes still flying over the fort. He was deeply moved. In the fervor of the moment, using the blank backs of a letter he had in his pocket, he wrote some lines and brief notes for a poem to describe what he had seen and felt, and to express his hope for the future of his country. (The letter is now owned by the Maryland Historical Society. Another copy, with Key's writing, is in the Library of Congress.)

After the battle, Key, Skinner and Dr. Beanes were put ashore. (Astonishingly, the combined land and sea assault resulted in only four Americans killed and 24 wounded. The British had heavy losses, including Major General Ross.) Key returned to Baltimore later that day and took a room at a tavern, where he completed his epic poem. He did not title it but gave it to his brother-in-law, Judge J. H. Nicholson. The judge was so impressed with it that he took it to the printing office of the *Baltimore Patriot*, a newspaper. The printer ran it off as a handbill, calling it, at Nicholson's suggestion, "The Defence of Fort M'Henry." The poem was printed as published on September 20, 1814. (Two copies of the broadside have survived.) Other newspapers published it; they changed the title to "The Star-Spangled Banner."

The words to it were, by Key's choice, set to the melody of an English drinking song about Anacreon, a 6th century B.C. Greek poet. The song, "To Anacreon in Heaven," was widely sung in this country at that time. It was borrowed from the Anacreontic Society, a group of amateur musicians formed in London in the mid-1760s. The Society hired composer John Stafford Smith to create music for the group. Once the melody made its way to North America, it was borrowed to create the campaign song for John Adam's campaign. Key's patriotic poem of the defense of Fort McHenry, set to that music, took the popular fancy and eventually became our national anthem.

Key later told an audience in his home town of Frederick, Maryland: "I saw the flag of my country waving over the city—the strength and pride of my native State—a city devoted to plunder and desolation by its assailants. I witnessed the preparation for its assaults. I saw the array of its enemies as they advanced to the attack. I heard the sound of battle; the noise of the conflict fell upon my listening ear, and told me that 'the brave and the free' had met the invaders." On another occasion he wrote, "Then, in that hour of deliverance, my heart spoke. Does not such a country, and such defenders of their country, deserve a song?"

Key went on to become a United States district attorney and, more important, America's great patriot-poet. He died in Baltimore in 1843 and was buried there, but his remains were removed in 1866 to Frederick, Maryland and reinterred in Mt. Olivet Cemetery. By a 1949 act of Congress, a flag flies continuously over the monument marking the site of Key's birthplace, Terra Rubra Farm, in Keymar, Maryland.

In the 1840s Key's song became regarded as a patriotic "national song." During the Civil War, soldiers sang it with new verses related to the war between the states. In 1889, the Secretary of the Navy ordered the song to be used at all naval flag-raising and flag-lowering ceremonies. In 1903, the U.S. Army decreed that the song should be used for special occasions, and when it was played, soldiers were to stand at attention.

According to the first edition (1910) of the Boy Scout manual *Handbook for Boys*, "The Star-Spangled Banner" was played "on all state occasions at home or abroad and is the response of our bands at all international gatherings. In the theatre, at a public meeting, or at a banquet—wherever it is played the people rise and remain standing to the end as a tribute to the flag of our country" (p. 331).

In 1913, Congress opened debate on declaring "The Star-Spangled Banner" as the national anthem. Debate raged about it for years. Some citizens said it was too hard to sing because of its high and low notes. Some objected to it because of its origin as a drinking song. Others, such as bandmaster John Philip Sousa, extolled it for its patriotic spirit. Still others supported Katharine Lee Bates's "America the Beautiful" (which is so beloved by Americans today that many call it "our second national anthem").

In 1928, the Veterans of Foreign Wars and other patriotic organizations began collecting signatures on a petition to have the song adopted. Two years later they presented Congress the petition with 5,000,000 signatures. The political pressure worked. Congress approved the resolution favoring "The Star-Spangled Banner." On

March 3, 1931, President Herbert Hoover signed it into law, officially making Francis Scott Key's song our national anthem. [2]   Even so, it has been described as the most difficult national anthem on Earth to sing.

As for Fort McHenry, it continued in active military service nearly a century after the battle. However, changing military technology eventually made it obsolete for coastal defense. Today the 43-acre fort is preserved as a national monument and historic shrine. The property is managed by the National Park Service and the flag is flown over the fort 24 hours a day. When Alaska and Hawaii joined the Union and our nation's flag changed its design from 48 to 50 stars, the new flag was raised for the first time at 12:01 a.m. on July 4, 1960, at the Fort McHenry National Monument.

## Sewing the First Star-Spangled Banner

The original Star-Spangled Banner was sewn in 1813 by a Baltimore seamstress and widow, Mary Pickersgill (1776-1857), and her 13-year-old daughter Caroline. They were assisted by the daughters of Mary's brother John and, presumably, by Mary's slaves.

Mary laid out the flag according to the provisions of the 1794 Flag Act. The flag contained four hundred yards of wool bunting purchased from a Baltimore dry-goods story. It required about half a million stitches. The stars were made of cotton, a luxury item at the time. It weighed 200 pounds and was so big that the Pickersgills couldn't assemble it at their home. They had to take it to a nearby brewery where they could stretch it all out. Each of its fifteen stripes were two feet wide; the stars also were two feet in diameter. At Fort McHenry, a crew of many men was needed to handle it.

Major Armistead, the fort's commander, and other military planners had foreseen a British invasion so, as a gesture of defiance, he wanted a flag the British would have no difficulty in seeing from a distance. He also felt it would be a much-need morale booster for the Americans.

Technically called a garrison flag, it was ordered from Mary by Armistead in June 1813. A garrison flag is a giant flag flown at forts and military posts. The dimensions of the flag were 30 feet high by 42 feet long. Armistead also ordered a smaller storm flag whose dimensions were 17 feet high by 25 feet long. Mary agreed to produce the garrison flag for $405.90 and the storm flag for $168.54, for a total bill of $574.44.

The flags were delivered to Fort McHenry on August 19, 1813, a full year before the Battle of Baltimore.

A few weeks after the battle, Major Armistead was promoted to lieutenant colonel for his leadership in defending the fort. He decided to keep the flag as a memento, so he signed his name and rank on it and the date of the battle.

During the night of the bombardment, the storm flag flew in the rain which had begun falling the that afternoon. Just before dawn on September 14, the rain stopped, the storm flag was taken down and the garrison flag run up. This was the flag which Key saw with his telescope at dawn. So, according to Margo Turner and John Tiffany, in an article entitled "Who Really Created the Star Spangled Banner?" (*Barnes Review*, September/October 2004, p. 78), rather than singing "our flag was still there," technically it should be that "our other flag was now there."

The fate of the storm flag is unknown although, Turner and Tiffany state, it may well have been destroyed because the flags were only intended to be flown for about two years, after which time they were customarily discarded without ceremony.

The fate of the garrison flag, however, is well known. Shortly after the battle, the widow of a soldier killed in the bombardment asked Armistead for a piece of the flag as a remembrance, and he complied. Thereafter, when he wished to make a gift to a friend, he would cut a strip from the flag and present it with his compliments. Thus he established a military practice which continued until the end of the Civil War. As a result, over the decades the flag was snipped away for relic hunters and reduced in size by "souveniring" to its present dimensions of 30 feet by 34 feet. One of the stars and eight feet of its leading edge are missing, but it is still as tall as a three-story building.

When Armistead died in 1818, Mrs. Armistead inherited the Star-Spangled Banner but kept it private and practically unseen. In 1873, their daughter Georgiana stated that the flag was a family heirloom and allowed a photograph to be taken of it for inclusion in a history of the American flag. Calling it "my treasure" and "this time honored relic," she said the family heirloom should not remain in private hands forever. On January 1, 1876, for the nation's centennial celebration, it was placed on view for the first time since it flew over Fort McHenry. In 1907 it was transferred to the Smithsonian Institution by Eben Appleton, Georgiana's son, for an exhibition. Five years later he presented the flag as a gift to the Institution. It was tattered and in fragile condition.

Carefully preserved and restored, it is on display in the Institution's Flag Hall at the National Museum of American History in Washington, D.C. To show what the flag looked like full-size, the missing portion was reproduced using material much like the original, and the new piece was hung just behind the old. The colors of the faded flag were not duplicated exactly, nor was the new piece attached to the old. Thus, the authenticity of the 1814 flag is retained, but at the same time visitors can visualize it in its original dimensions.

The home of Mary Pickersgill, where she lived from 1807-57 and where she and her daughter Caroline began work on the Star-Spangled Banner, is now a National Historic Landmark known as The Star-Spangled Banner Flag House. It stands at the corner of Albemarle and Pratt Streets in Baltimore and is operated by an independent nonprofit association. The American flag is flown over the house 24 hours a day. The Baltimore flag maker is not as well known as Betsy Ross, but her legacy to America is very real.

## How Our Flag Got the Name "Old Glory"

The first person to refer to the flag as Old Glory was a sea captain, William Driver of Salem, Massachusetts. Driver was the young master of the brig *Charles Daggett*. On his 21st birthday, March 17, 1824, as he was about to leave Salem for the South Pacific on one of many voyages, his mother and some friends presented him with a beautiful, new 24-star flag. He had it hoisted aloft. As it unfurled and opened to the ocean breeze, he exclaimed in pride "Old Glory!" Some say he exclaimed more expansively, "I name thee 'Old Glory'!"

Whatever the case, the name stuck—forever. Captain Driver associated his name for our national flag with the resplendent beauty and beatific happiness of heaven. Just as the Great Seal of the United States depicts on its reverse side a pyramid representing America watched over by the Eye of Providence surrounded by "a glory" (as the designer wrote in explaining the seal's symbolism), Driver poetically reiterated the view of our Founders that God, in all His glory, is the foundation of our nation.

Old Glory accompanied Driver whenever he went to sea. In 1837, after many voyages, he quit the sea and settled in Nashville, Tennessee, taking his treasured flag with him. On patriotic occasions and on his own birthday, Old Glory could be seen flying from a rope extending from Driver's house to a tree across the street. By the time of the Civil War, the residents of Nashville were familiar with Old Glory and some rebels were determined to destroy it. However, Old Glory mysteriously vanished. Despite repeated searches, they never found Driver's flag.

On February 25, 1862, Union forces captured Nashville and raised a small American flag over the state capitol. People began asking Driver if Old Glory still existed. It did. He had hidden it in his bed cover, sewn between the quilt-top and the batting. He gathered up the flag and, accompanied by cheering soldiers of the victorious Sixth Ohio Regiment, returned to the capitol.

Then the nearly 60-year-old Driver climbed up to the capitol tower and replaced the smaller Union flag with the original 24-star flag beloved as Old Glory. The Sixth Ohio Regiment cheered and saluted—and later adopted the nickname "Old Glory" as their own, telling and retelling the story of Driver's devotion to the flag of our republic.

One day, shortly before he died, Driver placed a bundle in the arms of his daughter, saying, "Mary Jane, this is my old ship flag, Old Glory. It has been my constant companion on many voyages. I love it as a mother loves her child; take it and cherish it as I have cherished it, for it has been my steadfast friend and protector in all parts of the world, among savages, heathen and civilized. Keep it always."

Old Glory was kept and guarded as a precious heirloom in the Driver family until 1922, when it was sent to the Smithsonian Institution in Washington, D.C., where it is today, carefully preserved under glass.

Driver's grave is located in the old Nashville City Cemetery. It is one of the few places authorized by an act of Congress where the Flag of the United States may be flown 24 hours a day.

## The History of Flag Day

The Stars and Stripes first flew in a Flag Day celebration in Hartford, Connecticut, in 1861, during the first summer of the Civil War. The first national observance of Flag Day occurred on June 14, 1877, the centennial of the original flag resolution. In 1885, Dr. Bernard J. Cigrand, a school teacher, led pupils in the Fredonia, Wisconsin Public School, District 6, in observing June 14 as "Flag Birthday." He continued advocating the observance via magazine and newspaper articles and public addresses. In 1889, George Balch, a kindergarten teacher in New York City, planned ceremonies for the children at his school, and his idea of observing Flag Day was adopted by the State Board of Education of New York. On June 14, 1891, the Betsy Ross House in Philadelphia held a Flag Day celebration and on June 14, 1892, the New York Society of the Sons of the Revolution celebrated Flag Day.

The idea spread widely. By the mid-1890s the observance of Flag Day on June 14 was a popular event. Mayors and governors began to issue proclamations in their jurisdictions to celebrate this event. Public sentiment for a national Flag Day intensified. In 1894, Dr. Cigrand and Leroy Van Horn of Chicago founded the American Flag Day Association for the purpose of promoting Flag Day exercises. Under its auspices, the first general public school children's celebration of Flag Day in Chicago was held in five Illinois public parks, with more than 300,000 children participating.

In 1914, Secretary of the Interior Franklin K. Lane delivered a Flag Day address in which he repeated words which he said the flag had spoken to him that morning: "I am what you make of me; nothing more. I swing before your eyes as a bright gleam of color, a symbol of yourself."

Two years later, President Woodrow Wilson officially established the occasion as a national event by a proclamation. Issued on May 30, 1916, Wilson said: "It has, therefore, seemed to me fitting that I should call your attention to the approach of the anniversary of the day upon which the Flag of the United States was adopted by the Congress as the emblem of the Union, and to suggest to you that it should this year and in the years to come be given special significance... I therefore suggest and request that throughout the nation, and, if possible, in every community, the fourteenth day of June be observed as Flag Day, with special patriotic exercises, at which means shall be taken to give significant expression to our thoughtful love of America...our determination to make it greater and purer..."

President Calvin Coolidge likewise expressed his thoughts about the meaning of the flag and a day devoted to honoring it. "We identify the flag with almost everything we hold dear on earth," he said. "It represents our peace and security, our civil and political liberty, our freedom of religious worship, our family, our friends, our home. We see it in the great multitude of blessings, of rights and privileges that make up our country."

But, he added, "when we look at our flag and behold it emblazoned with all our rights, we must remember that it is equally a symbol of our duties. Every glory we associate with it is the result of duty done. A yearly contemplation of our flag strengthens and purifies the national conscience."

In 1949, Congress made June 14 a permanent observance by resolving "That the 14th day of June of each year is hereby designated as Flag Day..." The measure was signed into law by President Harry Truman on August 3, 1949. Although Flag Day is not celebrated as a federal holiday, Americans everywhere continue to honor the history and glorious heritage it represents.

The flag of our nation—long may it wave o'er the land of the free and the home of the brave!

---

## FOOTNOTES

[1] Early manuscripts of the lyrics have many inconsistencies with spelling and punctuation, including use of a hyphen in the title. Most sheet music will have "The Star Spangled Banner" as the title. However, in recent years, "The Star-Spangled Banner" has become the preferred spelling for usage within text. I have adopted that usage throughout this book for both the title and the text to be consistent.

2 Playing "The Star-Spangled Banner" at the opening of sporting events actually preceded its status as our national anthem. The first time it was played was September 5, 1918, during a Boston Red Sox-Chicago Cubs World Series baseball game in Wrigley Field, Chicago. The First World War was raging in Europe and the U.S. had just entered it. Patriotism was high. When the World Series moved to Fenway Park in Boston a few days later, the precedent set in Chicago was followed. Thereafter, however, the national anthem was generally reserved for Opening Day in baseball until the Second World War, when it became standard before most professional and college baseball games. This led *Sports Illustrated* writer Frank Deford to quip that many fans think the last two words of the anthem are "Play ball!"

## Sidebar 15

# THE COMPLETE VERSES OF "THE STAR-SPANGLED BANNER"

"The Star-Spangled Banner" was made our official national anthem by an Act of Congress on March 3, 1931. Do you know the words to it? (Surveys in 2004 show that 61% of Americans don't.)

Respect for our national anthem is shown in the same way you show respect for the national flag. When you hear it played or sung in public, stand up at attention, be silent, salute if you are in uniform, or place your right hand over your heart if you are in civilian clothes—and think of the sacrifices made by so many to give you a future under that star-spangled banner.

The verses of "The Star-Spangled Banner" can be found in many hymnals. Do you sing them in your church, synagogue, temple or mosque? If not, why not—at least on national holidays? All Americans should be familiar with the words and, equally important, the great heritage enshrined in them.

Oh, say, can you see, by the dawn's early light,
What so proudly we hailed at the twilight's last gleaming,
Whose broad stripes and bright stars, through the perilous night
O'er the ramparts we watched were so gallantly streaming?
And the rockets' red glare, the bombs bursting in air,
Gave proof through the night that our flag was still there.

*Chorus*
Oh, say does that star-spangled banner yet wave
O'er the land of the free and the home of the brave?

On the shore dimly seen through the mists of the deep,
Where the foe's haughty host in dread silence reposes,
What is that which the breeze o'er the towering steep,
As it fitfully blows, half conceals, half discloses?
Now it catches the gleam of the morning's first beam,
In full glory reflected, now shines on the stream.

*Chorus*
'Tis the star-spangled banner, Oh, long may it wave,
O'er the land of the free and the home of the brave!

And where is that band, that so vauntingly swore
That the havoc of war and the battle's confusion

A home and a country should leave us no more?
Their blood has washed out their foul footsteps' pollution.
No refuge could save the hireling and slave,
From the terror of death and the gloom of the grave;

*Chorus*
And the star -spangled banner in triumph shall wave
O'er the land of the free and the home of the brave.

Oh, thus be it ever when freemen shall stand,
Between their loved homes and foul war's desolation;
Blest with victory and peace, may the heaven-rescued land
Praise the power that hath made and preserved us a nation!
Then conquer we must, when our cause it is just,
And this be our motto: "In God is our trust!"

*Chorus*
And the star-spangled banner in triumph shall wave
O'er the land of the free and the home of the brave.

Some people argue that the words and sentence structure of this 18th century poem are too difficult to understand . Replying to those critics, Ed Goodman, an editor for the [Waterbury, Connecticut] *Republican American*, writes (13 February 2011, p. 11A):

As frequently occurs in verse of the period, clarity is sacrificed to the demands of rhyme and rhythm. By modern standards, the order of the words and images is jumbled, meaning those trying to understand the verse need to take a minute or two to figure out what the author is trying to say. However, put into modern prose, the meaning is simple, clear and moving, though nowhere near as well-expressed as by Key:

*Now that it's the earliest light of dawn, can you tell me if our flag is still flying over Fort McHenry? Yesterday, in the last glimmer of twilight, we felt proud when we saw the flag's broad stripes and stars gallantly streaming over the fort's ramparts. During the night, we were reassured when we caught glimpses of it, lit up by the red glare of rockets and by airborne explosions from the bombardment. . . . Does the star-spangled banner still wave over our brave, free land?*

…That people have to know a little bit of history and think a little bit about the words and word order to understand what the song says and means hardly should count against it.

**Chapter 14**

# WHAT SHOULD YOU DO WITH A WORN OUT FLAG?

The American flag represents what we are all about.... Flags deserve a reverent retirement after their honorable service.

– John Wright, former U.S. Marine

If a good friend of yours retired from work after decades of service, you'd want that person to have a nice retirement ceremony, wouldn't you?

The flag of our nation, although a symbol, is considered to be a living thing. (See Section 176 (j) of the U.S. Flag Code on p. xxx.) Not only a living thing, but a dear friend named Stars and Stripes and also Old Glory who has spent its life in service to our nation. Therefore, like your friend who retired from work, Old Glory should be treated with respect when it is retired. If it is unserviceable and can no longer perform its "work," don't just throw it in the garbage or use it as a rag.

How do you retire a flag from service? What should be done with a flag when it's unserviceable?

Most Americans don't know. But veterans do. The American Legion and the Veterans of Foreign War have rituals for retiring a worn out flag properly. Their Post Commander's handbooks have complete details about the ceremony and some posts conduct public flag retirement ceremonies on Flag Day (Flag Day is June 14, the birthday of our flag. It commemorates that day in 1777 when the Continental Congress adopted the Stars and Stripes as the official flag of the United States.) The short answer to the questions above, based on the veterans organizations' experience, is: You burn the flag.

Burn it? Like millions of Americans, I fly the flag daily at my home to express patriotic gratitude for the blessings of liberty we citizens of the republic have in such abundance. Also, like millions of Americans, I feel badly when someone burns a flag to express disrespect for our nation and the heritage behind Old Glory.

However, the issue is not flag burning per se; the issue is flag desecration. In and of itself, burning a flag is not improper. Ceremonial burning is neither illegal nor disrespectful. According to the U.S. Flag Code (see Appendix 1), when an American flag is no longer a fitting emblem for display because of an unserviceable condition, it should be destroyed in a dignified way. Unserviceable means faded, tattered, torn, soiled or otherwise worn out; it is disrespectful to our nation to fly such a flag. The traditional military manner of retiring a flag from service is consigning it to the flames. The Flag Code designates burning as the preferred means of disposing of a flag. It is reduced to ashes so it is unrecognizable as a former flag. In military parlance, such a flag is retired from service.

If you choose to burn a flag, the U.S. Flag Code says to fold the flag in its customary manner. Make sure your fire is large enough and of sufficient intensity to completely burn the flag. After placing the flag on the fire, come to attention, salute the flag, recite the Pledge of Allegiance and have a brief period of silent reflection.

Anyone can burn an unserviceable flag privately at home or in public, treating it in a respectful manner. It's when the burning is intended to desecrate the Stars and Stripes that patriots object. That's what the Flag Protection Amendment now pending in Congress is all about: prohibiting physical desecration to the flag of our nation. (See Chapter 12.)

Although burning is the preferred method, it is also acceptable simply to cut the flag into small pieces so it is no longer recognizable as a flag. Then, whether the remainder is ashes or pieces of cloth, it may be buried or simply sealed in a bag or box for trash collection. The latter is not disrespectful and, for those without access to a plot of land, may be the only viable means of disposal. Some veterans' posts scatter the ashes on land, at sea or from the air.

## Flag Day in Cheshire, Connecticut

In my home town of Cheshire, Connecticut, the American Legion and Veterans of Foreign Wars posts used to burn hundreds of flags annually on Flag Day. (Age and dwindling numbers have required us to alter that; I'll describe the new method in Footnote 1 below.) Using the ritual prescribed by the American Legion, we conducted a reverent public ceremony to retire flags no longer fit to be flown. (The VFW ritual prescribes that it be done by the post privately.) Our ceremony was held in the parking lot of the community center, where a simple 55-gallon drum served as the incinerator. The public was invited, of course. The event lasted about half an hour.

Several months before Flag Day, we invited Girl Scout troops to obtain and decorate half a dozen large boxes with patriotic decorations and a sign we provide. The sign reads:

FLAG COLLECTION BOX
FOR UNSERVICEABLE AMERICAN FLAGS
The flags will be retired on Flag Day in a dignified public ceremony.
It will be conducted by Cheshire's American Legion Post 92 and VFW Post 10052.

Time: Thursday, June 14, 7 p.m.
Place: VFW Hall/Rochford Community Center
1220 Waterbury Road, Cheshire
This box was decorated by Girl Scout Troops 252 and 268 of Chapman School.

A month prior to Flag Day, the Girl Scouts placed the collection boxes around town so people could conveniently drop off unserviceable flags. A news release to the local paper called attention to the boxes and the upcoming ceremony. Veterans collected the flags just before the ceremony.

Also prior to Flag Day, the Police Department was notified of the event, the fire marshal issued a permit for the ceremonial fire and the Fire Department committed to have a fire truck nearby, just in case. So everything was in readiness for the event.

The ceremony was held at 7 p.m. so entire families could attend. A fire, lit earlier, was tended by a veteran. After the color guard presented the colors, the sergeant-at-arms announced to the ceremony commander that a number of flags were present for retirement. The commander called for inspection of a single flag, representing all which were to be burned. Veterans recited the ritual lines in a formal manner. The flag was declared to be unserviceable and was recommended for retirement. Then the commander told the ceremonial detail and assembled viewers:

## The Meaning of the Flag

"A flag may be a flimsy bit of printed gauze or a beautiful banner of finest silk. Its intrinsic value may be trifling or great; but its real value is beyond price, for it is a precious symbol of all that we and our comrades have worked for and lived for, and died for—a free nation of free men, true to the faith of the past, devoted to the ideals and practice of justice, freedom and democracy.

"Let these faded flags of our country be retired and destroyed with respectful and honorable rites and their places be taken by bright new flags of the same size and kind, and let no grave of our soldier or sailor dead be unhonored and unmarked. Sergeant-at-Arms, assemble the Color Guard, escort the detail bearing the flags and destroy the flags by burning."

With everyone at attention, the chaplain offers a prayer: "Almighty God, captain of all hosts and commander over all, bless and consecrate this present hour. We thank Thee for our country and its flag, and for the liberty for which it stands. To clean and purging flame we commit these flags, worn out in worthy service. As they yield their substance to the fire, may Thy holy light spread over us and bring to our hearts renewed devotion to God and country. Amen."

The flag is placed in the fire by the sergeant-at-arms, while all members of the ceremony salute. That ends the ceremony. Then, while the fire tender continues burning flags, the commander of the ceremony and other veterans speak to the assembled citizens about the history of Flag Day and the meaning of the flag. The Girl Scouts are recognized for their role and are invited to address the group. Then the people gathered are invited to share their feelings about the flag. The flag-folding ritual is also demonstrated. (See Sidebar 8.) Afterward, the post continues to burn flags. [1]

According to Ernest DiPietro, former commander of Cheshire's American Legion Post 92, "We want to see the flag of our nation treated with dignity and respect. Our flag retirement ceremony demonstrates how Old Glory should be treated when it's necessary to dispose of a flag. It also provides a public service so residents can properly dispose of flags. Consigning them to the flames is the traditional military way of doing it, and by doing it publicly, we raise the level of patriotic expression in our town."

That thought is echoed by veterans across our country. In Closter, New Jersey, for example, American Legion Post 111 and its counterpart VFW post in Northvale showed school children at St. Mary's School and Tenakill Middle School how to properly dispose of an American flag. The wave of patriotic expression which swept America after the September 11, 2001 terrorist attacks saw flags proudly displayed everywhere, but by the following Spring, many of them had become tattered and damaged by wind. So the two posts took action: they performed the flag retirement ritual in the school parking lot. As reported by the *New Jersey Record* (13 March 2002, p. L-5), Joe Organo, vice commander of the American Legion post, told the students, "This is not just a rag to be thrown away. People have died believing in what this flag stands for. Do not mistreat my flag." Post Commander Jack Kelly finished the thought. "Rather than just throw it in the garbage, give it to us."

As another example, in Jeffersontown, Kentucky, American Legion Post 244 respectfully retires thousands of flags each year through ceremonial burning. Flags are collected from Jefferson County, surrounding Kentucky counties and from Indiana neighbors to the north. On the day of the semiannual event, flags are taken to the crest of a hill, placed on wooden pallets and soaked with a flammable liquid. Prior to ignition, Legionnaires carry out solemn sunset ceremonies. Post member John Wright, quoted above from *The American Legion* magazine (December 2003, p. 54) said, "We don't simply pile up a bunch of flags and set them on fire. We honor each flag collectively in formal services the way we would honor a fallen comrade on the battlefield."

America's veterans everywhere send that message to you.

---

## FOOTNOTES

[1] If the number of flags to be consigned to the fire is large, it could take many hours to burn them all. So our approach, following the lead of other posts, is to display the entire collection of unserviceable flags—which is in the hundreds—in the collection boxes, then burn a sufficient number to demonstrate the process and fulfill the needs of the ceremony. Beyond that, we have arranged with a local funeral home to have the flags reduced to ashes in its crematorium. This cremation service, graciously offered without charge by the patriotic staff, provides a dignified ending to the unserviceable flags. Post members are relieved of the need to remain on duty at the ceremonial fire for hours after the ritual has ended.

## Sidebar 16

# A PATRIOT'S CALENDAR

The National Flag represents our nation as a living experience and vital heritage. It is emblematic of the respect and pride Americans have for our country. It should be displayed on all days in good weather, but especially these. It is the universal custom to display the flag only from sunrise to sunset on buildings and on stationary flagstaffs in the open. However, the flag may be displayed outside at night when it is desired to produce a patriotic effect; in such instances, the flag should be illuminated. Also, all-weather flags (identified as such by the manufacturer) may be flown in bad weather.

| | |
|---|---|
| January 1 | **New Year's Day** |
| January 20 | **Inauguration Day**. Celebrates beginning a new term of office by The President of the United States. |
| Third Monday in January | **Martin Luther King, Jr. Day** |
| February 12 | **Abraham Lincoln's birthday** |
| February 22 | **George Washington's birthday** |
| Third Monday in February | **President's Day** |
| Variable (early Spring) | **Easter Sunday** |
| May 1 | **Loyalty Day.** Recognizes that America is our heritage. |
| Second Sunday in May | **Mother's Day** |
| May 15 | **Peace Officers Memorial Day.** (Flag flies at half-staff until noon.) |
| Third Sunday in May | **Armed Forces Day.** Honors men and women currently serving in America's armed forces. |
| Last Monday in May | **Memorial Day.** Honors deceased men and women who gave their lives in military service to America. (Flag flies at half-staff until noon.) |

| | |
|---|---|
| June 14 | **Flag Day.** Honors the birthday of "Old Glory." |
| July 4 | **Independence Day.** Honors the day when the Declaration of Independence was adopted and America was officially founded. |
| July 27 | **National Korean War Veterans Day** |
| First Monday in September | **Labor Day.** Honors American workers. |
| September 17 | **Constitution Day.** Honors the Constitution of the United States of America, which was signed on September 17, 1787, and expresses appreciation for being a citizen of the United States of America. |
| September 24 | **National Recognition Day.** Honors American POWs and MIAs. |
| Second Monday in October | **Columbus Day.** Honors the discovery of America by Christopher Columbus. |
| October 27 | **Navy Day.** Honors the U.S. Navy. |
| First Tuesday in November | **Election Day.** It is the right and responsibility of Americans to vote for candidates and on civic/political issues in our system of self-government. |
| November 11 | **Veterans Day.** Honors living men and women who served in America's military services. |
| Fourth Thursday in November | **Thanksgiving Day.** Designated as a national day for giving thanks to God for the gift of America. |
| December 7 | **Pearl Harbor Remembrance Day.** Honors those who lost their lives in the 1941 surprise attack on Pearl Harbor, Hawaii. |
| December 15 | **Bill of Rights Day.** Marks the ratification of the Bill of Rights, the first 10 amendments to the U.S. Constitution, in 1791. |
| December 25 | **Christmas Day** |

All election days.

All state and local holidays.

Birthdays of states (dates of admission).

Such days as may be proclaimed
by the President of the United States.

# VETERANS—STILL ON DUTY FOR AMERICA

Today is Veterans Day, a national holiday when America honors a group of citizens who have earned special recognition and treatment: military veterans. Their deserving status has been recognized since the founding of America. Veterans' benefits are not welfare, handouts or charity; they are payback for service rendered. Veterans' benefits are earned; they are part of the price of freedom.

The purpose of our armed forces is to provide national security. Our warriors protect our freedom. However, we vets understand that the price of freedom is eternal vigilance against all enemies, whether foreign or domestic, so even though we're not in the armed forces any more, we're still on duty. That's the responsibility of citizenship. Whether you've left the service or never were in it, you're always on duty as an American citizen to preserve freedom and keep our nation strong.

When we were in the military, we reported to the President, who is Commander-in-Chief. However, as civilians, we don't report to the Commander-in-Chief; we report to the Founding Fathers, to the Constitution and to God, who is the source of our liberty, our sovereignty, our equality, our rights, our justice and our human dignity. That is what the Declaration of Independence says this nation is all about and that is what we veterans uphold.

So we say to the young people today:

You are going to inherit this great nation someday, but will you keep it? The strength of America resides in citizens who understand and perform their obligations in a country dedicated to a way of life based on self-government, with liberty and justice for all. You young people must understand the sacred debt you owe to the men and women of the armed forces who have kept America safe and strong for you. Many of them died in defense of liberty; they gave up their tomorrows for your today. Without your understanding and performance of the duties of citizenship, America will weaken and eventually cease to exist. I say that because youth is 20% of the population but 100% of the future. If you don't appreciate and honor what America is all about, in a few generations, there won't be an America.

We veterans want you to keep America, and we'll help you however we can. We are mindful of providing a role model for you. During World War Two, America had 132,000,000 citizens and 16,000,000 of them served in the armed forces. That was one out of every eight people. With so many men and women in uniform, almost every civilian knew one or more veterans—because they were family and neighbors—and respected them for the effort they made to win the victory. Young people of that era, such as me, grew up with a powerful willingness to serve our nation, thanks to our parents and thanks to the role modeling of veterans.

Today America has a population more than double that. We have 300,000,000-plus citizens but only a little more than 1,500,000 of them are in the military. The ratio of veterans to civilians is much smaller now. Veterans are becoming invisible in the general population, especially as the World War Two and Korean vets make their final roll call. There are fewer and fewer new vets to join The American Legion, the Veterans of Foreign Wars and other such organizations which keep patriotism alive. If America were faced again with a world war, could the high school seniors of today handle another invasion of Normandy, another Battle of Iwo Jima? Remember, the average age of the warriors who died in those actions was 19.

As I said, if young people don't understand what America is all about, soon there won't be an America. But whose fault would that be? If young people don't learn patriotism and the significance of America at home, in school, in church, temple and mosque, and from the words and deeds of public officials and opinion makers, it is not their fault. It is ours. That's why we're here today. As we honor those who served in the armed forces, we also show to young people our love and devotion to freedom, to the American republic, to one nation under God.

So as a citizen and veteran, I ask you adults: What are you doing to educate youth about the principles of American society? What are you doing to educate youth about the values and traditions which built our nation? What are you doing to educate youth about the price of freedom? Does your example support your words?

Freedom is not free. Its price is paid in blood, sweat and tears. With so much strife and tyranny in the world, to be born free is a great privilege, but to die free is a great responsibility. As citizens of America, we have the responsibility to preserve freedom by instilling patriotism in our young people through personal example, through public events such as the Memorial Day and Veterans Day ceremonies, through showing respect for the flag, for the national anthem and for veterans, and by the simple, everyday demonstration of good citizenship. On behalf of all veterans, I urge you, young and old alike, to keep faith with those before us who pledged allegiance to America. With God's help and your service to our country, we will remain free and strong, and hold the torch of liberty high for all the world.

*These remarks were delivered on November 11, 2005, in Cheshire, Connecticut during a Veterans Day ceremony.*

**Chapter 16**

# "WITH LIBERTY AND JUSTICE FOR ALL"— THE UNITED STATES OF THE WORLD

Our cause is noble; it is the cause of mankind.

– George Washington,
Letter to James Warren, 1779

The cause of America is in great measure the cause of all mankind.
– Thomas Paine, *Common Sense*, 1776

God grant that not only the love of liberty, but a thorough knowledge of the Rights of Man, may pervade all the nations of the Earth, so that a philosopher may set his foot anywhere on its surface, and say, "This is my country."

– Benjamin Franklin

Justice is the will to secure to everyone his own right.
– President John Quincey Adams

And so, my fellow Americans, ask not what your country can do for you: Ask what you can do for your country.

My fellow citizens of the world: Ask not what America will do for you, but what together we can do for the freedom of man.

– President John F. Kennedy, Inaugural Address, 1961

We are the heirs of the great American Revolution. As this millennium draws to a close and the 21st century approaches, let us pause to honor the very idea of America. America mirrors the world's diversity, yet it remains united in the struggle to uphold fundamental freedom. We believe our nation's happiness still evolves from liberty, from opportunity and from the vision of equality set forth by our country's Declaration of Independence. And today our nation stands as a symbol of freedom and inspiration to people all over the world. There is nothing wrong with America that cannot be corrected by what is right with America. And there is nothing wrong with the world that cannot be cured by the ideals America represents. Those principles have no borders, and we look forward to a day when those principles, extended beyond our borders, will have circled the globe. The quest for democracy must continue until all of the people of the world enjoy the freedom we must always fight to preserve. The spirit of America is as bright and hopeful today as it was in July of 1776. And we are ready to carry our great national experiment forward into the next millennium.

– President William J. Clinton,
in his recorded speech in the Hall of Presidents
at Liberty Square, Walt Disney World, Florida

Americans are a free people, who know that freedom is the right of every person and the future of every nation. The liberty we prize is not America's gift to the world; it is God's gift to humanity.

— President George W. Bush,
in his 2003 State of the Union Address

We do not seek to impose our way of life on anyone, but rather to let it shine as an example. We will shine for everyone to follow.

— President Donald J. Trump,
in his 2017 Inaugural Address

It is not coincidence that the deity is mentioned four times in the Declaration of Independence. Our Founders saw clearly that God is the almighty Author of our very being and the source of our freedom, our sovereignty, our equality, our rights, our justice and our human dignity. The Declaration was a brilliant, innovative political document, but equally important, it is a *spiritual* document. Its essence is actually a restatement of a universal wisdom tradition about deity going back thousands of years.

As I noted in the first chapter, that tradition has been called the Perennial Philosophy, the Ageless Wisdom, the Timeless Wisdom and the Primordial Tradition. It is humanity's collective highest understanding about our nature and our destiny. The sum of it is this:

There is a meaning, purpose and direction to life. It is to express God, the source of our existence, evermore fully, thus glorifying God. For us humans, the purpose of life is to consciously realize God and then manifest that realization in every aspect of our lives, thereby glorifying God in the highest manner possible. To put it another way, it is seeing God in all things and all things in God, and then living in accordance with that understanding of divine nature. That is God-realization or, as it has also been called, liberation, unity consciousness, cosmic consciousness, nondual consciousness, spiritual freedom, enlightenment.

Enlightenment is the goal of human history, for the individual and for the race. The wonderful thing about enlightenment is that it is democratically available to everyone. We are evolving toward enlightenment, individually and collectively. God is drawing us all to His kingdom through a vast process involving all time and space.

How can that transcendent wisdom, that visionary insight of the Perennial Philosophy be put to work effectively? How can it be made practical around the world? How can the One who created us all and embraces us all be recognized as the basis for worldwide sister-and-brotherhood? How can human society be changed from its traditional divisions and divisiveness to a unified and universal community? How can patriotism—the national form of love of family—be extended to the entire family of Man? How can we develop a politics of enlightenment or God-realization for all humanity?

The answer is simple: America. The spiritual foundations of America are wholly congruent with the Perennial Philosophy. They are eternal and immutable because they reflect aspects of God. If they articulate that toward which humanity is evolving— enlightenment—then America, in its ideal form, represents the best political means devised so far to create societal conditions for nurturing, and even hastening, human evolution to enlightenment.

## Enlightenment Is for Everyone

The Perennial Philosophy declares that enlightenment is for everyone, awaiting us as the fulfillment of our human potential. Consider what that means for societal transformation and world peace. A simple syllogism expresses it:

1. Enlightenment is the goal of human history.
2. The essence of America is enlightenment.
3. Therefore, the essence of America is the goal of human history.

American patriotism differs from that of all other nations because it is based on love of God—love of the Spirit of Liberty—and reflected in society through the people, traditions and institutions comprising the American experience. American patriotism recognizes that our national identity consists not of territorial or ancestral origins but rather—to repeat what I said in the first chapter—it consists of the ideals, principles and values which flow (as the reverse of the Great Seal of the United States depicts) from the metaphysical to the physical, from the transcendent to the material, from God to the nation, where they are embodied in the laws, customs and practices of our civic and political life.

Thus, American patriotism is an understanding of this nation as a means whereby God's kingdom is being built on Earth. By offering to all nations the privilege of joining the Union (with appropriate preconditions for preparing them to become responsible American citizens—see below), a United States of the World could envelop the planet. Through a direct and unadulterated extension of our political heritage, American patriots can fashion a society which—again, to repeat from Chapter 1—builds world unity while honoring global diversity, exactly as the words *E pluribus unum* indicate, and which removes institutional forms of bondage and barriers to freedom and equality of opportunity in a world without borders.

John Adams, in a speech to the House of Representatives on July 4, 1821, highlighted the quintessential character of America as "the march of the mind." America's glory, he said, is not dominion, but liberty. "Her march is the march of the mind. She has a spear and a shield: but the motto upon her shield is Freedom, Independence, Peace. This has been her declaration: this has been, as far as her necessary intercourse with the rest of mankind would permit, her practice."

The spirit of Thomas Jefferson pervades this book, all the way from the Declaration of Independence and his words for our previous national motto, *E pluribus unum,* to his vision of global freedom and universal self-rule. Jefferson was not simply a visionary, however. He understood well that vision must be grounded in practicable forms and institutions of governance. In an 1816 letter to his friend Samuel Kercheval, he said:

> I know…that laws and institutions must go hand in hand with the progress of the human mind. As that becomes more developed, more enlightened, as new discoveries are made, new truths disclosed, and manners and opinions change

with the change of circumstances, institutions must advance also, and keep pace with the times.

My advocacy of the American political tradition is based on recognizing the human potential for growth to God-realization. I am not an uncritical defender of America, as my comments in this book should make clear. My observations are critical but documented. On that basis, I nevertheless state without reservation: ***America is the most advanced political system thus far along the evolutionary path to an enlightened global society because it is consciously and deliberately constructed to acknowledge and encourage that condition.***

In the spirit of Thomas Jefferson, what I propose is not a mere expansion of American hegemony but rather is, I maintain, a transcendent and truly cosmopolitan vision of what can become the basis for a genuine global union which honors all cultures, preserving them while refining and advancing them on the basis of free choice by the members of those cultures: The United States of the World. From that stance, I'll now offer a proposal for advancing freedom and attaining world peace.

## The United States of the World

In the Introduction, I urged Americans to turn The American Century into the beginning of The American Millennium because I believe it is humanity's only hope for a truly free and peaceful world. Here's how I think that can be attained. But first consider the words of Strobe Talbott in a 1992 essay he published in *Time* magazine:

> The best mechanism for democracy, whether at the level of the multinational state, or that of the planet as a whole, is not an all-powerful Leviathan or centralized superstate, but a federation, a union of separate states that allocate certain powers to a central government while retaining many others for themselves.
>
> The U.S. is still the best example of a multi-national federal state. If that model does indeed work globally, it would be the logical extension of the Founding Fathers' wisdom.

If another country or territory were to join the Union, the citizens of that new state would then begin, or continue, the educational process of inculcating American patriotism. Since American patriotism can encompass the whole of humanity, all nations, theoretically speaking, could change their status and join these united States. (The authority for that is Article 4, Section 3 of the Constitution.) America could embrace humankind through the benign extension of our political heritage to become The United States of the World.

What would develop from that? The result would be a true world community with responsible self-governance. The result would be a planet at peace rather than in pieces. The result would be America writ large upon the face of Earth—not arrogantly as a superstate, imperium, colonial power or American Empire but humbly as a God-realized Pax Americana. America would wage peace upon the world—the peace (*pax*) of God which passes all understanding. Our Constitution and its amendments, especially the Bill of Rights, would establish a global society in which war ends, freedom flourishes and prosperity abounds, as spiritual unity is promoted while cultural, racial, religious and ethnic diversity are honored. People everywhere could continue to love the lands of their birth as geographical locations; that would not conflict with loving America as their country of choice because those lands would be included in the territory of America. All sense of national identity which now so divides people into warring factions would be transformed into a sense of American identity, just as citizens of, say, Connecticut, Colorado and California love their home states but are unified in their identity as Americans. Honoring America as a global democratic republic would be synonymous with honoring Earth and creation itself, while simultaneously honoring one's previous national identity preserved as a sovereign state of the Union. As was said about the British flag at the height of British power in the 19th century, the sun would never set upon the star-spangled banner.

As I pointed out in the first chapter, since patriotism is the national form of love of family, love of America would be identical with love of the entire human family. It would also provide the global ethic which many spiritual groups are seeking in their quest for a better world based on love for humanity and the planet.

There would be no need for the United Nations because the world would be united as one nation. There would be planetwide freedom of speech, worship, assembly, the press, education, travel and trade. There would be no more NAFTAs, GATTs, WTOs and G-8s. If there are no nations to set tariffs, duties, trade barriers and trade balances against one another, why would we need all those treaties and agreements? Do the 50 states of America operate that way? Obviously, no.

The need for military forces and armaments would be virtually eliminated. There would be no more NATOs and SEATOs (ASEAN). If there are no nations to make war on one another, what is the need for soldiers, tanks and bombs? Do the 50 states of America settle differences that way? Obviously, no.

The United States of the World would provide the ultimate national security and military defense strategy for America. It would eliminate all our enemies by the peaceful and benign process of their conversion to Americanism. It would also eliminate the internal strife of tribal genocide, killing fields and brutal military dictatorships which oppress people in so many other countries.

The English language and the American dollar, which already are the *de facto* standard for international business, would become officially so. Just as we Americans now move freely throughout our land without Customs inspections, bureaucratic regulations and the need to exchange currency when we cross the border from one state into another, so would the entire population of Earth. Just as we Americans now enjoy a common heritage and identity which embraces many cultures, so would the entire population of Earth. America's best would become the world's best. American sovereignty and the American way of life would be preserved from shadowy international forces now seeking to destroy it. [1] In fact, the very word *international* would become obsolete. America would embrace the world and Americans everywhere would literally pledge allegiance to Earth as "one Nation under God, indivisible, with liberty and justice for all." It would accomplish what John Philip Sousa proudly proclaimed as "The Stars and Stripes Forever," which is the national march of the United States. (See Appendix 3.) It would fulfill Thomas Paine's description of global patriotism in *Rights of Man*: "The world is my country, all mankind are my brethren, and to do good is my religion." It would crown America's good with sister-and-brotherhood, across the Seven Seas, through the creation of a global nation and a world without borders.

## A Vision for Americans

That is my vision, my American dream. It is grounded in the God of our Founders, the Spirit of Liberty. It is loyal to the Declaration of Independence and the Constitution, which embody the ideals, principles and values of the Enlightenment tradition of our Founders. But it is also a new expression by Spirit-in-action of the world's enlightenment traditions, who is identical with the God of our forefathers and mothers, and is the Divine Source of the ongoing revelations and extensions of the American Spirit—this one and others yet to appear.

I pray it happens. The barriers to it are many and mighty. There are vast linguistic, religious, political, economic, legal, educational and cultural differences standing in the way of developing responsible citizenship in those potential new Americans. Other obstacles are brutal and corrupt governments, international criminal and terrorist organizations, vested financial interests and longstanding hatreds among diverse peoples. There is the absence of democratic traditions and citizen empowerment in many nations, and there is simple ignorance and complacence. There is also—let us think about it in practical terms—the challenge of conducting a Congress enlarged by representatives of Earth's nearly 200 nations which would become new states. And what about redesigning our flag to add a new star for every one of those new nation-states? As I said, there are many and mighty obstacles. However, I believe all those obstacles are surmountable and the goal is infinitely preferable to all other political possibilities for world government because they are antithetical to freedom.

## The UN vs. Freedom

The thrust of human history is toward ever-greater unity on all levels of our being, including the political, reflecting the unifying spirit of God. The Preamble to the Constitution puts it thus: "...to form a more perfect union." However, the way world affairs are going at present, we have nation warring against nation and faction fighting against faction, and the organization which is supposed to be a forum for the peaceful settlement of differences among belligerents—the United Nations—is, first of all, badly ineffective in performing that job and, second, has gotten "mission creep." What began as an international organization of sovereign nations is now attempting to become a world government to absorb all other governments into it. The 1994 UN publication *United Nation's Report on Human Development* states unequivocally, "Mankind's problems can no longer be solved by national governments. What is needed is a World Government" (p. 88). Now, guess who that world government will be.

An article by Herbert W. Titus (contained on the web site of Libertarian Answers (at http://libertariananswers.com/does-the-un-seek-to-usurp-the-sovereignty-of-its-nation-states-how-would-this-affect-the-individuals) explains why the UN threatens American sovereignty and that of other countries:

It is commonly assumed that the Charter of the United Nations is a treaty. It is not. Instead, the Charter of the United Nations is a constitution. As such, it is illegitimate, having created a supranational government, deriving its powers not from the consent of the governed (the people of the United States of America and peoples of other member nations) but from the consent of the peoples' government officials who have no authority to bind either the American people nor any other nation's people to any terms of the Charter of the United Nations.

Our individual sovereignty is certainly threatened when we can be bound to a contract without our express consent.

Former Rep. Ron Paul of Texas—a staunch defender of the Constitution and advocate for American sovereignty—has said the United Nations is not a government body, it has no legal right to create laws, and it has no legal right to enforce criminal prosecution of anyone. I agree.

Moreover, the UN is neither democratic nor representative. The citizens of the world do not vote for their representatives to the UN in free elections, nor do the citizens of the world have the power to impeach unfit or undesirable representatives. They have no right of direct appeal and no right of direct redress of grievances or wrongs. Yet membership in the UN obligates its members to abide by a set of international laws (disingenuously called accords) which limit the rights of their citizens while pretending to grant them unlimited democracy. Every step the UN takes to assert its control over the planet, its resources and its people—and even outer space—is not open to debate except within the legislatures of member nations, and when a certain minimum of them vote in favor of something—no matter how small an amount of territory or how few people the minimum collectively represents—the UN arrogantly says that step becomes binding on all other nations, regardless of their nonacceptance or rejection of it. The UN regards itself as the ultimate world authority and is answerable to no one! That is not "the consent of the governed." That is naked dictatorship and tyranny. [2]

In addition, the UN's Universal Declaration of Human Rights is hopelessly flawed. There is no transcendent basis recognized in it on which our liberty, our sovereignty, our equality, our rights, our justice and our human dignity are established. According to the Universal Declaration, human beings have rights because "they are endowed with reason and conscience." The source of humanity's reason and conscience is not named, even in explanatory UN publications. One UN publication notes, "Because man is a rational and moral being, he is different from other creatures on earth and therefore is entitled to certain rights and freedoms which other creatures do not enjoy." Nowhere is there recognition of God as the source of our existence and the goodness toward which humanity strives to build a peaceful world. [3]

Rather, the human rights enumerated in the Universal Declaration are predicated on the idea that the UN controls everything, including the definition of rights, and no one can oppose that. In the UN's view, government, not God, is the source of all authority—specifically, the UN itself as a world government. Article 29 states: "These rights and freedoms may in no case be exercised contrary to the purposes and principles of the United Nations." Article 30 states: "Nothing in this Declaration may be interpreted as implying for any State, group or person any right to engage in any activity or to perform any act aimed at the destruction of any of the rights and freedoms set forth herein."

Compare that with the Declaration of Independence: "...to secure these rights, Governments are instituted among Men, deriving their just powers from the consent of the governed. ...whenever any Form of Government becomes destructive of these ends, it is the Right of the People to alter or to abolish it, and to institute new

Government, laying its foundation on such principles and organizing its powers in such form, as to them shall seem most likely to effect their Safety and Happiness."

The UN way won't work. When government bestows rights, government can abolish those rights because they are not inherent and inalienable. That, to repeat, is why our Founders created a federal government with minimal delegated authority and firmly constrained by the principles and practices of liberty. Throughout history, government has been the principal enemy of freedom. A world government which bestows rights would therefore be the world's principal enemy of freedom. The UN way is the way to global tyranny. That's the way freedom will perish from the earth. 4 That's the way to a requiem for America.

Only a direct and unadulterated extension of the Declaration of Independence and The Constitution of the United States of America can bring a truly free, peaceful and unified world. Of all political documents in history, only those two make the Perennial Philosophy workable by offering a theory and practice of enlightened government. Collectively, they address all levels of our being.

First and foremost, they recognize God, the **Spirit of Liberty**, as the source of all life, all liberty, all equality, all personal sovereignty, all rights and all good. Next, in the Declaration of Independence, they enunciate the basic **principles of liberty** descending from God to be applied in the body politic. Then, in the Constitution, they articulate the **architecture of liberty**, which describes how our federal government is constructed, and the Bill of Rights, which enumerates the *inalienable rights of each individual* citizen, no matter what any government body or group of people may want to do otherwise. These make secure the blessings of liberty as they establish justice, insure domestic tranquility, provide for the common defense and promote the general welfare. Last of all, they demand and encourage elected officials and civil servants of integrity, calling on them to enact and enforce **laws, policies and practices of liberty** which honor the sovereignty of the individual citizen. At every level of human activity, from the physical through the mental and the social to the spiritual, from the individual through local, state and national government to the global human family, they declare God as the divine basis of our existence. Collectively, they make conditions for God-realization politically workable through the freedoms we enjoy to worship, speak, publish, assemble, travel and so forth.

God is the Founding Spirit of America, operating through the Founders. That is the source of the American Revolution. That is the truth which can set us free on all levels of our existence. It is universal and all-embracing truth, encompassing the entire cosmos. No other nation on Earth has such a basis.

## Implementing the Dream

U.S. citizenship confers responsibilities as well as rights, and those responsibilities must be recognized and accepted by potential new citizens. If nations or territories are to vote for statehood, Congress should set up strict conditions by which they would become qualified for admission to the Union. The voting of nations or territories should be by plebiscite—a direct vote by their residents—which genuinely expresses the opinion of the common people and is populist, not elitist. The majority of a nation—of say, England, France, Germany or Japan, which are relatively wealthy and free—might prefer their present status and not want admission to the Union, even though special interests in the government or business community might favor it and attempt to manipulate their legislative bodies to vote for admission. On the other hand, dictators presently holding power might try to derail a nation's popular wish to join the Union. So only a truly democratic vote should be the basis for statehood. There must be free, informed and voluntary assent to become Americans; anything less than that would violate the American Spirit.

There are major obstacles to responsible citizenship which must be overcome before the status of "American" is conferred on any foreign populace. English is our national language; it should be learned by all because our national unity depends upon a common tongue. Their public and private school curricula should have mandatory courses on American history, civics and political theory, the Declaration of Independence and the Constitution, and the responsibilities of citizens to vote, serve on juries, pay taxes and otherwise participate in the processes of our political and civic life.

What about showing respect for the American flag and displaying it properly in public? What about learning our national anthem and showing respect for the music when it is played in public? What about learning the Pledge of Allegiance, the national motto and other guiding inscriptions and symbols—and their meaning? What about observing national holidays such as Independence Day, Memorial Day and Veterans Day? What about learning of our nation's military structure—the branches of the armed forces, the chain of command from the President to the lowest rank of enlistees, the Medal of Honor and the Purple Heart, and the oath to support and defend the Constitution of the United States? And, in general, what about inculcating the sentiment of patriotism for America?

Being a patriotic American means showing informed, intelligent love of country. It means honoring our country's past, present and future. It means understanding and appreciating the fundamental principles, ideals, values, events, traditions, goals and dreams which have built our nation. ***True patriotism is best shown by responsible citizenship to preserve and extend America's freedom.***

All that can't be learned in an instant. Yet without it, citizenship is meaningless and even destructive of America. It's just a highway to the welfare trough. Therefore, in the event of statehood for another nation or territory, I think a twenty-year program of gradual integration to the Union would be appropriate to ensure that those people are properly prepared for citizenship and the American way of life. That means earning the privilege of citizenship by demonstrating they are ready, willing and able to assume its responsibilities and obligations. That means no mass migration to America to feed at the welfare trough, but rather an education in the basics of American citizenship—i.e., understanding the sacred and indivisible nature of freedom and the connection of its personal, economic, social and political aspects—so that our nation is enlarged by responsible, knowledgeable citizens, not people incapable of self-reliance and self-government.

## Raising the World's Standard of Living

My vision of The United States of the World has this additional benefit: introduction of the American way of life into a potential new state would raise its standard of living so that the material benefits of American society are realized there and the likelihood of mass migration of new citizens is eliminated. The reason people emigrate to America is to obtain the personal freedom and economic opportunity offered here. However, if "here" becomes "there," emigration becomes unnecessary. I propose to extend our freedom and opportunity to other lands. Statehood would confer both those conditions on any potential new state; a twenty-year probationary period would allow those conditions to bear fruit and equalize the new state's socioeconomic status with that of heartland America or at least approximate it. Our rule of law and our military strength would establish internal safety and external security for that new state. Our free market economy would elevate the level of goods and services—the standard of living —available in that nation to heartland America standards or nearly so. Our political structure would eliminate concern about the balance of trade with that former country because all trade would be internal between states.

With freedom from political fear and economic want—two of Franklin D. Roosevelt's "Four Freedoms" [4]—established in those provisional territories, heartland American citizens would not be faced with the nightmare of housing and feeding millions of poor, uneducated, unskilled migrant citizens who cannot communicate in English. Thus, the residents of, say, Vietnam, Haiti, Somalia or Bosnia would have no urgent need to leave their homelands to seek political asylum or to get on the public dole. Travel to heartland America would be changed from a desperate desire to escape oppression into a sociable wish to visit friends and relatives or take a vacation. In a world without war and want, in a world which proclaims and protects freedom and individual rights, people would be content to reside in their native lands, honoring and preserving their culture while enjoying the blessings of liberty which we Americans now have in abundance. Their racial, ethnic, religious and cultural diversity would remain— but modified to American norms of liberty, equality and justice—just as generations of immigrants from those nations have already done in pursuing happiness and "the good life" for themselves and their posterity here. And that would drive a stake through the heart of the New World Order.

By implementing this vision, by drawing down the dream, we Americans can ignite a political movement which extends the American Spirit to the entire world through unity-in-diversity. As a nation, we can so shine our light into the darkness of oppression, poverty, ignorance and fear that freedom is proclaimed throughout the world and the blessings of liberty are extended to all people. Then we would truly have a planet at peace and a world without need for armies. That is the age-old dream of humanity. It is also the promise of America.

## America as a Form of God-Realization

Before the founding of America, governments were predicated on limiting the liberty and rights of people by a supreme ruler or ruling body to whose government the populace was subservient; they were subjects, not citizens. That remains the case for large parts of Earth even today. America, however, is predicated on a revolutionary political idea which had never before been tried: expanding the freedom of individual citizens while keeping governmental power to a necessary minimum and government employees as servants of We the People. Before the founding of America, the "divine right of kings" governed society. The monarch was sovereign, subject to no one, and the government existed to support him, apart from the people.

America radically transformed that. In America, everyone is a king, figuratively speaking. The individual citizen is sovereign, titles of nobility are prohibited, and the government is subject to us and exists to serve us in our pursuit of happiness by protecting our freedom. The Constitution which created the federal government is intended to govern the government, not the people. The Constitution doesn't grant us freedom and rights because they are inherent in us before government even existed. Rather, the Constitution prohibits government from taking them away.

American patriotism differs from the patriotism of all other nations by that which distinguishes America itself from all other nations: namely, freedom, personal sovereignty, inalienable rights, justice and dignity for each citizen, derived from God—not from any human institution—and implemented in a self-governing society through democratically elected representatives serving in a constitutional republic characterized by a three-part division of federal power. The power of the federal government is strictly limited in its scope; it is constrained by the Constitution through the deliberately narrow definition of its authority and enumerated powers, and through a system of checks and balances to prevent or correct any attempts to overreach its authority.

In America, there are equal rights for all but special rights for none. The phrase "all men are created equal" meant to the Founders—and still means today—that no one should have special rights or privileges before the law or in dealing with the government because of who their parents were. There is no involuntary servitude, no monarchy or aristocracy or hereditary titles, and no arbitrary rule of despots. No one is above the law; everyone has equal protection under the law but no judicial privileges. Following elections, there is peaceful transfer of governmental power rather than military coup, thus assuring civic continuity rather than social disruption. Thanks to the wisdom, courage and sacrifice of the Signers of the Declaration and the Framers of the Constitution, America, the fortress of freedom, has contributed more to the betterment of the common people than any other political body in history. As Abraham Lincoln put it, "Freedom is the last best hope of earth."

That meaningful liberty is why, as the Statue of Liberty symbolizes, America is a beacon of hope and opportunity for the oppressed of humanity. The political experiment called America begun more than two centuries ago is Earth's greatest opportunity for every human being to use his or her talents, effort and property, in the pursuit of happiness, to build a satisfying life in a context which encourages civic responsibility, social justice and spiritual unity. I can think of nothing more desirable short of enlightenment for all humanity, which would be the full manifestation of the kingdom of heaven on Earth.

American patriotism is an understanding of this nation as a political form of God-realization. Our nation is an evolutionarily advanced political means of expressing God in our lives, and in its ideal form is wholly in line with what the Perennial Philosophy prescribes for peace on Earth. That tradition guides society toward God-realization, the goal of life. That is the Spirit of Liberty in action—not just political liberty but absolute truth and ultimate freedom itself. Of all the nations on Earth, the foundational ideals, principles and values of America are most aligned with the Perennial Philosophy and thus—to repeat—America represents the best political means devised so far to create societal conditions for supporting human growth to enlightenment. Therefore, the essence of America is the future of the world, the goal of history. [5]

However, the Perennial Philosophy does not proselytize; it informs and educates in a benign manner, never forcing or coercing, but only trying to persuade and convince on the basis of reason, realization and direct experience. It operates by attraction, not promotion. That is why so many people have come to America. They are attracted by the freedom and opportunity to find happiness and a better future for themselves, their families and their descendants. Although they may understand that attraction only in material and social terms, the potential is there for understanding and attaining the highest aspect of America: spiritual freedom, God-realization, unity/nondual/cosmic consciousness, liberation, enlightenment.

The War for Independence is over but the American Revolution goes on because it is a spiritual revolution of global dimensions. American patriots carry forward humanity's sacred love of freedom and the hard-won wisdom of our national experience which preserves our freedom and sovereignty against tyrants—of both the classes and the masses—so that, some day, all the inhabitants of Earth may enjoy the blessings of liberty—and liberation. [6] To truly understand America—its metaphysical foundation and its holy ideals, principles and values—is to stand at the threshold of enlightenment. To truly implement America—its potential for developing a United States of the World— could, at long last, bring a pledge of allegiance to "one Nation under God" in a magnificent act of planetary patriotism and global self-governance, with liberty, justice, equality of opportunity and prosperity for all.

*America! America!*
*May God thy gold refine*
*Till all success be nobleness*
*And every gain divine!*

I'm grateful to be American! I'm proud to salute the flag and pledge allegiance to the republic for which it stands! May God continue to bless America, this wonderful land I love! And for the good and the God of all humanity, I humbly but heartily say: **May the American Spirit embrace the world!**

---

# FOOTNOTES

[1] Those shadowy international forces include a longstanding conspiracy to create a world government which will eliminate our liberty and sovereignty, both individual and national. It is commonly known as the New World Order. What is it and how does it operate?

I see four levels to the process by which the New World Order is being implemented. Call it the Four C's: conspiracy, collusion, consensus and complacence. The process is structured like a pyramid.

At the top is actual ***conspiracy*** among a small number of plutocratic elites and their minions whose objective, largely unrecognized even by themselves, is to replace God and become Masters of the Universe. The most visible signs of such plutocratic conspiracy can be seen in the Bilderberg Group, the Trilateral Commission, the Council on Foreign Relations and others whom some collectively call "the Insiders," "the Invisible Government" and the Empire Elite.

The second level of the pyramid is ***collusion*** among globalist organizations set up by the plutocrats to do their bidding, but whose membership often doesn't recognize that. Most notable among those organizations are the World Bank, International Monetary Fund, Export-Import Bank, Federal Reserve System, World Trade Organization, and the United Nations and all its spinoffs. The world's central banks are taking control of the global economy; the world government is being set up through the UN. The number who collude is significantly larger than the number of primary conspirators, but is still only a small percentage of the many thousands of people who are employees of those organizations. The rank-and-file of such organizations, by and large, are decent people unaware of their role in the larger scheme. They fall into the third level of operation in the scheme to establish a New World Order.

The third level is ***conditioned consensus***. This level has predisposed large numbers of people—millions in America alone—to accept in sheep-like fashion the actions and social-political positions of the conspiratorial elite. That consensus is achieved through manipulation of the news, school curricula and other sources of information, and cultural institutions in general. The controlled major media, both print and broadcast, bias their reportage in favor of the globalist perspective held by their owners, who are among the plutocratic elite conspiring to become Masters of the Universe. Thus the elite are given an aura of respectability and wisdom as they act toward the apparently noble objective of unified global governance.

The fourth level—the base of the pyramid—represents the largest number of people who are unknowingly assisting the New World Order: ***complacent citizens***. These are the ones who take no interest in the political process or social-economic issues, but settle for ignorance and a superficial life of "bread and circuses" via government handouts and the various forms of mind-dumbing, moral-numbing entertainment which destroy all sense of civility and refinement in life. Judging by the number of voters who did not exercise their responsibility to cast a ballot in recent national elections, this level is fully half of the adult American population.

Why does the New World Order conspiracy exist?

What the architects of the New World Order intend is essentially ***the destruction of America*** and the creation of what amounts to *a **global plantation***. And why do they intend that? The answer is simple: They have an arrogant, elitist view of themselves and, in their inflated self-delusion, believe they know better than anyone else how the world should be run, so they will force that upon humanity, no matter what. Since they believe themselves to be godlike in their wisdom, and since—I say this in their favor— they are motivated in part by genuine concern for global problems which will affect them and their families, and are therefore not wholly evil people, they take the view that the end justifies the means and are working to create a world government in which everything can be run to their satisfaction. The bottom line: they want to control Planet

Earth, its natural and cultural resources and the people of the world, and have been covertly working toward that objective for decades.

Now, a world government has much to recommend itself, as I noted above. I would be delighted if national borders were someday eliminated so that I didn't have to go through Customs when traveling. I would be delighted if I didn't have to exchange currencies because there was a unified monetary system for the planet. I would be delighted if I didn't have to go through the postal system's international rates and fees when mailing outside the U.S. And I would be profoundly grateful if the world didn't waste trillions of dollars on armies and military might, so that wars between nations and ethnic groups were a thing of the past, and differences between belligerent groups were settled peacefully, rationally and justly in a forum such as the United Nations or a World Court. All that is part of the age-old global dream of peace and prosperity and true community/brotherhood on Earth.

So why am I against the New World Order? Because it is a scam. Because it is a counterfeit—a total prostitution of that age-old dream. Because it is a deliberate but covert and stealthy attempt to impose an ideology called socialism, a bankrupt philosophy which has failed everywhere because the centralized power it requires inevitably leads to tyranny. Moreover, any element of high-mindedness on the part of the principals involved is secondary to their primary motivation, which is to remake the world in their own image. That motivation is the hallmark of Satan, of extreme self-centeredness and inflated egotism which leads directly to totalitarianism, collectivism and the abrogation of every civil liberty and human right which humanity, with America at the vanguard, has worked and fought and died for over centuries. The result of the New World Order will be political, economic and social slavery—period.

Note that the hallmark of the New World Order is essentially a rejection of God and His plan for human salvation via enlightened living—that is, living in accordance with the ideals, principles and values of the Perennial Philosophy, which is the collective highest wisdom of humanity's enlightenment traditions and which—I've said throughout this book—is the essence of the American Spirit. Heaven on earth results from living in a God-centered manner; hell on earth results from living in a self-centered manner. We have the free will to choose either. The architects of the New World Order have chosen the latter, and then delude themselves that they are doing good. Their model, although they are not really conscious of it, is Satan as depicted in John Milton's epic poem *Paradise Lost*. There, Satan defies God and declares *"Non serviam,"* I will not serve. "I would rather reign in Hell than serve in Heaven," Satan says, and then sets about trying to remake the universe in his own image. That is precisely the mindset of the architects of the New World Order.

Note also that the characteristics of the New World Order conspirators are secrecy, deception and lies. "By their fruits ye shall know them" says the Bible, and it is still the truest test of character and intent.

Last of all, note that the people who make the best slaves are people who (1) are unaware they are slaves, (2) love their masters and (3) wear golden shackles in the form of government welfare and subsidies which chain them to the state, relieving them of the responsibility to think for themselves and to support themselves via honest labor. The "dumbing down of America" has placed mental and moral blinders of people while glamorizing politicians to make them attractive celebrities rather than genuine servants of the people. As Frederick Douglass said in *My Bondage and My Freedom* (1866): "To make a contented slave, it is necessary to make a thoughtless one (and) to annihilate the power of reason. He must be able to detect no inconsistencies in slavery, he must be made to feel that slavery is right."

***We the people of America are facing a clear choice about our future and the human future: Enslavement or enlightenment?*** I am in favor of a true world community but not a New World Order. The United States of the World is the community I espouse.

The obvious choice is enlightenment, but how do we get there? How do we get to a true world community rather than a New World Order? My answer: a true world community would be a Noetic World Order.

Noetics is the study of consciousness. The term has been used since the 1960s and was given widespread public recognition by Dr. Edgar Mitchell, Apollo 14 astronaut and the sixth man on the moon. After his lunar voyage, he retried from military service and formed an organization to study the powers of the human mind in order to apply its findings to personal and planetary transformation. That organization is The Institute of Noetic Sciences (IONS), located in Petaluma, California, and open to public membership. Author Dan Brown gave further visibility to noetics in his recent novel *The Lost Symbol,* which explicitly names IONS and noetic research as the key to unfolding the human potential for attaining enlightenment. Noetics can be regarded as the meeting of science and spirit—a meeting in which reason and revelation mutually engage each other on a respectful basis, opening deeper understanding than intellect alone can offer but doing so in a way which protects reason from going astray in the exploration of consciousness. For more on a Noetic World Order, see Appendix 3, "Noetic Patriotism and Global Society."

2 In a *Wall Street Journal* series about the UN ("The U.N.: Searching for Relevance," 16 December 2003, p. 1), the organization was described in these words: "Charged with everything from preventing war to regulating international mail, the U.N. and its galaxy of agencies, funds and programs appear accountable to nobody, yet micromanaged by many."

3 According to a personal communication from now-deceased British historian Charlotte Waterlow, author of *The Hinge of History* (One World Trust: London, England, 1995), when the UN's Universal Declaration of Human Rights was being drafted, Eleanor Roosevelt, who was a delegate to the Commission which wrote the United Nations Charter, personally intervened to block all references to God in order to make the Declaration acceptable to Communist nations.

4 In my judgment, the United Nations is the greatest threat to world freedom, bar none. Although it has no authority to function as a government, it is nevertheless attempting to perform governmental functions such as:

• direct taxation of the citizens of the world (it has proposed a tax on all computer mail, phone calls, stocks and bonds in retirement plans, airline tickets and various other schemes) with a global IRS to keep tabs on every American citizen,

• creating a permanent standing army (being formed through the NATO Alliance, including U.S. soldiers, sailors, marines and airmen who will serve under foreign officers and wear UN uniforms),

• consolidating all international agencies under its direct authority,

• regulating all transnational corporations and financial institutions,

• requiring global registration of all firearms,

• confiscating land and resources from nations via the Law of the Sea Treaty, its concept of "global commons" and its international Biosphere Reserves program (which involves huge tracts of U.S. land stretching from Alabama to Virginia),

• establishing a Marxist plan for elimination of private property and global redistribution of wealth via worldwide welfare-state programs,

• and numerous other activities aimed at seizing control of the entire planet, its people, institutions and resources.

The UN already has its own judicial system, the International Criminal Court (ICC), in which the rights and protections we Americans have under the Constitution are undermined and even eliminated. Among our rights and protections are: to be considered innocent until proven guilty, to confront our accuser, to have a speedy trial by jury in the state and district where the alleged crime was committed, to be released on bail, to avoid self-incrimination, to appeal the verdict to a higher court and so forth. The ICC eliminates all that. It claims jurisdiction over everyone on Earth. It claims the right to arrest anyone anywhere and try them in the Netherlands before foreign judges on vaguely defined charges such as "crimes against humanity." In short, the ICC acts as prosecutor, judge and jury. That's not justice; that's a kangaroo court.

The former Secretary General of the UN, Kofi Annan, proclaimed the UN's worldwide jurisdiction over "human rights and fundamental freedoms." Its Universal Declaration of Human Rights, Annan said, "must and will take precedence over concerns of State sovereignty." However, many of its committees are a farce because nations such as China, Cuba and Libya, which are gross abusers of human rights, rotate into the chairmanship of the Commission on Human Rights, and Iraq, when Saddam Hussein was its dictator, headed up the UN Commission on Disarmament. Its treaties and proclamations on topics such as the rights of children and families undermine fundamental principles of American society; they elevate socialism to positions of authority, making the state the head of the family and children wards of the state. In America, the Charter of the United Nations unconstitutionally usurps power reserved to the states and to the people by the Tenth Amendment.

The UN Charter broadly asserts its authority for armed intervention in the domestic turmoil of nations; that was its basis for sending troops into Haiti and Somalia, which were "nation-building" disasters. It ordered Iraq to disarm itself of weapons of mass destruction, yet for 12 years nothing was accomplished. Its inaction on situations such as the Hutu-Tutsi tribal warfare in Rwanda, which resulted in the death of an estimated 800,000 Africans in the mid-1990s, and in the killing fields of Cambodia where an estimated 3,000,000 were killed by Khmer Rouge, is indicative not only of the UN's political ineffectiveness but also of its moral indifference. Moreover, the UN supports brutal regimes around the world.

Last of all, the United States contributes 25 percent of the UN's $12 billion annual budget and has paid more than $30 billion since its creation in so-called "dues" and through international foreign aid (such as food, clothing, shelter, medicine and manpower) administered through the UN and through "peacekeeping" operations. Yet the UN, with 191 members, allows us only one vote, the same as the smallest, poorest countries who pay practically nothing. Moreover, the UN provides a platform for terrorist-harboring nations to issue their anti-American diatribes. In other words, we underwrite their name-calling, their false charges and their hatred of us. The only thing the "United" Nations seems united about is harming the United States.

Altogether, the United Nations is an institution whose endgame, although clothed in noble-sounding rhetoric about democracy and human rights, is in reality a totalitarian world government—which is being created right now. It would be in the best interests of America and the world to get the U.S. out of the UN and the UN out of the U.S. Recently former Rep. Ron Paul introduced a bill in Congress, H.R. 1146 - The American Sovereignty Restoration Act, to end U.S. membership in the UN. It was put to a vote but lost, 350-74. Nevertheless, that is a sizable number of congresspeople who are waking up to the fact that the UN is hostile to American sovereignty and American society. Ron Paul's son, Senator Rand Paul, is carrying on the work and has introduced his own bill to attain the same goal. I urge your support of it.

4 President Franklin D. Roosevelt's famous speech entitled "The Four Freedoms" (which was actually his 1941 State of the Union Address) said, "...we look forward to a world founded upon four essential human freedoms. The first is freedom of speech and expression—everywhere in the world. The second is freedom of every person to worship God in his own way—everywhere in the world. The third is freedom from want...everywhere in the world. The fourth is freedom from fear...anywhere in the world."

5 Shortly after I finished this part of the book, I had a dream which I regard as confirmation of my stance that the spiritual foundations of America are congruent with the ideals, principles and values of the Perennial Philosophy. In the dream, I was laying down in a nonspecific location, gazing into the sky. No identifying features were visible, so it may have been simply the earth itself on which I rested. My entire field of vision was contained by the sky. The daylight blue of the foreground faded into the near-black of night as my vision penetrated to the outer limits of the atmosphere and then beyond, into the cosmos. As I gazed upward, an American flag appeared midway between me and infinity. The flag was composed of some ethereal substance, giving it a translucent appearance. The colors of the flag were muted, not bright. The flag itself gently waved in a soft, silent celestial wind. I could see the flag clearly, but I could also see through it to the vanishing point of vision. The dream consisted of nothing more than that image from my steady, heavenward gaze; there was no other action or sound.

Upon waking, the image was still clear in my mind. It was immediately obvious that the dream was an endorsement—from my unconscious, from God, from whatever is the source of dreams—of my effort to bridge mainstream American values with enlightenment traditions and millennial hopes for global peace and world unity. It confirmed that the fundamental principles governing our human existence and our political life in the American experience are one and the same.

6 Not only will God ultimately decide history's outcome, that outcome is known through God's revelation in Jesus Christ and other godly men and women who provide inspiring example and wise teachings to guide us. Consider the case of Joseph in the Old Testament.

Joseph, an Israelite, was sold into slavery by his jealous brothers, but Joseph's faith in God and his purity of heart and mind brought him into a position of power second only to the Pharaoh in all of Egypt. When Joseph's brothers came to Egypt to buy grain during a famine, Joseph revealed himself to them. They were afraid, and rightly so, that he might have them killed or imprisoned for their criminal behavior against him years earlier. But Joseph's words provide an unfailing basis for hope in the face of adversity. When the brothers asked Joseph why he didn't punish them, he replied, "You meant evil against me; but God meant it for good, to bring about that many people should be kept alive, as they are today." (Genesis 50:20, RSV.)

That is a lesson for us all. The hidden hand of God is guiding world affairs according to His divine plan, which is the salvation of fallen humanity. Knowledge of that plan is widely and plainly available in the holy scriptures of Judeo-Christianity and other sacred traditions which likewise recognize the fatherhood of God and the brotherhood of man. There will never be a better world until there are better people in it, and the place to start building better people is with ourselves, using the Bible and other "operating manuals" for holy living.

## Afterword

# IF YOU VALUE FREEDOM

My country, 'tis of thee,
Sweet land of liberty,
Of thee I sing;
Land where my fathers died,
Land of the pilgrims' pride,
From every mountain-side
Let Freedom ring.
— Rev. Samuel Francis Smith
July 4, 1831

Shortly after the tragedy of September 11, 2001, I attended a local prayer breakfast at which service club members, clergy and town officials gathered to consider the Pledge's phrase "one Nation under God."

As I reflected on that theme, it occurred to me that Osama bin Laden, al Queda, and their cohorts—the Taliban of Afghanistan—might also say their objective is "one Nation under God." After all, they speak of the "nation of Islam" and call for an Islamic theocracy.

A theocracy, Mr. Webster tells us, is a state governed by immediate divine guidance or by officials—a monarch, council or junta—who are regarded as divinely guided. What distinguishes the Islamists' version of nationhood from ours?

Let's start with the Declaration of Independence, our founding document. Through its four references to deity, it states that God is the source of our liberty, our sovereignty, our equality, our rights, our justice and our human dignity, and that the purpose of government—which exists legitimately only when it has the consent of the governed—is to guarantee those blessings are not violated because each individual citizen is sacred and sovereign. Did bin Laden and the Taliban, which hosted him, offer anything comparable?

Look at Afghanistan under the Taliban. Where was the freedom we cherish—freedom of religion, freedom of conscience, freedom of speech and the press, freedom to assemble, freedom to criticize the government, freedom to seek redress of grievances, freedom from unreasonable search and seizure, freedom to work and marry as we wish, freedom of education, freedom to travel and so forth? The Taliban suppressed all that. Radio, TV and entertainment were forbidden except for government-approved forms. There were no minority parties campaigning for election because critics of the government were publicly executed. People were jailed for the "crime" of teaching about Christianity.

The Declaration of Independence also states that all men—meaning all people—are created equal. Did bin Laden and the Taliban have anything comparable? Just look at the condition of women under their rule. They had to be covered from head to foot, including their face; they were beaten on the street for showing even an ankle. They couldn't vote. They couldn't go to school or work outside the home. Female teachers couldn't teach. Even female doctors, whose medical services were badly needed, were forbidden to practice their profession. (Please note that this terrible treatment of women is not inherent in Islam, but was due to the twisted mentality of the Taliban.) As for other religions, Christians were persecuted and Hindus were forced to wear a symbol on their clothing to identify themselves as non-Muslim. Ancient Buddhist sculptures regarded by the world as art treasures were blown up.

Noble-sounding words can be misused to disguise something totally opposite to their meaning. That is what the Taliban, bin Laden and their followers did. Their version of "one Nation under God" was a brutal totalitarian dictatorship—the antithesis of everything for which America stands (and, according to many Muslim clerics and scholars, the antithesis of what Islam stands for also). Adding insult to injury, consider what the airplane hijackers of 9/11 did in America besides going to flight school. They reportedly drank in topless bars, watched pornographic videos and gambled in casinos, thereby demonstrating gross hypocrisy in their adherence to Qur'anic law intended to instill religious goodness and moral purity in practitioners of Islam.

## Freedom in China?

Well, if a theocratic dictatorship in Afghanistan offers no freedom, would an atheistic government such as the People's Republic of China do better?

An Associated Press article (27 August 2000) tells of terrible oppression in Chinese-ruled Tibet. According to it, monks were expelled from Tibetan Buddhism's holiest shrine, the 1,300-year-old Jokhang Temple in Lhasa, capital of Tibet. There used to be thousands of monks at the temple, but the Chinese government set a limit of 120 monks for it. Moreover, any monks who leave may not be replaced.

In addition, government teams began house-to-house searches in Lhasa, looking for religious objects and for pictures of the Dalai Lama, Tibet's temporal and spiritual leader who is now in exile in India. Any religious objects found were thrown into the nearby Tsangpo River.

Last of all, the general population was ordered to teach children atheism. The children were warned not to attend temples. These actions are part of a years-old campaign to break the fervently Buddhist Tibetan people's allegiance to the Dalai Lama, the AP said.

It has been widely reported that when the Chinese Communists invaded and conquered Tibet in 1950, claiming it was Chinese territory, they killed one million Tibetans, including thousands of monks, and they destroyed 6,000 Buddhist temples. The Dalai Lama, who lived in the Potala Palace in Lhasa, was put under house arrest. For nine years he tried to restore sovereignty to his nation, without success. In 1959 an uprising by Tibetans against Chinese rule failed. The Dalai Lama was forced to flee for his life; he slipped out of the palace at night with a small party of followers and trekked for weeks over the Himalayas into the safety of India. He still resides there, in the northern Indian town of Dharamsala, where he heads Tibet's government-in-exile and works for Tibetan autonomy.

## Oppression of Falun Gong and Christianity

There have also been media reports over the last few decades about the Chinese government oppressing followers of a Chinese spiritual system called Falun Gong, which has a set of beliefs about God and the universe, and a meditational practice for self-healing. Beijing officials have declared Falun Gong to be a cult and dangerous to the people; hundreds of Falun Gong members have been imprisoned.

Last of all, there have been media reports of Christians in China being persecuted, imprisoned, even killed, because of their faith.

What is the essential difference between Communist China and the United States of America? It is our theory of government, which declares that all people have been endowed by God with inalienable rights to life, liberty and the pursuit of happiness, and that government is instituted to assure that for its citizens, which it serves. The individual is sovereign because of our spiritual nature; the state may never violate that.

In Communist China, however, whatever freedom and rights people have are granted by the government and may be taken away whenever it suits the government because citizens are subjects of the government. With regard to religion, *The Wall Street Journal*, in an editorial entitled "The Chinese Martyrs" (29 September 2000, p. W17), noted that the Chinese foreign ministry declared that Pope John Paul II's plans to canonize 120 Chinese martyrs—the first Chinese saints in Catholicism—were "slanders against the Chinese people." The ministry spokesman insisted that those being honored were nothing more than lackeys of Western imperialism who deserved to die. The *Journal* continued:

> Beijing claims that it has nothing against religion, just foreign interference. But that doesn't explain why the Dalai Lama must live in exile from Tibet, why unregistered 'house Protestants' find themselves clapped into prison for reading their Bibles, why the Falun Gong is treated as China's number-one security threat, indeed why China has its own FBI, the Religious Affairs Bureau, dedicated solely to keeping tabs on believers.

## Imagine an America

Now, fellow citizens, imagine an America in which you are spied upon for being religious or arrested for expressing political dissent. Imagine an America in which your house can be searched without a warrant by soldiers looking for religious objects or other evidence that you worship God. Imagine an America in which you can be tried—in secret and without witnesses or an attorney—and sent to prison for such "crimes" or simply executed on the spot, without judicial appeal. Imagine an America in which your place of worship, whether church, synagogue, temple or mosque, can be raided by soldiers and destroyed because it is "harmful" to the social order. Imagine an America where schools are required to teach atheism as the official view of the government or where they are forbidden to teach about any religion other than the official one. Imagine an America where women are forbidden education and employment outside the home, and can be beaten on the street for failure to be clothed from head to foot. Imagine an America where all minority opinion is suppressed and those who dare to express it are imprisoned or executed. Imagine an America where all your other freedoms are likewise prohibited. In that case, the phrase "one Nation under God" would be changed to "one Nation under surveillance"—by Big Brother—and the all-seeing Eye of Providence on the Great Seal would be replaced by government controlled TV cameras, pilotless drones and spy satellites watching us.

Whether you believe in God or not, ***if you are American, you should understand the profound difference which our theory of government makes for us from all other theories and forms of political organization.*** I've stated the foundational idea of America repeatedly throughout this book: Our liberty, our sovereignty, our equality, our rights, our justice and our human dignity are bestowed upon us by God and guaranteed by the Constitution; all that may not be violated or taken away by laws, court decisions, executive orders or social majorities who think otherwise. Rather, the primary role of government is to protect all that from anyone who seeks to harm it or override it. As the Declaration of Independence puts it, governments are instituted to ensure those God-given rights. We should recall the statement by James Madison, quoted earlier, commenting on the significance of God in the social and political dimensions of human affairs:

> The belief in a God All Powerful wise and good, is so essential to the moral order
> of the world and to the happiness of man, that arguments which enforce it cannot
> be drawn from too many sources nor adapted with too much solicitude to the
> different characters and capacities impressed with it.

## America Is a Theocracy

If God is the foundation of America, we can rightly say ***this nation is a theocracy***. Remember the definition of a theocracy: a state governed by immediate divine guidance or by officials who are regarded as divinely guided. However, unlike all other theocracies in history, past and present, ***America is a democratic nonsectarian theocracy operating through a constitutional republic.*** America is governed by We the People rather than an autocratic religious junta such as the Taliban. Our Founders wisely separated church and state to prevent just that.

Unlike the former condition of Afghanistan with the Taliban and unlike the former condition of China or Japan with their emperors, clerics and divine-right monarchs do not rule here and the First Amendment assures they never will. The individual comes first, not the state, not an establishment of religion, not a clerical caste, not a ruler regarded as semidivine. By virtue of what the Declaration of Independence says is our spiritual nature and our moral equality, in American society *every citizen* is a direct representative of God. And by virtue of the Constitution of the United States of America, *every citizen* is a full and equal member of the ruling body known as "we the people."

Ideally speaking, therefore, ***America is a theocracy because it is governed by God through the total population of our divinely guided citizenry*** who are the true heads of state and who are educated in the religio-moral ideals, principles and values of our society. They provide the governance of our society from which the representatives of our government are elected. Our national character is the seedbed from which our public officials grow.

That is a radically new form of theocracy—both new and better. It is unique in history and fundamental for the future of freedom—your freedom. It is an advancement in establishing a God-centered society beyond even that which our Pilgrim forefathers intended, which was a theocracy, a Holy Commonwealth of the elect. The Pilgrims were separatists; they separated from England in order to set up a society in which God, not the King, was head of state. "No king but Jesus," they said.

Yet for all the debt of gratitude we owe our Pilgrim forefathers, we must not overlook the fact that their theocracy was a decidedly narrow, restrictive one, and intolerant of divergent religious beliefs. In fact, it was oppressive enough to send Roger Williams into the Rhode Island wilderness to establish a colony more hospitable to religious freedom for all. (Williams described the religiously pluralistic society he sought as one in which "all men may walk as their consciences persuade them, everyone in the name of his God.")

A century and a half later, in 1789, George Washington endorsed the principle of religious liberty when he said to the Quakers in their annual meeting, "The liberty enjoyed by the people of these states of worshiping Almighty God agreeably to their conscience, is not only among the choicest of their blessings, but also of their rights."

So understanding the magnificence of our Founders' achievement—a theocracy based on freedom of religion and freedom of conscience for all people, including even those who deny the existence of God—is critical for the future of freedom around the globe. They achieved a theocracy based on freedom of religion and freedom of conscience for all people, including atheists who demand freedom from religion. (*Note to atheists:* Move to Taliban City and see how long your right to say there is no God lasts.) Under the Constitution, even the godless are assured protection of their beliefs. (*Note to atheists*: But woe to your freedom and protection under the law if God is expelled from America and our theory of government.)

What follows from that theory of government is the marvelous liberty of our nation in which people can worship, speak, write, assemble, work, marry, travel and live as they wish—in short, can pursue happiness as they wish—so long as they do not violate another's right to do the same. Yes, that marvelous liberty has been abused by some citizens. And, yes, because liberty carries inherent responsibility, it requires a conscience, a sense of civic duty and a sense of respect for public decorum—in short, voluntary compliance—to live properly in accordance with our national ideals, principles and values. As Thomas Jefferson said, the qualifications for self-government are not innate; they are the result of habit and long training. But without that spiritual foundation asserting your right to life, liberty and the pursuit of happiness, and without the constitutional protection guaranteeing your freedom and your rights... well, renounce your American citizenship, move to Beijing or Taliban City and find out for yourself what follows. President Calvin Coolidge's defense of the Declaration of Independence provides the perfect commentary about the universal and absolute truths on which America is founded.

> If all men are created equal, that is final. If they are endowed with inalienable rights, that is final. If governments derive their just power from the consent of the governed, that is final. No advance, no progress can be made beyond these propositions. If anyone wishes to deny their truth and their soundness,

the only direction in which he can proceed historically is not forward, but backward toward the time when there was no equality, no rights of the individual, no rule [by] the people. Those who wish to proceed in that direction cannot lay claim to progress. They are reactionary.

*To be born free is a great privilege; to die free is a great responsibility.*

We Americans should thank God for the blessings we have: personal, economic, political, religious and social freedom, the right to self-determination of our lives and the opportunity to pursue happiness as we define it for ourselves, rather than being forced into abject, slavish service to a totalitarian state run by despots claiming to be divinely guided. And while all that is meaningful in and of itself, it also means something more— something unprecedented, something unique in political and world history. It means we have the opportunity not simply as solitary individuals but ***as a society*** to attain spiritual freedom, which is the goal of life, the destiny of all humanity.

We should express that gratitude through lives which serve others, all the way from the nuclear family to the human family, through the Golden Rule of enlightened self-interest. We should also gratefully honor those who went before us—often in great hardship, suffering and bloodshed—to build and defend a haven for us in the wilderness of man's longstanding inhumanity to man. Last of all, we should be vigilant, active citizens who work to preserve the blessings of liberty so they may be passed on to our posterity and the boundaries of our haven—the frontiers of freedom—may be enlarged to encompass all humanity. We should do all that in the name and spirit of what Thomas Jefferson called "the common Father...of man": nature's God, Divine Providence, the Supreme Judge of the world, our Creator.

## *America—love it and live it!*

# APPENDIXES

## Appendix 1

# THE U.S. FLAG CODE

The U.S. Flag Code is the guide for proper handling and display of the United States Flag. It was drawn up in 1923 and adopted by Congress in 1942. From time to time it has been amended.

The Flag Code prescribes flag etiquette for a variety of circumstances. It states specific ways in which the flag should be used and not be used, so that our flag's honor is upheld and no disrespect is shown to it. It is intended to assure that our principal national symbol is treated properly.

Notice that it says "code," not "law." The way our flag should be treated and honored is not law, but a code which has been developed over the years. It is the standard, it is what is right, it is what each of us should want to know and follow. The Flag Code does not impose penalties for misuse of the U.S. flag or enforcement provisions for noncompliance. That is left to the states and to the federal government for the District of Columbia. Each state and the District of Columbia has its own flag law, and each locality determines the penalties.

The Flag Code is contained within the United States Code, the official compilation of the federal laws of a general and permanent nature which are currently in force. The U.S. Code is divided into 50 titles by subject matter. Each title is divided into sections. Sections within a title may be grouped together as subtitles, chapters, subchapters, parts, subparts, or divisions. Titles may also have appendices which may be divided into sections, rules and/or forms. The sections pertaining to the U.S. Flag are given below.

Finally, the Flag Code is for civilian use. Each military branch has its own flag code, but of course there is much similarity among them with the U.S. Flag Code.

The United States Code is available for purchase in printed format and on CD-ROM from the Government Printing Office. For telephone orders, call 202-512-1800, Monday through Friday, 8 a.m. to 4 p.m. EST. Orders can be sent by mail to:

Superintendent of Documents
U.S. Government Printing Office
P.O. Box 371954
Pittsburgh, PA 15250-7954

The following text is abbreviated from the U.S. Code. It is available on line at http://www.usflag.org/uscode36.html.

## UNITED STATES CODE
## TITLE 36
## CHAPTER 10

# PATRIOTIC CUSTOMS

170. National anthem; Star-Spangled Banner.
171. Conduct during playing.
172. Pledge of allegiance to the flag; manner of delivery.
173. Display and use of flag by civilians; codification of rules and customs; definition.
174. Time and occasions for display.
175. Position and manner of display.
176. Respect for flag.
177. Conduct during hoisting, lowering or passing of flag.
178. Modification of rules and customs by President.
179. Design for service flag; persons entitled to display flag.
180. Design for service lapel button; persons entitled to wear button.
181. Approval of designs by Secretary of Defense; license to manufacture and sell; penalties.
182. Rules and regulations.
182a to 184. Repealed.
185. Transferred.
186. National motto.
187. National floral emblem.
188. National march.
189. Recognition of National League of Families POW/MIA flag.

## 173. Display and use of flag by civilians; codification of rules and customs; definition

The following codification of existing rules and customs pertaining to the display and use of the flag of the United States of America is established for the use of such civilians or civilian groups or organizations as may not be required to conform with regulations promulgated by one or more executive departments of the Government of the United States. The flag of the United States for the purpose of this chapter shall be defined according to sections 1 and 2 of title 4 and Executive Order 10834 issued pursuant thereto.

## 174. Time and occasions for display

(a) Display on buildings and stationary flagstaffs in open; night display

It is the universal custom to display the flag only from sunrise to sunset on buildings and on stationary flagstaffs in the open. However, when a patriotic effect is desired, the flag may be displayed twenty-four hours a day if properly illuminated during the hours of darkness.

(b) Manner of hoisting

The flag should be hoisted briskly and lowered ceremoniously.

(c) Inclement weather

The flag should not be displayed on days when the weather is inclement, except when an all weather flag is displayed.

(d) Particular days of display

The flag should be displayed on all days, especially on New Year's Day, January 1; Inauguration Day, January 20; Lincoln's Birthday, February 12; Washington's Birthday, third Monday in February; Easter Sunday (variable); Mother's Day, second Sunday in May; Armed Forces Day, third Saturday in May; Memorial Day (half-staff until noon), the last Monday in May; Flag Day, June 14; Independence Day, July 4; Labor Day, first Monday in September; Constitution Day, September 17; Columbus Day, second Monday in October; Navy Day, October 27; Veterans Day, November 11; Thanksgiving Day, fourth Thursday in November; Christmas Day, December 25; and such other days as may be proclaimed by the President of the United States; the birthdays of States (date of admission); and on State holidays.

(e) Display on or near administration building of public institutions

The flag should be displayed daily on or near the main administration building of every public institution.

(f) Display in or near polling places

The flag should be displayed in or near every polling place on election days.

(g) Display in or near schoolhouses

The flag should be displayed during school days in or near every schoolhouse.

## 175. Position and manner of display

The flag, when carried in a procession with another flag or flags, should be either on the marching right; that is, the flag's own right, or, if there is a line of other flags, in front of the center of that line.

(a) The flag should not be displayed on a float in a parade except from a staff, or as provided in subsection (i) of this section.

(b) The flag should not be draped over the hood, top, sides, or back of a vehicle or of a railroad train or a boat. When the flag is displayed on a motorcar, the staff shall be fixed firmly to the chassis or clamped to the right fender.

(c) No other flag or pennant should be placed above or, if on the same level, to the right of the flag of the United States of America, except during church services conducted by naval chaplains at sea, when the church pennant may be flown above the flag during church services for the personnel of the Navy. No person shall display the flag of the United Nations or any other national or international flag equal, above, or in a position of superior prominence or honor to, or in place of, the flag of the United States at any place within the United States or any Territory or possession thereof: Provided, That nothing in this section shall make unlawful the continuance of the practice heretofore followed of displaying the flag of the United Nations in a position of superior prominence or honor, and other national flags in positions of equal prominence or honor, with that of the flag of the United States at the headquarters of the United Nations.

(d) The flag of the United States of America, when it is displayed with another flag against a wall from crossed staffs, should be on the right, the flag's own right, and its staff should be in front of the staff of the other flag.

(e) The flag of the United States of America should be at the center and at the highest point of the group when a number of flags of States or localities or pennants of societies are grouped and displayed from staffs.

(f) When flags of States, cities, or localities, or pennants of societies are flown on the same halyard with the flag of the United States, the latter should always be at the peak. When the flags are flown from adjacent staffs, the flag of the United States should be hoisted first and lowered last. No such flag or pennant may be placed above the flag of the United States or to the United States flag's right.

(g) When flags of two or more nations are displayed, they are to be flown from separate staffs of the same height. The flags should be of approximately equal size. International usage forbids the display of the flag of one nation above that of another nation in time of peace.

(h) When the flag of the United States is displayed from a staff projecting horizontally or at an angle from the window sill, balcony, or front of a building, the union of the flag should be placed at the peak of the staff unless the flag is at half-staff. When the flag is suspended over a sidewalk from a rope extending from a house to a pole at the edge of the sidewalk, the flag should be hoisted out, union first, from the building.

(i) When displayed either horizontally or vertically against a wall, the union should be uppermost and to the flag's own right, that is, to the observer's left. When displayed in a window, the flag should be displayed in the same way, with the union or blue field to the left of the observer in the street.

(j) When the flag is displayed over the middle of the street, it should be suspended vertically with the union to the north in an east and west street or to the east in a north and south street.

(k) When used on a speaker's platform, the flag, if displayed flat, should be displayed above and behind the speaker. When displayed from a staff in a church or public auditorium, the flag of the United States of America should hold the position of superior prominence, in advance of the audience, and in the position of honor at the clergyman's or speaker's right as he faces the audience. Any other flag so displayed should be placed on the left of the clergyman or speaker or to the right of the audience.

(l) The flag should form a distinctive feature of the ceremony of unveiling a statue or monument, but it should never be used as the covering for the statue or monument.

(m) The flag, when flown at half-staff, should be first hoisted to the peak for an instant and then lowered to the half-staff position. The flag should be again raised to the peak before it is lowered for the day. On Memorial Day the flag should be displayed at half-staff until noon only, then raised to the top of the staff. By order of the President, the flag shall be flown at half-staff upon the death of principal figures of the United States Government and the Governor of a State, territory, or possession, as a mark of respect to their memory.

In the event of the death of other officials or foreign dignitaries, the flag is to be displayed at half-staff according to Presidential instructions or orders, or in accordance with recognized customs or practices not inconsistent with law. In the event of the death of a present or former official of the government of any State, territory,or possession of the United States, or the death of a member of the Armed Forces from any State, territory, or possession who dies while serving on active duty, the Governor of that State, territory, or possession may proclaim that the National flag shall be flown at half-staff, and the same authority is provided to the Mayor of the District of Columbia with respect to present or former officials of the District of Columbia and members of the Armed Forces from the District of Columbia. When the Governor of a State, territory, or possession, or the Mayor of the District of Columbia, issues a proclamation under the preceding sentence that the National flag be flown at half-staff in that State, territory, or possession or in the District of Columbia because of the death of a member of the Armed Forces, the National flag flown at any Federal installation or facility in the area covered by that proclamation shall be flown at half-staff consistent with that proclamation. The flag shall be flown at half-staff thirty days from the death of the President or a former President; ten days from the day of death of the Vice President, the Chief Justice or a retired Chief Justice of the United States, or the Speaker of the House of Representatives; from the day of death until interment of an Associate Justice of the Supreme Court, a Secretary of an executive or military department, a former Vice President, or the Governor of a State, territory, or possession; and on the day of death and the following day for a Member of Congress. As used in this subsection (1) the term 'half-staff' means the position of the flag when it is one-half the distance between the top and bottom of the staff; (2) the term 'executive or military department' means any agency listed under sections 101 and 102 of title 5; and (3) the term 'Member of Congress' means a Senator, a Representative, a Delegate, or the Resident Commissioner from Puerto Rico.

(n) When the flag is used to cover a casket, it should be so placed that the union is at the head and over the left shoulder. The flag should not be lowered into the grave or allowed to touch the ground.

(o) When the flag is suspended across a corridor or lobby in a building with only one main entrance, it should be suspended vertically with the union of the flag to the observer's left upon entering. If the building has more than one main entrance, the flag should be suspended vertically near the center of the corridor or lobby with the union to the north, when entrances are to the east and west or to the east when entrances are to the north and south. If there are entrances in more than two directions, the union should be to the east.

## 176. Respect for flag

No disrespect should be shown to the flag of the United States of America; the flag should not be dipped to any person or thing. Regimental colors, State flags, and organization or institutional flags are to be dipped as a mark of honor.

(a) The flag should never be displayed with the union down, except as a signal of dire distress in instances of extreme danger to life or property.

(b) The flag should never touch anything beneath it, such as the ground, the floor, water, or merchandise.

(c) The flag should never be carried flat or horizontally, but always aloft and free.

(d) The flag should never be used as wearing apparel, bedding, or drapery. It should never be festooned, drawn back, nor up, in folds, but always allowed to fall free. Bunting of blue, white, and red, always arranged with the blue above, the white in the middle, and the red below, should be used for covering a speaker's desk, draping the front of the platform, and for decoration in general.

(e) The flag should never be fastened, displayed, used, or stored in such a manner as to permit it to be easily torn, soiled, or damaged in any way.

(f) The flag should never be used as a covering for a ceiling.

(g) The flag should never have placed upon it, nor on any part of it, nor attached to it any mark, insignia, letter, word, figure, design, picture, or drawing of any nature.

(h) The flag should never be used as a receptacle for receiving, holding, carrying, or delivering anything.

(i) The flag should never be used for advertising purposes in any manner whatsoever. It should not be embroidered on such articles as cushions or handkerchiefs and the like, printed or otherwise impressed on paper napkins or boxes or anything that is designed for temporary use and discard. Advertising signs should not be fastened to a staff or halyard from which the flag is flown.

(j) No part of the flag should ever be used as a costume or athletic uniform. However, a flag patch may be affixed to the uniform of military personnel, firemen, policemen, and members of patriotic organizations. The flag represents a living country and is itself considered a living thing. Therefore, the lapel flag pin being a replica, should be worn on the left lapel near the heart.

(k) The flag, when it is in such condition that it is no longer a fitting emblem for display, should be destroyed in a dignified way, preferably by burning.

## 177. Conduct during hoisting, lowering or passing of flag

During the ceremony of hoisting or lowering the flag or when the flag is passing in a parade or in review, all persons present except those in uniform should face the flag and stand at attention with the right hand over the heart. Those present in uniform should render the military salute. When not in uniform, men should remove their headdress with their right hand and hold it at the left shoulder, the hand being over the heart. Aliens should stand at attention. The salute to the flag in a moving column should be rendered at the moment the flag passes.

## 178. Modification of rules and customs by President

Any rule or custom pertaining to the display of the flag of the United States of America, set forth herein, may be altered, modified, or repealed, or additional rules with respect thereto may be prescribed, by the Commander in Chief of the Armed Forces of the United States, whenever he deems it to be appropriate or desirable; and any such alteration or additional rule shall be set forth in a proclamation.

## Appendix 2

# THE U.S. FLAG CODE'S NATIONAL ANTHEM SECTION

[Laws in effect as of January 7, 2003]
[Document not affected by Public Laws enacted between
January 7, 2003 and February 12, 2003]
[CITE: 36USC301]

## TITLE 36—PATRIOTIC AND NATIONAL OBSERVANCES, CEREMONIES, AND ORGANIZATIONS

Subtitle I—Patriotic and National Observances and Ceremonies

Part A—Observances and Ceremonies

### CHAPTER 3—NATIONAL ANTHEM, MOTTO, FLORAL EMBLEM, AND MARCH

Sec. 301. National anthem

(a) Designation.—The composition consisting of the words and music known as the Star-Spangled Banner is the national anthem.
(b) Conduct During Playing.—During a rendition of the national anthem—
(1) when the flag is displayed—
(A) all present except those in uniform should stand at attention facing the flag with the right hand over the heart;
(B) men not in uniform should remove their headdress with their right hand and hold the headdress at the left shoulder, the hand being over the heart; and
(C) individuals in uniform should give the military salute at the first note of the anthem and maintain that position until the last note; and
(2) when the flag is not displayed, all present should face toward the music and act in the same manner they would if the flag were displayed.

# Appendix 3

# THE TEN PRINCIPLES OF AMERICAN PATRIOTISM

The Declaration of Independence says there are self-evident truths which provide the foundation for American government and society. They are fundamental principles on which America stands. Our national experiment in self-government is predicated on them. These ten principles or truths are essential to understanding, defending and preserving the theory and practice of the American way of life.

However, public understanding of those truths is being lost; they are no longer self-evident to many Americans. This appendix "unpacks" the meaning of the term "self-evident truths." It identifies ten principles or truths which are essential to understanding, defending and preserving the theory and practice of the American way of life.

1. The fountainhead of American government and society—the most fundamental idea of all—is this: *God is the mighty author of our being and the moral authority for our laws.* The Declaration of Independence contains four references to deity. They are "Nature's God," "Creator," "Supreme Judge of the world" and "divine Providence." These make clear that in the political theory articulated by the Founders of America, God, not government, is source of our freedom, our sovereignty, our equality, our rights, our justice, our human dignity and all else which creates a good society and a society which is good. Therefore patriots recognize that we are "one Nation under God" and honor it in word and deed.[1]

2. The corollary idea to that, which our Founders likewise held, is this: *We are made in the image and likeness of God, and by virtue of our spiritual nature, every human being is sacred, sovereign and inviolable.* Therefore patriots recognize that "all men are created equal" and honor it in word and deed.

3. *Freedom applies to all aspects of our existence*, from the physical through the intellectual-emotional and the social-political to the spiritual. Liberty is a subset of freedom and refers to the social-political aspect of freedom. (Incidentally, John Adams called God "the Spirit of Liberty." I'll discuss that when we get to the tenth principle.)

4. *Freedom is indivisible, so its various aspects are intimately related*. Any diminishment of freedom in one aspect of our lives (such as economic, civil, religious or political) diminishes freedom in all other aspects.

5. *God's purpose in granting us freedom is to use it to show forth His glory in our entire existence.* (Some Founders, such as Thomas Jefferson, John Adams and Benjamin Franklin, referred to America as the New Jerusalem and the New Israel. By that they meant not a Jewish nation but rather a God-centered society whose will was to reflect heaven on earth. In that way, our pursuit of happiness would be permanently and abundantly fulfilled.)

6. *Because all freedom comes from God, it carries an inherent responsibility to use it properly—i.e., morally and lawfully—to fulfill our obligation to our Creator.* Freedom and responsibility are therefore intimately related; without

responsibility, liberty becomes libertinism or immoral, destructive behavior. Freedom is never license to do as we please, but only as we ought.

7. ***Our political experiment in self-government is predicated on each citizen governing himself morally and taking personal responsibility for his or her words and deeds.*** The result is a godly society dedicated to glorifying our Creator. However, an immoral people is incapable of self-government. Any government it may set up will devalue honor, honesty and civility; it will legalize plundering, abridge rights and erode freedom. Patriots are therefore responsible, law-abiding members of society who uphold the principles of American government and honor our national heritage.

8. ***Government has always been the greatest enemy of freedom***, and therefore our Founders wrote a Constitution which established a minimal government for what was deemed necessary at the federal level, leaving all other powers and rights to the states and to the people themselves. The authority of the federal government was delegated by We the People and its powers were strictly enumerated and narrowly defined. Our Founders wanted *freedom from* government, not *dependence on* government. The Constitution and the Bill of Rights are, in simplest terms, a carefully devised system to govern the government, not the people. They were not written to restrict the citizens of America; they were written to restrict the government and to protect our inherent liberties and rights.

9. Although God is not explicitly mentioned in the Constitution, ***the principles expressed in the Declaration of Independence provided the philosophical framework for the system of ordered liberty established by the Constitution.*** Moreover, the Founders and Framers expected that government officials would conduct themselves in accord with that religio-moral view of life. In fact, the American theory of government has a clear demand for moral behavior by those holding governmental office; it reflects the Founders' understanding that God demands moral behavior of us all as the foundation for growth to deeper understanding of our nature and destiny. Elected officials are required to take an oath or to affirm that they will support the Constitution. Obviously, supporting the Constitution means upholding and honoring the fundamental principles which it embodies. An official who egregiously violates that understanding is subject to impeachment, whether his or her misconduct involves high crimes (violations of law) or misdemeanors (grossly immoral misbehavior).

10. ***Our Founders wisely separated church and state, but not God and state***. How could they when the Declaration of Independence says God is the basis of our nation? We have a secular government but a religious society. Our government makes no religious test of civic officials but nevertheless requires moral behavior of them, using moral standards arising from religious traditions, especially the Ten Commandments of Judeo-Christianity which became the basis of English—and hence American—civil law. God and nation are one. However, the Creator whom we recognize as the fountainhead of American government and society is not the exclusive property of any denomination. The First Amendment prohibits any denomination from becoming the established, official religion of America; likewise it prohibits government from interfering with religious freedom and thereby allows We the People to have full public expression of religion according to one's conscience.

Of all political documents in history, only the Declaration of Independence and the Constitution offer a seamless theory and practice of enlightened government. Collectively, they address all levels of our existence. Think of it as a pyramid such as the one on the Great Seal of the United States, with the Eye of Providence above the pyramid representing the nation.

First and foremost, our founding documents recognize God, **the Spirit of Liberty**, as the source of all life, all liberty, all rights and all good. That is the Eye of Providence above the pyramid.

Next, in the Declaration of Independence, they enunciate **the basic principles of liberty** descending from God to be applied in the body politic. That is the top of the pyramid.

Then, in the Constitution, they articulate **the architecture of liberty**, which describes how our federal government is constructed, and in the Bill of Rights they enumerate the inalienable rights of each individual citizen. That is the middle of the pyramid. These architectural plans make secure the blessings of liberty as they establish justice, insure domestic tranquility, provide for the common defense and promote the general welfare.

Last of all, they demand and encourage elected officials and civil servants of integrity, calling on them to enact and enforce **laws, policies and practices of liberty**, which are the base of the pyramid.

At every level of human activity, from the physical through the mental to the spiritual, from the individual through the local, state and federal government, they declare God as the divine basis and governor of our existence.

However, without public recognition of the self-evident truth that God is the transcendental basis of our government, our social order and our moral character as a people, this nation will not stand. And while it is true that America was founded primarily by Christians, the God to whom we Americans appealed in the Declaration of Independence is the transcendent and nondenominational Creator of the world. God, in America, can never become the exclusive property of any denomination or religion; the First Amendment assures that and religious tolerance for all. God remains, in Thomas Jefferson's words, "the common Father...of man."

---

# FOOTNOTES

[1] Principle 1 is a summary of the traditional Judeo-Christian view of humanity's duty to God. Principle 2 is a summary of the traditional Judeo-Christian view of humanity's duty to humanity. Together, they elaborate in social-political terms the statement of Jesus when he was asked by the Pharisees, "Which is the great commandment in the law?" Jesus replied that there are two correlated ideas. First, he said, quoting the Torah's summary statement of Judaism (given by Moses in Deuteronomy 6:5): "Thou shalt love the Lord thy God with all thy heart, and with all thy soul, and with all thy mind, and with all thy strength. This is the great and first commandment." Then, echoing Rabbi Hillel on the second idea, he said, "And the

second is like it, you shall love your neighbor as yourself. On these two commandments depend all the law and the prophets." (See Matthew 22:34-40, Mark 12:28- 34 and Luke 10:25-28.)

# Appendix 4

# "THE STARS AND STRIPES FOREVER"
# —OUR NATIONAL MARCH

You've often heard it played by bands, and perhaps even know it by name. But did you know that John Philip Sousa's stirring composition "The Stars and Stripes Forever" is the official march of the United States of America? It is so stated in the U.S. Code, Title 36, Chapter 10, by an act of Congress in 1987. It was the result of a grassroots movement which presented petitions to Congress with more than 250,000 signatures in support of the legislation. So, like our national anthem, our national march honors our nation's flag.

John Philip Sousa (1854-1932), known as the March King, was a composer, conductor and patriot. Over the course of his life, he composed 140 military marches. He was born in Washington, D.C., the third of ten children of John Antonio Sousa (born in Spain of Portuguese parents) and Maria Elisabeth Trinkhaus (born in Bavaria). His father played trombone in the U.S. Marine Band, so Sousa grew up around military band music.

Sousa began his musical education around age six, studying voice, violin, piano, flute, cornet, baritone, trombone and alto horn. His father enlisted him in the Marines at age 13 as an apprentice after he attempted to run away to join a circus band. He published his first composition, "Moonlight on the Potomac Waltzes," in 1872. In 1875 he was discharged from the Marines and began performing on violin, touring and eventually conducting theater orchestras. He conducted Gilbert & Sullivan's H.M.S. Pinafore on Broadway.

In 1879 Sousa married Jane van Middlesworth Bellis. The next year he returned to Washington to assume leadership of the U.S. Marine Corps Band, which he led for 12 years, until 1892. During that time he also conducted "The President's Own" Marine Corps Band, serving under presidents Hayes, Garfield, Cleveland, Arthur and Harrison. In 1881 he became a Freemason and remained so for 51 years. After two successful but limited tours with the Marine Corps Band in 1891 and 1892, promoter David Blakely convinced Sousa to resign and organize a civilian concert band.

When Sousa retired, he gave a farewell concert on the White House lawn. An engraved baton was presented to him. That baton was given back to the Marine Corps after Souza's death by his daughters and is now traditionally passed to the new director of the Marine Band upon assumption of the duties.

The first Sousa Band concert was performed in 1892. The band became America's first superstar band. It was the first to go on a world tour, the first to log more than one million miles and the first to perform before one million listeners.

Sousa continued his successful career to the end of his life in 1932, making European and world tours. During World War I, at age 62, Sousa joined the U.S. Naval Reserve (at the symbolic salary of $1 a year) and was assigned the rank of lieutenant.

He trained Navy bandsmen and took a band of recruits on tour to raise money for war causes. After the war he continued to tour with his band. He composed many of today's popular marches, including "Semper Fidelis," "El Capitan" and "Washington Post." (Three of his marches, "The Crusader," "the Thunderer" and "Nobles of the Mystic Shrine" have Masonic origins.) He championed the cause of music education, received several honorary degrees and fought for composers' rights, testifying before Congress in 1927 and 1928. The sousaphone, designed by Sousa in 1899, continues to be a vibrant part of marching bands.

## How "The Stars and Stripes Forever" Was Composed

In late 1896, Sousa and his wife went to Europe on vacation. While there, he received word that David Blakely, who had become manager of the Sousa Band, had died suddenly. The band was scheduled to begin another cross-country tour soon, and Sousa knew he must return to America at once to take over the band's business affairs. Sousa tells the rest of the story in his autobiography *Marching Along*:

> Here came one of the most vivid incidents of my career. As the vessel [the *Teutonic*] steamed out of the harbor I was pacing on the deck, absorbed in thoughts of my manager's death and the many duties and decisions which awaited me in New York. Suddenly, I began to sense a rhythmic beat of a band playing within my brain. Throughout the whole tense voyage, that imaginary band continued to unfold the same themes, echoing and re-echoing the most distinct melody. I did not transfer a note of that music to paper while I was on the steamer, but when we reached shore, I set down the measures that my brain-band had been playing for me, and not a note of it has ever changed.

It was Christmas Day, 1896.

## Sousa's Later Life

Sousa, a man of letters and author of several books, also wrote words for "The Stars and Stripes Forever" (see below). The march was an immediate success, and Sousa's band played it at almost every concert until his death more than 25 years later. Veteran Sousa musicians said that it was always an inspiring experience to play the piece because, despite hundreds of repetitions, the tearful and heartfelt patriotic fervor communicated by the audiences to the musicians never seemed to fail.

Sousa said he had been born "in the shadow of the Capitol dome" and as he witnessed the sights and sounds of Civil War activities, his love of America grew. He loved his country with a passion seldom demonstrated more eloquently and he described his occupation as "a salesman of Americanism." At all of his 15,000 concerts, there was a sense of patriotism. He was described as the "Pied Piper of Patriotism." Late in his career, he was asked what single piece of music he would choose to hear just before he died. He replied, "'The Stars and Stripes Forever.' I would meet my Maker face to face with the inspiration that grows from its melodies and the patriotism that gives it meaning."

A few days before his death, Sousa said to his friend, Dr. James Francis Cooke, editor of the famous music magazine, *The Etude*, "I believe firmly in God. The trouble with modernistic music today is that it is written by men who don't believe in any kind of God. That is the reason why it won't last. Only that lasts which comes from God....All of my music, all of my melodies are not of my own making; no matter how light, they come from a higher source. I have listened to a higher power."

Sousa died of a heart attack on March 6, 1932 at age 77 in Reading, Pennsylvania, after conducting a band rehearsal. The last piece he conducted was "The Stars and Stripes Forever." It is considered by many to be the finest march ever written. The remains of America's most famous and beloved bandmaster were taken by train to Washington, D.C., where he lay in state for public viewing in the Marine Band auditorium and then was buried in Congressional Cemetery with military and Masonic honors. Thousands lined the curb to pay their lasts respects.

Sousa's life was portrayed in a 1952 Hollywood film, "Stars and Stripes Forever," starring Clifton Webb and Ruth Hussey as his wife.

A statue of Sousa now stands at the Marine barracks building in Washington, D.C., one block from the home where he was born.

Here are the words to "The Stars and Stripes Forever."

*Let martial note in triumph float*
*And liberty extend its mighty hand*
*A flag appears 'mid thunderous cheers,*
*The banner of the Western land.*
*The emblem of the brave and true*
*Its folds protect no tyrant crew;*
*The red and white and starry blue*
*Is freedom's shield and hope.*

*Other nations may deem their flags the best*
*And cheer them with fervid elation*
*But the flag of the North and South and West*
*Is the flag of flags, the flag of Freedom's nation.*

*Hurrah for the flag of the free!*
*May it wave as our standard forever,*
*The gem of the land and the sea,*
*The banner of the right.*
*Let despots remember the day*
*When our fathers with mighty endeavor*
*Proclaimed as they marched to the fray*
*That by their might and by their right*
*It waves forever.*

*Let eagle shriek from lofty peak*
*The never-ending watchword of our land;*
*Let summer breeze waft through the trees*
*The echo of the chorus grand.*
*Sing out for liberty and light,*
*Sing out for freedom and the right.*
*Sing out for Union and its might,*

*O patriotic sons.*

*Other nations may deem their flags the best*
*And cheer them with fervid elation,*
*But the flag of the North and South and West*
*Is the flag of flags, the flag of Freedom's nation.*

*Hurrah for the flag of the free.*
*May it wave as our standard forever*
*The gem of the land and the sea,*
*The banner of the right.*
*Let despots remember the day*
*When our fathers with mighty endeavor*
*Proclaimed as they marched to the fray,*
*That by their might and by their right*
*It waves forever.*

## Appendix 5

# DAVY CROCKETT'S LESSON FOR CONGRESS

David Crockett (1786-1836) was the legendary Davy Crockett from Tennessee, a buckskin-clad frontiersman and a hero of the Alamo, where he died. It is less known that he was a U.S. Representative in Congress. The following account of a speech he gave there, and its aftermath, illustrate a fundamental Constitutional principle which is sadly ignored today. It illustrates the statement made by James Madison, the Father of the Constitution, who said in the House of Representatives on January 10, 1794, "The government of the United States is a definite government, confined to specified objects. It is not like state governments, whose powers are more general. Charity is no part of the legislative duty of the government." The modern retelling of the story of Crockett speaking to the House of Representatives is drawn from the original source, *The Life of Colonel David Crockett*, written in 1884 by Edward S. Ellis.

In our very early American Republic, our young state legislators and our young national congressmen did make the MISTAKE of passing socialistic legislation occasionally, but these legal errors were definitely the EXCEPTIONS rather than the rule. During the first 150 years of our existence after the ratification of our Constitution in 1788, our American Republic survived relatively free of the evils of Socialism because most of our people, most of our state legislators, most of our national congressmen and national Supreme Court justices ALL clearly understood the principles of freedom, patriotism, and Americanism as defined by our founders. And because at that early time, these three principles were so simple for our people to easily understand, they could easily recognize socialist-American [SA] type legislators and judges, and when they did, they would either vote these elected SA type legislators out of office, or pressure our RA [Real American] type legislators to impeach the SA type judges. And the story of Davy Crockett PERFECTLY illustrates the truth of this statement regarding our earlier legislators in Congress....

Also, after Davy's story has been told, you should understand how EASILY even intelligent people can fall into the errors of Socialism, but also how EASILY sincere people with the virtues of honesty and humility can EASILY correct their ERRONEOUS thinking regarding the fallacious principles of Socialism.

Everyone is familiar with the famous Davy Crockett of Tennessee. He was a legendary American hunter, hostile Indian fighter, frontiersman, pioneer, and hero, who valiantly sacrificed his life fighting at the Alamo for Texas independence from Mexico in 1836. Everyone is familiar with his physical courage, and his mastery over the natural human emotion of fear. But fewer people are familiar with his metaphysical courage, which enabled him to stand up for what he believed in, and to verbally express his convictions, no matter what the cost to himself personally.

This is the story of Davy's metaphysical courage. Davy served six years as a member of our national Congress until 1835, one year before he died fighting at the Alamo. Did you remember that? While Davy was a congressman, a bill came up for a vote which proposed to use public money to pay financial benefits to the elderly widow of a highly decorated deceased naval officer veteran of our Revolution and War of 1812. It seemed like a worthy cause, and all of the discussion immediately preceding the vote appeared unanimously in favor of its passage. But Davy got the floor and rose to speak. This is what he said:

Mr. Speaker, I have as much respect for the memory of the deceased, and as much sympathy for the sufferings of the living, if suffering there be, as any man in this House, but we must not permit our respect for the dead or our sympathy for a part of the living to lead us into an act of injustice to the balance of the living. I will not go into an argument to prove that Congress has NO POWER to appropriate this money as an act of charity. EVERY MEMBER UPON THIS FLOOR KNOWS IT. We have the right, as individuals, to give away as much of our OWN money as we please in charity; but as members of Congress we have NO RIGHT so to appropriate a dollar of the public money. Some eloquent appeals have been made to us upon the ground that it is a debt due the deceased. Mr. Speaker, the deceased lived long after the close of the war; he was in office to the day of his death, and I have never heard the government was in arrears to him...

Every man in this House knows it is not a debt. We cannot, without the grossest corruption, appropriate this money as the payment of a debt. We have not the semblance of authority to appropriate it as a charity. Mr. Speaker, I have said we have the right to give as much money of our own as we please. I am the poorest man on this floor. I cannot vote for this bill, but I will give one week's pay to the object, and if every member of Congress will do the same, it will amount to more than the bill asks.

Remember now, Davy is speaking almost 50 years AFTER the ratification of our Constitution, and boldly claims that EVERY SINGLE CONGRESSMAN knows that they don't even possess the "semblance" of power or authority from the Constitution to appropriate the taxpayers' money for government charity, and that if they do, it would be an act of "grossest corruption." Can you believe it? Believe it.

When Davy sat down, no congressman replied, and when the vote was taken, the bill was soundly defeated.

The next day, one of Davy's fellow congressmen challenged him to justify his heartless-appearing position regarding the naval widow's bill, and Davy told the following story by way of explanation.

"Several years ago I was one evening standing of the steps of the Capitol with some other members of Congress, when our attention was attracted by a great light over in Georgetown. It was evidently a large fire. We jumped into a hack and drove over as fast as we could... In spite of all that could be done, many houses were burned and many families made houseless, and, besides, some of them had lost all but the clothes they had on. The weather was very cold, and when I saw so many women and children suffering, I felt that something ought to be done for them. The next morning a bill was introduced appropriating $20,000 for their relief. We put aside all other business and rushed it through as soon as it could be done...

The next summer, when it began to be time to think about the election, I concluded I would take a scout around among the boys of my district. I had no opposition there, but as the election was some time off, I did not know what might turn up... When riding one day in a part of my district in which I was more of a stranger than any other, I saw a man in a field plowing and coming toward the road. I gauged my gait so that we should meet as he came to the fence. As he came up, I spoke to the man. He replied politely, but, as I thought, rather coldly...

I began: 'Well, friend, I am one of those unfortunate beings called candidates, and—'

'Yes, I know you; you are Colonel Crockett. I have seen you once before, and voted for you the last time you were elected. I suppose you are out electioneering now, but you had better not waste your time or mine. I shall not vote for you again."

This was a shock...I begged him to tell me what was the matter.

'Well, Colonel, it is hardly worth-while to waste time or words upon it. I do not see how it can be mended, but you gave a vote last winter which shows that either you have not the capacity to understand the Constitution, or that you are wanting in the honesty and firmness to be guided by it. In either case you are not the man to represent me. But I beg your pardon for expressing it in that way... I intend by it only to say that your understanding of the Constitution is very different from mine; and...that I believe you to be honest... But an understanding of the Constitution different from mine I cannot overlook, because the Constitution, to be worth anything, must be held sacred, and rigidly observed in all its provisions. The man who wields power and misinterprets it is the more dangerous the more honest he is.'

I admit the truth of all you say, but there must be some mistake, for I do not remember I gave any vote last winter upon any constitutional question.

'No, Colonel, there's no mistake. Though I live here in the backwoods and seldom go from home, I take the papers from Washington and read very carefully all the proceedings of Congress. My papers say that last winter you voted for a bill to appropriate $20,000 to some sufferers by a fire in Georgetown. Is that true?'

It certainly is, and I thought that was the last vote which anybody in the world would have found fault with.

'Well, Colonel, where do you find in the Constitution any authority to give away the public money for charity?'

Here was another shock; for, when I began to think about it, I could not remember a thing in the Constitution that authorized it. I found I must take another tack, so I said:

Well, my friend; I may as well own up. You have got me there. But certainly nobody will complain that a great and rich country like ours should give the insignificant sum of $20,000 to relieve its suffering women and children, particularly with a full and overflowing Treasury, and I am sure, if you had been there, you would have done just as I did.

'It is not the amount, Colonel, that I complain of; it is the principle. In the first place, the government ought to have in the Treasury no more than enough for its legitimate purposes. But that has nothing to do with the question. The power of collecting and disbursing money at pleasure is the most dangerous power that can be entrusted to man, particularly under our system of collecting revenue by a tariff, which reaches every man in the country, no matter how poor he may be, and the poorer he is the more he pays in proportion to his means. What is worse, it presses upon him without his knowledge where the weight centers, for there is not a man in the United States who can ever guess how much he pays to the government. So you see, that while you are contributing to relieve one, you are drawing it from thousands who are even worse off than he. If you had the right to give anything, the amount was simply a matter of discretion with you, and you had as much right to give $20,000,000 as $20,000. If you have the right to give to one, you have the right to give to all; and, as the Constitution neither defines charity nor stipulates the amount, you are at liberty to give any and everything which you may believe, or profess to believe is a charity, and to any amount you may think proper. You will very easily perceive what a wide door this would open for fraud and corruption and favoritism, one the one hand, and for robbing the people on the other.' "

The farmer continued:

'Individual members may give as much of their OWN money as they please, but they have NO RIGHT to touch a dollar of the public money for that purpose. If twice as many houses had been burned in this county as in Georgetown, neither you nor any other member of Congress would have thought of appropriating a dollar for our relief. There are about two hundred and forty members of congress. If they had shown their sympathy for the sufferers by contributing each, one week's pay, it would have made over $13,000...The congressmen chose to keep their own money, which, if reports be true, some of them spend not very creditably; and the people about Washington, no doubt, applauded you for relieving them from the necessity of giving by giving what was not yours to give. The people have delegated to Congress, by the Constitution, the power to do certain things. To do these, it is authorized to collect and pay moneys, and for nothing else. Everything beyond this a USURPATION, and a VIOLATION of the Constitution.

'So you see, Colonel, you have violated the Constitution in what I consider a vital point. It is a precedent fraught with danger to the country, for when Congress once begins to stretch its power beyond the limits of the Constitution, there is no limit to it, and no security for the people. I have no doubt you acted honestly, but that does not make it any better, except as far as you are personally concerned, and you see that I cannot vote for you.

This farmer was truly a Real-American if ever there was one.

When the farmer finished his lecture, Davy humbly admitted that he had been wrong in this matter, and that his vote to appropriate public money for the victims of the Georgetown disaster had been UNCONSTITUTIONAL. But this farmer was not satisfied with Davy's apologies, and not satisfied with Davy's solemn oath not to vote for another unconstitutional law. The farmer continued:

'You have sworn to that once before, I obviously refer to the oath of office each congressman must STILL TAKE TODAY to uphold and defend the Constitution from all enemies, domestic and foreign, but I will trust you again upon one condition. You say that you are convinced that your vote was wrong. Your acknowledgment of it will do more good than beating you for it. If, as you go around the district, you will tell people about this vote, and that you are satisfied it was wrong, I will not only vote for you, but will do what I can to keep down opposition, and, perhaps, I may exert some little influence in that way.'

It is interesting that the farmer would agree to trust Davy just one more time, even though Davy admitted to violating his original oath of office to uphold and defend our Constitution. The quality of mercy is not strained...to err is human...to forgive is divine.

Davy agreed to publicize his mistake as widely as possible, and kept his promise to the farmer to do just that. Because he did, the farmer gave Davy his full support for re-election, and the two men became close friends. Right before the election, Davy visited his former critic, and later reported:

"Though I was considerably fatigued when I reached his house, and, under ordinary circumstances, should have gone early to bed, I kept him up until midnight, talking about the principles and affairs of government, and got more real, true knowledge of them than I had got all my life before...

I have known and seen much of him since, for I respect him—no, that is not the word—I reverence and love him more than any living man, and I go to see him two or three times every year; and I will tell you, sir, if every one who professes to be a Christian lived and acted and enjoyed it as he does, the religion of Christ would take the world by storm...Now, sir, you know why I made that speech yesterday."

Davy Crockett was a congressman who had the courage of his convictions in the principles of freedom, patriotism, and Americanism. He was not afraid to admit his socialistic mistake, and because he loved the country which our founders gave us, he would never again vote for Socialism, no matter how worthy a cause appears, or how emotional was its appeal. Davy realized that he was not elected by the people of Tennessee to give away their tax dollars for so-called welfare or government charity. His farmer friend made Davy realize the American principle that he could donate his own money in true charity, but that the public's money was not his to TAKE TO GIVE AWAY.

And it is interesting that Davy did not consider Christ to be a Socialist by any stretch of the imagination. In fact, Davy knew that Christ never lobbied the Roman government to tax one to give to another. That would be legal theft, pure and simple. And Socialism....

Now during the first 150 years of our existence after the ratification of our Constitution in 1788, the individuals on our state Supreme Courts and our national Supreme Court fulfilled their true legal obligation of striking down as unconstitutional, null and void, almost every socialistic law which members of our State Houses and national Congress made the mistake of passing. These personal freedom-protecting actions on the part of the patriotic judges of our land helped to keep the country which our founders gave us, free of un-American, unconstitutional Socialism. But of course, Supreme Court action was seldom necessary.

Our patriotic justices on our states' and national Supreme Court for 150 years correctly viewed their function as the LAST-RESORT protectors of their respective Constitutions, and that their proper functions was to INTERPRET THE LAWS passed by state and national congressmen TO MAKE SURE THAT THOSE LAWS WERE CONSTITUTIONAL.

These patriotic justices on our states' and national Supreme Court for 150 years paid attention to George Washington's Farewell Address, warning that unconstitutional, socialistic law-passing is a "usurpation" of power, which appears that it "in one instance may be the instrument of good, it is the CUSTOMARY weapon by which free governments are destroyed." Remember? These patriotic justices for 150 years lived by our fearless spirit's warning to NEVER allow a change to occur in our state or national Constitutions through the simple House-Senate type law-passing procedure, but only through the more cumbersome, slow, cautious, time-consuming, everybody paying attention, widespread publicity causing, debate generating, AMENDMENT PROCESS. And for your information, our founders did their job of writing our national Constitution so well that it has been amended only 26 times in the last 200 years, with the 26th amendment ratified in 1971, recognizing the right of all citizens 18 years old and older to vote in every political election, at every level of government within the United States. [1]

So Supreme Court justices did their patriotic jobs for 150 years after our national Constitution was ratified, and after their state constitutions were ratified, striking down as null and void almost every socialistic law our state and federal legislators made the mistake of passing. And our people were able to maintain glorious freedom because of these Supreme Court actions.

But the last time our national Supreme Court CORRECTLY struck down as socialistic and unconstitutional a law passed by our national Congress was in 1935. Since that time, the Socialist-American justices on our formerly patriotic national Supreme Court HAVE BEEN DECLARING SOCIALIST LAWS CONSTITUTIONAL, and CONSTITUTIONAL LAWS AS UNCONSTITUTIONAL. What a tragedy. What a tragic reversal of their true function.

Today, and for the last 50 years, our Socialist-American national Supreme Court has been the CHIEF PROTECTOR of socialistic legislation, and these socialistic justices on our national Supreme Court view it as their proper function to INTERPRET OUR CONSTITUTION to justify as constitutional almost every socialistic law our Socialist-American Congress passes, and which our Congress has been passing for the last 50 years. What an absolute and complete reversal of the judicial system for which our founders fought and died to give us.

---

## FOOTNOTES

[1] Since the text was written, a 27th amendment was made in 1992 regarding the compensation for the services of the Senators and Representatives. JWW.

This appendix is reprinted by permission from *Uncommon Sense: The Real American Manifesto* by "A Real American" (William James Murray). See Acknowledgments for more information.

## Appendix 6

# SOME FUNDAMENTALS OF LAW AND PUNISHMENT

Some basic principles are being overlooked by those who argue in favor of viewing criminals as sick people needing treatment rather than as lawbreakers deserving punishment. The consequences of that misguided view are detrimental to society and actually encourage more lawlessness. Here are the main points they overlook.

1. **In the American theory of government, everyone has fundamental and inalienable rights to life, liberty, property and the pursuit of happiness.** Government is instituted primarily to assure and protect those individual rights. All the rest of government is secondary to that, including rehabilitation of convicts.

2. Even with protection of liberty, property and individual rights as the primary mission of local, state and federal government, there isn't always a cop on the corner when you need one. Criminals and violent people abound. You'd probably think you were safe while eating in a restaurant or riding on a train, wouldn't you? Well, think of the 22 people killed at a restaurant in Killeen, Texas, by the madman who drove his truck through the plate glass window and then stepped out, firing an M-16-type rifle. Think of the 15 people killed on the Long Island Railroad by a deranged racist firing a semiautomatic handgun.

Therefore, **everyone has the right to defend her/himself against violation of those fundamental and inalienable rights**. The Second Amendment in the Bill of Rights is intended to assure that; in America you have the right to keep and bear arms for self-defense. (The Second Amendment was the original Department of Homeland Security.) You can use a measure of force commensurate with the attack upon you, up to and including lethal force. That is your right under the American system of government. If the 22 dead people in the restaurant or the 15 commuters killed on the train had been armed and trained for self-defense, there would have been only two deaths in each situation—the shooter's first victim and the shooter himself (or even, depending on the training of the people involved, only the shooter himself).

3. **The purpose of our judicial system is to deliver justice, not compassion.** Consideration of mitigating factors, where compassion or mercy might be appropriate, is entirely secondary to the question of innocence or guilt. If the person committed the crime, he is guilty—period. Then punishment must be meted out; otherwise the justice system becomes a travesty. What kind of punishment and how severe—i.e., whether to be merciful—are appropriate questions only at that point. But to absolve a guilty wrongdoer of his responsibility for his actions because of his state of mind is to undermine the American theory of government and justice (see point 4 below), and to make society unsafe for everyone. Mercy is not the primary consideration in a trial; that

is why judges, when delivering a sentence of capital punishment, say to the guilty party, "May God have mercy on your soul." If swift, stern punishment is deserved, mercy is left to God or—to use a term from the Declaration of Independence—the Supreme Judge of the world. The Pledge of Allegiance does not say liberty and compassion for all. It says liberty and justice for all.

4. **In a free society such as ours, laws are made to control behavior, not states of mind**. In determining whether a person broke the law, it doesn't matter if that person is insane, retarded, suffering from postpartum depression, high on drugs or alcohol or even demonically possessed, etc. If he did it, he's guilty—end of story. Why he did it is secondary and becomes proper for consideration only after the finding of innocence or guilt.

5. **Prisons are not intended for rehabilitation and therapy.** Prisons are intended to keep criminals off the street and out of society. Whether the prisoner becomes penitent or rehabilitated is not the primary concern of the prison system, the warden or the staff. They are primarily concerned with incarcerating criminals who've been sentenced to prison. Enlightened penal institutions can indeed offer adjunct services intended to help rehabilitate, but that is a social policy issue to be decided by legislation which has to fund such services. To offer privileges (seen by social engineers as "rehabilitative") and luxuries (such as television and fitness equipment) to prisoners the moment they are incarcerated undermines the purpose of prison, which is punishment. Privileges and luxuries should be earned through good behavior indicating true repentance and reform.

6. **The threat of imprisonment does indeed keep the crime rate down**. Just look within yourself and ask how many times you've refrained from some tempting violation of law or rights because you were afraid of getting caught and punished.

7. **Capital punishment works.** It permanently removes vicious criminals from society so they cannot repeat their crimes. Concern about the possibility of executing an innocent, wrongly convicted person is, of course, proper and of utmost importance for a civil society. Legislation to restore capital punishment should therefore include measures to assure that only the guilty are executed, and the same applies where capital punishment is used already. But if an innocent person is wrongly executed, that is not the fault of capital punishment; that is a failure of the judicial system through which the investigation and trial took place.

8. **To eliminate crime at the root cause requires enlightened parenting, schooling and socialization of children** through moral training at home, in churches/synagogues/temples/mosques and through reinforcement of that via the words and deeds of public authorities and other figures of influence. Enlightened parenting includes reinforcement of social behavior codes such as the Ten Commandments (Judeo-Christian), the Eightfold Path (Buddhist), the Sharia (Muslim) or whatever rules are established or accepted by the parents to determine simple right and wrong conduct for young children so that they grow up to obey the law and respect duly constituted authority.

For an adult criminal set in his ways, the threat of punishment (loss of life, liberty or property—such as fines, imprisonment, capital punishment or, if the citizen is not native-born, deportation) will never fully deter him; it will only make him more crafty in his criminal mindset. John Wayne Gacey sodomized and killed 33 boys in Illinois, but prior to his apprehension he was perceived by his community as a "role model of good behavior" (he was a Scoutmaster at one point). That was crafty of Gacey—sick as hell, but crafty. How to prevent such monsters from being created in the first place is of paramount importance, but dismantling or watering down the criminal justice system is not the answer. That will only make things worse for society.

## Appendix 7

# LIBERTARIAN VS. LIBERATIVE GOVERNMENT

I have great respect for the libertarian approach to politics and government, but I am dissatisfied with it in one fundamental aspect. The dominant school of libertarian thought, which takes its orientation from philosopher Ayn Rand, is characterized by atheism and ethical humanism. Like the classical liberalism of our Founders, it is based on reason and Natural Law. But unlike the classical liberalism of our Founders, it is incomplete because it has little to no recognition of the *source* of reason and Natural Law. It is contrary to the perspective of the great libertarian Thomas Jefferson because there is no transcendent and eternal basis in it for the liberty which libertarians rightly extol. Reason and Natural Law are necessary but not sufficient for enduring liberty. As Thomas Jefferson said in *Notes on the State of Virginia*, "And can the liberties of a nation be thought secure when we have removed their only firm basis, a conviction in the minds of the people that these liberties are the gift of God?"

The Randian school ignores the fundamental principle which our Founders stated in the Declaration of Independence: God is the source of our liberty, our sovereignty, our equality, our rights, our justice and our human dignity—and all else which creates a good society and a society which is good. To our Founders, that was self-evident. Everything else in our free society flows from that. To derive a theory of liberty from mere human reasonableness, ethical humanism and/or atheistic freethought is to build one's house on sand.

Conservatives, with their emphasis of godly living, have preserved that key insight of the American theory of liberty. However, they don't understand its proper application. They try to legislate morality and force it on everyone to the point of thought control. They end up shooting themselves in the foot because much of their legislative agenda actually reduces liberty while enlarging government. Think, for example, of the conservative-supported federal Department of Education and the War on Drugs, and how much tax money is wasted on their totally ineffective actions by an ever-expanding bureaucracy which is replacing individual freedom, local control and self-government with a federal monster.

The task now is for libertarians to learn from conservatives about the theory of liberty and for conservatives to learn from libertarians about the practice of liberty.

### God as the Spirit of Liberty

John Adams called God "the Spirit of Liberty." Why is that insight absent from libertarianism? George Washington and other Founders stated that morality cannot survive in the absence of the religious principle, i.e., reverence for God as the Supreme Lawmaker and Judge. Why is that insight absent from libertarianism? The ministers of New England who spoke forcefully from the pulpit in support of American liberty during the Revolutionary era often quoted St. Paul: "Where the spirit of the Lord is, there is liberty" (2 Corinthians 3:17). Why is that insight absent from libertarianism?

The dilemma which libertarianism vs. conservatism sets before us is this: An immoral people is incapable of self-government, but so is a people totally dominated by authoritarian moralists. The solution? God must become central to libertarian thought; liberty must become central to conservative thought.

## God as the Essence of Freedom

Liberty is actually a subset of freedom and refers only to the social-political aspect of human existence. Freedom embraces every aspect of our being, from the material through the emotional, intellectual and social-political to its highest aspect, the spiritual.

The essence of freedom is having a choice. Our God-given free will allows us to choose, for good or ill, on all levels of our existence. However, since all freedom comes from God, we have an inherent responsibility to use it properly—i.e., morally and lawfully—to fulfill our obligation to our Creator. Freedom and responsibility are therefore intimately related. Without responsibility, liberty becomes libertinism or immoral behavior —i.e., abuse of liberty. Freedom is never license to do as we please, but—as Lord Acton, the libertarian Catholic author of *The History of Freedom*, put it—only to do as we ought.

A synonym for spiritual freedom is liberation. The world's religions and sacred traditions are agreed that the purpose of human life is to attain liberation or enlightenment. They are in unison when they say that our Creator, our Divine Source wants us to remove from ourselves all the spiritual blindness, self-centered thought and immoral behavior which separates us from the realization that we are one with the Divine Creator because that God-realization can transform the world into what it should be—heaven on earth.

Spiritual freedom, not merely liberty, is the goal of our human journey. Why? The corollary, which our Founders held, to the principle about the source of freedom answers that: Humanity is made in the image and likeness of God, and the purpose of our life is to glorify God by expressing God in every aspect of our existence—i.e., by attaining liberation, enlightenment, spiritual freedom as the basis for our daily living. That alone can provide an enduring basis not only for social-political freedom or liberty, but also for freedom from vice, immorality, negative emotions, self-aggrandizement, antisocial behavior and everything else which prevents us from recognizing the presence of God in all others and thereby building heaven on earth. Our choice, not simply as Americans but as human beings, is between that and a godless society.

It was no accident that some of our Founders (notably Benjamin Franklin and John Adams) spoke of America as the New Jerusalem and the New Israel. By that they did not mean a Jewish nation; rather, they meant a God-centered society whose collective will was to glorify God and reflect heaven on earth. They rightly separated church and state so that, in the name of freedom of conscience, no particular denomination could ever become established as the state religion. But they never separated God and state. How could they? Through their four references to deity in the Declaration of Independence (Nature's God, Creator, Supreme Judge of the world and Divine Providence), God is proclaimed as the mighty author of our being and the moral authority for our government and our society—the very basis of America.

## God and American Government

Without a recognition of God as the central fact of the American theory of government, libertarianism will remain incomplete and unable to respond to the depths of the human hunger for freedom. That hunger will not end until the source of freedom is recognized and embraced, thereby yielding spiritual freedom and its byproduct, true and enduring happiness.

The name I offer for the perspective which recognizes both the strengths and the shortcomings of the libertarian and the conservative stances, and which integrates the best aspects of them while discarding their errors, is an amalgam word: *liberative*. It denotes spiritual freedom and the source of spiritual freedom as the basis of everything in our lives, including liberty. It also explains why it is right—intellectually, philosophically and morally—to pledge allegiance to America and to declare that we are one nation under God.

*This appendix was published as an essay in the June 2003 edition of* Libertarian News, *which is the newspaper of the Libertarian Party. For a full discussion of the meaning of "liberative government" see my book* America, Freedom and Enlightenment: An Open Letter to Americans about Patriotism and Global Society.

## Appendix 8

# THE JAMESTOWN AND PLYMOUTH COLONIES: SEEDBEDS OF FREE MARKET CAPITALISM

There is no better justification for the free market capitalist system of economics than the story of the first two permanent English settlements in America, Plymouth and Jamestown. Both colonies would have failed completely if their leaders had not recognized that their initial economic system, communism, was not working but rather was leading to their destruction.

I do not mean Marxist communism, which emerged centuries later, based on atheism, materialism and naked military-political force. No, the economic system put in place at both colonies could properly be called Christic communism.

Why that term? Both colonies or plantations, as they were called, were distinctly Christian in character, and both implemented a form of economics which was based on the New Testament. With no disrespect intended, Jesus can be regarded one of the earliest communists in history, coming from an Essene background which was distinctly communal. The early Christians therefore, following in his way, also lived communally or communistically—i.e., had collective ownership and use of property. This is shown in the Book of Acts, which is the oldest record of how the earliest Christians lived. Specifically, in Acts 2:44 and 4:32, they are described by St. Paul as living communally by selling all they had, contributing their wealth to the group, and having "all things in common." Various monastic orders and communes still do that today.

Why didn't Christic communism work at Jamestown and Plymouth? The answer is simple: ego or human self-centeredness. That is the reason the plantations nearly failed and so many other utopian experiments in history have failed. The key to success in Christic communal living is the radical transformation of consciousness which Jesus called his followers to attain—a God-centered rather than self-centered state of mind called enlightenment or "the peace which passeth understanding." It was not present at Jamestown and Plymouth—at least not in sufficient degree—to sustain the economic system. The self-centeredness of the people living there undermined what was intended as a noble way of living based on the Bible.

Within a few years, each community found that some of its members were lazy, irresponsible and willing to take advantage of others, simply by not contributing to the communal establishment while nevertheless taking from it. Governor William Bradford in *Of Plimouth Plantation: 1620-1647,* his history of the Plymouth Colony, wrote this about what he called simply "communism," noting that it was a failed experiment in "communal service": "At Plymouth some men had not exerted themselves because tangible evidence was lacking that their efforts in any way contributed to their personal well being." Similarly, Captain John Smith, who had charge of the Jamestown Colony, recorded:

When our people were fed out of the common storehouse and labored jointly together, glad was he who could slip away from his labor or slumber over his task. He cared not, presuming that howsoever the harvest prospered, the general storehouse must maintain him. Even the most honest among them would hardly take so much true pains in a week under the public ownership and common storehouse system, as now for themselves they will do in a day. So that, we reaped not so much corn from the labor of thirty as now three or four would provide for themselves.

The egotism—the lazy, irresponsible self-centeredness—of those parasitic people thought, "Why should I work when I can rely on others to provide my living?" (Sound like the welfare system today?) And on the other side of the question were those whom Bradford described a few sentences later in his history of Plimouth Plantation: "For the young men, that were most able and fitte for labor and service, did repine that they should spend their time and strength to worke for other men's wives and children without any recompense." (Sound like fed-up taxpayers today?)

Governor Bradford applied the commandment which St. Paul gave to the early Christians in Thessalonia, where the same problem existed. He actually posted the text to make his position clear. St. Paul had put it very simply. He said he had heard that some members of the community were "living in idleness, mere busybodies, not doing any work." His solution: "If any one will not work, let him not eat." (II Thessalonians 3:10-11)

That is precisely what the Jamestown and the Plymouth elders learned, and that is why they changed their economic system from a socialistic commonwealth—in which land and its agricultural products were communally owned and cultivated—to free enterprise capitalism and private ownership of land. Allowing the colonists to keep most of what they produced was an incentive to labor and increased production. (Some food was required as taxation for the support of those who worked in government and other nonfarming activities.) Again from Governor Bradford:

At last after much debate of things, the governor gave way that they should set corn everyman for his own particular... That had very good success for it made all hands very industrious, so much [more] corn was planted than otherwise would have been... The experience that was had in this common course and condition, tried sundrie years, and that amongst Godly and sober men, may well evince the Vanities of the conceit of Plato's and other ancients, applauded by some of later times; that the taking away of propertie, and bringing into commone wealth, would make them happy and flourishing, as if they were wiser than God.

The famine of 1623 which nearly wiped out the Pilgrims gave way to a period of agricultural abundance. That, in turn, enabled the Massachusetts settlers to put down roots, prosper and play an indispensable role in the ultimate success of the American experiment. Free market capitalism, meaning the right to own private property and the right to conduct commerce freely while keeping the profits, harnesses egotism or self-interest in a way which actually benefits all. (That is also an objective of Christic communism, but it requires the "mind of Christ" rather than ego-based mind to work properly.)

Free market capitalism also provides greater opportunity and incentive for individuals to rise on the basis of their own talent and effort. It is the means by which the poorest and otherwise most hopeless people can pull themselves up by their own bootstraps (or sandalstraps, as the case may be). Not all make it, of course; there are competitive and monopolistic factors to be reckoned with. But as demonstrated so well and so often in American history, free enterprise capitalism is a major reason this nation is regarded as the land of opportunity. Personal, economic, social and political freedom are intimately related in the American way of life—much more so than in any other nation.

Anything economic which supports freedom, personal choice and the responsibility and accountability for those choices, can in principle be regarded as supportive of the process of growth to enlightenment or the peace which passeth all understanding. Capitalism is the only socioeconomic system based on the recognition that each individual owns his life; it is the only system in which individuals are free to pursue their rational self-interest, to own property and to profit from their actions. That "profit" is as much spiritual as it is economic, with regard to learning that one's actions have consequences for which the person must be responsible.

## The Primary Value of Free Enterprise Capitalism

The primary value of free enterprise capitalism is its respect for and expression of certain fundamental moral principles. Foremost is individual freedom, which in the American perspective on human society is regarded as a natural, inalienable right. Next, free enterprise capitalism functions on the basis of exchanges which require honesty and honor in the parties involved; dishonest people or people without integrity soon earn a reputation which drives away further business for them, leading to failure or legal sanction. (However, practice does not always live up to theory, so *Caveat emptor*, "Let the buyer beware," is still wise advice.)

Free enterprise capitalism also functions on the basis of giving customers the most value at the lowest price. Unless someone has a monopoly in business, that person must compete with others for customers. Hence there is constant pressure for increased value and lower prices of goods or services. (Moreover, businesses generally follow a policy of credit or refund if a customer is not satisfied.)

This has two benefits. First, it spurs technological innovation, so that "the best" is always improving and the standard of living rises across society. ("A rising tide lifts all boats.") Second, it forces businesses to become more productive. This results in lowered expenses and increased profits which are shared with employees (in order to retain their skills, experience and morale) and stakeholders (in order to retain their investments and good will), thus improving their standard of living and, more generally, their society's standard of living.

In addition, businesses constantly scrutinize their competitors and are quick to denounce dishonest or questionable practices. Thus, free enterprise capitalism has still another benefit: it tends to be self-policing, and nearly all industries, trades and professions have their own regulatory boards which seek to uphold the reputation of their group by requiring ethical activity from those in it. (The Better Business Bureau is an American invention.) On the other side of the topic, organizations representing various industries offer surveys of "best practices" and thereby share freely methods of improving their own industry.

All this helps to place society on a moral foundation of honesty, responsibility and accountability, which is a necessary precondition for societal self-government and personal growth to enlightenment. Annual surveys which rate countries as places to do business constantly rank America at or near the top because the moral climate of this nation rejects bribery, payoffs, false accounting and other forms of dishonest dealings which are deeply entrenched in the Asian and Middle Eastern countries at the bottom of the ranking. (Note that the Enron Corporation accounting scandal was an exception, not the rule, and it resulted in public outrage and government prosecution.)

The brilliance of the free market economy is this: it harnesses the force of the ego's self-interest into a system which functions to produce enlightened self-interest. The choices of the individual produce something which is best for both the individual and the many in an economic, social and moral sense by preserving freedom while improving the material quality of life.

In short, the free market economy is an expression of the highest spiritual principle: freedom. It is a partial embodiment, at the level of mass consciousness, of the ancient concept of liberation, which is a fundamental tenet of the Perennial Philosophy. Thank you, Jamestown and Plymouth.

## Appendix 9

# A PROCLAMATION FOR USE BY TOWNS AND CITIES TO HONOR INDEPENDENCE DAY

This proclamation, which I wrote, has been issued several times by successive mayors of my home town. Its purposes are (1) to get people to fly the flag on national holidays—and, ideally, year-round—and (2) to get people thinking about the meaning of the flag. The kind of patriotism America needs is informed, thoughtful love of country based on awareness and understanding of our nation's history, ideals, principles, values and its potential for building a world community with liberty and justice for all.

Note that the format of this proclamation can be adapted to any other patriotic occasion and thereby be used for further instruction in the fundamentals of America.

## A PROCLAMATION

**Whereas** The United States of America was founded on July 4, 1776 at great cost in hardship, sacrifice and bloodshed to secure the blessings of liberty for the inhabitants thereof and their posterity; and

**Whereas** that daring and unprecedented political experiment based on the principles of individual freedom and inalienable rights granted to us by God, limited constitutional government by the consent of the governed, separation of church and state in government, equality and justice under the rule of law, local self-government and free enterprise has produced the greatest nation on earth; and

**Whereas** America is the oldest democratic constitutional republic in history and has established a society with political, economic, social and religious freedom admired around the world; and

**Whereas** the Town/City of XYZ is a secure, prosperous, beautiful community as a direct result of that; and

**Whereas** the citizens of XYZ enjoy in abundant measure the blessings of liberty which the Founders of our country so nobly intended for us;

**Now therefore** I, _____, Mayor of XYZ, proclaim that all citizens of _____ should patriotically demonstrate their gratitude, loyalty and love for our country by flying the flag of the United States of America daily at their homes, schools, places of work, places of worship, public meetings and other gatherings.

I proclaim further that all citizens of XYZ should learn the proper manner of demonstrating respect for our flag and our national anthem when in public gatherings, so that the youth of XYZ are shown good examples to follow in their education as citizens of our town/city, our state and our nation.

I proclaim further that all citizens of XYZ should deepen their understanding of America—its history, its democratic traditions, its principles of self-governing society, and its dependence upon moral citizens behaving responsibly, charitably and with civic pride—so that our precious national heritage is preserved for our posterity and is upheld in honor before all the world.

Signed: John or Jane Doe, Mayor

## Appendix 10

# A PROCLAMATION FOR USE BY TOWNS AND CITIES TO HONOR SCOUTS BSA AND GIRL SCOUTS

This proclamation, which I wrote, has been issued several times by successive mayors of my home town. Its purposes are (1) to publicly thank and honor the young people of Scouting and their adult leaders, and (2) to encourage young people and adults who are not in Scouting to get involved. The timing of issuance of this proclamation is best when it coincides with the national Scout BSA Recognition Week in February, when Scouts are encouraged to wear their uniform to school as a means of increasing their visibility as Scouts and showing pride in their organization.

## A PROCLAMATION

**Whereas** the Scouts BSA and Girl Scouts of America are the world's largest organizations dedicated to helping girls and boys everywhere build character, gain skills for success in the real world, and develop conviction about their own potential and self-worth which will serve them all their lives, and

**Whereas** Scouting has helped millions of young people to confront difficult situations and make responsible decisions, and

**Whereas** the Scouting movement has played an important role in the growth and preservation of America for more than a century, and

**Whereas** Scouting instills civic values and virtue in young people which are integral with the ideals, morals. principles and values which America embodies, and

**Whereas** Scouting develops a sense of respect and care for the environment and the world of nature, and

**Whereas** Scouting in XYZ has been of great benefit to our town through its emphasis on character development, citizenship training, and mental and physical fitness, and

**Whereas** Scouting in XYZ has contributed to the beautification of our town in the form of planting flower barrels in the center of town, creating hiking trails, erecting signage marking the Linear Trail and Medal of Honor Plaza, installing a courtyard for XYZ School and numerous other projects which enrich the appearance and culture of XYZ,

**Now therefore I**, _____, Mayor of XYZ, proclaim [day/month/year] to be Scouting Recognition Day.

I proclaim further that all citizens of XYZ should feel proud and grateful to have the various Scouting organizations for young people available to the town through the committed adult volunteers who make Scouting possible.

Signed: John or Jane Doe, Mayor

## Appendix 11

# CONGRESSIONAL RESOLUTION CALLING FOR AMERICAN RELIGIOUS HISTORY WEEK

## 110TH CONGRESS
## 1ST SESSION H. RES. 888

Affirming the rich spiritual and religious history of our Nation's founding and subsequent history and expressing support for designation of the first week in May as "American Religious History Week" for the appreciation of and education on America's history of religious faith.

---

## IN THE HOUSE OF REPRESENTATIVES
## DECEMBER 18, 2007

Mr. FORBES (for himself, Mr. MCINTYRE, Mr. AKIN, Mr. BARRETT of South Carolina, Mr. CULBERSON, Mr. DOOLITTLE, Mr. FEENEY, Mr. GINGREY, Mr. GOHMERT, Mr. HAYES, Mr. HENSARLING, Mr. HERGER, Mr. JONES of North Carolina, Mr. MCHENRY, Mrs. MUSGRAVE, Mr. PEARCE, Mr. PENCE, Mr. PITTS, Mr. RYAN of Wisconsin, Mrs. SCHMIDT, Mr. WALBERG, Mr. WILSON of South Carolina, Mr. WOLF, and Mr. YOUNG of Florida) submitted the following resolution; which was referred to the Committee on Oversight and Government Reform

---

## RESOLUTION

Affirming the rich spiritual and religious history of our Nation's founding and subsequent history and expressing support for designation of the first week in May as "American Religious History Week" for the appreciation of and education on America's history of religious faith.

Whereas religious faith was not only important in official American life during the periods of discovery, exploration, colonization, and growth but has also been acknowledged and incorporated into all three branches of American federal government from their very beginning;

Whereas the Supreme Court of the United States affirmed this self-evident fact in a unanimous ruling declaring "This is a religious people....From the discovery of this continent to the present hour, there is a single voice making this affirmation"; 1

Whereas political scientists have documented that the most frequently-cited source in the political period known as The Founding Era was the Bible; 2

Whereas the first act of America's first Congress in 1774 was to ask a minister to open with prayer 3 and to lead Congress in the reading of four chapters of the Bible; 4

Whereas Congress regularly attended church and Divine service together *en masse*; 5

Whereas throughout the American Founding, Congress frequently appropriated money for missionaries and for religious instruction 6 –a practice that Congress repeated for decades after the passage of the Constitution and the First Amendment; 7

Whereas in 1776, Congress approved the Declaration of Independence with its four direct religious acknowledgments referring to God as the Creator ("All people are endowed by their Creator with certain unalienable rights, that among these are life, liberty and the pursuit of happiness"), the Lawgiver ("the laws of nature and nature's God"), the Judge ("appealing to the Supreme Judge of the world"), and the Protector ("with a firm reliance on the protection of Divine Providence"); 8

Whereas upon approving the Declaration of Independence, John Adams declared that the Fourth of July "ought to be commemorated as the day of deliverance by solemn acts of devotion to God Almighty"; 9

Whereas four days after approving the Declaration, the Liberty Bell was rung;

Whereas the Library Bell was named for the Biblical inscription from Leviticus 25:10 emblazoned around it: "Proclaim liberty throughout the land, to all the inhabitants thereof";

Whereas in 1777, Congress, facing a national shortage of "Bibles for our schools, and families, and for the public worship of God in our churches," 10 announced that they "desired to have a Bible printed under their care & by their encouragement" 11 and therefore ordered 20,000 copies of the Bible to be imported "into the different ports of the States of the Union"; 12

Whereas in 1782, Congress pursued a plan to print a Bible that would be "a neat edition of the Holy Scriptures for the use of schools" 13 and therefore approved 14 the production of the first English language Bible printed in America that contained the congressional endorsement that "the United States in Congress assembled... recommend this edition of the Bible to the inhabitants of the United States"; 15

Whereas in 1782, Congress adopted (and has reaffirmed on numerous subsequent occasions) the National Seal with its Latin motto "Annuit Coeptis," meaning "God has favored our undertakings," along with the eye of Providence in a triangle over a pyramid, and the eye and the motto "allude to the many signal interpositions of Providence in favor of the American cause"; 16

Whereas the 1783 Treaty of Paris officially ended the Revolution and establishing America as an independent nation begins with the appellation "In the name of the most holy and undivided Trinity"; 17

Whereas in 1787 at the Constitutional Convention in Philadelphia, Benjamin Franklin declared, "God governs in the affairs of men. And if a sparrow cannot fall to the ground without His notice, is it probable that an empire can rise without His aid?…Without His concurring aid, we shall succeed in this political building no better than the builders of Babel"; 18

Whereas the delegates to the Constitutional Convention concluded their work by placing a religious punctuation mark at the end of the Constitution in the Attestation Clause, noting not only that they had completed the work with "the unanimous consent of the States present" but they had done so "in the Year of our Lord one thousand seven hundred and eighty seven"; 19

Whereas James Madison declared that he saw the finished Constitution as a product of "the finger of that Almighty Hand which has been so frequently and signally extended to our relief in the critical stages of the Revolution," 20 and George Washington viewed it as "little short of a miracle," 21 and Benjamin Franklin believed that its writing had been "influenced, guided, and governed by that omnipotent, omnipresent, and beneficent Ruler, in Whom all inferior spirits live, and move, and have their being"; 22

Whereas in 1787-1788, State conventions to ratify the U. S. Constitution not only began with prayer 23 but even met in church buildings; 24

Whereas in 1795 during construction of the Capitol, a practice was instituted whereby "public worship is now regularly administered at the Capitol, every Sunday morning, at 11 o'clock"; 25

Whereas in 1789, the first federal Congress—the Congress that framed the Bill of Rights, including the First Amendment—appropriated federal funds to pay chaplains to pray at the opening of all sessions, 26 a practice that has continued to this day, with Congress not only funding its congressional chaplains but also the salaries and operations of more than 4,500 military chaplains; 27

Whereas in 1789, Congress, in the midst of framing the Bill of Rights and the First Amendment, passed the first federal law touching education, declaring that "Religion, morality, and knowledge, being necessary to good government and the happiness of mankind, schools and the means of education shall forever be encouraged"; 28

Whereas in 1789, on the same day that Congress finished drafting the First Amendment, it requested President Washington to declare a national day of prayer and thanksgiving, 29 resulting in the first federal official Thanksgiving proclamation that declared "it is the duty of all nations to acknowledge the providence of Almighty God, to obey His will, to be grateful for His benefits, and humbly to implore His protection and favor"; 30

Whereas in 1800, Congress enacted naval regulations requiring that Divine service be performed twice every day aboard "all ships and vessels in the navy," with a sermon preached each Sunday; 31

Whereas in 1800, Congress approved the use of the just-completed Capitol structure as a church building, with Divine services to be held each Sunday in the Hall of the House, 32 alternately administered by the House and Senate chaplains;

Whereas in 1853 Congress declared that congressional chaplains have a "duty…to conduct religious services weekly in the Hall of the House of Representatives"; 33

Whereas by 1867, the church at the Capitol was the largest church in Washington, D. C., with up to 2,000 persons per week attending Sunday service in the Hall of the House; 34

Whereas by 1815, over two thousand official governmental calls to prayer had been issued at both the state and the federal levels, 35 with thousands more issued since 1815;

Whereas in 1853 the U. S. Senate declared that the Founding Fathers "had no fear or jealousy of religion itself, nor did they wish to see us an irreligious people…they did not intend to spread over all the public authorities and the whole public action of the nation the dead and revolting spectacle of atheistical apathy"; 36

Whereas in 1854 the United States House of Representatives declared "It [religion] must be considered as the foundation on which the whole structure rests.…Christianity; in its general principles, is the great conservative element on which we must rely for the purity and permanence of free institutions"; 37

Whereas, in 1864, by law Congress added "In God We Trust" to American coinage; 38

Whereas in 1864, Congress passed an act authorizing each state to display statues of two of its heroes in the United States Capitol, 39 resulting in numerous statues of noted Christian clergymen and leaders at the Capitol, including Gospel ministers such as the Revs. James A. Garfield, John Peter Muhlenberg, Jonathan Trumbull, Roger Williams, Jason Lee, Marcus Whitman, and Martin Luther King Jr.; Gospel theologians such as Roger Sherman; Catholic priests such as Father Damien, Jacques Marquette, Eusebio Kino, and Junipero Serra; Catholic nuns such as Mother Joseph; and numerous other religious leaders;

Whereas in 1870, the federal government made Christmas (a recognition of the birth of Christ, an event described by the U. S. Supreme Court as "acknowledged in the Western World for 20 centuries, and in this country by the people, the Executive Branch, Congress, and the courts for two centuries" 40) and Thanksgiving as official holidays; 41

Whereas beginning in 1904 42 and continuing for the next half-century, 43 the Federal government printed and distributed *The Life and Morals of Jesus of Nazareth* for the use of Members of Congress because of the important teachings it contained;

Where in 1931, Congress by law adopted the Star-Spangled Banner as the official National Anthem, 44 with its phrases such as "may the Heav'n-rescued land Praise the Power that hath made and preserved us a nation," and "this be our motto, 'In God is our trust!' "; 45

Whereas in 1954, Congress by law added the phrase "one nation under God" to the Pledge of Allegiance; 46

Whereas in 1954 a special Congressional Prayer Room was added to the Capitol with a kneeling bench, an altar, an open Bible, an inspiring stained-glass window with George Washington kneeling in prayer, the declaration of Psalm 16:1: "Preserve me, O God, for in Thee do I put my trust," and the phrase "This Nation Under God" displayed above the kneeling, prayerful Washington;

Whereas in 1956, Congress by law made "In God We Trust" the National Motto, 47 and added the phrase to American currency; 48

Whereas the constitutions of each of the fifty states, either in the preamble or body, explicitly recognize or express gratitude to God; 49

Whereas America's first Presidential Inauguration—that of President George Washington—incorporated seven specific religious activities, including (1) the use of the Bible to administer the oath; 50 (2) affirming the religious nature of the oath by the adding the prayer "So help me God!" to the oath; 51 (3) inaugural prayers offered by the president; 52 (4) religious content in the inaugural address; 53 (5) civil leaders calling the people to prayer or acknowledgement of God; 54 (6) inaugural worship services attended *en masse* by Congress as an official part of congressional activities; 55 and (7) clergy-led inaugural prayers 56—activities which have been replicated in whole or part by every subsequent president;

Whereas President George Washington declared "Of all the dispositions and habits which lead to political prosperity, religion and morality are indispensable supports"; 57

Whereas President John Adams, one of only two signers of the Bill of Rights and First Amendment, declared "As the safety and prosperity of nations ultimately and essentially depend on the protection and the blessing of Almighty God, and the national acknowledgment of this truth is not only an indispensable duty which the people owe to Him"; 58

Whereas President Jefferson not only attended Divine services at the Capitol throughout his presidency 59 and had the Marine Band play at the services 60 but during his administration church services were also begun in the two Executive Branch buildings under his direct control: the War Department and the Treasury Department, 61 thus allowing worshippers on any given Sunday the choice to attend church at either the United States Capitol, the War Department, or the Treasury Department if they so desired;

Whereas Thomas Jefferson urged local governments to make land available specifically for Christian purposes, 62 provided Federal funding for missionary work among Indian tribes, 63 and declared that religious schools would receive "the patronage of the government"; 64

Whereas President Andrew Jackson declared that the Bible "is the rock on which our Republic rests"; 65

Whereas President Abraham Lincoln declared that the Bible "is the best gift God has given to men… But for it, we could not know right from wrong"; 66

Whereas President William McKinley declared that "Our faith teaches us that there is no safer reliance than upon the God of our fathers, Who has so singularly favored the American people in every national trial and Who will not forsake us so long as we obey His commandments and walk humbly in His footsteps"; 67

Whereas President Teddy Roosevelt declared "The Decalogue and the Golden Rule must stand as the foundation of every successful effort to better either our social or our political life"; 68

Whereas President Woodrow Wilson declared that "America was born to exemplify that devotion to the elements of righteousness which are derived from the revelations of Holy Scripture"; 69

Whereas President Herbert Hoover declared that "American life is built, and can alone survive, upon…[the] fundamental philosophy announced by the Savior nineteen centuries ago"; 70

Whereas President Franklin D. Roosevelt not only led the nation in a six-minute prayer during DDay on June 6, 1944, 71 but he also declared that "If we will not prepare to give all that we have and all that we are to preserve Christian civilization in our land, we shall go to destruction"; 72

Whereas President Harry S. Truman declared that "The fundamental basis of this Nation's law was given to Moses on the Mount. The fundamental basis of our Bill of

Rights comes from the teachings which we get from Exodus and St. Matthew, from Isaiah and St. Paul"; 73

Whereas President Harry S. Truman told a group touring Washington, D. C., that "You will see, as you make your rounds, that this Nation was established by men who believed in God... You will see the evidence of this deep religious faith on every hand"; 74

Whereas President Dwight D. Eisenhower declared that "Without God there could be no American form of government, nor an American way of life. Recognition of the Supreme Being is the first—the most basic—expression of Americanism. Thus, the founding fathers of America saw it, and thus with God's help, it will continue to be" 75—a declaration later repeated with approval by President Gerald Ford; 76

Whereas President John F. Kennedy declared that "The rights of man come not from the generosity of the state but from the hand of God"; 77

Whereas President Ronald Reagan, after noting "The Congress of the United States, in recognition of the unique contribution of the Bible in shaping the history and character of this Nation and so many of its citizens, has...requested the President to designate the year 1983 as the 'Year of the Bible'," officially declared 1983 as "The Year of the Bible"; 78

Whereas every other president has similarly recognized the role of God and religious faith in the public life of America;

Whereas all sessions of the United States Supreme Court begin with the Court's Marshal announcing, "God save the United States and this honorable court"; 79

Whereas a regular and integral part of official activities in the Federal courts—including the United States Supreme Court—was the inclusion of prayer by a minister of the Gospel; 80

Whereas the United States Supreme Court has throughout the course of our Nation's history said that the United States is "a Christian country," 81 "a Christian nation," 82 "a Christian people," 83 "a religious people whose institutions presuppose a Supreme Being," 84 and that "we cannot read into the Bill of Rights a philosophy of hostility to religion"; 85

Whereas Justice John Jay, an author of the *Federalist Papers* and original Justice of the U. S. Supreme Court, urged "The most effectual means of securing the continuance of our civil and religious liberties is always to remember with reverence and gratitude the Source from which they flow"; 86

Whereas Justice James Wilson, a signer of the Constitution, declared that "Human law must rest its authority ultimately upon the authority of that law which is Divine....Far from being rivals or enemies, religion and law are twin sisters, friends, and mutual assistants"; 87

Whereas Justice William Paterson, a signer of the Constitution, declared that "Religion and morality...[are] necessary to good government, good order, and good laws"; 88

Whereas President George Washington, who passed into law the first legal acts organizing the Federal judiciary, asked, "Where is the security for property, for reputation, for life, if the sense of religious obligation desert the oaths in the courts of justice?"; 89

Whereas some of the most important monuments, buildings, and landmarks in Washington, D.C., include religious words, symbols, and imagery; Whereas in the United States Capitol the declaration "In God We Trust" is prominently displayed in both the United States House and Senate Chambers;

Whereas around the top of the walls in the House Chamber appear images of 23 great lawgivers from across the centuries, but Moses (the lawgiver, who—according to the Bible—originally received the law of God,) is the only lawgiver honored with a full face view, looking down on the proceedings of the House;

Whereas religious artwork is found throughout the United States Capitol, including in the Rotunda where the prayer service of Christopher Columbus, the Baptism of Pocahontas, and the prayer and Bible study of the Pilgrims are all prominently displayed; in the Cox Corridor of the Capitol where the words "America! God shed His grace on thee" are inscribed; at the east Senate entrance with the words "Annuit Coeptis"—Latin for "God has favored our undertakings"; and in numerous other locations;

Whereas images of the Ten Commandments are found in many federal buildings across Washington, D. C., including in bronze in the floor of the National Archives; in a bronze statue of Moses in the Main Reading Room of the Library of Congress; in numerous locations at the U. S. Supreme Court, including in the frieze above the Justices, the oak door at the rear of the Chamber, the gable apex, and in dozens of locations on the bronze latticework surrounding the Supreme Court Bar seating;

Whereas in the Washington Monument not only are numerous Bible verses and religious acknowledgements carved on memorial blocks in the walls, including the phrases: "Holiness to the Lord" (Exodus 28:26, 30:30, Isaiah 23:18, Zechariah 14:20), "Search the Scriptures" (John 5:39), "The memory of the just is blessed" (Proverbs 10:7), "May Heaven to this Union continue its beneficence," and "In God We Trust", but the Latin inscription Laus Deo—"Praise be to God"—is engraved on the monument's capstone;

Whereas of the five areas inside the Jefferson Memorial into which Jefferson's words have been carved, four are God-centered, including Jefferson's declaration that "God who gave us life gave us liberty. Can the liberties of a nation be secure when we have removed a conviction that these liberties are the gift of God? Indeed I tremble for my country when I reflect that God is just, that His justice cannot sleep forever";

Whereas the Lincoln Memorial contains numerous acknowledgments of God and citations of Bible verses, including the declarations that "we here highly resolve that… this nation under God…shall not perish from the earth"; "The Almighty has His own purposes. 'Woe unto the world because of offenses; for it must needs be that offenses come, but woe to that man by whom the offense cometh' (Matthew 18:7)"; "as was said three thousand years ago, so still it must be said 'the judgments of the Lord are true and righteous altogether' (Psalms 19:9)"; "one day every valley shall be exalted and every hill and mountain shall be made low, the rough places will be made plain, and the crooked places will be made straight and the glory of the Lord shall be revealed and all flesh see it together" (Dr. Martin Luther King's speech, based on Isaiah 40:4-5);

Whereas in the Library of Congress, The Giant Bible of Mainz and The Gutenberg Bible are on prominent permanent display and etched on the walls are Bible verses, including "The light shineth in darkness, and the darkness comprehendeth it not" (John 1:5); "Wisdom is the principal thing; therefore, get wisdom and with all thy getting, get understanding" (Proverbs 4:7); "What doth the Lord require of thee, but to do justly, and to love mercy, and to walk humbly with thy God" (Micah 6:8); and "The heavens declare the Glory of God, and the firmament showeth His handiwork" (Psalm 19:1); 90

Whereas numerous other of the most important American government leaders, institutions, monuments, buildings, and landmarks both openly acknowledge and incorporate religious words, symbols, and imagery into official venues; and

Whereas such acknowledgments are even more frequent at the state and local level than at the Federal level, where thousands of such acknowledgments exist;

Whereas the first week in May each year would be an appropriate week to designate as "American Religious History Week": Now therefore be it

Resolved, That the House of Representatives –

(1) Affirms the rich spiritual and diverse religious history of our Nation's founding and subsequent history, including up to the current day;

(2) Recognizes that the religious foundations of faith on which America was built are critical underpinnings of our Nation's most valuable institutions and form the inseparable foundation for America's representative processes, legal systems, and societal structures;

(3) Rejects, in the strongest possible terms, any effort to remove, obscure, or purposely omit such history from our nation's public buildings and educational resources; and

(4) Expresses support for designation of an "American Religious History Week" every year for the appreciation of and education on America's history of religious faith.

---

1 *Church of the Holy Trinity v. U. S.*, 143 U. S. 457, 458, 465-468, 471 (1892).

2 Donald S. Lutz, *The Origins of American Constitutionalism* (Baton Rouge: Louisiana State University Press, 1988), pp. 141-142; see also Donald S. Lutz, "The Relative Influence of European Writers on Late Eighteenth Century American Political Thought," *American Political Science Review*, Vol. 78, Issue 1, March 1984, p. 191.

3 *The Journals of the American Congress, from 1774 to 1788* (Washington, D. C.: Way and Gideon, 1823), Vol. I, p. 8, September 6, 1774.

4 John Adams, *Letters of John Adams, Addressed to His Wife*, Charles Francis Adams, editor (Boston: Charles C. Little and James Brown, 1841), Vol. I, pp. 23-24, to Abigail Adams on September 16, 1774; John noted that Duche "read several prayers in the established form, and then read the collect of the seventh day of September, which was the thirty-fifth Psalm"; an examination of the prayer book covering that year (The Book of Common Prayer (Cambridge: John Archdeacon, 1771), p. 24) shows that in addition to the "collect"—the lesson—that was read by Duche (Psalm 35), three other chapters of the Bible played prominent parts in "the established form" which was followed by him on that day, some being passages being prayed as well as read.

5 See, for example, *Journals of the Continental Congress* (Washington: Government Printing Office, 1905), Vol. II, p. 192, July 19, 1775; this activity was repeated on numerous other occasions, including the Inauguration of George Washington on April 30, 1789 (Senate: *Annals of Congress* (1834), Vol. I, p. 25, April 27, 1789; House: *Annals of Congress* (1834), Vol. I, p. 241, April 29, 1789).

6 See, for example, *Journals of the Continental Congress* (Washington: Government Printing Office, 1906), Vol. IV, p. 267, April 10, 1776; Vol. IV, p. 111, February 5, 1776; Vol. VII, p. 72, January 30, 1777; Vol. XV, pp. 1181-1182, October 16, 1779; Vol. XXVIII, pp. 306-307, April 26, 1785; Vol. XXVIII, p. 399, May 27, 1785; Vol. XXVIII, pp. 407-408, 417, June 1 & 2, 1785; Vol. XXXIV, pp. 485-487, September 3, 1788; etc.

7 See, for example, *American State Papers* (Washington: Gales & Seaton, 1832), Vol. IV, p. 546, "Treaty Between the United States and the Oneida, Tuscorora, and Stockbridge Indians, dwelling in the Country of the Oneidas," Dec 2, 1794, Proclamation, Jan 21, 1795; *Debates and Proceedings* (Washington: Gales and Seaton, 1851), p. 1332, 7th Cong., "An Act in Addition to an Act, Entitled, 'An Act in Addition to an Act Regulating the Grants of Land Appropriated for Military Services, and for the Society of the United Brethren for Propagating the Gospel Among the Heathen' " (April 26, 1802); *Debates and Proceedings* (Washington: Gales and Seaton, 1851), p. 1602, 7th Cong., 2nd Sess., "An Act to Revive and Continue in Force An Act in Addition to an Act, Entitled, 'An Act in Addition to an Act Regulating the Grants of Land Appropriated

for Military Services, and for the Society of the United Brethren for Propagating the Gospel Among the Heathen,' and for Other Purposes" (March 3, 1803); *Debates and Proceedings* (Washington, D. C.: Gales and Seaton, 1852), 8th Cong., p. 1279, "An Act Granting Further Time for Locating Military Land Warrants, and for Other Purposes" (March 19, 1804); *American State Papers: Documents, Legislative and Executive of the Congress of the United States* (Walter Lowrie & Matthew St. Claire Clarke eds., Washington, D. C.: Gales and Seaton, 1832), Vol. IV, p. 687, "The Kaskaskia and Other Tribes" (1803); *Journal of the Senate* (Washington: Gales & Seaton, 1821), 17th Congress, 1st Session (Communicated to the Senate March 5, 1822, in reference to the act passed June 1, 1796); see also *American State Papers: Public Lands,* (Washington: Duff Green, 1834), Vol. 3, p. 467, No. 354 "Grants to the United Brethren in trust for certain Christian Indians," *Statutes at Large* (Boston: Little, Brown & Co, 1856) 28th Congress, 2nd Session, pp. 766-777, March 3, 1845 Annuity to the Christian Indians; *Statutes at Large* (Boston: Little, Brown & Co, 1862), Vol. 9, pp. 544-545, September 30, 1850, Christian Indians, Restates the act of May 26, 1844 for permanent $400 annuity, *Statutes at Large* (Boston: Little, Brown & Co, 1862), Vol. 9, pp. 574-575, February 27, 1851, Christian Indians, Restates the act of May 26, 1844 for permanent $400 annuity; *Statutes at Large* (1855), Vol. X, p. 41, August 30, 1852; *Statutes at Large* (1855), Vol. X, p. 226, March 3, 1853; *Statutes at Large* (1859), Vol. XI, pp. 65-69, August 18, 1856; *Statutes at Large* (1863), Vol. XII, pp. 1191-1194, "Treaty with the Pottawatomies." November 15, 1861, Article VI; *Statutes at Large* (1868), Vol. XIV, p. 650, June 9, 1863, "Treaty between the United States of America and the Nez Perce Tribe of Indians," proclaimed April 20, 1867; *Statutes at Large* (1868), Vol. XIV, pp. 309-310, "Chap. CCXCV.—An act for the relief of the Trustees and Stewards of the Mission Church of the Wyandot Indians," July 28, 1866; etc.

8 The Declaration of Independence.

9 John Adams, *Letters of John Adams, Addressed to His Wife*, Charles Francis Adams, editor (Boston: Charles C. Little and James Brown, 1841), Vol. I, p. 128, to Abigail Adams on July 3, 1776.

10 *Letters of the Delegates to the Continental Congress*, Paul H. Smith, editor (Washington D. C.: Library of Congress, 1981), Vol. VII, p. 311, n1.

11 *Letters of the Delegates to the Continental Congress*, Paul H. Smith, editor (Washington D. C.: Library of Congress, 1981), Vol. VII, p. 311, "Committee on Publishing a Bible to Sundry Philadelphia Printers," on July 7, 1777.

12 *Journals of the Continental Congress* (Washington: Government Printing Office, 1907), Vol. VIII, p. 734, September 11, 1777.

13 Memorial of Robert Aitken to Congress, 21 January 1781, original in the National Archives, Washington, D.C.; see also the introduction to the *Holy Bible As Printed by Robert Aitken and Approved & Recommended by the Congress of the United States of*

*America in 1782* (Philadelphia: R. Aitken, 1782) or the New York Arno Press reprint of 1968.

14 *Journals of the Continental Congress* (Washington: Government Printing Office, 1914), Vol. XXIII, p. 574, September 12, 1782; see also cover page of the "Bible of the Revolution," either the 1782 original or the 1968 reprint by Arno Press.

15 *Journals of the Continental Congress* (Washington: Government Printing Office, 1914), Vol. XXIII, p. 574, September 12, 1782.

16 Richard S. Patterson and Richardson Dougall, *The Eagle and the Shield* (Washington: Department of State, 1976), p. 85, citing from the report adopted by Congress on June 20, 1782, available at *Journals of the Continental Congress* (Washington: Government Printing Office, 1914), Vol. XXII, p. 339, available online at http://memory.loc.gov/cgibin/ ampage?collId=lljc&fileName=022/ lljc022.db&recNum=348&itemLink=r%3Fammem%2Fhlaw%3A%40field %28DOCID %2B%40lit%28jc0221%29%29%230220001&linkText=1.

17 *The New Annual Register or General Repository of History, Politics, and Literature, for the Year 1783* (London: G. Robinson, 1784), p. 113; opening line of final Treaty of Peace.

18 James Madison, *The Papers of James Madison*, Henry D. Gilpin, editor (Washington: Langtree and O'Sullivan, 1840), Vol. II, pp. 984-986, June 28, 1787.

19 U. S. Constitution, Article VII.

20 Alexander Hamilton, John Jay, & James Madison, *The Federalist* (Philadelphia: Benjamin Warner, 1818), p. 194, James Madison, Federalist #37; see also Federalist #2 (p. 12) and Federalist #20 (p. 105) for other acknowledgments of the blessings of Providence upon America.

21 George Washington, *The Papers of George Washington, Confederation Series*, W. W. Abbot, editor (Charlottesville: University Press of Virginia, 1997), Vol. 6, p. 95, letter from George Washington to Marquis de Lafayette on February 7, 1788, (at http:// gwpapers.virginia.edu/documents/constitution/1788/lafayette1.html); see also a: similar sentiment in *The Papers of George Washington, Presidential Series,* Dorothy Twohig, editor (Charlottesville: University Press of Virginia, 1987), Vol. 2, p. 83, his letter on April 20, 1789 in which he said: "When I contemplate the Interposition of Providence, as it was visibly manifested, in guiding us thro' the Revolution in preparing us for the reception of a General Government, and in conciliating the Good will of the people of America, towards one another after its Adoption, I feel myself oppressed and almost overwhelmed with a sense of the Divine Munificence."

22 Benjamin Franklin, *The Works of Benjamin Franklin*, Jared Sparks, editor (Boston: Tappan, Whittemore, and Mason, 1837), Vol. V, p. 162, from "A Comparison of the

Conduct of the Ancient Jews and of the Anti-Federalists in the United States of America."

23 See, for example, *The Debates in the Several Conventions, on the Adoption of the Federal Constitution*, Jonathan Elliot, editor (Washington: Printed for the Editor, 1836), Vol. II, p. 2, Massachusetts Convention, January 9, 1788; Vol. II, p. 207, New York Convention, June 17, 1788; Vol. III, p. 1, Virginia Convention, June 2, 1788; etc.

24 *The Debates in the Several Conventions, on the Adoption of the Federal Constitution*, Jonathan Elliot, editor (Washington: Printed for the Editor, 1836), Vol. IV, p. 1, North Carolina Convention, July 21, 1788; see also Vol. II, p. 2, Massachusetts Convention, January 9, 1788.
25 *Federal Orrery*, Boston, July 2, 1795, p. 2.

26 *Journal of the Senate of the United States of America* (Washington: Gales and Seaton, 1820), p. 67; see also, *The Public Statutes at Large* (Boston: Little & Brown, 1845), 1st Cong., 1st Sess., pp. 70-71, September 22, 1789, "An Act for allowing compensation to the Members of the Senate and House of Representatives of the United States, and to the Officers of both Houses (c)."

27 As of June 2006, there were 1,432 Army chaplains; 825 Navy chaplains, and 602 Air Force chaplains, for a total of 2,859 regular duty chaplains. Additionally, there are 433 chaplains in the Army Reserve National Guard, 500 chaplains in the U. S. Army Reserves, 237 chaplains in the U. S. Navy Reserves, 254 in the Air National Guard, and 316 in the U. S. Air Force Reserves, for a total of 1740 reserve chaplains. This makes a combined 4,599 federally funded chaplains in the regular and reserve military. From information provided from the office of U. S. Congressman Bobby Jindal (LA) on September 28, 2006.

28 *The Public Statutes at Large* (Boston: Little & Brown, 1845), Vol. I, pp. 50-53, available online at http://memory.loc.gov/cgi bin/ampage?collId=llsl&fileName=001/llsl001.db&recNum=173 =; see also *Acts Passed at a Congress of the United States of America Begun and Held at the City of New-York, on Wednesday the Fourth of March, in the Year 1789* (Hartford: Hudson & Goodwin, 1791), p. 104, August 7, 1789; see also *The Constitutions of the United States of America With the Latest Amendments* (Trenton: Moore and Lake, 1813), p. 364, "An Ordinance of the Territory of the United States Northwest of the River Ohio," Article III.

29 *The Debates and Proceedings in the Congress of the United States* (1834), Vol. I, pp. 949-950, September 25, 1789.

30 George Washington, *The Writings of George Washington,* Jared Sparks, editor (Boston: Ferdinand Andrews, 1838), Vol. XII, pp. 119-120, October 3, 1789; see also James D. Richardson, *A Compilation of the Messages and Papers of the Presidents* (Published by Authority of Congress, 1897), Vol. I, p. 56, October 3, 1789.

31 *Acts of the Sixth Congress, First Session, Statutes at Large*, 6th Congress, Session 1, Ch. 33, 1800. page 45. Approved April 23, 1800, "An Act for the better government of the navy of the United States" on April 23, 1800, Article II; see also B. F. Morris, *Christian Life and Character of the Civil Institutions of the United States, Developed in the Official and Historical Annals of the Republic* (Philadelphia: George W. Childs, 1864), p. 283. "The Act "for the better government of the navy of the United States."

32 *Debates and Proceedings in the Congress of the United States* (Washington: Gales and Seaton, 1851), p. 797, Sixth Congress, December 4, 1800.

33 *The Reports of Committees of the Senate of the United States for the Second Session of the Thirty-Second Congress, 1852-53* (Washington: Robert Armstrong, 1853), p. 2; see also, B. F. Morris, *Christian Life and Character of the Civil Institutions of the United States, Developed in the Official and Historical Annals of the Republic* (Philadelphia: George W. Childs, 1864), pp. 324-325.

34 James A. Hutson, *Religion and the Founding of the American Republic* ( Washington, Library of Congress, 1998), p. 91 note; see also http://www.loc.gov/exhibits/religion/rel06-2.html.

35 Deloss Love (*The Fast and Thanksgiving Days of New England* (Boston: Houghton, Mifflin and Company, 1895), pp. 464-514, "Fast and Thanksgiving Days Calendar"), in a non-exclusive list, identifies at least 1,735 proclamations issued between 1620 and 1815. Additionally, numerous state and private libraries and repositories of historical documents own hundreds of proclamations not listed in Love's work. Therefore, while the exact number of government-issued prayer proclamations is unknown, it is certain that they number in the thousands.

36 *The Reports of Committees of the Senate of the United States for the Second Session of the Thirty-Second Congress, 1852-53* (Washington: Robert Armstrong, 1853), pp. 1-4.

37 *Reports of Committees of the House of Representatives Made During the First Session of the Thirty-Third Congress* (Washington: A. O. P. Nicholson, 1854), pp. 1, 6, 8-9.

38 *Statutes at Large*, March 3, 1865, 38th Congress, 2nd Session, Chapter 100, Sect. 5, pp. 517-518; similar laws passed on April 22, 1864 and March 3, 1865 and February 12, 1873; see current 31 USC §5112(d)(1)(2000).

39 http://www.uschs.org/04_history/subs_articles/04e_07.html.

40 *Lynch v. Donnelly*, 465 U. S. 668, 669-670 (1984).

41 *The Public Statutes at Large* (Boston: Little & Brown, 1845), 41st Cong., 2nd Sess., p. 168, June 28, 1870, (http://memory.loc.gov/cgi-bin/ampage?collId=llsl&fileName=016/llsl016.db&recNum=203) (currently at 5 U.S.C. §6103).

42 *The Life and Morals of Jesus of Nazareth, Extracted Textually from the Gospels in Greek, Latin, French, and English,* Thomas Jefferson, editor, introduction by Cyrus Adler, Librarian of the Smithsonian (Washington, D. C.: Government Printing Office, 1904), pp. 17-19.

43 Thomas Jefferson*, Jefferson's "Bible": The Life and Morals of Jesus of Nazareth*, compiled with introduction by Judd W. Patton (Grove City: American Book Distributors, 1996), p. iii, "Introduction."
44 46 Stat. 1508 (codified at 36 U.S.C. §301).

45 *The Analectic Magazine* (Philadelphia: Moses Thomas, 1814), Vol. IV, pp. 433-434.

46 Law passed on June 15, 1954 (codified at 4 U.S.C. §4).

47 Law passed on July 20, 1956 (codified at 36 U.S.C. §302).

48 Law passed on July 20, 1956 (codified at 31 U.S.C. §5114(b)).

49 See, for example, *The Federal and State Constitutions: Colonial Charters, and Other Organic Laws of the States, Territories and Colonies Now or Heretofore Forming the United States of America*, compiled and edited under the Act of Congress of June 30, 1908, by Francis Newton Thorpe (Washington: Government Printing Office, 1909), 7 volumes; see also http://www.constitution.org/cons/usstcons.htm; http://www.congress.org/congressorg/bio/userletter/?id=20004&letter_id=1514769741; http://www.legis.state.wv.us/Educational/Publications/Manual_PDF/13-WV_State_Constitution.pdf; http://www.yale.edu/lawweb/avalon/states/stateco.htm; etc.

50 See, for example, *The History of the Centennial Celebration of George Washington as First President of the United States,* Clarence Winthrop Bowen, editor (New York: D. Appleton and Company, 1892), p. 51; Benson J. Lossing, *Washington and the American Republic* (New York: Virtue & Yorston, 1870), Vol. III, p. 93; and numerous others.

51 See, for example, *The History of the Centennial Celebration of George Washington as First President of the United States,* Clarence Winthrop Bowen, editor (New York: D. Appleton and Company, 1892), p. 52; Benson J. Lossing, *Washington and the American Republic* (New York: Virtue & Yorston, 1870), Vol. III, p. 93; and numerous others.

52 James D. Richardson, *A Compilation of the Messages and Papers of the Presidents* (Published by Authority of Congress, 1897), George Washington, Vol. 1, p.44, April 30th, 1789.

53 James D. Richardson, *A Compilation of the Messages and Papers of the Presidents* (Published by Authority of Congress, 1897), George Washington, Vol. 1, pp. 44-45, April 30th, 1789.

54 *The Daily Advertiser*, New York, Thursday, April 23, 1789, p. 2; see also *The History of the Centennial Celebration of George Washington as First President of the United States,* Clarence Winthrop Bowen, editor (New York: D. Appleton and Company, 1892), p. 41, and many other sources.

55 Senate: *Annals of Congress* (1834), Vol. I, p. 25, April 27, 1789; House: *Annals of Congress* (1834), Vol. I, p. 241, April 29, 1789.

56 George Bancroft, *History of the Formation of the Constitution of the United States of America* (New York: D. Appleton and Company, 1882), Vol. II, p. 363; see also *The History of the Centennial Celebration of George Washington as First President of the United States,* Clarence Winthrop Bowen, editor (New York: D. Appleton and Company, 1892), p. 54, and many other sources.

57 George Washington, *Address of George Washington, President of the United States and Late Commander-in- Chief of the American Army, to the People of the United States, Preparatory to His Declination* (Baltimore: George and Henry S. Keatinge, 1796), pp. 22-23.

58 John Adams, *The Works of John Adams, Second President of the United States*, Charles Francis Adams, editor (Boston: Little, Brown, and Company, 1854), Vol. IX, p. 169, proclamation for a National Thanksgiving on March 23, 1798.

59 See, for example, William Parker Cutler and Julia Perkins Cutler, *Life, Journal, and Correspondence of Rev. Manasseh Cutler* (Cincinnati: Colin Robert Clarke & Co., 1888), Vol. II, p. 66, 119, in a letter to Dr. Joseph Torrey on January 3, 1803; see also his entry of December 12, 1802 (Vol. II, p. 113) and December 26, 1802 (Vol. II, p. 114); Bishop Claggett's (Episcopal Bishop of Maryland) letter of February 18, 1801, available in the Maryland Diocesan Archives; *The First Forty Years of Washington Society*, Galliard Hunt, editor (New York: Charles Scribner's Sons, 1906), p. 13; James Hutson, *Religion and the Founding of the American Republic* (Washington, D. C.: Library of Congress, 1998), p. 84; etc.

60 James Hutson, *Religion and the Founding of the American Republic* (Washington, D. C.: Library of Congress, 1998), p. 89.

61 James Hutson, *Religion and the Founding of the American Republic* (Washington, D. C.: Library of Congress, 1998), p. 89; see also John Quincy Adams, *Memoirs of John Quincy Adams*, Charles Francis Adams, editor (Philadelphia: J. B. Lippincott & Co., 1874), Vol. I, p. 265, October 23, 1803.

62 Letter from Thomas Jefferson to Bishop Carroll (Sept. 3, 1801) (on file with the Library of Congress, #19,966).

63 *American State Papers: Documents, Legislative and Executive of the Congress of the United States,* Walter Lowrie and Matthew St. Claire Clarke, editors (Washington, D. C.: Gales and Seaton, 1832), Vol. IV, p. 687, "The Kaskaskia and Other Tribes"; *Debates and Proceedings* (Washington, D. C.: Gales and Seaton, 1851), 7th Cong., p. 1332, "An Act in addition to an act, entitled 'An act in addition to an act regulating the grants of land appropriated for military services, and for the Society of the United Brethren for propagating the Gospel among the Heathen'"; *Debates and Proceedings* (Washington, D. C.: Gales and Seaton, 1851), 7th Cong., 2nd Sess., p. 1602, "An Act to revive and continue in force an act, in addition to an act, Entitled 'An act in addition to an act regulating the grants of land appropriated to military services, and for the Society of the United Brethren for propagating the Gospel among the Heathen,' and for other purposes."; *Debates and Proceedings* (Washington, D. C.: Gales and Seaton, 1852), 8th Cong., p. 1279, "An Act Granting Further Time for Locating Military Land Warrants, and for Other Purposes.

64 Letter from Thomas Jefferson to the Nuns of the Order of St. Ursula at New Orleans on May 15, 1804, original on file with the New Orleans Parish.

65 American Presidency Project, "Ronald Reagan: Proclamation 5018—Year of the Bible, 1983, February 3rd, 1983" (http://www.presidency.ucsb.edu/ws/?pid=40728); see the same quote in a proclamation from President George H. W. Bush on February 22, 1990, "International Year of Bible Reading," in *Code of Federal Regulations* (Washington, DC: U. S. Government Printing Office, 1991), p. 21.

66 Abraham Lincoln, *The Collected Works of Abraham Lincoln,* Roy P. Basler, editor (New Brunswick, NJ: Rutgers University Press, 1953), Vol. VII, p. 542, reply to Loyal Colored People of Baltimore upon presentation of a Bible, September 7, 1864.

67 American Presidency Project, "William McKinley: Inaugural Address, March 4th, 1897" (http://www.presidency.ucsb.edu/ws/index.php?pid=25827).

68 Theodore Roosevelt, *American Ideals, The Strenuous Life, Realizable Ideals* (New York: Charles Scribner's Sons, 1926), pp. 498-499.

69 Woodrow Wilson, *The Papers of Woodrow Wilson,* Arthur S. Link, editor (Princeton, New Jersey: Princeton University Press, 1977), Vol. 23, p. 20, An Address in Denver on the Bible, May 7, 1911.

70 American Presidency Project, "Herbert Hoover: Radio Address to the Nation on Unemployment Relief, October 18, 1931" (at http://www.presidency.ucsb.edu/ws/?pid=22855).

71 American Presidency Project, "Franklin D. Roosevelt: Prayer on D-Day, June 6th, 1944 (http://www.presidency.ucsb.edu/ws/index.php?pid=16515&st=&st1=).

72 American Presidency Project, "Franklin D. Roosevelt: Address at Dedication of Great Smoky Mountains National Park, September 2nd, 1940" (at http://www.presidency.ucsb.edu/ws/?pid=16002).

73 American Presidency Project, "Harry S. Truman: Address Before the Attorney General's conference on Law Enforcement Problems," February 15, 1950" (at http://www.presidency.ucsb.edu/ws/?pid=13707).

74 American Presidency Project, "Harry S. Truman's Address to the Washington Pilgrimage of American Churchmen, September 28th, 1951" (at http://www.presidency.ucsb.edu/ws/?pid=13934); see also "Address at the Cornerstone Laying of the New York Avenue Presbyterian Church, April 3rd, 1951 (at http://www.presidency.ucsb.edu/ws/?pid=14048).

75 American Presidency Project, "Dwight D. Eisenhower: Remarks Recorded for the "Back-to-God" Program of the American Legion. February 20th, 1955" (http://www.presidency.ucsb.edu/ws/index.php?pid=10414&st=&st1=).

76 American Presidency Project, "Gerald Ford: Proclamation 4338—National Day of Prayer, 1974, December 5th, 1974" (http://www.presidency.ucsb.edu/ws/index.php?pid=23888).

77 American Presidency Project, "John F. Kennedy: Inaugural Address, January 20th, 1961" (http://www.presidency.ucsb.edu/ws/index.php?pid=8032).

78 American Presidency Project, "Ronald Reagan: Proclamation 5018—Year of the Bible, 1983, February 3rd, 1983" (http://www.presidency.ucsb.edu/ws/?pid=40728).

79 http://www.supremecourtus.gov/about/procedures.pdf .

80 See, for example, *New Hampshire Gazette* (Portsmouth), May 26, 1791; *Columbian Centinel* (Boston), May 16, 1792; *Newport Mercury* (Rhode Island) of June 25, 1793; *United States Oracle* (Portsmouth, NH), May 24, 1800; see also *Documentary History of the Supreme Court,* Vol. II, p. 192, Vol. II p. 412, Vol. II, p. 276, Vol. III, p. 436; and B. F. Morris, *Christian Life and Character of the Civil Institutions of the United States, Developed in the Official and Historical Annals of the Republic* (Philadelphia: George W. Childs, 1864), p. 646, relating the first court convened in the Northwest Territory, in Ohio, where the prayer was offered by the Rev. Dr. Cutler; etc.

81 *Vidal v. Girard's Executors*, 43 U. S. 127, 198 (1844).

82 *Church of the Holy Trinity v. U. S.*, 143 U. S. 471 (1892).

83 *United States v. Macintosh*, 283 U. S. 605, 625 (1931).

84 *Zorach v. Clauson*, 343 U. S. 306, 313 (1952).

85 *Zorach v. Clauson*, 343 U. S. 306, 315 (1952).

86 William Jay, *The Life of John Jay: With Selections from His Correspondence and Miscellaneous Papers* (New York: J. & J. Harper, 1833), Vol. I, pp. 457-458, to the Committee of the Corporation of the City of New York on June 29, 1826.

87 James Wilson, *The Works of James Wilson,* Bird Wilson, editor (Philadelphia: Bronson and Chauncey, 1804), Vol. I, pp. 104-106, "Of the General Principles of Law and Obligation."

88 *United States Oracle* (Portsmouth, NH), May 24, 1800; see also *The Documentary History of the Supreme Court of the United States, 1789-1800*, Maeva Marcus, editor (New York: Columbia University Press, 1988), Vol. III, p. 436.

89 George Washington, *Address of George Washington, President of the United States...Preparatory to his Declination* (Baltimore: George and Henry S. Keatinge, 1796), p. 23.

90 *Library of Congress*, "The Thomas Jefferson Building: A Virtual tour of the Library of Congress" (http://www.loc.gov/jefftour/firstfloor.html ), *Library of Congress,* "On These Walls" (http://www.loc.gov/loc/walls/jeff1.html, http://www.loc.gov/loc/walls/jeff2.html).

## Appendix 12

# AFROCENTRISM IS WRONG FOR AMERICANS

A newspaper article, "Teaching a New Perspective" (*New Haven Register*, 22 October 2000, p. B1), reported that teacher Maguena Adedona was using an Afrocentric perspective in teaching her all-black kindergarten class at the Nannie Helen Burroughs School. "We're not excluding anything or anyone," she told the *Register*. "But if you're going to tell it, tell it right and tell the whole story."

It is indeed important for children to learn of their racial and ethnic roots and to develop a healthy respect for their ancestral heritage. However, as described in the article, Ms. Adetona was not telling the whole story or telling it right. She was doing a disservice to her students.

Those children are American, not African. Their culture is Western, not African. Their skin may be black, but In the melting pot of America, the only colors which matter are red, white and blue. Those colors stand for God-given liberty, inalienable rights and human dignity in a democratic republic based on rule of law. That is what should be at the center of Ms. Adetona's perspective. Do her students learn that the history of freedom on Earth begins with Christianity and its emphasis on the moral equality among all individuals, whether freeborn or slave? That is the basis on which slavery in America was finally eliminated. That is why America is leading the world toward liberty and justice for all, while Africa is locked in centuries-old destructive tribal warfare, with slavery still being practiced in some areas.

So far as I know, black or sub-Saharan Africa has not contributed a single idea, invention, discovery, scientific insight, religious doctrine, social value, philosophic speculation or anything else which has had a formative effect on the Euro-American culture sustaining Ms. Adetona and her students. In other words, in the process of cultural evolution, whatever glory Africa might have had centuries ago is now merely museum dust, however much glory was deserved then. (The same can be said for all other tribal societies around the world, including Native Americans.) The Malian expedition to Central America in 1311 was historically interesting, but it didn't do anything to advance the creation or rise of Western civilization which built America. It is no more or less important than the similarly little known "discoveries" of America by the Celts in 5,000 B.C., the Phoenicians in the fifth century B.C., Brendan the Navigator (Irish) in 500 A.D., Leif Ericcson (Viking) in 1000 A.D., Prince Madoc of Wales in 1171 A.D. and Prince Henry Sinclair of Scotland in 1398 A.D. They, too, are part of telling what Ms. Adetona calls "the whole story."

However, even naming all those explorers doesn't remove my principal objection to Ms. Adetona's Afrocentric curriculum. Here's why.

For whatever reasons, the black man in Africa simply did not develop or place importance on abstract reasoning, philosophical inquiry, theoretics and technology.

Afrocentric historians have not made a convincing case for their counterclaims. For example, the wheel, the plow, literacy, the calendar and the scientific method were virtually unknown to black Africa. Inventiveness and speculation are either European or Asian (Chinese, Japanese, Indian). Moreover, the traditional African perspective values community cohesion over the freedom of the individual—i.e., the tribal status quo over the innovator. I challenge Ms. Adetona to name even one negroid African or black American who has influenced Euro-American culture in terms of traditional African values and African thinking. Every black man and woman whom school children learn about, from Singbe/Cinque, Sojourner Truth, Frederick Douglass, George Washington Carver and Booker T. Washington to Malcolm X, Martin Luther King, Nelson Mandela and Bishop Tutu, is notable for his or her actions which were essentially based on Western values, Western mentality, Western perspective and Western technology. That statement applies even to actions—such as those of Marcus Garvey and Stokely Carmichael/Kwame Touré—which were opposed to Western culture or simply an attempt to break away from it and return to Africa.

Am I wrong? I would welcome being shown so (and I note one possibility below). Am I a racist? No, I have no racial axe to grind. I'm simply looking—without bias, as objectively as I can—at the historical process by which cultures emerge, rise, fall and are superseded by other cultures. That includes all races. Where are the Hittites, the Etruscans, the Mayans, the Roman Empire, the Clovis people of the American Southwest, Kenniwick Man? Euro-American culture is the evolutionary high point of cultural development thus far in time and should be appreciated as such. Yes, it certainly has its deplorable aspects, its shameful actions, its reprehensible moments. Despite that, it deserves our support and appreciation, and those "old dead white men" of Western civilization whom many scorn deserve our respect for achieving something unprecedented and wonderful in history: a truly global perspective exalting the individual over the tribe or the state, and the means to communicate and advance it on a worldwide scale. Let freedom ring throughout the Earth, and give America greatest credit for advancing that.

Having stated my case, I must say there appears to be one exception to it—but it is an exception which nevertheless does not refute my position. According to Michael Bradley in his 1988 book *Holy Grail Across the Atlantic* and, building on that, William F. Mann's 1999 *The Labyrinth of the Grail,* by the 14th century the Emperor of Mali had ships going to the New World, as Ms. Adetona points out, and other Africans had crossed much earlier. Mayan stone statues of men with negroid features in Central America are mute testimony to this extraordinary achievement. It could not have been done without the development of a method to measure longitude. That means Africans solved the problem of determining longitude at sea long before Europeans did. However, the knowledge was lost and apparently had no influence on the solution developed by Europeans in the 18th century.

Why it was lost and why Malian seafaring culture declined are topics for research. The Bradley-Mann thesis contends that knowledge of longitude measurement was passed from Mali to Arabic culture, and thence to the Knights Templar, whose interactions with Arab Muslims in the Middle East were sometimes friendly rather than hostile. The Knights Templar, in turn, kept that knowledge secret, using it for their own purposes. Those purposes may have included voyages to the New World a full century before Columbus, through Prince Henry Sinclair of Scotland, who reached Nova Scotia and the coast of Massachusetts in 1398. Sinclair's forebears had granted shelter in Scotland to fugitive Knights Templar when the King of France and the Pope disbanded the Order of the Temple in 1307. Those Knights Templar in turn made Rosslyn Castle, the ancestral home of the Sinclairs, their center of operations. Rosslyn Chapel was begun in the mid-1400s and completed before the end of that century. It contains carvings of maize (Indian corn) and aloe, plants which are native to the New World. (Also see *The Hiram Key: Pharaohs, Freemasons and the Discovery of the Secret Scrolls of Jesus* by Christopher Knight and Robert Lomas and *The Lost Treasure of the Knights Templar* by Steven Sora.)

# ABOUT THE AUTHOR

## A Biographical Profile

JOHN WARREN WHITE is an internationally known author who writes about the human mind and spirituality and their relationship to political, social and cultural affairs. He has published 20 books, including *America, Freedom and Enlightenment, Celebrating America in Poem and Song, The Meeting of Science and Spirit, What Is Enlightenment?, A Practical Guide to Death and Dying* and (for children) *The Christmas Mice.* His forthcoming book is *Enlightenment 101: A Guide to God-Realization and Higher Human Culture.* His writing has appeared in *The New York Times, The Wall Street Journal, Reader's Digest, Esquire, Woman's Day, Saturday Review, Omni, Science of Mind, New Age, The New American* and many other newspapers and magazines around the world. His books have been translated into ten languages.

Mr. White was born in 1939. He holds a Bachelor of Arts degree from Dartmouth College (1961) and a Master of Arts in Teaching from Yale University (1969). He has taught English and journalism on the secondary and college levels and has served on the directing and advisory boards of various academic and research organizations. He also has served on the editorial boards of various scholarly journals and popular magazines.

After college, Mr. White served four years in the U.S. military as a naval officer, primarily in antisubmarine warfare and nuclear weaponry. He is a Vietnam veteran. From 1965-1969, he taught English in his hometown high school. He then joined the public relations department of a Connecticut utility company. In 1972, Mr. White joined with Apollo 14 astronaut Edgar Mitchell to begin The Institute of Noetic Sciences, a research organization founded by Dr. Mitchell to study the human potential for personal and planetary transformation. He remained with the Institute for two years and then began a career as a freelance writer. In 1981, he joined another Connecticut utility company as a communications specialist. He is now retired and devotes full time to communicating "information for transformation," both personal and planetary, including America's leading role in that process.

Mr. White lives in Cheshire, Connecticut, where he is active in veterans affairs, Freemasonry, Scouting, youth education and the grassroots level of politics. He and his wife Barbara have been married more than 50 years. They have four children and seven grandchildren.

## A Personal Statement

You may wonder: Who is this person offering his views and opinions? Simply a concerned American citizen who is grateful for the blessings of liberty and who wants to pass them on to my grandchildren and succeeding generations. I'm a teacher and writer by profession. Governmentally speaking, I am a Jeffersonian constitutionalist. Religiously speaking, I stand with the Founders of our nation who recognized that God is the author of our being and the source of morality, law and freedom. Economically speaking, I am a free enterprise capitalist. Politically speaking, I am active in the Republican Party (having left the Democratic Party in 1993 after nearly 30 years of largely inactive membership), but I also have membership in the Libertarian Party. Philosophically speaking, I am in the conservative wing of libertarian thought but reject the atheism which some libertarians say is a necessary element of the philosophy.

My mother, Jane Zobel White, descended (via her mother) from the Warrens of Virginia, a 17th century English colonial family, and (via her father) from the Zobels of Berlin, Germany. My father, Robert Paul Weiss, descended (via his father) from the Weisses of Germantown, Pennsylvania and (via his mother) from the Henleins of Greenville, Pennsylvania. So I descend from English and German immigrants. I was born John Warren Weiss in 1939, but in 1941 my father and his brother Americanized their last name to White (Weiss is German for White) to avoid the anti-German sentiment of the time.

During the Civil War my Virginian forebears fought against the Union, so although I grew up in the North (Maryland until age 11 and then Connecticut) I am also a Son of the Confederacy. Additionally, because my Virginia forebears predate the War for Independence, I regard myself as a Son of the American Revolution. Strictly speaking, I am not a full member of that hereditary patriotic organization but I was made an honorary member of it in the General David Humphries Chapter of the SAR in Connecticut.

On my mother's side, one of my Virginia ancestors is described in a 19th century census as an unnamed "mulatto." That could mean having either Negro or Native American blood, but the census does not specify it.

Although I was raised as an Episcopalian, three of my grandparents were Jews and I am qualified, under Israel's Law of Return, for Israeli citizenship. (However, I want only American citizenship.) Among my relatives who remained in Germany, it is quite likely that some of them died in the Holocaust, simply for being Jews.

In a common American fashion, therefore, I am ethnically, racially and religiously mixed.

Speaking of religion, I no longer call myself Christian. I am, however, trying to become Christed by following the teaching of Jesus of Nazareth, the exemplar of perfected humanity who called people to follow in his Way. Jesus did not intend to form a new religion (Christianity) or even reform an old one (Judaism). Rather, he intended to *trans*form the consciousness of humanity from self-centered to God-centered so that a society would develop based on the same sense of unity which he enjoyed with God. If that can be accomplished, we would truly have heaven on earth, with people following their conscience—the still, small voice of God within us all—so faithfully that man's law would be little needed and a godly society would envelop the planet.

At the moment, however, religions struggle among themselves, creating ever-greater disunity and disharmony. The Founders of America saw things differently. Although they belonged to various denominations of Christianity, they nevertheless had a clear sense of the ultimate unity of religions beyond all denominationalism by recognizing that our loving Creator blesses us with ongoing divine providence, even when human self-centeredness tries to block its flow. Therefore, I honor all religions but belong to none—only to God.

Understanding that transcendent unity which recognizes the presence of God in our lives and in all things is the heart of the American Spirit. If America is to survive, that sense must be restored. Without it, America will join the list of failed societies in history. I therefore embrace William Penn's succinct advice on how religion should be lived: "In essentials, unity. In nonessentials, liberty. In all things, charity."

No one can be totally objective, but through self-knowledge you can recognize your biases and be honest about them. Those are some of mine—and I regard them as direct expressions of the Spirit of Liberty.